LUSITANIA

LUSITANIA

———

TRIUMPH, TRAGEDY, AND THE END OF THE EDWARDIAN AGE

———

Greg King and Penny Wilson

 ST. MARTIN'S GRIFFIN ⚲ NEW YORK

LUSITANIA. Copyright © 2015 by Greg King and Penny Wilson. All rights reserved. Printed in the United States of America. For information, address St. Martin's Press, 175 Fifth Avenue, New York, N.Y. 10010.

www.stmartins.com

Designed by Jonathan Bennett

The Library of Congress has cataloged the hardcover edition as follows:

King, Greg, 1964–
   Lusitania : triumph, tragedy, and the end of the Edwardian age / Greg King and Penny Wilson. — First edition.
      p. cm.
   Includes bibliographical references and index.
   ISBN 978-1-250-05254-4 (hardcover)
   ISBN 978-1-4668-7637-8 (e-book)
   1. Lusitania (Steamship)   2. Shipwreck victims—North Atlantic Ocean—Anecdotes.   3. Ocean travel—North Atlantic Ocean—Anecdotes.   4. Upper class—Social life and customs—20th century.   5. Upper class—United States—Biography. I. Wilson, Penny, 1966– II. Title.
   G530.L87 2015
   910.4'52—dc23

                                                                    2014040843

ISBN 978-1-250-08035-6 (trade paperback)

Our books may be purchased in bulk for promotional, educational, or business use. Please contact your local bookseller or the Macmillan Corporate and Premium Sales Department at 1-800-221-7945, extension 5442, or by e-mail at MacmillanSpecialMarkets@macmillan.com.

First St. Martin's Griffin Edition: April 2016

10 9 8 7 6 5 4 3 2 1

In memory of my beloved
mother, Helena

Greg

To my parents, Edward
and Mary O'Hanlon, with love

Penny

ACKNOWLEDGMENTS

The writing of any book can be a complicated and challenging process; at best, it also offers scope for expression and a useful outlet for energies and ideas that might otherwise rumble endlessly around in one's head. This book, born in and written under less than ideal circumstances, has ultimately provided the kind of experience for which every author hopes: new friendships, generous fellow researchers, intellectual exercise, and ultimately the transformation of concept into reality.

This book was really the brainchild of two people who believed in the idea and who helped to push it to fruition: our agent, Dorie Simmonds, in London, and Charles Spicer, our editor at St. Martin's Press. Even when energies, effort, and attention were flagging, both remained constant sources of encouragement. Charlie in particular has understood late developments and deadline extensions that might otherwise have proved catastrophic. And April Osborn, assistant editor at St. Martin's Press, has helped answer queries and been an often sorely needed source of good news.

The idea for this book was first discussed in the summer of 2013, at a time when Greg's beloved mother, Helena, was in declining health, and much of his attention was thus diverted elsewhere. Helena had enthusiastically supported Greg throughout his efforts. Her death in September, just a month after this project began, was an unexpected blow, as Greg and his father, Roger, struggled through a difficult mourning process.

Greg thanks his beloved father for his encouragement and invaluable support in this especially trying time.

Reassuring relatives also helped: Greg would like to especially note the thoughtful and much appreciated attentions of his aunt and uncle Virginia and Willard Pearson; his cousin Jeannine Evans; his aunt and uncle George and Ann Cline; and his aunt Anna King. Everyone mourns in a different way: this book—demanding so much of Greg's time and attention each day—became an invaluable outlet for his energies and helped focus his mind at a time when concentration was difficult.

Greg would also like to thank a truly supportive group of friends, even if the last few years have often left him preoccupied with other concerns: Janet Ashton, Bob Atchison, Antonio Pérez Caballero, Diana and Nick de Courcy-Ireland, Simon Donoghue, Professor Joseph Fuhrmann, Coryne Hall, Ceceilia Hamilton-Brown, Sophie von Hohenberg, Chuck and Eileen Knaus, Marlene Eilers Koenig, Angela Manning, Susanne Meslans, Ilana Miller, Rob Moshein, Mike Pyles, Karen Roth, Debra Tate, Katrina Warne, and Sue and Mike Woolmans. Brad Swenson, of Buy and Sell Video in Everett, Washington, not only kept him entertained but also came to his technological assistance during research. And Arturo Beéche, editor and publisher of the *European Royal History Journal,* has provided enthusiastic support and a diverting mixture of projects to keep him current in the royal history universe.

Penny would like to thank her family for their support: Peter and Lynne O'Hanlon of Providenciales, Turks & Caicos Islands;

James and Tricia Manara of Phoenix; Jon Phillips of Tucson; Peggy, Darren, Eric, and Ryan Cartwright of Riverside, California; Barbara Wilson of Riverside, California; and Mary Kelsey of San Diego. Above all, thanks to Tom Wilson, for midnight repairs on Penny's computer, for buying and building extra bookshelves, for taking over at home during archival visits, and for generally enduring life with a writer for almost twenty years.

Penny would also like to thank her employees and coworkers at Riverside City Gym, who have carried on keeping the doors open when the boss was unavailable: James Brown, Justin DeSoucy, Daniel Early, Nicole Flaherty, Gino Gonzalez, Gio Gonzalez, Alex Howard, Haley Hyland, Clayton Nicodemus, Wellington Porter, Jennifer Rider, James Shearer, Josh Sweeten, Casey Watson, David Watson, Jisel Wilson, and Alvin Wright. Thanks also to Bent Corydon, Ivan Crystal, Rosie Pérez, and Guillermo Pérez. And many thanks to Eugene Mejia, Don Lowrey, and Chris Schaper.

And thanks to the many gym members who have pitched in and helped, supporting Penny through the flood of Labor Day Weekend 2013 and generally through the last two years. You guys are awesome!

Occasionally in life, one comes across a person wiser and stronger than his years. Penny thanks Andrei Karlin, hope of the future, for being himself, which is a wonderful thing to be. We wish him nothing but the very best, though he already has much of that in his family.

Penny thanks Simon Donoghue, for years of friendship, laughter, and historical shenanigans. She looks forward to meeting him in person one day. She also thanks Oscar Shearer for his friendship and everything that means, from workouts to diet tips, conversations to arguments on subjects as varied as cars, Middle Eastern politics, and Spartan warfare. She looks forward to many more years of the same.

❧

Finally, thanks to Penny's longtime PS friends, most of them never met in person, but all of them valued as much as those met every day.

In researching this book, we have been lucky to draw upon the patient and amiable help of a number of institutions and archives. We would like to thank Aya Ito and Bill Barker for access to the Hoehling and Hoehling Archive at the Mariners' Museum, Christopher Newport University, Newport News, Virginia; Matthew Chipping of the BBC Archives, Perivale Park, London; the staff of the McCord Museum in Montreal, for help in researching the family of Marguerite Allan; Michaela Strong at the National Archives and Records Administration in Maryland; Darren Yearsley of the CBC Radio Archives, Ottawa, Ontario, Canada; and especially Carol Leadenham of the Hoover Institution on War, Revolution, and Peace, at Stanford University in Stanford, California. Carol not only allowed us access to the Bailey and Ryan Archive there but also took the time to show us the handle of an oar inscribed *Lusitania,* which was donated to the Hoover Institution, and which allegedly came from one of the lifeboats used on May 7, 1915.

Chris Lands, of Seaocean Book Berth in Seattle, located many of the obscure maritime works we used.

We also thank Joan Blacker, Interlibrary Loan Specialist at the Everett Public Library, and the Everett Public Library's reference staff for their thorough and diligent research and work in locating some of the rare and obscure materials on which this book draws. Their assistance proved invaluable.

We are happy to thank Mary Carpenter of Riverside, California. Mary is the granddaughter of *Lusitania* passengers Gladys and Albert Clay "Chris" Bilicke. She provided us with anecdotal information regarding her family, which corrected some of the misinformation about them that has seeped into the historical record. She has also shared photographs of her grandparents for use in this book.

Oscar Shearer provided much-needed advice and technological expertise in preparing the illustrations in this book. We thank him for his patience and generosity.

Lusitania historian Michael Poirier not only shared rare, previously unpublished images from his own collection but also contacted researchers and relatives of passengers on our behalf. Thanks to him we have been able to include a number of important photographs, unpublished memoirs, letters, and accounts of the tragedy. We would like to thank Chris Anagnos, the family of Albert Bestic, Mary Jolivet, Paul Latimer, Chester Nimitz Lay and Richard Bailey, Peter Lordan, Marika Pirie, and Rick Timmis for their generosity. We would also especially like to thank Demetrio Baffa Trasci Amalfitani di Crucoli and his family for information on survivor donna Angela Papadopoulos.

A number of people read through this book and gave us much-needed feedback, corrections, and suggestions, as well as helping with research. Janet Ashton kept us up to date on breaking developments and spent time researching Ian Holbourn's book *The Child of the Moat* so that we could include details here. Simon Donoghue endured several drafts of the manuscript and was always ready with sage advice. Sue Woolmans also diligently worked on our behalf, offering a multitude of information on *Lusitania* and her last voyage that has helped shape the book.

Susanne Meslans again proved herself an invaluable friend during the days and weeks after the death of Greg's mother. She matched her emotional support with research, repeatedly sacrificing her time and money to obtain materials in which she had no personal interest so that we could explore disparate topics. She also endured reading a less than polished manuscript and offered helpful advice on arrangement and the social background of the era.

Although we had both had long-standing interests in the *Lusitania* story, we came to this book almost by accident, outsiders in a world of historians steeped in the ship's history. The prospect was intimidating. Yet we were delighted to find that people like Eric Sauder, Jim Kalafus, and Michael Poirier—researchers and authors who have devoted decades to the ship and the passengers on her last voyage—were welcoming and supportive. Eric answered queries and shared information and images with us, for which he has our thanks. Jim Kalafus and Michael Poirier run the *Lusitania Resource,* the world's foremost Web site on the ship and those aboard on her last voyage. Anyone wishing to know more about these passengers and their experiences can discover a wealth of information at www.rmslusitania.info, where Jim and Mike so graciously share their years of accumulated research. Jim also read an early version of the manuscript: his corrections and forthright comments helped shape portions of the book and ensure its accuracy.

And finally, there is Mike Poirier. Mike had the unenviable job of suffering through numerous versions of the manuscript, always making time in his busy life to advise and assist us in ways that have proved invaluable to the finished product. His helpful critiques led us to a complete—and much needed—rewrite.

He not only shared rare accounts, memoirs, letters, and newspaper clippings from his extraordinary personal archive but also contacted numerous relatives of those aboard *Lusitania* during her final voyage seeking information and illustrative materials.

There is little we can say in thanks: quite simply, Mike made this book what it is. We can only hope that, in some small way, it helps the ongoing efforts to put a human face to this tragedy.

AUTHORS' NOTE

In this book, readers will encounter a number of figures indicating costs of travel, personal fortunes, and amounts paid for various parties. We have given these as contemporary sums, but here include a modern rendering of current valuation, following the formula that a 1915 $1 is equal to $23 today; the exchange rate of dollars to pounds sterling in 1915 was $1=£4.70. Even so, these figures are approximations. Owing to inflation and taxation, the actual purchasing power of any given sum in 1915 would have been much greater than it is a century later.

For *Lusitania*'s last voyage, Cunard had reduced Second Class fares from the usual $70 to $50 ($1,610 and $1,150, respectively, in 2015 figures). A typical First Class fare began at roughly $115 ($2,645 in 2015 currency); it cost approximately $1,500 ($34,500 in 2015), each way, to stay in one of the ship's Parlor Suites; a passenger who booked one of her two Regal Suites could expect to spend approximately $2,250 ($51,750 in 2015), one way.[1]

A look at some typical 1915 costs helps set these figures in perspective. The average annual household income for a professional in America was some $2,000 ($46,000 in 2015 figures);

most people, though, earned less than half of this. A Ford would set the buyer back by $490 ($11,270 in 2015), although most good quality motorcars began at well over $1,000 ($23,000 in 2015). A luxurious apartment in New York City might run between $3,000 and $5,000 ($69,000–$115,000 in 2015 currency) a year; bed and board in a respectable lodging house cost approximately $5 ($115 in 2015) a week, while one could rent a room in a squalid tenement for just $1 ($23) a month. A good dinner at a fashionable New York City restaurant like Delmonico's began at $3 ($69) per person, including wine. A men's suit from Lord & Taylor might cost $17.50 ($172.50 in 2015); an unpretentious dress might go for $2–$4 ($46–$92), with upwards of $125 ($2,875) spent on a fashionable dress from Paris. A pair of good ladies' shoes began at $4.25 ($97.75), while ladies' silk stockings started at 25 cents a pair ($5.75); a child's velvet playsuit could be had for $2.95 ($67.85); it took $650 ($14,950) to buy a grand piano. A 32-ounce box of corn flakes cost 8 cents ($1.84); a can of sliced peaches went for 22 cents ($5.06); a smoked ham sold for 15 cents a pound ($3.45); an oak desk could be purchased for $35 ($805), while a good-quality metal bed might run $3.95 ($90.85); and a pack of ten cigarettes could be had for a nickel.[2]

CAST OF CHARACTERS

Adams, Annie, age 46, British, traveling with her British husband, Henry (58), to return home.

Adams, William, age 19, American, traveling with his father to enlist in British Army.

Allan, Lady H. Montague (Marguerite), age 47, British Canadian, traveling with her two daughters, Anna (16) and Gwendolyn (15), and with maids Emily Davis and Annie Walker, to establish army hospital in England.

Baker, Amelia (Millie), age 27, American, traveling with Charles Williamson to Paris.

Bates, Lindon W. Jr., age 31, American, traveling to join war relief efforts in Belgium.

Bernard, Oliver, age 34, British, escorting Stewart and Leslie Mason and returning home to London.

Bilicke, Albert, age 54, American, traveling with his wife, Gladys (48), on holiday.

Boulton, Denis Duncan Harold Owen (Harold), age 22, British, returning to Europe hoping to join French Red Cross.

Braithwaite, Dorothy, age 24, British Canadian, traveling to be with her widowed sisters.

Brandell, Josephine, age 23, American opera singer.

Brooks, James (Jay), age 41, American, traveling on business.

Brown, Mary, age 55, American, traveling with her daughter, Beatrice Witherbee, and grandson Alfred Witherbee to reunite with family.

Burnside, Josephine, age 49, British Canadian, traveling with her daughter, Iris (20), to see her estranged husband.

Byrne, Michael, age 47, American, traveling on business.

Conner, Dorothy, age 25, American, traveling with her brother-in-law, Dr. Howard Fisher, to join war relief efforts in Belgium.

Depage, Marie, age 43, Belgian, traveling with Dr. James Houghton to return to war relief efforts in Belgium.

Dunsmuir, James A. Jr., age 21, British Canadian, traveling to enlist in British Army.

Fisher, Dr. Howard, age 49, American, traveling with his sister-in-law, Dorothy Conner, to join war relief efforts in Belgium.

Forman, Justus, age 39, American, traveling with Charles Frohman party.

Freeman, Richard, age 28, American, college friend of Dr. James Houghton.

Friend, Edwin, age 28, American, traveling with Theodate Pope to meet English spiritualists.

Frohman, Charles, age 58, American, traveling on theatrical business.

Gorer, Edgar, age 43, British, returning to London.

Hammond, Ogden, age 46, American, traveling with his wife, Mary (29), to join war relief efforts in Belgium.

Holt, William Robert Grattan (Robert), age 15, British Canadian, returning to school.

Home, Thomas, age 50, British Canadian, traveling on business.

Houghton, Dr. James T., age 29, American, traveling with Marie Depage to join war relief efforts in Belgium.

Hubbard, Elbert, age 58, American, traveling with his wife, Alice (53), hoping to interview Kaiser Wilhelm II.

Jeffery, Charles, age 39, American, traveling to sell his tanks to France.

Jenkins, Francis, age 29, British, traveling on business.

Jolivet, Marguerite (Rita), age 25, French, traveling to see her brother.

Kessler, George, age 52, American, traveling on business.

Klein, Charles, age 48, British, traveling with Charles Frohman party.

Lane, Sir Hugh, age 39, British Irish, traveling on business.

Lassetter, Elisabeth, age 43, British Australian, traveling with her son, Frederic (22), returning to his regiment.

Lauriat, Charles, age 40, American, traveling on business.

Lehmann, Isaac, age 36, American, traveling on business.

Loney, Allen, age 43, American, traveling with his wife, Catherine (37), and daughter, Virginia (15), to work for British Red Cross.

Mackworth, Lady Humphrey (Margaret), age 32, British, traveling with her father, D. A. Thomas (59), and his secretary, Arnold Rhys-Evans (23), returning home from business trip.

Mason, Stewart, age 30, British, traveling with his new wife, Leslie (28), escorted by Oliver Bernard, on honeymoon.

Moodie, Ralph, age 26, British, traveling with fellow cotton broker Robert Timmis on business.

Orr-Lewis, Frederick, age 49, British Canadian, traveling with his valet, George Slingsby (26), on business.

Papadopoulos, Michael, age 43, Greek, traveling with his wife, Angela (32), returning home from business trip.

Pearl, Frederick (Warren), age 46, American, traveling with his wife, Amy (34), their four children, Stuart (5), Amy (2), Susan (1), and Audrey (3 months), and two nurses, British Alice Lines (18) and Danish Greta Lorenson (23), to join Red Cross relief.

Pirie, Robinson, age 59, British Canadian, traveling on business.

Pope, Theodate, age 48, American, traveling with Edwin Friend and with her maid, Emily Robinson, to meet English spiritualists.

Ryerson, Mary, age 56, British Canadian, traveling with her daughter, Laura (23), to see wounded son.

Schwabacher, Leo, age 43, American, traveling with Henry Sonneborn.

Slidell, Thomas, age 41, American, journalist traveling on business.

Smith, Jessie Taft, age 39, American, traveling to bring her husband plans for a military aircraft engine.

Sonneborn, Henry, age 43, American, traveling with Leo Schwabacher.

Stephens, Frances, age 64, British Canadian, traveling with her grandson, John (18 months), to see wounded son.

Timmis, Robert, age 51, British, traveling with fellow cotton broker Ralph Moodie on business.

Vanderbilt, Alfred, age 37, American, traveling with valet Ronald Denyer (30) to donate to British Red Cross.

Vernon, George (Butler), age 45, British, brother-in-law of Rita Jolivet, traveling to secure Russian munitions contract.

Williamson, Charles, age 44, American, traveling with Amelia Baker to Paris.

Witherbee, Beatrice (Trixie), age 24, American, traveling with mother, Mary Brown, and son, Alfred Witherbee Jr. (3), to reunite with family.

SECOND CLASS PASSENGERS ABOARD *LUSITANIA*

Amory, Phoebe, age 65, British Canadian, traveling to see sons serving in the war.

Anderson, Emily, age 24, British, traveling with her daughter, Barbara (nearly 3), to reunite with family and obtain medical treatment.

Cowper, Ernest, age 32, British Canadian, journalist traveling on business.

CAST OF CHARACTERS

Dolphin, Avis, age 12, British Canadian, traveling with nurse Hilda Ellis to attend school in England.

Foss, Dr. Carl, age 27, American, traveling to join war relief efforts in Belgium.

Holbourn, Ian, age 43, British, returning home.

Meriheina, William, age 26, Russian, traveling on business.

Naish, Belle, age 49, American, traveling with her husband, Theodore (59), to meet his family.

OFFICERS AND CREW ABOARD *LUSITANIA*

Anderson, James (Jock), age 48, British, staff captain.

Bestic, Albert, age 24, British Irish, junior third officer.

Gadd, Lott, age 45, British, *Lusitania* barber.

Hawkins, Handel, age 25, British, cellist in *Lusitania*'s band.

Lewis, John Idwal, age 29, British, senior third officer.

McCubbin, James, age 62, British, purser.

Morton, Leslie, age 18, British, signed on *Lusitania* as an able-bodied seaman with his brother, John (21).

Turner, William Thomas, age 58, British, captain of *Lusitania*.

INTERESTED PARTIES

Churchill, Winston, First Lord of the British Admiralty.

Fisher, Admiral Sir John (Jackie), First Sea Lord of the British Admiralty.

Horgan, John J., conducted first inquiry into the sinking as coroner at Kinsale, Ireland.

Mayer, Judge Julius, presided over American *Lusitania* liability trial, 1918.

CAST OF CHARACTERS

Mersey, John Bigham, Lord, presided over the official British Board of Trade Inquiry into the sinking of *Lusitania*.

Schwieger, Kapitänleutnant Walther von, age 30, captain of U-20.

Sumner, Charles, Cunard Line agent in New York City.

PREFACE

A beam from the lighthouse high atop the Old Head of Kinsale cut through the May twilight, its arc revealing, then concealing the grisly scene. Pillows, torn clothing, lifebelts, bits of ornately carved woodwork, dolls, purses, letters—all surged forward with each wave, littering the rocky Irish coast with the tragedy's debris. A lifeless arm appeared now and then, as if waving from the surf; babies with blue lips and tiny fingers curled in death floated peacefully; men in tweed suits, broken bones jutting through sickly gray skin, careened in the water; ladies, still clad in elegant afternoon ensembles now covered in soot and oil, twisted and turned as the current pummeled them toward land. The scene was ghastly, almost unbearable.

A few miles northeast, and a century later, a winged bronze angel peacefully gazes out over Casement Square in Cobh, the collection of streets and hills formerly known as Queenstown. Arms outstretched, head bowed, and feet planted atop a sword, she looks down on two sculpted sailors adorning the beautifully restrained monument. A simple inscription commemorates the terrible event: "To the Memory of All Who Perished by the Sinking of the *Lusitania*."

PREFACE

On the afternoon of May 7, 1915, a German U-boat fired a torpedo into the side of British ocean liner *Lusitania*; 1,198 passengers and crew perished. "Enlist!" evocative posters soon urged: the tragedy became a call to arms in the Allied battle against a cruel and callous nation of bloodthirsty "Huns" who killed women and children without mercy. There had been no shortage of shocking moments in the ongoing Great War, as the new twentieth century struggled to make sense of machine guns and mustard gas. The sinking of an unarmed passenger liner, though, signaled that not even civilians were immune from the effects of total warfare.

Just three years earlier, *Titanic* had gone to the bottom of the Atlantic after her fatal encounter with an iceberg. Wrapped in an aura of romantic myth and self-sacrifice, *Titanic* has long overshadowed *Lusitania*. Time has transformed a rather ordinary passenger liner into the height of luxury, an example of man's triumph over nature. Legend surrounds the two hours and forty minutes it took her to sink, when gentlemen stoically went to their deaths dressed in evening clothes, and ladies heroically refused to leave their husbands. Slipping beneath the frigid water, she took with her the last vestiges of a golden era of tradition and dignity. *Titanic* was a lesson in supreme arrogance, a Greek tragedy writ large, and a morality play that seemed to presage all the horrors of the coming war.

Lusitania, in contrast, took a mere eighteen minutes to sink; there was little time for heroics or self-analysis among panicked passengers and a largely inept crew. She fell victim to an ongoing conflict in which millions had already perished; within days of her sinking she again fell victim, this time to a propaganda war. Germany had warned passengers not to travel aboard British liners, which were regularly used to transport contraband and munitions; these facts gave Berlin its justification and allowed it to trumpet the sinking as a great achievement by the Imperial Navy. Elsewhere, revulsion turned to outrage by those favorably inclined toward Great Britain and her allies. The sinking, declared one contemporary, "marked the apex of horror" and revealed Germany's "diabolical barbarity." It had not been a disaster: it had been "butchery," the "slaughter of hundreds of women and children."[1] Yet word of the newest military campaigns, the latest atrocities against civilians, and the progress of the conflict itself soon overtook the sinking. Unease over being drawn into the Great War and decidedly mixed loyalties tempered the American reaction. *Lusitania*'s sinking did not, as is often said, draw America into the conflict: almost two years passed before the United States finally declared war on Kaiser Wilhelm II's Germany.

Titanic continued to live on in the public imagination; *Lusitania* faded from memory. She became a footnote in the history of the Great War, recalled for her end and, in time, for a host of controversies surrounding her final voyage. For the last half century, critics have unraveled conspiracies about her cargo; about the role of the British Admiralty and its First Lord, Winston Churchill, in her fate; and about a second, massive explosion that rattled through the liner after the torpedo's impact. *Titanic* has become a story of passengers and people; *Lusitania* has become a tale of intrigue, with whispers of illicit munitions and nefarious schemes designed to draw America into the war. This is not putting too fine a point on it: pick up nearly any book on *Lusitania* and almost inevitably one encounters plots, espionage, missing wireless messages, and political machinations woven into elaborate, Machiavellian tapestries.

This is all the more unfortunate in that *Lusitania*'s final story does not lack for high drama. When she went into service in 1907, *Lusitania* was the world's largest and most luxurious ocean liner, pride of the Cunard Line and proof that Britannia indeed still ruled the waves. By 1915, other liners had surpassed her in size and in ostentatious comforts, but *Lusitania* remained very much a grand lady of the Atlantic, plying her trade and attracting a glittering array of privileged passengers. In retrospect, her final voyage links two divergent threads. If *Titanic* seemingly ended the Gilded Age in America, so, too, did the First World War mark the death of the Edwardian Era in Europe. Looking back, it had seemed—at least for the privileged—a kind of long, golden Indian summer before the horrors of war burst forth, a time of genteel manners and leisurely pace, elegant gowns and glittering tiaras, bewhiskered monarchs and mechanical wonders. Even during the war, *Lusitania* lingered on as a tangible Edwardian survivor. Yet just hours before reaching Liverpool, she fell victim to one of the modern age's engineering wonders.

The human stories, all too often ignored in most works on *Lusitania,* provide a focus every bit as dramatic as persistent tales of conspiratorial intrigue and government malfeasance. At its heart, it is the story of a great liner in the Golden Age of Travel, a floating palace embodying the elegance and genteel traditions of an era doomed to oblivion. Passengers on her final voyage exemplified the shifting tide of society: millionaires and merchants; automobile manufacturers and race car drivers; suffragettes and shady social climbers; Red Cross volunteers and a witness to the shootout at the O.K. Corral; actors, singers, and writers; and even a pair of dedicated men who dared to live openly as a couple at a time when homosexuality was punishable with hard labor and lengthy prison sentences. All were randomly thrown together as they crossed the Atlantic; all shared the terrible trauma of her rapid, chaotic sinking. Many survivors were haunted to the end of their days by the agonizing sights and sounds they had witnessed on her decks and in the water.

In this book, we have largely focused on the lives and experiences of those traveling First Class (or Saloon Class, as Cunard called it) on *Lusitania*'s last voyage, with a sprinkling of Second Class passengers added to the narrative: we have not included those traveling Third Class. This decision stems not from class prejudices but rather from practicalities. Quite simply, the lives of the wealthy and well connected are better documented than those passengers who traveled in Steerage. In assembling our cast of characters, we looked for those who were well known before the tragedy, who occupied positions of prominence, or whose lives in some manner exemplified the era and provided an unsuspected bridge to themes still prevalent in the twenty-first century. By focusing tightly on this select group, we have tried to illuminate their lives and times, painting in portraits to depict *Lusitania*'s last voyage and hopefully help the ongoing effort to put a much needed and deserved human face to the tragedy.

LUSITANIA

PROLOGUE
SATURDAY, MAY 1, 1915

A rainy twilight fell over New York City on April 30, 1915. Spring was late that year: indeed, an unexpected blizzard had nearly paralyzed the city three weeks earlier. Rushing crowds filled the slippery sidewalks, dodging puddles and splashing water cast off by passing motorcars. Bells on trolleys clanged, horns honked, and horses pulling elegant carriages snorted and stomped along the wet pavement in a cacophony of sound that formed the city's own unique symphony of life.

New York City seemed caught in a surreal, parallel universe. Nearly a year earlier, the halcyon days of the Edwardian Era had given way to a new, terrifyingly modern age as the Great War spread across Europe. In muddy fields from East Prussia to Belgium, soldiers exchanged bullets from miserable trenches in a conflict whose scale eclipsed anything ever before witnessed. Despite intense pressure, isolationist, comfortably insular America was still untouched by the distant war. President Woodrow Wilson had insisted that "every man who really loves America will act and speak in the true spirit of neutrality." Too many people, he declared, would "excite passion" and try to divide the country into opposing camps.[(1)] Yet official policy could not override widespread worry: how long could America really remain neutral?

Here, in this prosperous, bustling metropolis, a different kind of war was being waged, a conflict between the dying Gilded Age and a new world of clinking cocktails and raucous jazz. Starting in the 1870s, a race of millionaires, speculators, and lavish hostesses invaded New York's proud old Knickerbocker society, all vying to stun the city with lavish spectacle and voluptuous wealth. The Gilded Age had burst with vibrant color on this sedate and drab world, replacing the "desiccated chocolate" brownstones of respectable society with new palaces of "white and colored marble," as H. G. Wells marveled.[2]

The exploits of The Mrs. Astor's famed 400 families of social merit had captivated and amused America for thirty years. They built their ornate palaces on Fifth Avenue and summered in hundred-room Newport "cottages" that, insisted a member, would have made "a Doge of Venice or a Lorenzo de Medici" envious.[3] Society reveled in extravagant parties, sleek yachts, and ever more brazen displays of excess. At a time when an average laborer made roughly $500 a year, one hostess spent $420,000 concealing black pearls in the oysters served to her guests; another piled her dining table high with sand and handed out little silver shovels from Tiffany, bidding guests to dig for party favors of emeralds, diamonds, and rubies.[4] They gave elaborate dinners for their favorite dogs; dressed as their own servants for balls; unleashed monkeys clad in tuxedos to leap upon startled guests; and had meals served while they sat atop horses in decorous hotel ballrooms.[5]

Such antics had once entertained and bemused: now, they repelled. The age of the imposing The Mrs. Astor had imperceptibly slipped into oblivion. Mansions still marched down Fifth Avenue in a parade of ostentatious Renaissance, Italianate, and

French facades, but office blocks like the towering Singer, Woolworth, and Metropolitan Life buildings now dominated. Since the controversial exhibitions at the New York City Armory in 1913, the avant-garde had replaced the sentimental in art. The handsome carriages that had once crowded Fifth Avenue had ceded their places to rumbling trolleys and weaving motorcars. Extravagant balls at Sherry's and fashionable dinners at Delmonico's had given way to noisy vaudeville revues, whose flirtatious chorus girls became celebrities. Operatic airs and refined waltzes disappeared, replaced by the popular songs of Irving Berlin, the tinkle of ragtime on a piano, and the exotic, sensuously dangerous coming of the Jazz Age.

Bevies of eager young couples, doing their best to emulate the popular Vernon and Irene Castle, fox-trotted, tangoed, and one-stepped across the city's nightspots.[6] People crowded the burgeoning motion picture houses, watching Mack Sennett's comedies, the antics of Charlie Chaplin, and the thrilling installments of *The Perils of Pauline*. The undoubted hit of the year was D. W. Griffith's epic *The Birth of a Nation,* a true spectacle that played to a packed house at Broadway's Liberty Cinema.[7]

Lights flashed and glasses clinked as couples danced that Friday evening into Saturday. There was incessant motion across town as well: throughout the night and into dawn, Pier 54 was a hive of activity. Wagons, vans, and trucks clogged the streets along Manhattan's West Side, stopping in the shadow of the darkened liner. Just three years earlier, this same pier had been the scene of heartrending pathos, as the Cunard liner *Carpathia* arrived bearing the lucky passengers rescued from the sinking of *Titanic*. Now, hour after hour, men deposited cargo, including 250 hefty canvas bags, filled with transatlantic mail.[8] Coal barges drew alongside the hull and spilled their loads through hatchway doors amid grimy black clouds. It took an enormous amount of coal to power the ship: at her top speed, she could consume up to a thousand tons a day.[9]

Wagons and carts delivered goods needed to sustain life during the liner's seven-day voyage. Passenger bookings had dropped considerably since the start of the war, but the vessel still needed an almost unbelievable amount of supplies: 45,000 pounds of beef; 17,000 pounds of mutton; 4,000 pounds of bacon; 40,000 eggs; 2,500 pounds of pork; 1,500 pounds of veal; 750 pounds of fresh salmon; 2,000 chickens, 150 turkeys, and 300 ducks; three barrels of live turtles; 100 pounds of caviar; 5,500 pounds of butter; 28 tons of potatoes; 6,000 gallons of cream; 3,000 gallons of milk; 1,600 pounds of coffee; hundreds of crates of fresh fruit and vegetables; boxes packed with rare truffles, pâté, crab, and lobster; and case after case of wine and champagne.[10] It was enough to sustain a small army.

Throughout the night, cranes lifted cargo into the liner's hold. Since the beginning of the war, British owners had used the vessel to transport contraband across the Atlantic. This spring of 1915, Great Britain faced a munitions shortage, and needed American war matériel in its fight. America was officially neutral, but in this case neutrality was a convenient pretense: U.S. industries regularly provided arms and other contraband to Great Britain. According to American law, it was all perfectly legal: a private firm could sell its goods to anyone without violating neutrality.[11] Yet the trade was generally one-sided: few goods or munitions went to Germany. Berlin strenuously and repeatedly complained that the American government, while claiming "an honorable neutrality," was aiding its enemies, but to no avail.[12]

Roughly two thirds of the cargo on this voyage consisted of matériel for military use, including brass, copper wire, and machine parts. Even the foodstuffs shipped in bulk were contraband—at least according to the British government's own definition

4

of the term. More lethal cargo loaded into the forward holds between the bow and bridge included 4.2 million rounds of Remington .303 rifle ammunition consigned to the British Royal Arsenal at Woolwich; 1,248 cases of shrapnel-filled artillery shells from the Bethlehem Steel Corporation, each case containing four 3-inch shells for a total of some fifty tons; eighteen cases of percussion fuses; and forty-six tons of volatile aluminum powder used to manufacture explosives.[13] According to American law, none of this fell under the category of ammunition forbidden aboard a passenger liner; instead, it was classified as a legal shipment of small arms.[14]

Work continued as dawn broke over New York City, revealing the Cunard Line's immense passenger liner *Lusitania*. Her sleek black hull, pierced by innumerable portholes, stretched some 787 feet from a sharply narrowed bow to a gracefully curved stern. Decks of yellow pine and teak crowned a gleaming white superstructure dotted with rows of lifeboats and ventilators; above, four sixty-five-foot-high funnels—raked at graceful angles—towered over the vessel. Once they had proudly sported the distinctive Cunard colors of reddish orange banded in black; now, they were cloaked in drab wartime gray.[15]

Less than a decade old, *Lusitania,* an onlooker once marveled, was "more beautiful than Solomon's Temple, and big enough to hold all his wives."[16] Subsidized by the British government on the understanding that in time of war she could be quickly converted to an armed auxiliary cruiser, she was immense. At just over 31,000 tons, *Lusitania* could accommodate three thousand persons, including crew, on her nine decks. At her maiden voyage in 1907, she had been the largest liner ever built, and until 1910 she was the fastest. *Lusitania* was a triumph: Man, through mastery of the Industrial Age, had finally tamed Nature.

By eight that Saturday morning, Pier 54 was crowded. Although the air was warm, clouds still cluttered the sky, releasing occasional bursts of rain over the scene.[17] Yet not even the weather could dampen spirits as friends and relatives embraced and shouted farewells. "Smartly-dressed officers" moved among the milling crowd as "great truck loads of luggage" and last-minute consignments of mail were rushed aboard.[18] Streets along the Chelsea Piers were clogged with a constant stream of wagons, vans, trucks, motorcars, and taxicabs, dispensing luggage and disgorging travelers destined for *Lusitania*. Passengers raced past newsstands where young boys loudly hawked the early editions. Within the papers lay an ominous announcement from the German embassy in Washington, D.C.:

NOTICE!

TRAVELLERS intending to embark on the Atlantic voyage are reminded that a state of war exists between Germany and her allies and Great Britain and her allies; that the zone of war includes the waters adjacent to the British Isles; that, in accordance with formal notice given by the Imperial German Government, vessels flying the flag of Great Britain, or of any of her allies, are liable to destruction in those waters and that travellers sailing in the war-zone on ships of Great Britain or her allies do so at their own risk.

IMPERIAL GERMAN EMBASSY

WASHINGTON, D. C., APRIL 22. 1915.

It was only an accident—though in retrospect, an ominous one—that the notice appeared next to an advertisement for *Lusitania*'s voyage. This warning had been the subject of worried debate among German officials in America. Ambassador to the United States Johann, Count von Bernstorff, had received the text several months earlier from Berlin but, "thinking it a great mistake" that would unduly antagonize the country, he had shoved it into a desk drawer and did his best to ignore its existence.[19] In April, Berlin had finally insisted that Bernstorff publish the warning. There was a week's delay: only on the morning of May 1 did the German notice finally appear in the press.[20] It had, a German spokesman said, merely been "an act of friendship."[21]

Staring up at *Lusitania*'s hull, seventeen-year-old Alice Lines, holding tight to a three-month-old girl named Audrey Pearl, was unnerved by the coming voyage. It wasn't the idea of the crossing itself: there had been frequent journeys across the Atlantic since the British nanny began working for the family of American Frederick Warren Pearl. A former surgeon-major during the Spanish-American War, Pearl had firsthand knowledge of the potential dangers: the family had been in Europe when the Great War erupted, and Germany had arrested Pearl as a spy. He wore English tweeds and carried a copy of *The Times* of London—all the proof they needed. His release sent the family—Pearl, his wife, Amy, five-year-old son Stuart, three-year-old daughter Amy (called "Bunny"), and one-year-old Susan, along with Alice—back to America, where a fourth daughter, Audrey, was born in early 1915. Now, Amy Pearl was expecting a fifth child as they again set off, this time for London, where her husband was to take up a Red Cross job with the American embassy. Luckily for Alice, a second nanny, a Danish girl named Greta Lorenson, had joined the household to help care for the children.[22]

Newsboys shouted the warning, and talk of a possible submarine attack rumbled through the waiting crowd. Still clutching baby Audrey, Alice scanned the German notice. The ship seemed so big and so fast, yet it was hard to forget the possible danger.

Now the Germans had practically advertised their intent to sink her. Nervously, Alice showed the notice to her employer's wife. "Take no notice, dear," Mrs. Pearl assured her, "it's just propaganda."[23]

Others echoed Amy Pearl's dismissal. Americans, a British journalist declared, were "as safe on Broadway" as they were aboard *Lusitania*; the warning was merely "a piece of impudent bluff . . . an infantile effort to make Americans afraid."[24] "Like many other passengers, I gave the notice no serious thought," recalled Boston bookseller Charles Lauriat. "No idea of canceling my trip occurred to me."[25] Oliver Bernard, a theatrical scenic designer, saw the warning as he read the morning newspaper over breakfast. He was "not seriously perturbed" by what he imagined was a gesture meant "to embarrass the United States Government and create further consternation in England." The speed of *Lusitania*, coupled with "the presence of so many American citizens on board," he thought, completely eliminated the possibility of a submarine attack.[26] Margaret, Lady Mackworth—returning to Great Britain with her father, David Thomas—paid no attention to the warning: "Feeling ran strong," she wrote, "and that we should be driven off our own boat by German threats, to take shelter on one of a neutral nationality after we had already booked our passage, was unthinkable."[27]

The German notice was not the only warning. That morning, thirty-seven-year-old millionaire Alfred Vanderbilt had sleepily struggled out of bed in his luxurious apartment at the Vanderbilt Hotel he had built on Park Avenue. He had spent the previous evening with his second wife, Margaret, at the theater, attending a performance of *A Celebrated Case*, a new Broadway play produced by David Belasco and Charles Frohman; today, he would sail aboard *Lusitania*.[28] At eight, the telephone rang. It was Vanderbilt's mother, Alice: had Alfred seen the notice in that morning's newspapers?[29] Alfred dismissed it as a joke. His valet, Ronald Denyer, then handed him a telegram: "Have it on good authority *Lusitania* is to be torpedoed. You had better cancel passage immediately." It was signed simply, "*Morte*."[30] It seemed absurd, and Vanderbilt dressed in a charcoal gray suit, a tweed cap atop his head, and a pink carnation jauntily adorning his lapel. Photographers and reporters swarmed around his motorcar as it pulled up at Pier 54 later that morning; spotting his friend, millionaire wine and champagne merchant George Kessler, Vanderbilt made his way through the crowd. He pulled the newspaper notice from his pocket, waved it at Kessler, and said, "How ridiculous this thing is! The Germans would not dare to make any attempt to sink this ship!"[31]

Broadway impresario Charles Frohman, whose play Vanderbilt had enjoyed the previous evening, was also bound for *Lusitania* that morning. "It seems to be the best ship to sail on," he wrote to a friend in London.[32] Actor John Barrymore unsuccessfully tried to dissuade Frohman from his trip. Barrymore's sister, actress Ethel, recalled that Frohman's voyage was "much against everybody's wishes." When she'd seen him earlier that week, the impresario told her, "Ethel, they don't want me to go on this boat," adding that he had received a message warning him off. He seemed determined to go; when Ethel left, he leaned over and kissed her cheek—something he had never before done.[33] To another friend, Frohman joked, "If you want to write me, just address the letter care of the German submarine." Now, as he arrived at the pier from his suite at the Knickerbocker Hotel, Frohman faced a bank of reporters. Asked if he was afraid of U-boats, the manager grinned, saying, "No, I am only afraid of IOUs."[34]

The notice troubled London merchant Henry Adams, head of the Mazawattee Tea Company. With his new wife, Annie, he was to return to Great Britain aboard *Lusitania,* but now thought a change of vessel might be best. He discussed the situation with Annie and argued that they should take a neutral liner, but his wife, who had relatives employed by Cunard, insisted that they sail as planned. "I have always been a confirmed Cunarder," she said.[35] Others were visibly anxious that morning. Twenty-six-year-old Dorothy Allen, nanny to the six young Crompton children traveling on *Lusitania* with their parents, stood at the pier, nervously crying at the idea of a potentially dangerous wartime crossing.[36]

An anxious Sidney Witherbee had rushed to the pier to make one last plea to his brother's family. Wealthy Alfred Witherbee, president of the Mexican Petroleum Solid Fuel Company, waited for his lovely young wife, Beatrice, their nearly four-year-old son, Alfred Jr., and his mother-in-law, Mary Brown, to join him at their new home in London. Vivacious Beatrice, called "Trixie," had hurriedly packed up clothing, furs, jewels, silver, porcelain, and linens—a mountain of belongings bound for *Lusitania*'s cargo holds. The previous night, Sidney had implored Beatrice to take another liner; now, having just read the German notice, he tried again. Beatrice dismissed his concerns: *Lusitania* was faster than any other ship, and the idea of some submarine successfully attacking her seemed so unlikely.[37]

Immensely wealthy Mary Hammond, too, refused to let the warning dampen the impending voyage: with her husband, Ogden, she would celebrate their eighth wedding anniversary aboard *Lusitania*. Ogden worried: *Lusitania* was a British ship, heading into a declared war zone—it somehow seemed foolish to sail aboard her when they could travel on a truly neutral American liner. He had even more cause to worry as they headed toward the ship that morning. A few days earlier, Mary's aunt had given the couple some stunning news. Count von Bernstorff happened to be a friend; hearing that the Hammonds were to sail to Europe, he had apparently warned her aunt, "Do not let anyone you know get on the *Lusitania*." Mary thought it was a joke, but Ogden took the warning seriously enough to ask an official at Cunard Line's New York office about the potential danger.[38] Traveling aboard *Lusitania,* he was assured, was "perfectly safe, safer than the trolley cars."[39] Ogden wasn't convinced: together with his brother, John, he tried his best to change his wife's mind. If Mary insisted, John said, at least she should have a will: she was a millionaire, with three young children, Mary, Millicent, and Ogden Jr. And so that Saturday morning, John came aboard *Lusitania,* presenting Mary with a hastily drawn-up document to sign before the ship sailed.[40]

Mary dismissed the warnings; so, too, did others. A few days earlier, two British cotton dealers working in Texas had boarded a train bound for New York: bulky Robert Timmis was delighted that his friend and fellow dealer Ralph Moodie would also be sailing on *Lusitania.* A few years earlier, Timmis had been blinded in one eye, but nothing could keep him from his annual trip to Europe. Now, he jokingly told his wife, "We may be torpedoed on this trip, but don't worry. If we should be, we probably will be near the Irish coast." Even when he saw the German notice that Saturday morning, Timmis maintained an air of jovial dismissal. "We thought little about it at the time," he recalled, convinced that he was embarking on "just another journey."[41]

Canadian Thomas Home was glad that he'd woken early: "Never before," he wrote, "have I seen so much crowd and so much baggage."[42] The buyer for a Toronto department store had just missed being on *Titanic* three years earlier.[43] Now he shuffled along the pier under the watchful eyes of Cunard officials who examined tickets; this, he knew, was unusual—and not a reassuring sign, especially in light of the German notice.[44]

Mountains of leather valises and wicker cases, steamer trunks and hatboxes, arrived throughout the morning. They contained all the worldly belongings of some passengers, setting off to embark upon new lives in the Old World; many more, though, were filled with a wide range of clothing and accessories necessary to maintain the sartorial traditions and comforts of First Class. Trunks ticketed "Not Wanted" were separated and hoisted into the cargo holds, while stewards supervised as those needed during the voyage were taken to cabins.[45]

These trunks and suitcases were a source of potential worry. Would a German spy or saboteur conceal some infernal machine amongst stockings or handkerchiefs? Security this May 1 was especially tight. Detectives checked papers and tickets before allowing passengers to approach the ship; luggage had to be personally claimed and identified before it was loaded, and all handbags, packages, and parcels were searched. Officials waiting at the foot of gangways double-checked tickets and papers before allowing passengers aboard.[46] Yet such measures were apparently haphazardly enforced. Forty-seven-year-old former deputy sheriff Michael Byrne, off to visit relatives in Ireland, arrived at the pier with his German-born wife and several friends, a large steamer trunk, two suitcases, and an umbrella bag. "No officer or anyone else questioned me or asked about my baggage," he recalled. Nor did anyone stop his wife and friends from following him aboard to inspect the ship.[47] Charles Lauriat was equally surprised when two members of his family, who had come to see him off, were also allowed to join him aboard the ship without any questions being asked.[48]

Crews cranked newsreel cameras as passengers shuffled along the pier; a few photographers, noting the German warning, joked that they were going to entitle their images "The *Lusitania*'s last voyage."[49] Charles Sumner, general agent for the Cunard Line in New York, seemed equally lighthearted. There was, he insisted, "no risk whatsoever" by sailing aboard *Lusitania*.[50] The ship, he promised, could make 25 knots; this was "too fast for any submarine. No German vessel of war can get near her."[51] As for the notice, Sumner—pointing at the lines of passengers—laughingly said, "You can see how it has affected the public."[52]

High on the liner's gently curved bridge, Captain William Turner surveyed the last-minute preparations. He dismissed worries that his ship might be in danger heading into a war zone patrolled by German U-boats as "the best joke I've heard in many days."[53] Turner was cavalier when questioned about the German notice and potential danger: "I wonder what the Germans will do next?" he mused. "Well, it doesn't seem as if they have scared many people from going on the ship by the looks of the pier and passenger list."[54] *Lusitania*, he insisted, was entirely safe. "Do you think all these people would be booking passage on board *Lusitania* if they thought she could be caught by a German submarine?" he asked reporters. "Germany can concentrate her entire fleet of submarines on our track and we would elude them." Besides, he added, "we shall be going faster than any submarine can travel; therefore, they are not likely to sneak up on us."[55] As the crew bustled over the liner's decks preparing for the voyage, a few of the more superstitiously minded whispered a piece of ominous news: Dowie, the ship's four-year-old black cat and unofficial mascot, had disappeared the previous night, and no one had seen him since.[56]

Lusitania had been scheduled to sail at ten that morning. On this voyage, she would carry the largest number of passengers since the beginning of hostilities.[57] Some were off to join the fighting in Europe; others were hoping to join relief efforts, or traveling to reunite with loved ones who were destined for the battlefield. But surprisingly, and considering the state of war and the risks of traveling through an area patrolled by hostile U-boats, many passengers sailed aboard *Lusitania* for holidays and family reunions.[58]

Following custom, the 373 Third Class passengers had begun forward boarding first, just after seven.[59] "This is not, as has been unkindly suggested," a guidebook warned, "because they only pay low fares, but because there are so many of them, because the number of children in that class is proportionately greater than in any other, and because sufficient time must be allowed for them to settle down before the voyage begins."[60] An hour later, the 601 Second Class passengers embarked, climbing gangplanks at the rear of the vessel. Helpful stewards examined tickets and directed people down decks and along corridors to their cabins.[61]

The 290 passengers traveling in First, or Saloon, Class began arriving shortly before nine.[62] This, as one contemporary noted, "is a more ceremonious affair, for they sometimes include persons of title, holders of high naval or military rank, colonial governors, millionaires, and even members of reigning families. Their arrival is interesting because there is about it a survival of the etiquette of the sailing-ship days, when the owners of the ships saw personally to their departure and were always careful to escort any exalted personages to the ship's side and present them to the captain." They disappeared into the pier building, temporarily shielded from clicking cameras as they presented papers and steadily neared the open doors at the side. Emerging into the light of day, they climbed narrow gangways above the dark Hudson that seemed to vibrate ominously with every tread. Once they had entered the hull of the vessel, crisply uniformed officers waited in the First Class Entrance Hall, decorously welcoming these ladies and gentlemen aboard the great *Lusitania*.[63]

"Such last minute excitement!" was how an earlier traveler described the scene aboard *Lusitania*. "All was confusion—stewards and stewardesses guiding passengers with their suitcases to their staterooms, lifts going up and down, bustle, noise, and hurrying everywhere."[64] Stewards rushed along corridors, bearing an assortment of farewell gifts sent on by friends and relatives of those sailing that morning. There were immense bouquets of flowers; bottles of fine wine and vintage champagne; carefully wrapped boxes of candy or hothouse fruits; packages of books; collections of teas from around the world; decorative tins of delicacies like caviar or exotic tropical jams; and a multitude of cards and letters wishing travelers a memorable voyage.[65]

More than a few passengers clustered in *Lusitania*'s Reading and Writing Room that morning. Architect and spiritualist Theodate Pope sat there with her traveling companion, Edwin Friend, browsing through the newspaper, when she spotted the German notice. "That means, of course, that they intend to get us," she commented.[66] Others penned farewell notes and letters to friends and relatives, to be sent off the ship when the pilot departed: these were the people who, as Lady Mackworth thought, were "fully conscious of the risk we were running."[67] Elaine Knight, traveling with her brother Charles, wrote out an eerie postcard to her niece: "I am mailing you this card just as we are going on board the *Lusitania*. Will write as soon as we reach the other side, if I am still alive."[68]

There was an unexpected delay that morning, when word came that the British Admiralty had abruptly requisitioned *Cameronia*, a smaller liner that was to sail from New York to Glasgow, to use as a troop transport. Forty-one of her passengers and their baggage were transferred to *Lusitania*.[69] The delay, Oliver Bernard noted, created some tension as people again worried over safety, though *Cameronia*'s former passengers were "obviously delighted" to find themselves aboard "a faster, and therefore safer, ship."[70] In all, 1,264 passengers sailed on *Lusitania*, less than half of her actual capacity; with a crew of 702, which included the ship's five musicians, this brought the total to 1,966. By noon, morning rain gave way to patches of sunshine, as a boy wandered over the ship shouting, "All ashore that's going ashore!"[71] Passengers lined *Lusitania*'s decks, shouting farewells and waving handkerchiefs to onlookers below. "It was almost like a personal triumph," a previous passenger remembered, "to be one of those who stood at the rail, looking down. . . . You were a part of the ship itself, although you were hardly more than a pinhead along the great expanse of deck rail."[72] An "eager, restless movement of the throng" aboard ship always marked such departures. Writer Theodore Dreiser likened the experience to "the lobby of one of the great New York hotels at dinnertime" as people scampered and scrambled.[73]

"Bells were ringing their signals for final preparation," Phoebe Amory remembered. "The shrill blasts from the tugboats announced that they were ready to begin their labor of moving the great ship from her moorings, and the deep, throaty reply from the chimes of the *Lusitania* voiced her assent."[74] Hatches were sealed, gangways pulled in, lines hauled up, and doors closed as the ship readied for her voyage. Cameras clicked and men along the pier cranked their newsreels, capturing Captain Turner as he looked out from the bridge.[75]

Deep below, a grimy contingent of shirtless trimmers rushed wheelbarrows filled with coal from bunkers to boiler rooms. Mustachioed Chief Engineer Archibald Bryce shouted orders and watched the gauges as stokers relentlessly fed the fuel into *Lusitania*'s blisteringly hot furnaces. Everything "clanked and rattled and hissed and squeaked" as the ship built up steam.[76] A deep rumble shivered through *Lusitania* as her steam turbine engines came to life.[77]

Members of the Royal Gwent Singers, returning home to Wales

after an American tour, loudly sang "The Star-Spangled Banner," while the ship's five-man band launched into "Tipperary" as the crowd along the pier cheered and waved. Three little tugs gently eased the black hull out into the Hudson.[78] Gulls swooped and circled as *Lusitania*'s four immense bronze propellers twisted and turned, churning behind them a wide wake of foam. Slowly, surely, *Lusitania* steamed past Ellis Island, the Statue of Liberty, and what Theodore Dreiser deemed "the magnificent wall of lower New York, set like a jewel in a green ring of seawater," as the city receded in the distance.[79] Smoke curled from her funnels and waves furrowed against her bow as *Lusitania* picked up speed. Across the Hudson, a line of German passenger liners, kept at dock for fear that British cruisers patrolling the waters outside of America's three-mile limit would sink them as potential enemy auxiliary cruisers if they attempted to return home, attracted much attention.[80] With the sun now shining on the brass letters of her proud name, *Lusitania* was on her way out of New York, bound for Liverpool on her 101st return voyage.

CHAPTER ONE

A wave of excited, enthusiastic adulation followed *Lusitania* out of New York harbor—a distant echo of a fine, early summer day nine years earlier, when another expectant crowd had gathered along the banks of Scotland's River Clyde. Then, the usual sounds of shouted orders, melding metal, and ceaseless hammering of rivets at the John Brown Shipyard had temporarily fallen silent, replaced by the rousing strains of "Rule Britannia." Gentlemen in frock coats or dark uniforms awash with shining medals had stood with ladies dressed in summer pastels, their faces shielded from the sun by wide picture hats adorned with flowers and a kaleidoscope of twirling parasols. All eyes gazed on the black-hulled vessel dwarfing the slipway. At half-past noon, a bottle of champagne cracked across her stately bow as she received the name *Lusitania*.[1] At the time of her launch, she was the largest, fastest, and most magnificent ocean liner in the world.

It was the Golden Age of the Steamship, a time when travel was not merely the means to an end but an end in itself. "How you traveled was who you were," and *Lusitania* was meant to attract the era's wealthy and well connected.[2] The funereal gloom of Queen Victoria's long reign had given way to an age of undisguised pleasures under her son King Edward VII. Aristocrats and millionaires bought their clothing in Belle Époque Paris and dined at Maxim's or at the Ritz; adorned themselves with tiaras and jewelry from Cartier and Fabergé; "took the waters" at Marienbad, Baden-Baden, and Bad Homburg; and gambled away fortunes at Monte Carlo's baize-covered tables. They shouted for their favorite horses at Longchamp, Ascot, and the Derby; yachted at Cowes and Kiel alongside Kaiser Wilhelm II; basked in the sunshine of Deauville, Biarritz, and Nice; and slaughtered hundreds of thousands of grouse, partridge, and pheasant at autumn shooting parties on vast country estates. With an almost frenzied delirium, people read Sigmund Freud, Rainer Maria Rilke, and Arthur Rimbaud; took coffee in Vienna's Art Nouveau cafés; watched the exotic dances of Serge Diaghilev's *Ballets Russes* and Isadora Duncan; and listened to the lyrical and cacophonous music of Gustav Mahler, Richard Strauss, Maurice Ravel, and Igor Stravinsky.

Fashionable society was constantly on the move. From New York, London, Berlin, and St. Petersburg, they traveled on liners and aboard luxurious private railway cars seeking diversion. An ocean voyage beckoned the elite with promises of romance, glamour, and luxury. It was not uncommon for a First Class passenger to travel with a dozen steamer trunks and pieces of luggage, hatboxes, and jewelry cases. Some brought their own maids and valets to tend to their needs while aboard ship; others refused to travel without their own lace pillows, imported linens, and favorite pets. The most exacting even dispatched cases of wine and champagne, or trunks filled with special delicacies, carefully stowed in the ship's vast refrigerators so that they could be enjoyed throughout the voyage.[3] These passengers wanted all the comforts of their mansions or country estates while at sea; mahogany-paneled drawing rooms, smoking rooms with crackling fires, and immense dining saloons offered elegant reassurance. Those from the Old World appreciated the air of tradition, with an attentive staff of deferential British waiters and stewards to look after them; Americans wanted not merely luxury but the latest innovations at sea: elevators, swimming baths, telephones, and, above all, speed.

Lusitania had been built to satisfy both the traditionalists and the modernists, though she owed her life to the more prosaic concerns of British pride and maritime supremacy. Since the advent of regular and reliable commercial transatlantic passenger service in 1818, countries and companies had vied with each other to offer the fastest crossing times. Great Britain had seemingly cornered the honor, and few ships proved to be as quick or as reliable as those belonging to the Cunard Steamship Company. Founded in 1838 by Halifax businessman Samuel Cunard to win mail contracts and subsidized by generous governmental loans, the line established an early dominance when, in 1840, its ship *Britannia* crossed the Atlantic in a record twelve days. Her feat won *Britannia* the fabled Blue Riband, an unofficial honor awarded to the fastest crossing between Great Britain and North America. Vessels belonging to the Collins, Inman, and White Star lines challenged Cunard over the next half century, but in the 1890s the company reclaimed its premier position with *Campania* and *Lucania,* ships whose speed cut the time at sea to just over five days.[4]

Then the Germans entered the game. The first of Queen Victoria's seemingly endless swarm of grandchildren, Kaiser Wilhelm II had always felt torn between ingratiating himself—often annoyingly—to his British relatives and insisting on Teutonic superiority in all things. Starting in 1898, a string of Norddeutscher Lloyd and Hamburg-Amerika Line vessels—marked with distinctive paired funnels and larger, more luxurious, and faster than their British counterparts—seized the Blue Riband and threatened perpetual dominance of the transatlantic trade.[5]

Things came to a head in 1902, when American financier J. P. Morgan purchased a controlling interest in both the Hamburg-Amerika and Norddeutscher Lloyd lines as well as in Britain's White Star Line for his International Mercantile Marine.[6] Soon, Morgan was pressing to buy Cunard—the only large shipping company still exclusively in British hands. The proposal sent shockwaves through the British Admiralty. The Royal Navy needed complete control over a fleet of liners that, in the event of a war, could be requisitioned and converted to troop transports or armed cruisers. With this in mind, the Admiralty partnered with Cunard and subsidized construction of two new liners. Cunard was given £2.6 million, which was to be repaid in annual installments over twenty years at the exceptionally low interest rate of 2.75 percent (the customary rate was 5 percent); in addition, the government would give Cunard an annual operating stipend of some £75,000 for each vessel and another £68,000 for carrying the mail. Provisions in the agreement demanded that the liners be capable of maintaining an average speed of 25 knots; that the Admiralty approve all plans; and that the vessels be subject to government requisition in time of war.[7]

From 1904 to 1907, work went on at a furious pace. At first, *Lusitania* and her sister ship, *Mauretania,* were to feature only three funnels, in contrast to their German rivals; however, passengers associated speed with the number of smokestacks, and so a fourth was added.[8] The Admiralty demanded that all engine and boiler rooms, as well as steering mechanisms, be placed below the waterline, where they would be safe from shelling if the vessel saw military action. There were four boiler rooms situated in the main section of the ship, with the forward space reserved for cargo and the engine rooms located aft. The designers abandoned the customary reciprocating engines in favor of new steam-driven turbines; twenty-five coal-fueled boilers, fired by 192 furnaces, could produce 68,000 horsepower to drive the four bronze propellers—faster than any other ship afloat. Lateral bulkheads divided her into twelve main watertight compartments, any two of which could be flooded without risk to the ship; thirty-five hydraulic watertight doors sealed them off, and a double bottom added further protection. Coal bunkers lined the ship's hull for two thirds of its length, providing longitudinal bulkheads as an additional safeguard.[9]

Everything about the finished *Lusitania* was both revolutionary and enormous. More than 4 million rivets studded the 26,000 steel plates composing her 782-foot, 2-inch hull; her anchor chains each weighed just over 10 tons. Over 200 miles of electric wiring snaked through the vessel, supplying power to more than 5,000 individual lights. At 31,550 tons, she became the world's largest ship, capable of carrying 2,198 passengers and 827 members of her crew.[10] On her trials, she managed a record speed of 26.7 knots; vibration from the turbine propellers, though, violently shook the Second Class accommodations located in the stern.[11] The space had to be completely redone, with new supports disguised as columns and ornamental arches in a not entirely successful effort to stabilize the accommodations.[12]

On her maiden voyage in 1907, *Lusitania* barely missed capturing the Blue Riband. She won it a month later, crossing from Liverpool to New York in 4 days, 19 hours, and 52 minutes. Her sister ship, *Mauretania,* bettered even this, though in 1909—after her triple-bladed screws were replaced with four-bladed propellers—*Lusitania* again took the title of fastest ship in the world. Her triumph was short-lived: in a month, *Mauretania* permanently reclaimed the title.[13]

Lusitania plied the Atlantic for seven years, collecting accolades and attracting a glittering, international clientele. In time, larger, more luxurious vessels challenged *Lusitania*'s primacy: White Star Line's *Olympic* and, briefly, *Titanic,* along with

Hamburg-Amerika's trio of massive liners, *Imperator, Vaterland,* and *Bismarck,* and even Cunard's own *Aquitania* of 1914. Yet *Lusitania* had a special appeal: she was, said one lady, "the most wonderful thing on the sea."[14] She was the floating embodiment of the Edwardian Era's Indian summer, a halcyon age that seemed destined to last forever.

Then came the summer of 1914, when a Serbian nationalist assassinated Archduke Franz Ferdinand, heir to the Austro-Hungarian throne, and his morganatic wife during their visit to Sarajevo. Austrian and Serbian diplomats traded pointed accusations, but few people actually believed that the assassination would lead to anything more dangerous than some incautious saber rattling. After all, they reasoned, there had been no major European war for more than four decades. Austria, not surprisingly, wanted the Serbian government—which had aided the assassination—punished, and appealed to her ally Kaiser Wilhelm II for German support. Serbia, little more than a Russian protectorate, invoked their shared Slav heritage and turned to Tsar Nicholas II. "Willy" and "Nicky" exchanged increasingly frantic telegrams, each imploring the other to exercise restraint as they mobilized their armies. Agreements and ententes steadily pushed nation after nation toward the abyss: by the first week of August, Great Britain, France, and Russia were at war with Germany and Austria-Hungary.

The Great War, most people had optimistically believed, would be over by Christmas. Naive enthusiasm characterized its first months: the brightest young men of their generation enlisted amid patriotic calls to arms, cheered by frenzied crowds toward miserable deaths in muddy wastelands. Yet the war did not end: Russian efforts in the east and French resistance along the Marne confused the carefully wrought plans of German generals. A deadly game of stalemate descended over trenches scarring the continent from Belgium to East Prussia; ugly barbed wire stretched for hundreds of miles, weaving through field and forest as artillery whizzed through the air and the desolate scenes rang with the incessant rattle of machine guns. Even civilians far away from the front lived in fear as airplanes buzzed the skies and zeppelins dropped bombs on the unsuspecting. By the spring of 1915, over three million soldiers lay dead.

The British Admiralty had subsidized *Lusitania* and *Mauretania* on the understanding that, in the event of war, they could be requisitioned and converted to troop transports or armed auxiliary merchant cruisers. Admiral Sir John "Jackie" Fisher, who ruled the Admiralty as First Sea Lord, and First Lord Winston Churchill, representing the cabinet, heartily disliked each other, but they did agree on one thing: *Lusitania* was unfit for war service. She was simply too large and it took too much coal to maintain her record speeds. Although still classed as a reserve merchant cruiser by the British Royal Navy, and listed as such in the latest editions of *Jane's Fighting Ships* and *Brassey's Naval Annual*, *Lusitania* returned to regular service.[15]

Cunard later insisted that it operated *Lusitania* "as a public service" during the war, and that the company did so without expecting any profit.[16] To save money, it shut down one of her boiler rooms, reducing her top speed from 26 to 21 knots.[17] This wasn't a secret: before leaving New York on Saturday, Captain Turner told reporters that she would be operating "under three sections of boilers, and will average about 22 knots if the weather is fine."[18] Yet Cunard didn't advertise the fact, and many passengers heard contrary information. "When buying my ticket," said Michael Byrne, "I was told that the *Lusitania* would make 25 or 28 knots an hour when we would sight the Irish coast."[19] Even as Turner stood on the liner talking about his slower speed, Cunard agent Charles Sumner on the pier below him was spewing disinformation, perhaps to assuage nervous passengers. *Lusitania,* he assured everyone, would be safe from any submarine, as she would run at a speed of 25 knots.[20]

Lusitania might be Cunard's liner, but as soon as she was three miles off the British or American coasts, she fell under Admiralty jurisdiction. "Not only has the Admiralty assumed charge of our line," Charles Stead, advertising manager for Cunard, later said, "but it has made this control so absolute that we have even been unable to reach our own vessels by wireless for any purpose."[21] All communication went through the Admiralty—suggestions, warnings, and instructions on how to navigate *Lusitania* through the waters off the Irish coast.

And those waters represented a potentially lethal threat. For eight months, Great Britain and Germany had escalated the war at sea. Britain had always prided herself on her naval superiority; the Kaiser's new fleet of *Unterseeboote,* or U-boats, offered a surprisingly deadly challenge. Few had initially regarded them as a serious threat. Lord Fisher had tried to warn his Admiralty colleagues, but to no avail: U-boats were largely untested, their capabilities crude, and their effectiveness in doubt. The very idea of prowling about beneath the water, attacking and destroying without direct confrontation, somehow seemed *so* ungentlemanly. Having dismissed the threat, Great Britain was now learning that these U-boats could be fearsome, deadly hunters. In a letter to his German counterpart, Grand Admiral Alfred von Tirpitz, an exasperated Lord Fisher assured him, "I don't blame you for this submarine business. I'd have done it myself."[22]

At first, the war at sea followed a gentlemanly set of informal regulations known as the Cruiser Rules, codified by The Hague Conventions in 1899 and 1907. An armed ship or U-boat encountering an enemy merchant vessel was expected to give warning either by a shot across the bow or by semaphore flags. The challenged ship was to stop and allow a search of its cargo; if no contraband was discovered, she could proceed. If she was found to be carrying munitions or war matériel, her crew and any passengers were to be allowed sufficient time to abandon ship before she was sunk. Merchant vessels were also obliged to follow certain rules: they were not to display false or neutral flags; they were not allowed to actively resist search or sinking; they were not allowed to flee from a challenge; and they were not allowed a military or an armed escort. Any of these actions meant that the challenged vessel lost its immunity and was not subject to warning before destruction.[23]

Such niceties may seem absurd in a time of war, yet in the first months of the conflict, as one author noted, with "typically Teutonic passion for legality" U-boats diligently followed the Cruiser Rules when they encountered enemy vessels, surfacing, firing warning shots, and allowing ample time for passengers and crew to abandon ship before sinking it.[24] Then, in January 1915, the Admiralty made a momentous, and ultimately fatal, decision.

That month, the Admiralty issued secret orders that not only violated the Cruiser Rules but also ensured that Germany would respond in kind. In addition to disguising a vessel's name and company colors on her funnels, British ships were advised that flying the false flags of neutral countries would confuse the enemy; "it is not in any way dishonorable," instructions insisted. If possible, merchant ships should fire on suspected enemy submarines, even if they had not yet signaled intent or challenged the vessel. Captains were not to stop if challenged by a submarine; any captain who disobeyed would be court-martialed. Instead, they were to evade submarines by any means necessary, including firing upon them or ramming them at top speed without warning.[25] Britain, it was said, not only "ruled the waves, but waived the rules."[26]

These orders seem logical, especially in a time of war, yet they clearly violated the Cruiser Rules. With them, the Admiralty arguably abandoned any expectation that Germany would follow rules that the British themselves willfully ignored. U-boats could no longer safely surface and fire a warning shot for fear of being rammed or fired upon. A neutral flag was no longer a guarantee of neutrality. It was no longer possible for a U-boat to give warning: to do so risked destruction of vessel and crew.[27] Later, Winston Churchill admitted as much, writing that, by forcing U-boats to operate in this way, Great Britain guaranteed that there was a "greater risk of mistaking neutral for British ships, and of drowning neutral crews and thus embroiling Germany with other Great Powers."[28]

Germany learned of these instructions a few days after they were issued, when it captured a British vessel and found the communiqué.[29] The previous autumn, Great Britain had declared the entire North Sea a war zone and mined the approaches; in the spring of 1915, she declared all foodstuffs to be contraband; nearly 750,000 Germans eventually perished in this attempt to starve their country into submission.[30] On February 4, 1915, the German government answered with its own declaration:

> The waters around Great Britain and Ireland, including the whole of the English Channel, are hereby declared to be a war zone. From February 18 onward, every enemy merchant vessel encountered in this zone will be destroyed, nor will it always be possible to avert the danger thereby threatened to the crew and passengers. Neutral vessels will also run a risk in the war zone because, in view of the hazards of sea warfare and the British authorization of January 31 of the misuse of neutral flags, it may not always be possible to prevent attacks on enemy ships without harming neutral ships.[31]

In response, President Woodrow Wilson warned that there would be "strict accountability" if a German submarine destroyed an "American vessel or the lives of American citizens."[32]

An air of tension now surrounded *Lusitania*'s crossings—something only heightened by the German notice in New York City newspapers that first Saturday in May. Responsibility for this ship, her cargo, and the lives of 1,965 passengers and crew rested heavily on Captain William Turner's stout shoulders. Just a few months earlier, Cunard had picked him to helm *Lusitania* in the aftermath of an international incident. In February, returning to Great Britain from New York, *Lusitania* had followed Admiralty instructions and flown a false flag—in this case, the Stars and Stripes. Germany immediately protested, and President Wilson was himself none too pleased at this breach of maritime law. Daniel Dow, *Lusitania*'s captain, first suggested that he had been entitled to fly the American flag because his ship carried mail from that country; when this didn't convince, he insisted that Americans on the vessel had begged him to fly the flag for their own safety.[33] The resulting controversy proved too much for the nervous Dow, and Cunard tapped Turner to take command.[34]

Turner loved the sea: it was in his blood. His father was a naval captain from Liverpool, but he wanted his son to be "respectable," and pushed for him to enter the Church. "How the old boy ever got such a notion," Turner's son Norman later said, "is beyond understanding, as anyone less likely to become a parson than my father would be hard to imagine." Declaring that he would never become "a devil dodger," the boy ran away to sea when he was thirteen.[35] The first ship on which Turner served foundered off the Irish coast. Despite this misfortune, Turner remained at sea. He joined Cunard in 1878 as fourth officer aboard *Cherbourg*; when *Cherbourg* accidentally collided with a smaller vessel Turner dove into the water and rescued two of the flailing crew members. On another occasion, Turner was swept overboard and literally fought back swarming sharks by punching them. That he was personally courageous no one doubted; in 1883, he also rescued a young boy who had fallen into the Mersey River, for which he received a medal for valor.[36]

In 1883 Turner wed his cousin Alice, who gave him two sons, Percy in 1885, and Norman in 1893, but the marriage eventually proved a failure. In 1903, Alice left, taking their two sons with her. Turner hired a young woman, Mabel Every, as his housekeeper, and the two soon became inseparable. Turner settled into a happy domestic routine, tending to his small garden and playing with his dog and cat. He was, Norman recalled, "a connoisseur of good food and wine, with a preference for German food," and enjoyed smoking his favorite pipe.[37]

Turner gradually rose through the ranks, receiving command of Cunard's liners *Carpathia* in 1904, *Caronia* in 1908, and *Lusitania* in 1910. Unlike other lines, Cunard tended to move its captains from one ship to another, and by 1913 Turner was at the helm of *Mauretania*. After being promoted to the rank of commander in the Royal Naval Reserve, Turner was given the new *Aquitania* when she made her maiden voyage to New York in 1914. A stint aboard the liner *Transylvania* followed, and in the spring of 1915 Turner was asked to replace the nervous Captain Dow aboard *Lusitania*.

A captain was expected not merely to safely navigate his ship but also to act as Cunard's official representative and host. It was his job to know his most important passengers, to pore over *Who's Who, Burke's Peerage,* society *Blue Books,* and the European *Almanach de Gotha* listing royalty and aristocrats. The most privileged passengers always demanded extraordinary consideration, from seating at the Captain's Table to special tours of the vessel. A captain, wrote one historian, had "to adjust disputes, pacify angry women, comfort frightened ones, and judge correctly just when to send one whose conduct is questionable to her room for the rest of the passage. He must know when to forbid the bartender to serve more liquor to a passenger who is drinking too much, and just when to post the notice in the smoking room that gamblers are on board. Passengers must not be antagonized unless they antagonize others more valuable to the company than themselves."[38]

Cunard believed in Turner, paying him a generous £1,000 a year, far more than most other captains received.[39] His crew held the gruff captain in great esteem, knowing that his strict, matter-of-fact manner ensured a tightly run ship.[40] Turner, one *Lusitania* passenger noted, was "not the picture postcard commodore of an Atlantic fleet." Instead, he seemed "a more ordinary type of old man, who wore, rather than carried, his gold braid as if conscious of his Sunday best."[41] Short and stocky, with "broad shoulders and powerful arms," Turner, said one comrade, was "a rugged old salt if ever there was one," a man known for being "taciturn and austere."[42]

Yet Turner failed miserably in the role of social butterfly. Many passengers, noted a guidebook, viewed a captain as "little more than a pleasant host," and vied with themselves to obtain seats at his table.[43] Turner loathed the social obligations accompanying his position, preferring to dine alone in his cabin rather than preside at his table in the Dining Saloon.[44] In private, he supposedly condemned most of his wealthy passengers as "bloody monkeys."[45]

With Turner purposely absenting himself as much as possible, it fell to the staff captain to serve as the ship's social leader.[46] Aboard *Lusitania,* this position was filled by forty-eight-year-old Liverpool native James Anderson. Known as "Jock," he was, said one acquaintance, "a man of sturdy character and fine knowledge of seamanship," someone whose genial nature better meshed with the expectations of the ship's privileged passengers.[47] Anderson, in turn, relied on his comrades to help tend to the passengers: Chief Officer John Piper; Extra Chief Officer John Stevens; First Officer Arthur Jones; Second Officer Percy Hefford, on his way to attend a relative's funeral; Senior Third Officer John Idwal Lewis; and recently married, twenty-four-year-old Dublin native Albert Bestic, who served as junior third officer.[48] Cunard laid down a series of rigid rules it expected its officers to follow, warning them not to drink with or become too friendly with the passengers and "on no account invite them to their cabins or vice-versa."[49]

Turner could rely on these officers, assured of their competence and loyalty. He couldn't be as certain when it came to his crew on this voyage. The demands of war had played havoc with the merchant fleet. When the conflict erupted, Cunard "lost all its Royal Naval Reserve and Fleet Reserve men" to the service. The lack of available capable seamen led Cunard to "take on the best men they could get, and to train them as well as might be in the time at their disposal."[50]

Eighteen-year-old Leslie Morton and his brother, John, were among those who signed on to *Lusitania* as last-minute deckhands. They had just spent several months at sea on "a particularly vicious passage," working their way from Liverpool to Australia and then to New York on the sailing ship *Naiad*. By the time they anchored in New York, both young men were exhausted. They also thought that the war would soon be over and wanting, "in our ignorance, to see something of it," decided to return to England. Their father wired them money for two Second Class fares aboard *Lusitania*, but a chance encounter with one of the liner's officers the night before sailing changed their minds.[51] "We have had ten of our deckhands run away this trip," the man told the brothers, adding, "I could use two boys like you." The Morton brothers told their comrades, and eventually talked several of the *Naiad*'s crew into joining them as hands on *Lusitania*.[52]

The Morton brothers, though, still had the money their father had wired, some £60 in all.[53] "This was a really large sum of money, as it was in those days," Leslie recalled.[54] With a free night to enjoy in New York City, the brothers had spent every penny, "in luxurious if doubtful surroundings," as Leslie admitted.[55] At a bar Leslie had ordered a Manhattan cocktail; by the time he was on his second drink, things became blurry. He briefly awoke to find himself sitting on Broadway, a burly policeman eyeing him suspiciously and twirling his nightstick, but remembered nothing else until sunrise the next morning, when he and his brother made their way to the pier. *Lusitania*, he said, "seemed as large as a mountain" as the young men boarded her to join the crew. Leslie spent his days washing the decks and painting lifeboats; occasionally, he entertained curious passengers by tying intricate knots as they applauded his expertise.[56]

A war zone, enemy submarines, a makeshift crew—these things should have weighed on Turner's mind as *Lusitania* cleared New York City, passed down the Hudson, and steamed past Ambrose Light toward the open Atlantic. As if these pressures weren't enough, Turner had spent the previous day ruminating about a captain's worst nightmare—the loss of his ship. Three years earlier, the confident superiority of the Edwardian Era, the perfectly ordered world of the Gilded Age, the invincibility of wondrous modern technology—it had all vanished one dark April night, when White Star Line's new *Titanic* struck an iceberg.

Edward Smith, like all good captains, had gone down with his ship; his actions largely escaped censure in the fevered accounting of heroic gentlemen and brave ladies who had met death in the frigid Atlantic. Not everyone was as forgiving: survivors and relatives of the disaster's victims sued White Star for negligence.

And so, Captain William Turner had found himself sitting in the New York City law offices of Hunt, Hill & Betts, ready to opine on the tragedy. Turner knew something about helming liners, and his blunt words did little to help White Star's case. The "heroic" Captain Smith, he declared, had been "foolish" to run his ship at such a high speed. He'd been told that potential danger in the form of ice lay ahead in his path, and had ignored the warnings. The whole thing had been avoidable. Yet Turner was sure that nothing had been learned from the disaster. Sooner or later, another great liner would meet some unnecessary and perfectly avoidable tragic end: "It will happen again," he declared.[57]

CHAPTER TWO

Gulls dove and swept around *Lusitania*'s funnels, following her as she steamed east. Travelers who braved the weather had watched as New York's skyline receded on the distant, gray horizon; the long silvery ribbon of foam churned by her propellers stretched along Long Island, where breezes brought a whiff of salt air as she neared the open Atlantic. One by one, passengers abandoned *Lusitania*'s decks, disappearing into a confusing maze of corridors as Saturday evening approached.

"The people who use these ships are not pirates," an exasperated designer once insisted. "They do not dance hornpipes. They are mostly seasick American ladies, and the one thing they want to forget when they are on the vessel is that they are on a ship at all."[1] *Lusitania* was born in the age of historicism, at a time when liners strove to attract impressionable travelers with luxurious, opulent decor evoking the past. Palladian lounges, Teutonic smoking rooms, Turkish baths, Parisian palm courts, and Jacobean dining saloons mingled side by side, in a jarringly abrupt mixture of conflicting styles and claustrophobic decoration. The interiors Scottish architect James Miller devised for *Lusitania*, though, were subtler in approach. Here, the understated elegance of the

Georgian Era predominated: rooms paneled in dark mahogany, bedecked with carved pilasters and columns, ringed by deep ornamental friezes, and crowned with vaulted skylights or graceful domes. The effect gave passengers the "pleasurable hallucination" that they were enjoying a stay at a luxurious hotel like the Ritz in London or the Waldorf-Astoria in New York.[2]

"The impression of bigness begins when you enter the ship," recorded one traveler.[3] The Grand Entrance on the Boat Deck formed the hub of the ship's First Class public rooms and served as a fitting introduction to Miller's style. Mahogany walls, enameled white and adorned with Corinthian pilasters and carving picked out in gilt, were washed with light from the large, leaded glass barrel-vaulted skylight above. At one end, a white marble fireplace, set in a nook and flanked by built-in sofas upholstered in rose-colored brocade and potted palms, offered respite; across the black and white tiled floor was the Grand Staircase, which twisted in a rectangle down six decks between elaborate railings of black wrought iron set with decorative ormolu swags, rosettes, and medallions.[4] "The treads were easy," remembered one passenger, "and the magnificent balustrades and thick pile carpets reminded one of a first class hotel instead of a ship."[5]

In the middle of the stairwell attendants in gold-trimmed uniforms guarded the ship's two nine-person elevators, with polished mahogany cars wrapped in ornate cages of aluminum topped with gilded rocailles echoing the design of the black and gilt railing.[6] The lifts could speed passengers down the decks at 150 feet per minute.[7] "These elevators, by the way, give you curious sensations when the ship is rolling," a traveler said. "You start at the bottom with a distinct leaning to the right; perhaps by the time you reach C Deck, you are headed straight for the zenith, and when you land on Deck A, the car is pointed to the left. Small wonder that a special corps of boys will have to be trained for this whimsical, zigzag service."[8]

Descending *Lusitania*'s Grand Staircase, First Class passengers faced corridors with "a vista many hundreds of feet long, which narrows in your sight," said a passenger, who noted the "doors of staterooms without number, until you feel that it must have taken a wilderness of mahogany to build this long street."[9] "If you have a berth and a stateroom with another person," a guidebook advised, "seek them out at the earliest possible opportunity and exchange cards. Occupants of the same room should practice mutual forbearance."[10] Many passengers, though, found no need to extend themselves. Despite "the extravagant waste of space which such a proceeding involves," a critic groused, "many of the best steamships are fitted with single-berthed state rooms, so that to be thrust into acquaintanceship with a perfect stranger is no longer essential for the whole voyage."[11]

Lusitania's suites and cabins did not escape the conflicting and chaotic decorative tastes of the day. "You may sleep in a bed depicting one ruler's fancy," an author opined of the typical liner, "breakfast under another dynasty altogether, lunch under a different flag and furniture scheme, play cards or smoke, or indulge in music under three other monarchs, have your afternoon cup of tea in a verandah which is essentially modern and cosmopolitan, and return to one of the historical periods experienced earlier in the day for your dinner. . . . It is a wonder that some arbiter of fashion has not decreed that the costumes of the passengers shall match the scheme of decorations."[12]

Saloon Class cabins and suites were disposed over the five top decks; the lower one went, the less imposing the accommodations. Ordinary cabins for one or two passengers were fitted with thick Brussels carpets and blue or crimson brocade hangings; wardrobes and desks of mahogany or walnut; and brass-plated beds or berths covered with quilted eiderdowns. All featured electric fans, individual heating, and basins with running water.[13] "Even in the inexpensive cabins you have a broad sofa with many pillows and a silk-shaded lamp in just the proper place to read by," marveled a passenger.[14] Even the crystal prisms in the ceiling fixtures were strung on rigid wires, so that they would not sway in foul weather.[15]

No detail was too small to escape scrutiny. The shared lavatories and bathrooms were praised as "truly magnificent," with their fittings "carried out in a manner not previously attempted on board ship."[16] Even the urinals in the shared Saloon Class bathrooms were separated with marble dividers.[17] "Everything," noted one press account, "has been designed to look as little like a ship as possible."[18]

A more prescient observer might have likened *Lusitania* to a gigantic stage set, awaiting its revolving cast of actors to play out their own social comedies, dramas, and—on this voyage—tragedies across her decks. What might popular British playwright Charles Klein have made of the journey on which he now embarked? Having come to New York in 1883 from his native London, Klein had cast a sharply acerbic eye on American social life, with its inequities, scandals, and unrestrained celebration of money. He satirized John D. Rockefeller in *The Lion and the Mouse,* painting him as an unscrupulous millionaire; attacked the American legal system in *The Next of Kin*; and even composed the libretto for John Philip Sousa's comic operetta *El Capitan.*[19] The public enjoyed his plays; critics were sometimes less enthusiastic, with one dismissing him as "content usually with hack work," while another thought that there was "something spurious about his plays," which made it "hard to take them quite seriously."[20]

Klein knew all about rejection. He had wanted to be an actor, but he was short, nervous, and tense, and had a clubfoot—qualities that had limited his dramatic possibilities.[21] But at least he could write for the stage—a new play was in the works as he boarded *Lusitania*. A few peaceful days at sea and a visit to England would restore his nerves and refresh his creativity. In 1912, Klein had booked passage on *Titanic*'s maiden voyage, but a business engagement forced him to cancel at the last minute; now, he laughed off warnings of a possible submarine attack on *Lusitania* as "trifles."[22]

Success on the London stage was also on the mind of fellow passenger Justus Miles Forman. After a career writing popular novels and articles for magazines, the thirty-nine-year-old Forman had just seen his first play produced, to disastrous results. *The Hyphen* addressed the wartime patriotism of German immigrants, certainly a topical subject but also one guaranteed to stir up emotions. Worried that a riot might erupt, policemen lined the aisles at its New York City premiere. There were a few hisses, "much unfavorable comment from citizens of German extraction," but no violence—and almost no interest in the less than compelling play. A trial run in Boston was even more disastrous, forcing the play to close after a week.[23]

Yet one passenger aboard *Lusitania* believed in *The Hyphen,* impresario Charles Frohman. Frohman liked *The Hyphen,* and now wanted to take it to London, offering to introduce Forman to his friends and see what could be done with the play.[24] And when it came to the theatrical world, no one's opinion mattered more than that of Charles Frohman.

Born in 1856 in Sandusky, Ohio, Charles Frohman was one of three brothers; when he was eight his family moved to New York City, where young Charles worked as a night clerk for the *New York Daily Graphic.* Soon, he joined his brother Daniel, who had become business manager at the Madison Square Theatre. His beginnings were small, selling tickets, but he gradually assumed control over several companies and took them to Boston, Chicago, and to London. In 1888, through sheer boldness, he managed to secure production rights to an obscure play called *Shenandoah*, which he opened to tremendous success at New York City's Star Theatre. In twelve months, the play had earned some $200,000: it was the start of his fortune. The impresario used the money to found the Charles Frohman Stock Company; in 1893, he built the Empire Theatre at the corner of Broadway and Fortieth Street. It was at the Empire in 1895 that Frohman introduced America to the work of Oscar Wilde, producing *The Importance of Being Earnest*.[25]

In 1896, Frohman formed the Theatrical Syndicate, which soon standardized and monopolized bookings across the United States.[26] Frohman cultivated stock actors into stars: among his favorites were Maude Adams, John and Ethel Barrymore, William Gillette, Constance Collier, Nat Goodwin, and Billie Burke. He insisted that American audiences, at least, cared less about the content of a play than about its stars.[27]

People thought that Frohman exercised an "almost hypnotic" influence over his company.[28] He was obsessed with details, sitting through countless rehearsals, selecting costumes, prompting actors, and commenting on scenery from the orchestra pit. Actress Billie Burke called him "a martinet. He demanded long hours of rehearsal, work all day and every evening."[29] Frohman favored light comedies and romances over heavier melodramas. Sooner or later, he worried, the New York stage would be dominated by "crook plays, shop girl plays, slangy American farce," and "nude women invading the auditorium, as in Paris."[30]

In 1904, Frohman convinced British novelist J. M. Barrie to let him stage *Peter Pan*. After proving a hit in London, Frohman brought it to Broadway in January 1905. The production, which starred Maude Adams, proved to be an instant success and made Frohman even wealthier.[31] He expanded his empire across the Atlantic, leasing and managing a number of theaters, and soon was staging successful plays in London.[32]

Frohman was fiercely protective of his private life. Rumors abounded over his relationship with Maude Adams. "He was in love with Maude Adams," Billie Burke thought. He "spoke of her as if she were a princess in an ivory tower." Burke heard the rumors that they had secretly married, but suspected—probably correctly—that Frohman preferred worshipping her from afar.[33] "Had I possessed a wife and family," Frohman once said, "I could never have taken the risks which, as a theatrical manager, I am constantly called upon to do."[34] His closest relationship seemed to be with bachelor playwright Charles Dillingham—"the favorite of his heart," as one newspaper delicately phrased it.[35] Friends called them "the two Charlies," and they shared a country house in White Plains.[36] It was there, in 1912, that Frohman fell off the porch and permanently injured his right knee. Though the bruise healed, rheumatism soon set in, and Frohman was forced to walk with a cane, which he jokingly referred to as his "wife."[37]

Though a giant in the theatrical world, Frohman was short, pudgy, and unprepossessing in person; Billie Burke recalled that, when he sat in his leather chair behind his desk, his feet actually dangled a few inches above the floor. He spoke in short, staccato sentences, often jabbing his forefinger for emphasis, "leaving sentences trailing in his wake, but sometimes snapping them like a whip with pungent, sharp twists of the tongue." Frohman took extreme care over his clothing, favoring beautiful and costly tailored suits, but despite his attire he gave the impression that he cared nothing about his appearance. He refused to carry a watch, insisting that if he needed to know the time he could ask someone; he almost never carried any money, relying on friends to pay bills on his behalf.[38]

Frohman rarely entertained, avoided dinners and parties, and evaded most social encounters, although he often played billiards with Mark Twain, letting the author win just to boost his ego.[39] "All I want is a good meal, a good cigar, good clothes, a good bed to sleep in, and freedom to produce whatever plays I like," Frohman once said.[40] He had an inordinate passion for sweets, especially pies, and never traveled without a box of candy.[41] His personality was contradictory: rival theatrical impresario David Belasco said that Frohman "had the warm, open heart of a child."[42] Yet he was irascible: when someone greeted him with "Good morning," he would usually snarl, "Is it? I doubt it!" He hated to read anything but scripts: he once said his favorite book was a guide to Parisian restaurants, yet he could recite nearly all of *The Adventures of Alice in Wonderland*, which he adored.[43] He preferred to secret himself in his office or in his apartment at the Knickerbocker Hotel, listening endlessly to his favorite gramophone recording of Irving Berlin's "Alexander's Ragtime Band" to cheer himself up.[44]

By 1915, Frohman was recognized as the most powerful theatrical producer in the world. In addition to his Theatrical Syndicate, he operated five theaters in New York, one in London, and more than two hundred others scattered across the United States. Some ten thousand people worked in his employ for a total payroll of upwards of $35 million a year. Such was his status, someone joked, that railway employees gave his luxurious private Pullman carriage "the same precedence of schedule" as they did for President Woodrow Wilson himself.[45]

That spring, Frohman decided to visit London to investigate theatrical possibilities as well as to attend to some business litigation. With him, he took his valet, thirty-six-year-old William Stainton. Although he jokingly dismissed warnings from worried friends, Frohman did seem to have a sense of uncertainty about the future. Before leaving he dictated the next season's theatrical program—something he had never before done.[46] Aboard the liner, he quickly made his way to a cabin on B Deck, where a pile of potential scripts awaited reading, along with a basket of cooked chicken and some bottled coffee sent from the Knickerbocker Hotel.[47] He was also delighted to find that a friend had sent a gift basket loaded with flowers, fruit, and a candy ship. Before *Lusitania* departed, he jotted her a note, writing, "This little ship you sent is more wonderful than the big one that takes me away from you."[48]

Much of the attention directed by *Lusitania*'s passengers to Frohman's coterie on the ship, though, centered on two beautiful women. Twenty-three-year-old Josephine Brandell was a rising opera star, who the previous year had enjoyed great acclaim in *Come Over Here*, produced at the London Opera House.[49] But the real object of fascination for many men aboard *Lusitania* was exotically beautiful, twenty-five-year-old Rita Jolivet, a living example of that most acclaimed of twentieth-century celebrities, an actress.

Born as Marguerite Jolivet in 1890, she was brought up in France, where her wealthy father owned a number of vineyards. Even as a young girl, she had adored the stage, reciting in French and English and performing for increasingly appreciative audiences. Drama lessons in London followed dance lessons in Paris; soon, the young ingenue joined the Elizabethan Stage Society and appeared to great acclaim in increasingly prominent roles. A 1908 marriage proved disastrous and ended in divorce. Taking advantage of her charm, talent, and ambition, she changed her name to the more theatrical Rita and returned to the stage, where her dark-haired, expressive-eyed beauty made her a rising star. Her American stage debut came in 1911, when she appeared in *Kismet* at the Knickerbocker Theatre. She left the production after two highly successful years, taking a number of roles that won her critical praise as "one of the truly great artists and truly unique personalities of the present day."[50]

In 1915, Jolivet decided to go to Europe to see her brother before he went off to fight in the Great War. Her friend actress Ellen Terry was also traveling to Europe, and Rita was to join her, booking passage aboard an American liner, which they believed to be safe from possible submarine attack. *Lusitania,* though, was leaving the same day and would reach England first. "I wanted to see my brother before he left for the Front," she later said. Not only was *Lusitania* faster, she was also larger and more luxurious, and carried Rita's friend Charles Frohman. At eight that Saturday morning, she decided to take the Cunard vessel.[51]

With the last-minute change, Rita had to rush to reach Pier 54 before *Lusitania* sailed. Boarding the liner, she found that she had been given "a very bad room" on D Deck, an inside cabin with no portholes. She had a second surprise, this one more welcome, as she roamed over *Lusitania*'s decks awaiting departure: her brother-in-law, George Vernon Butler, also traveling aboard the liner to see his wife, Rita's sister, Inez, in Europe.[52]

Inez was a talented violinist who had performed before Tsar Nicholas II of Russia and King Edward VII of Great Britain, but her husband was a more shadowy figure. George, who used Vernon as his surname, offered himself as a jack-of-all-trades: he had once been a banker, then acted as a concert singer, and also as an importer, though no one could quite pin down the actual source of his income. In fact, he was on his way to Russia: Nicholas II's feckless brother Grand Duke Michael Alexandrovich had apparently asked Vernon to broker a munitions deal for the tsar's army to purchase some $3 million of American rifles.[53]

An actress was indeed an unusual and diverting attraction for many of *Lusitania*'s more aristocratic passengers. "Women of the stage," Theodore Dreiser once mused, seemed "peculiarly suited to this realm of show, color, and make believe. The stage is fairyland and they are of it." Most actresses, he insisted with a fair bit of misogyny, "lie like anything. They never show their true colors, or very rarely. If you want to know the truth, you must see through their pretty, petty artistry, back to the actual conditions behind them, which are conditioning and driving them. Very few, if any, have a real grasp on what I call life."[54]

If an air of unreality swirled around Rita, it was one that had been carefully cultivated. Frohman, always on the lookout for a potential star, thought that the beautiful Jolivet might one day grow to rival Maude Adams in popularity. She had five films to her credit when she boarded *Lusitania*, including Cecil B. DeMille's new picture, *The Unafraid*. Yet for all of the publicity Rita had received, it was her voyage aboard *Lusitania* that, ironically, would become her greatest claim to fame.

CHAPTER THREE

Quiet, her decks empty and her lights extinguished, *Lusitania* steamed east through the night. She was in the ocean now, her crisp bow slicing through the undulating Atlantic, her path marked by a silvery ribbon of foam trailing in her wake. New York City's dismal weather had followed her: May 2 dawned cold and gray, rain pelting the liner as she rolled in uneven seas south of Nova Scotia.[1]

It was a Sunday. As much as he loathed the public side of his duties, Captain Turner was nothing if not a traditionalist, and that morning he conducted Protestant services in *Lusitania*'s Saloon Class Lounge—one of the few times when First and Second Class passengers were permitted to mingle; Catholic services took place in the Second Class Dining Saloon. Turner read out the lesson, and lent his gruff voice to the singing of hymns. He ended with prayers for the royal family, and for all those at sea.[2]

Even on the tranquil *Lusitania,* thoughts of the war—relatives fighting, friends killed, acquaintances lost—dominated. A few passengers, like rotund, thirty-six-year-old Isaac Lehmann, saw opportunity. Although officially described as an export broker from New York, Lehmann let it be known that he was actually on his way to Paris, hoping to sign a profitable deal to supply cloth to the French government for military uniforms. The prospect of wartime financial gain also led Jessie Taft Smith to book passage aboard *Lusitania*. John Smith, the Ohio native's inventor husband, had developed a new engine for French airplanes; hearing of its success, Great Britain hoped he could develop a similar mechanism to give their planes an advantage over the Kaiser's air corps. As Smith was already in London when the British request came, he asked his wife to carry over his mechanical plans for presentation and analysis.[3]

Thirty-nine-year-old Charles Jeffery was also on his way to Europe, hoping to sell his armored cars to the French army. By the turn of the century, his father, Thomas, had turned from manufacturing bicycles to automobiles, founding the Thomas B. Jeffery Company. His Rambler proved an early success, and within a decade the Wisconsin-based company was a multimillion-dollar enterprise. Charles took over the company after his father's death and expanded the business, producing roadsters and touring cars that started at $1,000; the United States Army purchased his trucks for field use. His Jeffery Quad trucks proved valuable to the Russian and French armies, and now he had developed a new armored car with mounted machine gun, which he hoped to contract out to the Allied nations.[4]

Others aboard *Lusitania* were driven by wartime patriotism. It was still the age of the gentleman soldier, when young aristocrats, hoping to serve King and Country, willingly abandoned lives of privilege and took commissions that ultimately shattered such illusions and destroyed the brightest men of their generation. Twenty-one-year-old James Dunsmuir was the scion of British Columbia's wealthiest and most socially prominent family. His father had served as lieutenant governor of the province, and he and his American wife, Laura, were accustomed to entertaining premiers and princes at Hatley Park, their $4 million baronial castle on a tranquil lagoon outside Victoria. It took an army of nearly a hundred to care for its fifty rooms, Japanese and Italian gardens, hundreds of acres of forest, and immense stables—a measure of the privilege surrounding young James Dunsmuir from birth.[5]

Known as "Boy," young James was his father's second son: the eldest, Robert, was a thorough wastrel and his disappointed father carefully groomed Boy to be his principal heir. Quiet and shy owing to his persistent acne, he'd been educated at Loretto in Scotland, winning a reputation as a boxer of some ability. Boy worked hard to please his father, taking a job at the Bank of Montreal for a modest salary to prove his worth. His only passion was horses: he loved to play polo, and kept two thoroughbred jumpers with which he won numerous prizes. The most remarkable thing about Boy, said a cousin, was that he "never complained" about anything. "He did not talk big and act small, nor had he the coarseness of the elder son."[6]

Full of patriotic fervor, Dunsmuir had rushed to enlist when war erupted in Europe, training as a lieutenant with the British Columbia Horse Regiment and then the Canadian Mounted Rifles. At the end of April 1915, disappointed that his regiment was still in Canada, he resigned his commission: he hoped to go to London, enter the Royal Scots Greys Regiment, and join the fight against Germany.[7] Boy had met the Kaiser on several occasions, when Wilhelm II visited the family at Kiel aboard their 218-foot steam yacht *Dolaura* and boldly signed its guest book as "Admiral of the Fleet."[8] Before leaving, Boy returned to Hatley to see his family. Strolling around the lagoon one afternoon, he spotted a heron, aimed his rifle, and killed the bird. "No good will come of that shot," a servant gravely warned. "To shoot a heron spells bad luck."[9] Within a few days, Dunsmuir was on his way to New York to board *Lusitania.*

Wartime patriotism also drove twenty-two-year-old British Denis Duncan Harold Owen Boulton, who one day would become 3rd Baronet Boulton. After attending elite Stonyhurst and graduating from Oxford, Boulton followed the usual aristocratic path, briefly joining the British Army until he was medically discharged in 1912. He'd then gone to America to represent a creosote company, but sitting out the Great War ate away at his pride. When a friend suggested he might join the French Red Cross, Boulton decided to return to Europe.[10]

Boulton "paid very little attention" to the notice in Saturday's newspapers—"we'd heard so many rumors of what the Germans were to do," he said. "Being young, I felt more adventurous." He thought to himself, "The hell with it!" and boarded *Lusitania,* "thinking I'd be safer in the long run than on some other ship."[11] He was surprised and delighted to find that Lieutenant Frederic Lassetter, an old friend from Oxford, was also traveling on *Lusitania* with his mother, Elisabeth. Originally from Australia, Lassetter had been on leave from the King's Own Light Scottish Infantry Regiment after being wounded, and with his mother had visited relatives in Los Angeles.[12] Boulton settled in for the voyage, but found it difficult to ignore the "undercurrent of anticipation" as *Lusitania* steamed toward the war zone.[13]

Anxiety and grief punctuated the tension aboard *Lusitania.* Only a week had passed since a lovely spring day in Montreal when Dorothy Braithwaite had received a devastating cable from her sisters in London. Both had husbands fighting in the war and, almost unbelievably, both received the tragic news that the men had been killed in action on the same day. Dorothy quickly packed a few things and rushed off to New York: she would celebrate a rather grim twenty-fifth birthday aboard *Lusitania,* on her way to comfort her grieving sisters.[14]

Another lady from Montreal, Frances Ramsay McIntosh Stephens, faced an equally worrisome situation: she was off to see her son Francis, who had fallen seriously ill while fighting in France. A veneer of marble concealed inner turmoil, but then, Frances Stephens had always known how to play to appearances. She had risen from relatively humble beginnings to become a formidable member of Montreal society. Frances owed her good fortune to the tragic 1876 death of her sister Elizabeth. Left a widower with a young son, Elizabeth's husband, George Washington Stephens, waited a mere two years before marrying his much younger sister-in-law. Originally from Vermont, Stephens was a prominent Montreal lawyer and politician who could provide Frances with a large and fashionable house, couture dresses, exquisite jewelry, and a place in society; Frances, in turn, provided her husband with two daughters and a second son, Francis, born in 1887. After George Washington Stephens's death in 1904, his widow—having inherited an estate worth over $1 million—set about playing the *grande dame,* funding Montreal's Unitarian Church, endowing charities, and blessing social events with her regal appearance, invariably adorned with a brilliant, lengthy rope of pearls. On the outbreak of the Great War, her stockbroker son Francis patriotically went off to fight with the British Expeditionary Force in France.[15] His wife, Hazel, followed him as far as England, bringing their young daughter, but she left their two-year-old son, John, with his grandmother in Montreal. Then, in spring 1915, the Canadian soldier developed a serious heart condition and had to be evacuated to England. His condition was so grave that his mother, with young John, a nanny, and a personal maid in tow, booked passage aboard *Lusitania.*[16]

Fellow Canadian travelers Mary Ryerson and her twenty-three-year-old daughter, Laura, also knew firsthand the terrible price that many had paid in the war. A fifty-six-year-old mother of five, Mary Amelia Ryerson enjoyed a prominent place in Toronto, where her physician husband, George—after serving in the Provincial Legislature—had helped establish the St. John Ambulance Association and the Canadian Red Cross. Mary and George traveled frequently: in 1909, they'd been presented to the ill-fated Archduke Franz Ferdinand. Word of his assassination in Sarajevo had shocked the couple—"it seemed such an objectless, political murder," George recalled. "Little did we dream that it would be seized upon as an excuse for a world war."[17]

The couple's four sons all enlisted and went off to join the fight in Europe; George, though troubled at the "seriousness of the situation," confessed himself "proud of the patriotic spirit they displayed, and told them it was their duty to serve Canada and the Empire." In the spring of 1915, Ryerson himself left for Europe, sailing on *Lusitania* to survey Red Cross work on the continent. A few weeks later, word came that, on April 23, the couple's eldest son, George, had been killed in action at Ypres, and his younger brother, Arthur, had been seriously wounded in the abdomen by a piece of shrapnel.[18]

"I cabled my wife to come over to help and comfort my son," Ryerson recalled, "because I thought this work would divert her mind from the loss of her first born and beloved son. There was such a singular understanding and attachment between these two dear people that I doubt if she would ever have recovered from the blow." As Ryerson had recently crossed safely on *Lusitania,* his wife decided that this would be the most reliable way to reach her critically injured son.[19] Mary boarded the ship with her daughter, Laura, who had been educated in Lausanne; both had reason to be uneasy about the voyage itself. Three years earlier,

George's cousin Arthur Ryerson had drowned when *Titanic* sank. It seemed an unfortunate omen as mother and daughter traveled aboard this liner bound for a potentially dangerous war zone.

Others traveled aboard *Lusitania* to embark on humanitarian missions. In November 1914, future American president Herbert Hoover organized the Commission for Relief in Belgium and called on his fellow countrymen to go to Europe and assist in the war effort. He made a special plea to the young, asking them to volunteer for hospitals and other organizations, knowing that they would receive little or no compensation but appealing to the idea that they would help save lives.[20]

Beautiful millionaire Mary Hammond had heard the call. She exemplified the spirit of selflessness that many of the privileged attempted, often unsuccessfully, to emulate. And privileged she certainly was: she was born in 1885, into a family whose ancestors had counted George Washington and Thomas Jefferson as personal friends. More immediate forebears had founded the city of Hoboken, New Jersey, and developed steam and railway travel in New Jersey and New York.[21] After attending Bryn Mawr, Mary had married Ogden Hammond in 1907, a real estate developer and insurance broker sixteen years her senior.[22]

Life was pleasant, as the Hammonds divided their time between a house in New York—where Ogden worked as president of the Broadway Improvement Company, directed the Standard Plunger Elevator Company, and served as vice president of the Hoboken Land and Improvement Company—and a sprawling summer estate at Bernardsville. There were children—Mary in 1908, Millicent in 1910, and Ogden Jr. in 1912—along with parties, dinners, and political fundraisers that helped Hammond win a seat in the New Jersey State Assembly.[23] But with the war in Europe, Mary felt impelled to fund and establish a Red Cross hospital in France. Her determination worried Ogden; it wasn't his wife's charitable intent, but rather her insistence that they travel aboard *Lusitania*. Nothing, though—not even a personal warning from the German ambassador to her aunt—could convince Mary to change her plans.

The call of war relief also brought immensely wealthy Allen and Catherine Loney to *Lusitania,* traveling with their nearly sixteen-year-old daughter, Virginia, on their way to Europe. Like Mary Hammond, Catherine had also made a will before sailing to protect her considerable assets—Lorillard tobacco money, stocks, and real estate that generated a considerable fortune each year in interest alone. Members of an international set, the Loneys seemed perpetually to race between "the hunting field or the regatta, the polo ground, the salmon river, or the grouse moor," as friend, noted author Henry James, said.[24] Although American, their sympathies were entirely British: from their country estate in Northampton, they hunted, mingled with aristocrats, and sent forth a succession of exquisite horses to compete at Epsom and in the Derby. With the outbreak of war, Allen Loney decided he owed something to his English friends, and he became a driver in the American Volunteer Motor Ambulance Corps operating in France and Belgium. He was, said Henry James, "one of the most ardent and active of our volunteers, friendly and devoted in every way."[25]

Twenty-five-year-old Dorothy Conner was a volunteer nurse from Oregon. After attending school in Germany, Dorothy had graduated from Wellesley College with a degree in history and moved with her mother to Oregon to operate a fruit orchard. When the war erupted, Dorothy abandoned her social life and earned her Red Cross nursing certificate. Her brother-in-law Harold Reckitt had established a military hospital at Ris-Orangis in Belgium, and now, heeding Herbert Hoover's call, she decided to volunteer her services at the facility.[26] Naively, she brought a fox stole, lace and silk evening gowns, and a multitude of jewelry.[27]

Dorothy traveled with another brother-in-law, Howard Fisher. After receiving his medical degree from Jefferson College in Philadelphia and serving as a missionary in India, Fisher married Sara Conner and settled in Washington, D.C., where his brother Walter had served as secretary of the interior under President William Howard Taft.[28]

Pro-British feelings and outrage over "German brutality" led Fisher to volunteer for work at his brother-in-law's hospital in France, where he hoped "to take part in Germany's defeat."[29] Dorothy and Fisher booked passage on *Lusitania*, as he said, because they were told it "would be the safest vessel to choose."[30] Once at sea, he noted some tense conversations among the passengers about the possibility of *Lusitania* being torpedoed. Still, he mused, "I felt sure that in case of being torpedoed, we would have ample time to take to the boats."[31]

Thirty-one-year-old Lindon Bates Jr. was off to join the Commission for Belgian Relief, which his father had chaired. Born in Portland, Oregon, in 1883, Bates had attended Harrow in England and graduated from Yale with a degree in engineering. Like his engineer father, he'd worked on a number of projects around America and traveled the world as a consultant; he'd taken advantage of this to write a number of entertaining travelogues. Passionate about politics, he was elected to the New York State Legislature in 1904 and reelected in 1909, though his bids for Congress in 1912 and 1914 ended in defeat. Now he'd left his position as vice president in the Bates Engineering Company in New York to volunteer his services in the Allied effort.[32]

Debonair, twenty-nine-year-old Harvard-educated Dr. James Houghton was also on his way to Belgium to assist in relief efforts. While waiting for the *Lusitania* to leave New York City, Houghton was "delighted" to find fellow Harvard graduate Richard Freeman aboard the ship, and the two stood on deck, chatting about their plans. Houghton recalled "congratulating" Freeman "upon having such a fine trip ahead of him."[33]

The real star of *Lusitania*'s war relief efforts, though, was the lovely Marie Depage, a forty-three-year-old nurse originally from Brussels. Born in 1872 as Marie Picard, she was distantly related to the Belgian royal family. After her 1893 marriage to Dr. Antoine Depage and the birth of three sons, Pierre, Lucien, and Henri, she'd studied anatomy and joined in his medical work. In 1907, when Pierre created the first Belgian school for nurses, she became treasurer, with English nurse Edith Cavell acting as trainer. The move was not without controversy: the Catholic Church protested that for centuries its nuns had served as nurses and were now being displaced. In 1912, with the outbreak of the Balkan Wars, Marie and Antoine led Belgian Red Cross relief workers to Turkey.[34] King Albert of Belgium made Antoine his personal surgeon, and in 1914 named him head of the Belgian Red Cross; at Queen Elisabeth's request, he organized a Red Cross hospital at La Panne, where Marie put her nursing skills to use.[35] "Why do you bother?" a wounded German soldier once asked her. "I'm your enemy."

"No, you're not," she assured him. "To me, you're just a wounded man who needs help."[36]

By 1915, resources were dwindling, and at Queen Elisabeth's request, Marie embarked on an American tour to solicit funds. She spent several months crossing the country, ultimately collecting over $100,000 for war relief. She was, said an official, "a lovely, attractive lady" who "endeared herself to everybody."[37] Author Charlotte Kellogg, who had met her in San Francisco, found Marie "fresh and charming." She was tireless as she "told, so simply and poignantly, her country's story," and appealed for donations.[38]

Pierre, Marie's eldest son, had already joined the fighting; while in America, she received word that her second son, seventeen-year-old Lucien, was about to enter the army. Hoping to see him before he left, she decided to return to Belgium. Originally, she wanted to travel aboard a neutral liner, *Lapland*. But this meant two extra days at sea—crucial days that might prevent her reunion. Not willing to risk the timing, she changed her passage to *Lusitania*.[39] Howard Fisher later recalled her "sad, anxious face" throughout the voyage, wondering, "Had she some prophetic vision of the coming disaster?"[40] Yet when James Houghton questioned her about a legal will in case something happened, Marie merely smiled: she'd prepared nothing, and called herself a "happy fatalist."[41]

Marie Depage might dismiss the concerns, but few passengers now aboard *Lusitania* failed to sense an air of tension; spoken, whispered, barely acknowledged, betrayed in an anxious look or a jocular comment—a kind of palpable, nervous energy seemed present as *Lusitania* steamed east. One earlier American passenger had recalled that traveling on the ship after 1914 "gave us our first intimation of warfare."[42] They could find some rather unsubtle propaganda: Cunard officials placed brochures in all of the public rooms, helpfully explaining how Germany had started the war.[43] Famed correspondent Richard Harding Davis had been most struck by the darkness that fell over the vessel at night as lights and windows were blacked out: "You can imagine," he wrote, "the effect of this Ritz Carlton idea of a ship wrapped in darkness."[44]

Darkness might prevent a submarine from spotting a potential victim; more reassuring was the popular belief that *Lusitania* actually had guns mounted on her decks. *Lusitania* and her sister had been designed to accommodate heavy artillery should the need arise: twelve 6-inch guns placed at intervals along the forecastle and shelter decks, capable of firing 6-inch shells some 3,000 yards and 4.75-inch shells nearly double that distance. Coupled with their great speed, this armament, a contemporary journal noted, would make the two ships "most effective additions to any fighting squadron."[45]

In June 1913, the *New York Tribune* reported that "high powered naval rifles" had been installed aboard *Lusitania*.[46] At the same time, Winston Churchill, as First Lord of the Admiralty, told Parliament that "substantial progress" had been made in arming the nation's top liners; he later added that the conversions made the vessels "indistinguishable in status and control from men-of-war."[47] The following year, a few months before the war began, Churchill again openly boasted about the large number of British merchant vessels that were being fitted with sizable guns.[48]

Churchill didn't mention specific ships, but *Lusitania* had been named in newspapers, and most assumed that the guns were in place. Early that Sunday morning, passenger Michael Byrne took to her decks with a specific purpose: he wanted to see if he could spot any of the rumored guns. As it happened, this was his thirteenth Atlantic crossing; familiar with *Olympic, Mauretania,* and *Imperator,* he now walked up and down the decks. "I took particular notice to see if they had any guns mounted or un-mounted," he wrote. "There were none." He "inspected every deck above the waterline, but found no guns of any description."[49] Byrne was unable to find anything because there was nothing to be found. At some point, disguised gun rings were installed on the ship's foredeck, concealed beneath coils of rope, but their contingent of artillery was not.[50] Her size and her immense consumption of coal, the Admiralty decided, made *Lusitania* unsuitable for duty as an auxiliary cruiser.

A few passengers might blithely dismiss the idea of a possible submarine attack but they couldn't ignore recent history. Anyone who doubted the potential danger of traveling aboard a British liner through a declared war zone had only to recall an event earlier that spring. On March 28, a German U-boat had caught the five-thousand-ton British liner *Falaba* off the Irish coast. Passengers and crew had been evacuating when *Falaba*'s captain launched distress rockets and called for help. Afraid that armed assistance would soon arrive and counterattack, the U-boat torpedoed the liner, and *Falaba* sank within ten minutes. Of the 242 people aboard, 104 perished, including mining engineer Leon Thrasher, who became the Great War's first American victim.[51]

From London, United States ambassador Walter Page warned his countrymen to avoid traveling to England unless they had "urgent business."[52] The fear cut into Cunard's revenue. In April, after dreaming of disaster at sea, Gilded Age heiress Elizabeth Drexel Lehr canceled her planned passage aboard *Lusitania*. Her friends ridiculed her fears but she finally managed to convince them to join her on an American liner. Such cancellations worried an image-conscious Cunard Line. Having lost six socially prominent passengers, its New York office sent a representative to plead with the group to reconsider. "Think what an effect it will have on our reputation when the papers learn you would not sail with us!" the agent declared, but to no avail.[53]

Cunard's worries extended not merely to bookings; now the company heard stories that several passengers, including Vanderbilt and Frohman, had actually received personal warnings not to travel aboard *Lusitania*. Such warnings suggested something more concrete than the vague threat implied in the German notice, demanding that Cunard and the Admiralty exercise every caution and use all measures to see the ship safely arrive in Liverpool. Late Saturday night, Cunard had cabled Captain Turner, asking if any passengers had indeed been warned before boarding the liner. Inexplicably, Turner replied: "No one received telegrams of the kind indicated."[54]

The only consolation to those now traveling aboard *Lusitania* was the belief that, once she reached the waters off Ireland, the British Admiralty would provide a Royal Navy escort. When buying his ticket, Charles Lauriat had specifically asked a Cunard official if a military convoy would escort *Lusitania* through the war zone. "Oh yes!" he was told. "Every precaution will be taken."[55] Though worried about the voyage, Theodate Pope had "comforted myself with the thought that we would surely be conveyed when we reached the war zone."[56]

Complaisant, lulled into a false sense of security, *Lusitania*'s passengers could only hope that the Admiralty and Captain Turner would protect them, that the great liner would indeed be able to outpace any nefarious German submarine. At sea, they were largely cut off from the world, unaware of a troubling interview one German official gave in New York City a few days after *Lusitania* had departed. "The British flag," he predicted, "will shortly be driven from the seas by Germany. As for the *Lusitania,* we will get her surely. She is not as fast as some of our latest submarines."[57]

CHAPTER FOUR

An exhausted Theodate Pope wakened from a fitful sleep that Sunday morning in her cabin on D Deck. She'd hardly slept. "There was a very noisy family next to me," she wrote to her mother.[1] The noise had come from the Crompton family: Paul, his wife, Gladys, and their six children, ranging in age from fourteen to eighteen months. They might be devoted and jovial—Crompton often took them along on business trips—but they were a bit too boisterous and loud for the middle-aged woman from Connecticut. Unwilling to endure another sleepless night, an irritated Theodate cornered the purser that morning: First Class was not fully booked, and soon she was on her way to an empty cabin on A Deck.

Overcoming difficulties—the woman born Effie Pope in 1867 knew something about that. The only child of millionaire industrialist Alfred Pope and his wife, Ada, she had always felt out of place, at war with expectation and the traditional limits imposed by her sex. She inherited her father's charm and love of art, and her mother's iron will. At a time when obedient conformity was a cardinal virtue, Effie openly questioned her teachers. With dark blond hair, blue eyes, and an angular face, she was not unattractive, but the empty social life of the era left her cold.[2]

Effie found redemption in travel. She loved the trips to Europe, where her father began collecting Impressionist paintings by Degas, Cassatt, Manet, Monet, and Whistler. Architecture, though, was her greatest discovery. "For years," she explained, "I have been keen on architecture and felt that the ugliness of our buildings actually menaced my happiness."[3] Arches, arcades, mullioned windows, thatched roofs, medieval chimneys—all whispered so evocatively to the young woman that, after a stint at the famed Miss Porter's School in Farmington, Connecticut, she embarked on this most unlikely of careers.[4]

With her father's money to pay for private tutors and lectures at Princeton and a determination that refused to be bowed, Effie plunged forward. She changed her name to Theodate: it not only recognized her paternal grandmother, but also sounded confusingly masculine at a time when very few women practiced architecture. Theodate was fortunate: independent women were just beginning to break free of expected roles, finding happiness and fulfillment on their own terms. Education and money opened doors previously closed, and Theodate set about seizing all the advantages her privileged background offered. After practicing ideas at her small country house in Farmington, she convinced her parents to build their own adjoining retreat.[5] The job went to the renowned architectural firm of McKim, Mead & White, but from the first, it was Theodate's project. Rather than ask the firm to design the house, Theodate decided to send them

the plans that I have been working over at intervals for some years to draw to scale and make an elevation of in the event of our coming to a mutual agreement. Consequently, as it is my plan, I expect to decide

in all the details as well as all more important questions of plan that may arise. This must be clearly understood at the outset, so as to save unnecessary
friction in the future. In other words, it will be a Pope
house instead of a McKim, Mead and White. In conclusion, I will say that I am not nearly as difficult to
deal with as this would seem, for I am very tolerant
of advice and always open to suggestions and good
reasoning.[6]

Hill-Stead, as the completed building was named, was a rambling farmhouse clad in gleaming white clapboards, dotted with
bay windows and adorned with a replica of the portico at George
Washington's Mount Vernon, which Theodate so admired. It became an architectural icon, called "perhaps the finest Colonial Revival house" in America.[7] Guests like Thornton Wilder, Edith
Wharton, and Henry James were stunned to find the rambling but
deliberately unpretentious house filled with "wondrous examples
of Manet, of Degas, of Claude Monet, of Whistler." Although
James found the mixture of studied colonial simplicity and refined
European art "of the queerest" taste, he deemed the effect "like
the sudden trill of a nightingale," startling and unexpected.[8]

Armed with newfound confidence, Theodate eventually opened
an office in New York City and took on several commissions, including renovation of the Westover School in Middlebury, Connecticut.[9] Her style was a variant on the then popular Arts and
Crafts Movement, harking back to medieval models in the search
for comfort. She loathed modern architecture, deeming it too
coldly clinical. "People," she said, "are building nests. You can't
take that out of human nature."[10]

These were difficult years, as Theodate not only struggled
against professional prejudices but also attempted to rationalize

her place in the world. Although her father's money had opened doors and allowed her to enter a traditionally male-dominated career, she found the idea of great wealth distressing. The poor seemed more genuine to her, and increasingly she spouted political ideas that left her parents aghast. "If you don't stop talking about Socialism," her mother once warned, "your father is going to leave you out of his will."[11]

More difficult was Theodate's struggle to understand herself. She was horrified by the notion that one day she must follow convention and become a wife and a mother. Early on, she had developed an intense crush on a young woman at Miss Porter's; ambivalent sexual feelings led her to reject at least one marriage proposal with the remark, "Perhaps I am not capable of loving a man."[12] Theodate had a brief but intense relationship with a woman she named only as Laura. "Will she ever love me?" she pondered in her journal. Then, Laura spent the night with her. "I only slept about an hour and a half," Theodate coyly confided to her journal. "I am just so happy today, it has changed the whole tenor of my mind."[13]

When the relationship ended, the emotionally fragile Theodate fell into a deep depression; at a particularly low point, she readily submitted to shock treatments, sitting in a tub of water while a wire with live current was thrust into the bath.[14] Whether this was some misplaced attempt to "cure" herself of her lesbian tendencies or merely an effort to treat her persistent depression and insomnia, the regular counseling sessions led her to emotionally latch onto her male therapist. Convinced that she was in love with him, she again rejected another marriage proposal from a friend and patiently awaited one from her new crush, a proposal that would never come.[15]

Against this background of questioning and analysis, Theodate increasingly turned to a new interest that soon dominated her thoughts. She had always been something of a religious and philosophical seeker, and her ideas were, for the time, rather startling. Christ, she believed, had only been a mortal man though one imbued with a unique morality, while she thought of God as an indefinite force present in all living things.[16] In 1900, she had joined the Unitarian Church, but soon she was drawn to spiritualism, and notions of the soul's survival after death.

Spiritualism was then at the height of its popularity, as many intellectuals pondered the meaning of life and sought definitive scientific proof of life after death. The Society for Psychical Research, founded in England, attracted such luminaries as Arthur Conan Doyle, Sigmund Freud, and Alfred, Lord Tennyson. William James, brother of novelist Henry James, contributed to the movement by writing extensively on questions of clairvoyance, telepathy, and theology.[17] Theodate studied the literature and, in 1907, when Professor James Hyslop of Columbia University formed an independent American branch of the Society for Psychical Research, she contributed $25,000 to help fund the cause.[18] She began visiting England with some regularity, including meetings with Sir Oliver Lodge, a professor of physics at the University College in Liverpool, who had long been a member of the society and penned a number of popular works on communication with the dead. After William James died, though, she infuriated his brother Henry by passing along a medium's claimed communication. "The *commonness* of it," the famed novelist wrote, "simply nauseates." Though he regarded Theodate as a person of "fine and true qualities," he was horrified that she would "pass on such a tissue of trash" and believe it had come from his late brother.[19]

When Alfred Pope died in 1913, he left an estate valued at some $5.5 million, not including his real estate and art collection.[20] She used her inheritance to provide James Hyslop with an assistant, twenty-eight-year-old Harvard graduate Edwin Friend, who had studied classics and philosophy both in America and in Berlin.[21] Theodate was drawn to the young man "endowed so richly in heart and mind," and to his wife, Marjorie, and provided them with housing on the Hill-Stead estate.[22] At her prompting, Friend became editor of the society's journal, with an annual salary of $2,000. Soon, he began to ignore Hyslop's articles in favor of his own, writing about séances and how his wife allegedly communicated with the dead. An infuriated Hyslop removed Friend as editor; shortly thereafter, both Friend and Theodate resigned from the society.[23] In the spring of 1915, she decided to form a new American psychical society, and sail with Friend to England to obtain the backing of Sir Oliver Lodge and other English spiritualists.[24] They booked passage on *Lusitania:* Theodate traveled with her maid, Emily Robinson, but Friend was forced to leave his pregnant wife behind.[25]

Now, assured of what she hoped would be a peaceful night's sleep, Theodate pondered the voyage. She was nervous: the crossing itself seemed fraught with potential danger and, on top of it, the German warning was too ominous to simply laugh off. She thought that many others aboard *Lusitania* shared her anxiety, noting, "We were a very quiet shipload." Hoping to take her mind off her own worries, she asked Friend to read aloud to her from Henri Bergson's *Matière et Mémoire.* This, she thought, "illustrated so wonderfully some of the common difficulties in communication." As she listened, Theodate "marveled to myself that such a man as Mr. Friend had been found to carry on the investigations. I felt very deeply the quality of my respect and admiration for him."[26]

A steady rhythm of marching feet interrupted the Sunday morning quiet of *Lusitania's* Boat Deck. Staff Captain Anderson led a contingent of officers and officials up and down, in and out, and back and forth as they inspected the liner deck by deck. Public rooms, staterooms, bathrooms, galleys, engine rooms, storage rooms, and crew quarters had to be clean, neat, and in good order, ready for any potential emergency. It was Cunard tradition.[27]

Passengers and crew would have been better served had Cunard paid less attention to tidiness and more to their lifeboat drills. The *Titanic* disaster had at least ensured that a liner like *Lusitania* now carried enough lifeboats to hold everyone aboard. They stood ranged down the length of the Boat Deck, eleven to each side, capable of holding 1,322 people within their wooden hulls; twenty-six collapsible lifeboats with wooden keels and canvas sides, fitted beneath them and set in cradles on deck, could carry another 1,238 passengers.[28]

At eleven every morning, *Lusitania*'s sailors conducted a boat drill. Two short whistles summoned ten members of the deck crew to muster. At a signal, they climbed into a single boat, hoisted the oars, and sat down. In a few seconds, they stood back up, replaced the oars, and climbed back down onto the deck. None of the falls—the ropes holding the boats to their individual davits—were checked or tested, none of the boats were raised or lowered, and no passengers were involved.[29]

For Captain Turner and the Cunard Line, this passed for a competent boat drill. The Royal Navy had taken the best sailors for the war; *Lusitania* had to make do with a haphazard crew of seamen, picked up here and there. Training had been minimal; Turner even complained that the men weren't proficient in handling the lifeboats.[30] As master of *Lusitania,* he was responsible for the 1,965 souls aboard his ship. A passenger liner had been torpedoed just a month earlier; he was taking *Lusitania* into a declared war zone; the German government had warned passengers with its newspaper notice. Yet Turner did nothing to rectify this lack of training. There were no extra drills, there was no additional practice for the sailors, and no attempt was made to advise passengers what to do if the ship should meet with tragedy.

These drills did nothing to calm *Lusitania*'s anxious travelers. Michael Byrne, horrified at the "pitiable exhibition," wondered why passengers were not included; at the very least, he thought, everyone should be shown how to properly put on and adjust their lifebelts.[31] "It is not necessary to offer any of the officers advice as to the navigation of the ship," one guidebook warned passengers. "They have been at sea longer than you have, and probably know more about it than you do."[32] Yet to many, the risk of deadly disaster outweighed the risk of offending. After watching one of these perfunctory lifeboat drills, burly wine merchant George Kessler complained to purser James McCubbin, "It's all right drilling your crew, but why don't you drill your passengers?" McCubbin merely referred Kessler to Captain Turner.[33]

Kessler wasn't accustomed to being summarily dismissed. Born in Mobile, Alabama, in 1863 and known derisively as "the Champagne King," the black-bearded man—who prided himself on his resemblance to King Edward VII—made a name for himself in Gilded Age New York as American agent for Moët & Chandon.[34] "A fine type of New York's self-made man," one journal said of Kessler; not only was he "a pleasant, courteous gentleman" but, as befitting the refined product he represented, he had "a natural affinity for beauty, and a pleasant and cultivated taste." He liked the finer things in life: his bachelor apartment on Fifth Avenue had been decked in expensive brocades and silks sewn with pearls, Moorish lanterns, and figures of marble, jade, and ivory set with diamond eyes.[35]

Eventually he opened his own import company in New York City, George A. Kessler & Company, married Cora Parsons, and grew wealthy thanks to the orchestrations of Harry Lehr, a flamboyantly bizarre man who acted as the indispensable advisor to

Gilded Age hostesses. Lehr liked nothing better than planning parties, or helping hostesses select elaborate evening gowns. "Oh, if only I could wear ladies' clothes," Lehr once sighed, "all silks and dainty petticoats and laces!"[36] He had married heiress Elizabeth Drexel, as he coldly told her on their wedding night, only for her money, and delighted in making her life miserable. "What a perfect fright you look!" Lehr hissed at her during prayers at Mass. "Why on earth did you put on those shoes?"[37]

Lehr was an opportunist, but then, so, too, was Kessler. One day, he called on Lehr and forthrightly declared, "You and I can be useful to one another. I will give you six thousand dollars a year to sell my champagne." The gamble worked, and soon enough the cellars of the Astors and Vanderbilts were filled with champagne they "did not particularly want" merely to please the powerful Lehr.[38] A born self-promoter, Kessler relentlessly pushed both Moët & Chandon and his own label, White Star Extra Brut, which Moët & Chandon sponsored. When dining out, he would look around, spot tables with the wealthiest and most important guests, and order complimentary bottles of his champagne promptly dispatched. He even bribed waiters at Sherry's and Delmonico's: they received 50 cents for each bottle sold, with a dollar lavished on those who cajoled patrons into purchasing a magnum—though Kessler demanded to see the corks as evidence.[39]

Kessler was no stranger to scandal. In 1902, he'd caused an international incident when he substituted his own White Star Extra Brut in place of a bottle of Söhnlein Rhine champagne sent from Germany to christen Kaiser Wilhelm II's new racing yacht in New Jersey. The shipyard manager pocketed a $5,000 bribe, but the outcry was so great that the German ambassador, who had missed Kessler's trick, was briefly recalled.[40] Four years later, Kessler happened to be in San Francisco when the great earthquake struck. Rushing from his hotel as it collapsed around him, he watched in horror as the city crumbled and burst into flames. It was, Kessler decided, the perfect opportunity for yet another publicity stunt: within days, crates of his champagne arrived aboard a railroad car, to be given free of charge to the shattered city's suffering victims.[41]

In time, Kessler also made a name for himself as a lavish host. Dividing his time between a house at Bourne End on the River Thames in England and New York City, he "used to lie awake at nights," a newspaper declared, "thinking of novel ways of spending some of his vast income, and he decided that freak dinners best suited his purpose."[42] There was a summer banquet in his English garden, where fifty thousand miniature electric lights sparkled on the trees to magical effect; another time, he re-created the North Pole in the Savoy Hotel's winter garden. Crossing a floor covered in artificial snow, guests walked past towering icebergs crafted from mounds of silver tissue to tables resembling snowdrifts, as an army of dwarves, dressed as snowmen, served dinner.[43]

Then there was his infamous Gondola Party in 1905. Kessler returned to London's Savoy Hotel for this bit of phantasmagoria. At first, he wanted to hire a dirigible to perch atop the roof; when his guests had climbed into the gondola, the lines would be let out and they could then dine several hundred feet above the city. After objections, Kessler exchanged an airborne gondola for one in the water.[44] A small fortune went to transform the Savoy's ballroom and courtyard into a vision of Venice. The courtyard was flooded to create a lagoon, the water tinted blue, and strewn with live goldfish, swans, and ducks; 120 electricians wired tiny electric lights into the ceiling to provide a twinkling nighttime sky. Eighty guests dined aboard an enormous, gilded gondola, served by waiters dressed as gondoliers while strolling musicians sang and famed tenor Enrico Caruso serenaded them with operatic selections. At the end of the evening, a baby elephant called Jumbo

Junior was led before the startled guests, carrying on his back an enormous cake. Compared with many Gilded Age entertainments, Kessler got off cheaply, spending only $15,000.[45] As Kessler hoped, the spectacle got people talking, though not exactly in the ways he had expected. Writer H. G. Wells marveled that the guests "were important, grown-up people," deriding the evening as an example of how "people of sluggish and uneducated imagination, who find themselves profusely wealthy, are too stupid to understand the huge moral burden."[46]

Kessler wasn't as worried about a torpedo hitting *Lusitania* as some of his fellow passengers. He was, though, worried about his money—especially if something should happen to the ship. He carried a case with some $2 million in stocks and bonds when he boarded. Passengers generally entrusted such valuables to the purser. Not Kessler: should there really be an emergency aboard the liner, he decided that his cabin was "much safer" than the purser's safe.[47]

"What would happen if all the boats had to be lowered?" mused passenger Oliver Bernard after watching that Sunday's drill.[48] Bernard knew something about seamanship: half a lifetime ago, after a miserable childhood, he'd run away, signing on as a deckhand and working his way across the Atlantic. One way or another, it seemed, he'd been running for most of his life. His parents had wanted nothing to do with him; on his father's death in 1894, his vain actress mother had shipped thirteen-year-old Oliver off from London to live with relatives in Manchester. After a stint as a stagehand, Bernard had gone to sea, working his way to New York, where he took jobs at several Broadway theaters. "Scenery, properties, and the operations of stage mechanics and lighting" fascinated him, and soon he was putting his artistic talents to use designing sets.[49]

Bernard appreciated the city's visual interest, where "towers of burnished brass welded into cliffs of bronze, smoldering above massive shadows descending far below where hordes of electric jewels glittered."[50] He was less enthused by the realities of life. New York, he thought, was not only thoroughly uncultured, but also "in the throes of a spectacular disease" he deemed to be a constant quest for money. Whether "standing, walking, sitting," or even "eating," all conversation seemed to turn on "dollars, dollars earned, won, lost, spent, stolen, saved, begged, borrowed or buried in a maelstrom." He concluded that "to those who refused to profit by any means available, New York was absolutely pitiless."[51]

Returning to London, the handsome, diminutive Bernard married a singer, Muriel Lightfoot; joined an opera company as scenic director on its Australian tour; and finally landed a job at the Royal Opera House, Covent Garden.[52] Growing deafness led to his rejection by the British Army; feeling ashamed, Bernard returned to America, taking a position as technical director of the Boston Opera House.[53] Bernard fumed at having to design sets for "a deplorable play" written by millionaire William Lindsey. Lindsey had made a fortune developing and selling ammunition belts to the British Army during the Boer War; he was "by occupation a millionaire, by inclination a successor of minstrels in Provence," and regarded himself as "New England's Bard."[54]

It was all too humiliating for the volatile Bernard. He seized on stories that, by the spring of 1915, the British Army was so desperate for men that it was now accepting recruits previously denied, and decided to return to London. Lindsey asked one final favor: his beautiful young daughter Leslie had just married Stewart Mason of Ipswich, and the couple—off to England on their honeymoon—would sail aboard *Lusitania* with Bernard. Would he act as chaperone? How, Bernard wondered, was he supposed to watch this couple, who "had everything that human beings could wish for: unlimited money, youth, fond parents, and the world?" But he agreed, with Lindsey's admonition, "Keep an eye on my little girl!" ringing in his head as they all had boarded *Lusitania* the previous day.[55]

Looking after the romantic Stewarts put Bernard in a foul mood. He thought that his fellow travelers "were less sociable than usual," which he put down to typical English reserve. Like many others, he had read the German notice in the newspaper on the morning he was to sail, but it did nothing to change his mind. He was "quite sure that this warning was entirely another bluff to embarrass the United States Government and create further consternation in England." Even so, as he prowled the liner on its first full day at sea, he secretly nursed the thought that "something would happen" during this voyage that would finally allow him to experience the reality of war.[56]

CHAPTER FIVE

Monday, May 3, began with dismal weather as *Lusitania* churned her way across the Atlantic. Although the voyage was relatively pleasant, a few passengers suffered from seasickness as the ship rolled and pitched through the ocean; *Lusitania* was known to be a roller in rough seas.[1] *Lusitania* had her own hospital, doctor, and nursing staff, but there was little that could be done to alleviate this most common of complaints. For much of the crew, being seasick, wrote one historian, "became synonymous with malingering," and those who suffered were often mocked and belittled for their "weakness." Sufferers usually took to their cabins; no one could quite agree on the best remedy. A traveler suffering from seasickness should get plenty of rest, or should exercise incessantly, or should read a book, or should stand up, or should eat oysters, or should avoid jam—no two guidebooks seemed to agree on a practical approach.[2] One handbook recommended a variety of treatments including drinking champagne or brandy; if the case was severe, it advised, relief could be found in doses of morphine and cocaine.[3]

Passengers were gradually becoming accustomed to life on the vessel. On boarding the ship, they could consult a booklet issued by Cunard, with information on the liner as well as practical advice on the voyage.[4] The curious could scan the printed passenger list, looking for names of friends and acquaintances who might also be on board.[5] For those in First Class, life settled into a comforting, familiar routine. Those ensconced in suites could telephone the Steward's Department with requests. "One may ask for anything," recalled a traveler, "and in a mysterious way, that 'anything' seems to appear."[6]

An important part of each morning was selecting one's attire. A war might be on, but appearances must be maintained, even at sea. The last vestiges of the already vanished Edwardian Era lived on at sea; it was, insisted an author, "probably the last period in history when the fortunate thought they could give pleasure to others by displaying their good fortune."[7] Those fortunate passengers who traveled with their own maids or valets could rely on years of expertise; others sorted through brassbound steamer trunks, leather suitcases and valises, and jumbles of boxes that carried their wardrobes. A lady might begin her morning in a lacy negligee and exotically decorated Japanese kimono if she remained in her cabin. Late morning and early afternoon called for a day dress, or skirt and shirtwaist, with matching jacket and, perhaps, a parasol to shield her from the rays of the sun. Little boxes offered an array of hats bedecked with feathers, fur, and flowers; others held stockings; underclothing; and shoes and boots for daytime, with delicate satin slippers reserved for the evening. Drawers in the trunks protected delicate shawls; a variety of gloves; lacy handkerchiefs wrapped in tissue paper; scarves; and an array of items necessary to complete a toilette. Only actresses or *demimondaines* used cosmetics: at most, a little face powder and rouge might nestle on dressing tables next to tooth powder, creams, and a variety of scents. Many ladies changed clothing again in late afternoon, donning a filmy dress to join fellow passengers in the Lounge for a highly ritualized tea. Evening called for another change of clothing, when dinner demanded more formal attire. Gentlemen needed fewer changes of clothing. A tweed or wool business suit, or even knickerbockers, a matching jacket, and a jaunty hat, were sufficient for most of the day. An overcoat was essential, especially for walks or time spent on deck. It was also important not to overdress aboard ship, to prefer simpler cuts and materials to the more elaborate concoctions that might be worn ashore.[8]

Passengers relied on the ship's crew for every request. There were deck stewards; barkeepers; three barbers; two lift attendants; a ship's typist and a ship's printer, who each morning published the liner's newspaper; two telegraph operators; an interpreter; a bugler to summon passengers to meals; nurses attached to the infirmary; and a number of young boys who acted as assistants to the stewards. Each day, *Lusitania*'s linen keeper tracked the hundreds of items that flowed through his office. "Just imagine a washing day," Cunard informed passengers, "with between 70,000–80,000 articles to be dealt with." Freshly laundered cloths were placed on the tables in the First and Second Class Dining Saloons before each meal, while those in Third Class were changed several times a week. Napkins had to be laundered, along with sheets, pillowcases, and towels. Clothing from passengers also arrived for cleaning, including gentlemen's collars and shirtfronts for starching.[9]

In First Class, nineteen cabin stewards and twenty-one cabin stewardesses—along with several additional helpers—tended to passengers. They ran errands, cleaned staterooms, made beds, and replenished linens and towels, all in an effort to keep passengers comfortable and content. "A more willing man than the average ship's steward," a guidebook explained, "does not exist."[10] Passengers whose accommodations did not include private facilities applied to stewards or stewardesses to arrange for baths. "All those having baths are expected to give gratuities," literature advised, generally $1 if more than one bath was taken during the voyage. Tips to stewards "should not be evaded," and were regularly paid at the end of the voyage. The amount was determined by the cost of the cabin, but generally somewhere between $2.50 and $4 was advised; stewardesses should only receive two thirds of the tip given to their male counterparts. A passenger occupying a large suite was expected to offer more generous remuneration.[11] "No great metropolitan hotel," a contemporary reported, "offered more in the way of service and facilities for enjoyment and comfort than this palace of the deep."[12] Above all, passengers should "remember that the ship's servants are human beings," deserving of considerate treatment.[13]

Breakfast was normally served in the Dining Saloon from 8 A.M. to half-past nine, though many preferred to have tea or coffee delivered each morning to their stateroom. They could follow the latest developments by consulting the ship's newspaper, the *Cunard Daily Bulletin*. Cunard had been the first line to print its own daily for passengers on the ship, relying on news wired from London and New York. Not only did this include helpful advertisements for hotels but it also kept passengers informed of any important events in the war and of the liner's daily array of activities.[14]

After taking breakfast, passengers dispersed about the ship. For children—at least those traveling First Class—*Lusitania* offered a number of diversions, designed to ensure that they were separated from adults. A nursery and playroom, walls adorned with scenes from nursery rhymes and fairy tales, offered games and a full staff to look after them. For meals, most children ate in their own Louis XVI–style dining room on C Deck.[15]

Freed from tending to their children, parents could thus take advantage of life at sea. Ladies might spend their mornings in the Reading and Writing Room, just off the Grand Staircase on Boat Deck. This was a place of sober refinement in the style of Robert Adam, fifty-two feet wide and forty-four feet long, with carved Corinthian pilasters framing panels of cream and gray silk brocade against enameled walls. Above, the large, circular leaded glass dome pierced a ten-foot-high ceiling swept with delicate stucco reliefs; below, mahogany sofas and chairs, upholstered in Rose du Barry silk matching the curtains at the etched glass windows, were arranged atop a rose-colored carpet. On one wall, a black and white marble mantel framed an electric fireplace; opposite stood a twenty-six-foot-long, nine-foot-high Georgian-style mahogany bookcase filled with the latest popular novels and works of non-fiction.[16] Here, twenty-six-year-old Harry Grisdale, the library steward, carefully noted the names of passengers taking books with them. "Books can be taken to staterooms," one guide advised, "but should be returned to the library steward before landing," as the cost of any replacements would be deducted from his salary.[17]

Inlaid mahogany writing desks, set with silk-shaded gilt lamps, held supplies of *Lusitania*'s stationery, adorned with a depiction of the ship at the top left corner. There was, commented a historian, "enormous prestige" in sending a letter on an elite liner's embossed stationery, and "reams of the stuff disappeared, some of it to reappear in the mailbox," with the rest "unused, into suit-cases to serve until something more elegant could be found in a hotel."[18] As such, the supply had to be replenished each morning. Although those on *Lusitania* could receive telegrams while at sea, Marconi Company operators Robert Leith and David Mc-Cormick were under orders that "no passengers' messages must be sent from the ship whatever," for fear that such transmissions would point German submarines to its route. The Cunard

Line itself was not allowed to communicate with the vessel: only messages approved by and passed on from the Admiralty were transmitted to the liner.[19]

Friendships were born and acquaintances renewed as an air of sociability took hold. A typical voyage, according to one chronicle, "should be one of ease, and after the first day or two it may be one of dignity also." Fellow passengers should be treated "with courtesy and civility," for one never knew if, after the voyage, the "unpretentious person" might be called upon to render assistance or exert influence in the future. Passengers should not "be too dignified or too assertive," and should not indulge in practical jokes. A crossing, at least in Saloon Class, would likely comprise "an assemblage of people as one would expect to meet at a first-class hotel."[20]

Life aboard *Lusitania* reflected British tradition and values, an atmosphere carefully cultivated to both entice and reassure her most privileged passengers that, even though they were at sea, they need not forgo the comforts or courtesies of home. Theodore Dreiser, traveling a few years earlier aboard *Mauretania,* was particularly struck by the exacting politeness of the crew. Being British, he thought, had made these stewards and stewardesses subservient in ways starkly contrasting with their American counterparts. There was, he thought, "an aloofness" about their service, yet they were unfailingly polite, deferential, and anxious to please; everywhere he went, the crew spouted, "Yes, sir," and "Thank you, sir."[21]

"It may be pretty accurately said," wrote social advisor Emily Post, "that the faster and bigger the ship, the less likely one is to speak to strangers and yet, as always, circumstances alter cases." The most exclusive passengers rarely sought out new acquaintances aboard ship for fear that unwelcome intimacy and unsuspected antecedents might somehow tarnish reputations. Transatlantic liners were the known hunting ground of a particular type of scoundrel, the Arriviste, armed with enough money to buy temporary membership in this exclusive club and always on the watch for opportunities to add prominent figures to his circle of acquaintances. Post warned passengers against those who attempted to force themselves on others and struck up conversations without proper introductions. When this happened, one should immediately be on guard. A "few minutes of conversation" were sufficient to assess intent and breeding; expressions of slang, lack of decorum, and pushiness would quickly reveal someone who was "grasping, calculating, and objectionable." If such was the case, Post advised, it was best to immediately leave or to divert one's attention to a book or to another passenger.[22]

After traveling for many months, Angela Papadopoulos and her husband, Michael, were looking forward to reuniting with their three children in Athens. Born in 1883, Angela was the daughter of Italian aristocrat Vincenzo Baffa Tasci Amalfitani di Crucoli. Brought up at her father's estate, she'd married Papadopoulos, a wealthy businessman who had cornered the market on exporting Oriental carpets from Turkey, Persia, and Central Asia, and settled into a comfortable life in Athens. They'd crossed the Atlantic in *Lusitania* that February, and saw no reason not to return aboard her to Europe. Settling into their stateroom on B Deck, thirty-two-year-old Angela "discovered with delight that in the cabin next to us were Mrs. Burnside and her daughter Iris, whom we met in Toronto."[23]

Josephine Eaton Burnside was probably happy to find a friendly companion to help occupy her time: she was on her way to see her estranged husband—just the latest development in her oddly contradictory life. She'd been born to Timothy Eaton, one of

Toronto's wealthiest men and the founder of Eaton's Department Store. Sly and farsighted, Eaton had used money-back guarantees and mail-order catalogues to build his network of mercantile shops into the country's largest commercial enterprise. In the process he'd become very rich: a 1907 estimate placed his fortune at roughly $5 million.[24] Yet he was a dedicated Methodist who disdained luxury, and Josephine was brought up in a comfortable, though not lavish, house. Fashionable Toronto society deemed the Eatons dull: they neither drank nor danced, and kept to themselves, dining every Sunday on what he deemed a good Irish supper of cold mashed potatoes mixed with buttermilk.[25]

Timothy approved when Josephine married Irish-born Thomas Burnside, but the union was miserable. Burnside hated Canada, and wanted to continue working in England; Josephine hated England, and refused to leave her beloved Toronto. No amount of Eaton money could persuade Burnside to maintain appearances, and so the couple agreed to live apart in their respective countries. Now, their twenty-year-old daughter, Iris, insisted on going to stay with her father. Dreading a dangerous crossing and possible attack by a German submarine, Josephine tried to put the voyage off; Iris stubbornly insisted, and so her mother reluctantly booked passage on *Lusitania*.[26]

Timothy Eaton's money was relatively new, and he had earned it "in trade." It bought access but not necessarily acceptance. Still, with its "enforced intimacy," *Lusitania* was something of a social leveler.[27] In this artificial world, an otherwise peculiar blend of aristocrats and traditionalists rubbed shoulders with celebrities, industrialists, and entrepreneurs unlikely, under other circumstances, to find themselves gathered in the same social milieu. Vigorously ambitious Americans, in particular, could temporarily abandon their self-made origins and travel in all of the luxury and style their money afforded.

Even in the midst of the war, there was no absence of luxury aboard *Lusitania*. Her two Regal Suites on B Deck were the pinnacle of indulgent comfort. Author Richard Harding Davis, who had occupied one of the suites in 1914, deemed it "so darned regal that I hate to leave it. I get sleepy walking from one end of it to the other."[28] Deploying decorative motifs drawn from the Palace of Fontainebleau and the Petit Trianon at Versailles, each suite was subtly different. That on the port side featured a dining room paneled in Italian walnut and adorned with gilded reliefs; meals or private parties could be catered from a small nearby pantry. Sliding doors inset with glass opened to a sitting room hung in "beautifully painted panels of flowers." Sofa, chairs, and a mahogany writing desk inlaid with satinwood were grouped around an ornamental marble mantelpiece above an electric fire; windows, draped in cream and green silk to match the upholstery, flooded the room with light, and a door allowed direct access to and from the deck beyond. "Designed in a sumptuous manner," the bedrooms featured brass beds and blue silk brocade hangings: delicate little Wedgwood-style cameos hung from gilded floral swags adorning the white enameled walls. Even the private bathroom was fitted with marble fixtures.[29] All of this luxury came at a price: $2,250 for a Regal Suite, one way.[30]

Two kinds of passengers usually booked *Lusitania*'s Regal Suites: the old-moneyed, titled traveler, and the nouveau riche passenger accustomed to luxury. And so it was on this voyage: socially prominent Marguerite, Lady Allan occupied the starboard suite, while self-made American entrepreneur Albert Bilicke and his wife, Gladys, had taken the one to port. Here, in these refined surroundings, the fifty-four-year-old California businessman hoped to recuperate from recent abdominal surgery.

By 1915, Bilicke had gone far in life and seen much. Born the son of German immigrants in Oregon, he'd graduated from a San

Francisco business college and followed his father, Carl, to Arizona Territory, opening and operating hotels in Globe and Florence before moving on to the bustling frontier town of Tombstone.[31] The discovery of silver ore in the surrounding hills saw the settlement quickly double in size, with gambling dens, shops, saloons, and Carl's Cosmopolitan Hotel rising along its dusty streets.

Tombstone was a wild and rough place, where frontier justice ruled: young Albert once shot the ear off a man who was attempting to rob his father.[32] Town marshal Virgil Earp tried to impose some sense of order; he made the Cosmopolitan his unofficial headquarters, meeting there with his brothers Wyatt and Morgan, and their friend Doc Holliday, as tensions between citizens and cowboys steadily rose. On the evening of October 25, 1881, Holliday got into an argument with a group of cowboys, led by brothers Frank and Tom McLaury; the cowboys were back the next day, drunkenly wandering the streets near the O.K. Corral and brandishing their guns. After the marshal wrestled a gun away from cowboy Ike Clanton, the latter's allies loudly threatened to shoot the Earp brothers.[33]

Twenty-year-old Albert Bilicke followed these scenes with growing apprehension. "Every good citizen in this city," he later explained, "was watching all those cowboys very closely." The day after Earp took Clanton's gun, Bilicke saw Tom McLaury walk into a shop; when he came out a few minutes later, Albert thought that he detected the unmistakable bulge of a gun in his pocket.[34]

McLaury joined his brother, and Ike and Billy Clanton, as they marched down Fremont Street. Ahead stood Virgil Earp, along with brothers Wyatt and Morgan, as well as Doc Holliday. Albert believed that one of the cowboys had first opened fire; in a few seconds, everyone was shooting. When the smoke cleared, Billy Clanton and both McLaury brothers lay dead, and Virgil and Morgan Earp were seriously wounded. At the subsequent trial,

Bilicke testified for the Earps and Holliday, insisting that he had seen Tom McLaury surreptitiously arm himself, presumably with the intent to kill the marshal and his brothers as well as Holliday.[35]

The gunfight at the O.K. Corral became the single most famous episode of Wild West justice. A few years after the incident, Albert returned to California, opening a hotel in Dunsmuir before moving to Los Angeles. In 1893, he took over operation of the city's exclusive Hollenbeck Hotel; ten years later, he was building his own establishment, the Alexandria, which "added much to the fame and luxurious hotel life of Los Angeles."[36] Investments in real estate and building companies made Bilicke extremely rich: within two decades, he had amassed a fortune worth $2,706,000.[37]

Bilicke married Illinois native Gladys Huff, six years his junior, at Niagara Falls in 1900, and the couple had three children: Albert, Nancy, and Carl. The family lived in a quarter-million-dollar, Mediterranean-style house on South Pasadena's Monterey Road, complete with terraced gardens and fruit orchards.[38] Here, Gladys worked tirelessly—not on her household, gardens, or entertaining, but rather as her husband's private secretary. She had an unusual aptitude for business, and served as Albert's "most intimate counselor in many of his transactions."[39]

In the spring of 1915, Bilicke fell ill and had to have abdominal surgery. To recover, he and Gladys took a holiday across America; when they ended up in New York, they decided to sail to Europe and booked passage on *Lusitania*. Just before the ship left New York, Bilicke jotted a postcard to a business associate in Los Angeles: "We are off and this is certainly a fine ship. Have crossed twice in her, and am acquainted with her speed and officers. Expect to get much rest this trip."[40]

Bilicke was just the sort of man fellow passenger and art

dealer Edgar Gorer would have wanted as a client: eager to leave a rough-and-tumble past behind, wealthy, and anxious to demonstrate his good taste. A "man of strong and aggressive personality," the British-born Gorer sold exquisite porcelains, delicate figurines, and rare objets d'art to connoisseurs and collectors around the globe.[41] The son of a silversmith and jeweler, Gorer had, said a rival, "forced himself into a leading position amongst London art dealers by sheer cleverness and courage."[42]

Early on, Gorer hit on the idea of producing beautifully illustrated catalogues of his Eastern and Asian porcelains that won him much attention. The rival Duveen Brothers, while admitting Gorer's cunning, openly questioned his expertise. They warned potential clients that Gorer might be passing off modern reproductions as antiques. Things came to a head in 1914, when Joseph Duveen learned that Gorer had arranged the sale of a rare Chinese vase to American collector Henry Clay Frick for $40,000. "That vase is not a genuine antique," Duveen warned Frick. Duveen insisted that "Gorer knows nothing about porcelains," adding that he meant to stop him "putting these fakes on the market." Frick quickly backed out of the agreement.[43] Insisting that Duveen had purposely set out to ruin his reputation, an infuriated Gorer filed a libel lawsuit against his rival, seeking $575,000 in damages for having "practically destroyed" his career. The suit was to be announced on May 7, while Gorer was still at sea on *Lusitania*.[44]

Gorer wasn't the only art dealer aboard *Lusitania*. Standing nearly six feet tall, thin, balding, and with a distinguished little beard and a mustache whose tips he habitually waxed, Sir Hugh Lane was quiet, charming, and mild-mannered; he was also, as *The Times* of London noted, "generally regarded as one of the soundest judges" of painting. In 1893, when Lane was eighteen, he got a job at a London gallery when his aristocratic aunt

Augusta, Lady Gregory, asked the Keeper of the Queen's Pictures to pull a few strings.[45] "How can you waste money on dinners when there are such beautiful things to buy?" Lane once asked a traveling companion.[46] Frugality allowed him to open his own showroom, and Lane began arranging exhibitions of Irish artists in London, with an eye to establishing a gallery in Dublin.[47]

"A Gallery of Modern Art in Dublin," he wrote, "would create a standard of taste, and a feeling for the relative importance of painters. This would encourage the purchase of pictures, for people will not purchase where they do not know. Such a gallery would be necessary to the student if we are to have a distinct school of painting in Ireland, for it is one's contemporaries that teach one the most."[48] Although named director of the National Gallery of Ireland in 1914, the now ennobled Sir Hugh Lane was frustrated in his attempts to establish a permanent modern collection. When it seemed the issue might drag on interminably, he lent his works by Manet, Degas, and Renoir to the National Gallery in London.[49]

Lane lived in considerable comfort at Lindsey House in Chelsea, surrounded by marbles, silks, Turkish carpets, and rare porcelains; although mild, he had the unfortunate habit of blurting out whatever crossed his mind. He once entered a friend's drawing room, raced across the carpet, and abruptly pulled down the curtains, crying, "You *really* must not have these in your house!"[50] Lane never married: his aunt thought that a marriage would have worked only if he and his wife "had lived in separate houses."[51] Noting his fastidious attention to dress and decoration, his love of art, and his "somewhat effeminate manner," people speculated that Lane was homosexual.[52] He left almost no paper trail to document his private life: given the times in which Lane lived, perhaps discretion was indeed advisable.

Having just sold a Titian and a Hans Holbein portrait to Henry

Clay Frick in New York, Lane was now on his way back to Europe.[53] He carried a handful of paintings bound for Dublin: there were rumors of watertight lead tubes; of works by Monet, Rubens, Titian, and Rembrandt; and of a $4 million insurance policy should the masterpieces be lost.[54] Although he dismissed talk of a possible U-boat attack as "too absurd" for words, Lane worried about traveling on the British liner.[55] Before departing New York, he wrote a new codicil to his will, leaving the Impressionist paintings then on loan to the National Gallery in London to the city of Dublin. Lane admitted to being "frightened," telling a friend he was "going into danger" by sailing aboard *Lusitania*.[56]

CHAPTER SIX

"As the days passed," recalled forty-year-old Boston bookseller Charles Lauriat of this voyage on *Lusitania,* "the passengers seemed to enjoy them more and more, and formed those acquaintances such as one does on an ocean crossing." Lauriat had crossed the Atlantic twenty-two times before on business, though this was his first trip aboard one of the truly majestic "greyhounds," and he found the experience exciting as he roamed the decks, doing his best to forget the German notice he had seen in New York.[1]

By Tuesday, May 4, the earlier, dismal weather had finally disappeared and people took to the decks. It was, wrote Frederick Orr-Lewis, "perfect weather" for most of the voyage, with "scarcely a ripple all the way across and sufficiently warm to go on deck without an overcoat."[2] *Lusitania*'s Promenade Deck, a sweeping expanse running the length of the main superstructure, offered both shelter and magnificent views over the sea: it was the perfect place to sit and enjoy the voyage. A deck chair or chaise, a guidebook warned, "is absolutely essential to comfort." Passengers were advised to apply to the ship's deck steward, who then assigned chairs at the rate of $1 for the duration of the crossing: once let, passengers should not move deck chairs from their assigned place.[3] On this voyage, the most desirable chairs were on the starboard side, where the sun was most likely to shine and the superstructure sheltered them from northern winds.[4]

Here, passengers could sit, laps covered by warm woolen rugs, as they chatted, read, and enjoyed the passing ocean.[5] Emily Post, at least, warned against deck chair friendships: "To have your next chair neighbor on deck insist on talking to you, if you don't want to be talked to, is very annoying, and it is bad form." The surest way to ward off the unwelcome was to utter a few "monosyllables" in reply, which "should be taken to mean that you prefer to be left to your own diversions."[6]

For the more adventuresome, there were usually plenty of activities to be found on deck. The more energetic might make daily circuits of the ship, while others joined in outdoor games usually arranged by the ship's quartermaster.[7] "Every day," recalled Toronto department store buyer Robinson Pirie, he joined a group of fellow Canadians, buyers for Eaton's Department Store, and "played deck quoits, shuffleboard, or something."[8] Deck quoits, a game involving the tossing of rope rings onto a hook, was always popular, as was bull board, where little bags of sand were tossed at a square divided into numbers. Shuffleboard was a perennial favorite, and there were even games of tennis, played using a badminton net stretched across the width of the deck. Ladies who declined to play were advised to bring needlework and embroidery to help fill the hours.[9]

Some gentlemen took to the deck; others seemed to spend most of their days in the Smoking Room, situated near the aft end of *Lusitania*'s Boat Deck. The First Class Smoking Room was meant to evoke the atmosphere of an exclusive gentlemen's club in London. Designed in a vaguely Queen Anne style, the roughly fifty-foot-square room featured walls paneled in Italian walnut set between finely wrought Corinthian pilasters. Sofas and chairs covered in red upholstery were scattered atop the Brussels carpet; above the wide, cream-colored cornice adorned with decorative reliefs stretched an immense stained glass barrel-vaulted skylight. To provide just the right atmosphere, the marble fireplace here burned coal to provide dancing flames.[10] The effect, wrote one periodical, was of a room "of quiet repose and richness, in pleasant contrast to the brightness of the white and gold of other public apartments."[11]

Beneath a fine haze of blue cigarette smoke and against the sound of ice clinking in tumblers of whiskey, passengers whiled away pleasant afternoons over games of bridge, whispered racy stories, or exchanged business cards and cemented potential deals. A liner typically carried thousands of cigars, numerous brands of cigarettes, and a variety of tobacco for pipes, but travelers were generally warned that it was better to bring their own supplies, carefully wrapped in tinfoil and waxed paper to avoid disintegration in the sea air.[12] Michael Byrne must have liked to smoke: he boarded *Lusitania* with three hundred cigars and eleven pounds of tobacco for his use.[13] Even if one didn't resort to Cunard's supplies, a passenger who frequented the Smoking Room was advised to tip the steward 50 cents at the end of the voyage.[14]

Playing cards at sea was always a risk. "A curious, but none the less dangerous, type of adventurer known as the ocean gambler and sometimes less politely as a sea-going sharper and swindler," warned one guidebook, "crosses the North Atlantic with great regularity."[15] In theory, gambling of any sort was not allowed on passenger liners; in practice, however, stewards tended to look the other way, especially as so many travelers seemed intent on violating the rule. It remained in force mainly to protect the shipping line if a disgruntled losing passenger attempted a lawsuit.[16]

Professional gamblers, cardsharps, and confidence tricksters were usually ingenious, charming, and well mannered. Some made their entire living crossing and recrossing the ocean, swindling the unsuspecting out of small fortunes. Passage on a liner like *Lusitania* was almost tailor-made for their activities. Few people knew each other, and circumstance brought together a heady mix of businessmen, industrialists, millionaires, and wealthy politicians, all relaxed, accustomed to striking up conversation with casual acquaintances, and all ripe for the picking. There was just enough time to mix and mingle, play out their games, and escape before suspicions were aroused.[17]

Passengers were warned to be particularly careful if approached by several men and asked to join a game already in progress.[18] To avoid unpleasant situations, most liners posted prominent notices alerting passengers to the danger of professional gamblers.[19] Shipping lines kept lists of such troublesome adventurers; some even denied passage to those who had previously been embroiled in a shipboard scandal. To thwart this, some relied on false identities, while others, fearful of being identified by watchful stewards, grew or shaved beards and mustaches and tried to alter their appearance. A seasoned and diligent Smoking Room steward was the naive traveler's best defense against such characters. Once, a steward spotted just such an adventurer sitting smugly at a table and wrestled him to the carpet before his fellow startled passengers; on another occasion, a steward walked up to a well-known gambler and loudly asked, "What name *this* time, Sir?"[20]

Two forms of gambling, though, were deemed safe: the Ship's Daily Run, and the Pool Auction, operated by the Smoking Room steward. The Daily Run was a long-established source of diversion for many travelers who, for minimal sums, could place bets as to how far *Lusitania* had traveled in the past twenty-four hours. The person with the closest number won the small pot.[21] The Pool Auction was a more expensive—though potentially more rewarding—affair. The day's previous run was posted and tickets were sold covering a range of some twenty numbers high and low of this. If the number was close to the run, a passenger might keep it; if he wanted a different number, he could place his up for auction, and bid on a ticket offered by a fellow traveler. Numbers closest to the average went for the highest amounts; a ticket might cost as little as a few dollars, or as much as $100, depending on its popularity. Storms, fogs, or other unsuspected delays could throw the system into disarray, and bidders often chased down officers, attempting to gain any inside information that would give them an edge. Every day at noon, a slip of paper, signed by an officer on the bridge, arrived in the Smoking Room and gave the run for the past twenty-four hours. The passenger with the closest number to this in the Pool Auction then won the previous day's pot—a prize that could be upward of a thousand dollars.[22]

Such conventional distractions didn't hold much appeal to Margaret, Lady Mackworth; her entire life had been a gamble, with higher stakes than the wagers exchanged in any smoking room. Like her fellow traveler Theodate Pope, Margaret exemplified a struggle against expectation. It was the age of the New Woman. By turns scorned and celebrated in popular works like Henry James's *Daisy Miller,* Henrik Ibsen's *A Doll's House,* and Elinor Glyn's *Three Weeks,* she was willing to defy tradition for personal happiness. It was no accident that, as with Theodate and Margaret, most of these adventurous women came from wealthy backgrounds: money afforded them education, allowed them to travel, and exposed them to new ideas where marriage no longer defined feminine opportunity. In the last few decades, they had entered the workforce, not as servants or seamstresses but as journalists, doctors, and lawyers. Increasingly, they marched through the streets of London and New York, demanding the vote as onlookers both applauded their efforts and assaulted them with derisive shouts and hurled tomatoes. Margaret Mackworth had dodged her fair share of tomatoes. Born the only daughter of Welsh coal magnate David Thomas and his wife, Sybil, in 1883, Margaret later complained that her early education had been filled with useless "trifles."[23] She rectified this with diligent study that eventually led her to Somerville College, Oxford, but chafed at the restricted opportunities allowed to young ladies of her time and class. Hers was a childhood of conflicted influences. Her tall, imposing father, who served as a Liberal Member of Parliament for Wales, was "imperious" and temperamental, yet "honest and straightforward."[24] "I don't see what difference it makes what other people think of me," he once said. "I have a very good opinion of myself."[25] He derided the "groveling snobbery" surrounding the royal family, yet secretly yearned for a title.[26]

Somewhat short, with brown hair worn in a fashionable pompadour, and "soft gray eyes" that seemed "the epitome of femininity," Margaret reluctantly allowed her father to launch her into London society, but the efforts failed miserably.[27] The shy Margaret "became an inarticulate lump of diffidence" at parties, and felt hopelessly out of place in this world of shallow pleasures.[28] Finally, on July 9, 1908, out of expectation and convenience, she married Welsh neighbor Humphrey Mackworth, a dozen years her senior, the son of Colonel Sir Arthur Mackworth, and the man who would in time become 7th Baronet. They were, she admitted, "an oddly assorted couple."[29]

At first, Margaret tried to act as chatelaine of her husband's manor house and play the expected part of wife of Master of the Foxhounds. Humphrey adored hunting; Margaret loathed it, insisting that the pursuit was "entirely uncivilized and non-adult, really utterly indefensible, and of a cruelty which did not bear thinking about." She far preferred to spend her days reading; her husband, sure enough, disliked reading and thought it was a most unsocial pursuit.[30] It did not take long for unhappiness to set in: within a few months, Margaret felt trapped in her loveless marriage and despaired of the claustrophobic future that spread out before her.

Then, "like a draught of fresh air" in her "padded, stifled" life, Margaret discovered the women's suffrage movement. "For me, and for many other young women like me," she recalled, "militant suffrage was the very salt of life." For the first time, she had a "sense of being some use in the scheme of things, without which no human being can live at peace."[31] Humphrey Mackworth was bewildered, but this didn't stop his determined wife, who eagerly devoured the latest political tracts and philosophical works on equality. She vividly recalled "reading Havelock Ellis's *Psychology of Sex*. It was the first thing of its kind I had found. Though I was far from accepting it all, it opened up a whole new world of thought to me. I discussed it at some length with my father, and he, much interested, went off to buy the set of volumes for himself; but in those days one could not walk into a shop and buy *The Psychology of Sex*; one had to produce some kind of signed certificate from a doctor or lawyer to the effect that one was a suitable person to read it. To his surprise he could not at first obtain it."[32]

Margaret openly battled Prime Minister Herbert Henry Asquith, once breaking through a police cordon and jumping on his motorcar to protest his opposition to granting women the vote.[33] She made speeches, dodged insults, and reluctantly agreed that the movement demanded militancy and sabotage. Early goals centered on burning postal boxes. Although she initially worried that such actions would harm innocent people by destroying their mail, she decided that "everyone knew we were doing it, and therefore knew that they ran the risk of not getting their letters." "The end justifies the means," she reasoned.[34]

One day, Margaret went off to a secret meeting and received "a flimsy covered basket" filled with crude explosives. Transporting the materials home so unnerved her that she actually buried them in her garden for a week before finally deciding to act. Her attempt, though, went disastrously wrong, and police apprehended Margaret while she was trying to destroy a postal box. An unsympathetic judge sentenced her to a month in a cold, dank prison cell. Humphrey, mortified, rushed to free her, but Margaret, more interested in the cause than in temporary discomfort, refused to leave. Instead, like many suffragettes, she embarked on a hunger strike, although she was horrified at the idea of being force-fed through a tube in her nose.[35] Official government policy was to let the hunger striker reach the point of death and then release her; then, when she had recovered, she was rearrested—a vicious cycle that only increased the acts of militancy.[36] Five days after her incarceration, authorities released Margaret; she left prison weakened but unbroken, determined to continue the fight until women had the right to vote.[37]

Luckily for Margaret, there was no rearrest: the outbreak of the Great War brought a cessation to most of the suffragettes' more militant campaigns. Her father-in-law died and her husband inherited his baronetcy, but Margaret escaped marital unhappiness by taking on the role of her father's personal assistant and business partner. "I must have been about eleven or twelve when he first talked business to me," she recalled, "that is, poured out a stream of description of some deal he was engaged on at the time without any explanations."[38] David Thomas increasingly relied on his somewhat scandalous daughter; Margaret, in turn, now had an outlet for her formidable energies and talents as she attended board meetings, drafted letters, and accompanied her father on his business trips.

One such trip, made when future British prime minister David Lloyd George asked her father to investigate potential munitions deals, took Margaret and Thomas to America in the spring of 1915. "Part of the joy of New York," she recalled, "was that there was no war there, and to come from England to America was like stepping from under a thundercloud into brilliant sunshine. After the strained tension of life at home the relief of this carefree place was just wonderful."[39]

By the end of April, Thomas's work was done, and father and daughter—along with his secretary, Arnold Rhys-Evans—decided to return home aboard *Lusitania*. While waiting for the ship to sail, they had strolled around the deck Saturday morning. Margaret was especially surprised to see so many children aboard the vessel: with the German warning, she thought, it seemed too great a risk for families to travel on *Lusitania* just then. "There was tension on board," she remembered, "and the passengers were frankly anxious."[40] Tension eased with the passing days, but both father and daughter appeared preoccupied. Sharing a table with them, Howard Fisher thought that Thomas seemed "very grave, ate sparingly, and neither at table nor elsewhere was inclined to casual conversation."[41] Nor did Margaret have reason to celebrate. After her brief holiday in the "brilliant sunshine" of New York, she was returning to war-torn England—and to her loveless marriage.

Being a suffragette didn't make Margaret Mackworth a social outcast: indeed, many fashionable and aristocratic women had involved themselves in the cause, though perhaps not quite as actively. The threat of being ostracized, though, hung heavily over two men traveling aboard the liner. The ever-observant George Kessler had spotted them walking, taking tea, dining, and disappearing into their shared cabin on B Deck. They "kept to themselves" throughout the voyage, never mixing or mingling with other passengers. People noticed their studied discretion; a few passengers wondered if they might be Germans—identities that, aboard *Lusitania* during the war, would perhaps raise concerns or even lead to unkind comments.[42] The truth was more dramatic: Leo Schwabacher and Henry Sonneborn were a couple, at a time when homosexuality was punishable with harsh prison terms and hard labor.

If the individual struggles of Theodate Pope and Margaret Mackworth stood as precursors to the societal battles of a rapidly changing twentieth century, so, too, did Schwabacher and Sonneborn represent liberation and an increasingly growing homosexual subculture. They'd met in 1900, when Henry's parents let a room above their Baltimore tavern to twenty-seven-year-old Leo Schwabacher. Originally from Peoria, the tall, slender Schwabacher came from a fairly wealthy family of liquor merchants but now worked as a bookkeeper. The same age as Leo, the handsome Henry also lived above the tavern, managing a coal distribution company with his brother. The friendship between the two young men blossomed: they apparently shared a love of music and art, and the Sonneborns happily treated Leo as if he was a member of their family: Henry's mother, Wilhelmina, even referred to him as "a second son."[43]

But what the Sonneborns might accept and indulge, society at large condemned. It was a time when homosexuality was hidden, condemned, and prosecuted. Less than a decade earlier, Oscar Wilde had been convicted of "gross indecency" and imprisoned; in 1903, New York City police raided a bathhouse and arrested some two dozen men for various criminal acts. Four years later, newspapers around the world entertained their readers with scandalous stories about Kaiser Wilhelm II's homosexual friend Prince Philip of Eulenburg. Baltimore was not safe: Maryland, like all other states, had anti-sodomy laws that could lead to imprisonment and hard labor, not to mention financial ruin.

Uniquely, when many homosexuals fell victim to persecution, guilt, and self-loathing, Leo and Henry apparently made peace with themselves and their relationship. Nothing remains in the way of a paper trail to document their feelings, though at one point both bachelors described themselves as "married" on official documents. Perhaps this was an effort to conceal their status as a couple, or perhaps a tacit admission of how they viewed their own relationship. Starting in 1906, they began traveling to Europe with some frequency, dispatching postcards back to Henry's nephew signed by them both. For a time the two lived in Paris; France was one of the very few countries to have decriminalized sodomy, and Paris boasted a vibrant homosexual subculture. In autumn 1914, though, the two men returned to America—aboard *Lusitania*—and moved back in with Henry's mother in Baltimore.[44]

In the spring of 1915, Leo and Henry decided to return to Europe. Perhaps it was the war that drove their thoughts to the future: Leo purchased a mausoleum, where he and Henry could one day be entombed together, and both men changed their wills, each naming the other as sole beneficiary, before boarding the ship. At the last minute, Wilhelmina rushed to New York, pleading with her son to cancel the trip for fear of attack by a German submarine. But Henry assured her that all would be well. "Don't worry," he said, "we'll send a telegram when we arrive safely."[45] Wilhelmina never saw either man again.

CHAPTER SEVEN

Adventurous or indolent afternoons on *Lusitania* invariably gave way to slower, more refined pleasures as evening approached. The exodus from deck usually began shortly after four. Passengers disappeared into suites and staterooms, relaxing, refreshing toilettes, and changing clothing before gathering in the First Class Lounge just aft of the Grand Staircase on A Deck. Although it was executed in a refined Georgian style, a previous traveler thought that the Lounge, with its deep bay windows and airy atmosphere, "had none of the formalism associated with a liner." A twenty-foot-high, barrel-vaulted skylight, with stained glass panels representing the twelve months of the year, circled the room above a deep, ornate plasterwork cornice of sea nymphs and shells in contrasting ivory; at night, concealed electric bulbs illuminated the stained glass panels. Corinthian pilasters dotted richly veneered walls of polished French mahogany; a jade green carpet sporting yellow floral designs softened the effect. At either end of the eighty-six-foot-long room, alcoves featured fourteen-foot-high green *fleur de pêche* marble fireplaces, flanked by Corinthian columns and topped with decorative enameled panels framed in silver depicting *The Glory of Sunrise* and *The Conquest of the Sea*. Satinwood and mahogany

GREG KING and PENNY WILSON

sofas and chairs, "beautifully upholstered" in green and yellow floral silk, "stood about promiscuously," offering intimate areas to relax as the hours passed.[1]

At five, the bells of *Lusitania*'s clocks chimed the hour as crisply uniformed stewards appeared with afternoon tea. Following British custom, this was a substantial meal of its own, with delicate little sandwiches, an assortment of cheeses, French pastries, cakes and petit fours, and a variety of teas and coffee.[2] Helen Losanitch Frothingham, traveling aboard *Lusitania* a few months earlier, had noted that "fresh roses and carnations are on the small tables, and the passengers sit in comfortable easy chairs, some smoking, others reading the mail which awaited them aboard ship, still others sipping tea and chatting." In such surroundings, she thought, "it doesn't seem possible that elsewhere in the world people are homeless and starving."[3]

This very English ritual particularly appealed to *Lusitania*'s Canadian passengers. Most prided themselves on being more British than the British themselves. "The Empire is my country," said one lady. "Canada is my home."[4] They celebrated royal weddings, births, and jubilees with garden parties and balls; when the monarch died, they mourned as the bells of their churches tolled incessantly.[5] And now, with the British Empire, "the mainstay of freedom and civilization throughout the world," as Mary Ryerson's husband, George, so patriotically put it, at war, Canadians were determined to demonstrate their loyalty to the crown.[6]

One particular group in *Lusitania*'s Lounge appreciated the nod to British tradition. All were from Montreal, where the rich, commented one historian, "enjoyed a prestige in that era that not even the rich deserved."[7] They formed the city's Anglo-Canadian elite, living along the southern base of Mount Royal in an area called the "Golden Square Mile." Together, they controlled fully 70 percent of Canada's wealth: most had grown up with each other, many had married into each other's families, and they enjoyed the same dinners, balls, hunts, and winter carnivals that filled Montreal's social season.[8]

There was the imposing Frances Stephens, exchanging pleasantries with Dorothy Braithwaite; Frederick Orr-Lewis, president of the Canadian division of shipbuilding and armaments giant Vickers, crossing and recrossing the Atlantic on war business with his faithful valet, twenty-six-year-old George Slingsby; and William Robert Grattan Holt, the solidly built, fifteen-year-old son of Sir Herbert Samuel Holt.[9] A lot of baggage came with being Holt's son: his father was not only the wealthiest man in Canada, controlling assets worth more than $2 billion, but he was also perhaps the most hated.[10] Herbert Holt had absolutely no sympathy for the workingman: he railed against providing employees with a living wage, insisting that this would strip them of initiative to work harder. "Nobody liked him personally," was the usual verdict.[11] Eight months into the war, Holt decided that it was safe enough for William, who went by the name of Robert, to return to his school, Marlborough College in Wiltshire, and booked the young man passage aboard *Lusitania*.

No Canadian aboard *Lusitania,* though, was quite as prominent as Marguerite, Lady Allan. Privilege had surrounded Marguerite Ethel MacKenzie since her birth in 1873. Her father, Hector MacKenzie, not only served as director of the Hudson's Bay Company and vice president of the Merchant's Bank of Montreal, but he was also president of the Montreal Philharmonic Society. Lively and intelligent, Marguerite inherited her father's passion for music and art; she also shared his taste for adventure and mischievous sense of humor. When his pretty, dark-haired daughter married Hugh Montague Allan on October 18, 1893, Hector decorated the windows of his French-inspired mansion on Montreal's Sherbrooke Street with thousands of white marguerite blossoms in tribute.[12]

Marguerite married into the very pinnacle of Montreal society. The Allans served as directors of banks they founded, represented the Montreal Board of Trade, and controlled mills, mines, telegraph companies, and real estate stretching from Liverpool to New York. But they were best known as owners of the Allan Shipping Line, Canada's most successful passenger service crossing the Atlantic.[13] The money poured in: Marguerite's new husband had inherited an estate valued at between $6 million and $10 million.[14]

Conventional and proud of their place in Montreal society, the Allans expected much of themselves and of others. Marguerite learned that she had not merely married a man but also a very different way of life. She got an early taste of this shortly after moving into Ravenscrag, the massive mansion her husband's late father had built. Marguerite had grown up passing by the imposing Italianate house, hidden behind its wrought iron fence on a hillside high above Montreal. What most appealed to Marguerite, though, was its velvety green lawn. She never forgot the day when her proper, sedate in-laws came to call on her shortly after her marriage. They found her turning somersaults, skirts flying in the air as she hurtled down the slope like an excited teenager. She took one look at their dour, disapproving faces and burst out laughing.[15]

Yet Marguerite now found herself proud chatelaine of the largest house Montreal had ever seen. Ravenscrag stood in splendid isolation against the tree-clad slopes of Mount Royal, its rough granite walls pierced with rounded windows and broken by arcaded loggias and projecting bays. At the center, a seventy-five-foot-high tower offered sweeping views over Montreal to the St. Lawrence River, the Laurentians, and the Adirondacks to the distant Green Mountains of Vermont. The restrained masculinity of the exterior gave way to very feminine rooms adorned with ornate plaster reliefs picked out in gold, vibrantly colored frescoes, and sumptuous, gilded furniture. Marguerite presided over society teas in her rococo drawing room, a frothy space of gilded pilasters and cartouches of mythological scenes. During the winter social season, she could entertain up to four hundred in her immense ballroom, where crystal chandeliers swirled from a painted ceiling. Couples could dance across a floor inlaid with rare and contrasting woods, to music provided by an orchestra in wrought iron balconies above.[16] When they tired of dancing, they could stroll into the adjoining conservatory, "a dream of fragrance and beauty," where colored lights illuminated palm trees and banks of exotic flowers.[17] Here, marveled one visitor, it was "easy, even in the depths of a Canadian winter, to imagine oneself in the tropics."[18]

An entire wing at Ravenscrag, along with rooms in the basement and attics, was needed to house the family's domestic staff. "It's like a hotel for servants!" Hugh Allan's father once complained.[19] His son and daughter-in-law increased the size of their household to eighteen servants, most of whom lived in. Richard Chambers, the British butler, was the highest paid, earning $60 a month; there were two governesses; a lady's maid; two footmen who wore specially designed livery; two housemaids; two laundresses; a scullery maid; a maid of all work; a coachman; three grooms; a gardener; and a man whose sole duty was to stoke the coal furnaces and lay fires in the fireplaces.[20]

Marguerite was like Edwardian Montreal itself, "conscious of a proper and clearly defined pride," as one chronicler wrote, but effortlessly charming and vigorous in enjoying life.[21] She had, said one newspaper, the "gift for doing the right thing, always in the right way."[22] Marguerite was careful to bring up her four children in the right way: Marguerite, called Martha, was born in 1895, followed by Hugh in 1897, Anna in 1898, and Gwendolyn, called Gwen, in 1900. Martha went off to finishing school in Paris, while Hugh was sent to Eton; Anna and Gwen remained in Montreal, where they could often be seen riding in their own elaborate carriage pulled by a smart pony from their father's extensive stables.[23] Marguerite was also devoted to her little white Pekingese dog called Peek-a-Boo. To avoid having him quarantined on her travels, she usually drugged him and slipped him into a bag. She hated the idea of putting him in a kennel. "I left him to their tender mercies once before," Marguerite explained, "and the poor darling almost starved to death. He wouldn't eat a thing because he was parted from me."[24] And, as expected of a lady of her position, Marguerite immersed herself in charitable work, serving on the Local Council of Women of Montreal and the Central Council of the Victoria League, and acting as honorary president of the Daughters of the British Empire in Montreal.[25]

But Marguerite's principal role was that of social leader: it came with being H. Montague's wife and mistress of Ravenscrag. She welcomed dignitaries and diplomats, governors and princes to her house. In 1906, it was Prince Arthur of Connaught, whose stay she marked with a ball for three hundred; a year later, Prince Fushimi Hiroyasu, the Mikado's brother, enjoyed the Allan hospitality. And there were royal rewards. In 1904, King Edward VII created Marguerite's husband a Knight Bachelor in the Order of the British Empire; the new Lady Allan was presented at Buckingham Palace in 1906, and a year later the king named Sir Hugh Montague Allan a Commander in the Royal Victorian Order.[26]

From late September to the middle of February, Ravenscrag was the center of the Montreal social world. An invitation from the Allans was regarded as little short of a royal command. "Recipients who did not 'accept with pleasure,'" noted one journalist, "were only debarred from doing so by unavoidable causes."[27] Once, when a gentleman was unable to escort his wife to a Ravenscrag ball, he could only alleviate her great disappointment by presenting her with a magnificent pearl necklace that had cost thousands of dollars.[28] Frosty Saturday mornings found the driveway filled with stomping, snorting horses as the Montreal Hunt gathered to ride with its Master of Foxhounds. "The Union Jack flew from Ravenscrag," recalled a member, "the hounds bayed joyfully in front of the house; the hour for breakfast was ten, but members showed such a disregard for time that it was nearly eleven before the majority moved off."[29] On other nights, the Montreal Snow Shoe Club met at Ravenscrag for nighttime expeditions up Mount Royal. Wrapped in heavy white coats and red caps and deemed "very picturesque and very Canadian" by a visiting Marchioness of Dufferin, the crowd left the house and set out along the snowy paths circling to the park above, making a "fiery serpent winding among the trees" with their flaming torches. At the end of their invigorating adventure, they returned to Ravenscrag for a buffet supper.[30]

When summer came, the Allans—along with servants and dozens of steamer trunks—fled Montreal's stifling heat and humidity, decamping to the scenic Charlevoix region along the shores of the St. Lawrence River. Here, at Saint-Georges-de-Cacouna, they built a large Colonial Revival–style house called Montrose, a comfortable place of porches and chintz-hung rooms on a bluff high above the river.[31] There was riding, boating, and lawn tennis; sometimes, Marguerite found the pace too relaxed. When bored, she crossed the river to La Malbaie (Murray Bay), to enjoy the band playing on the Manoir Richelieu Hotel's wide veranda, join friendly games of bridge, and play golf with future American president William Howard Taft.[32]

It seemed a pleasant annual routine of social obligations,

parties, and relaxation as the Edwardian Era lingered on in the great houses of the Golden Square Mile. The momentous summer of 1914 forever shattered this world: suddenly the Royal Dominion of Canada found itself at war. In the city's exclusive clubs, Montreal's leading figures puffed away at cigars, assuring themselves that the conflict "would not last more than six months, because business would not allow it."[33] At the beginning, the streets of Montreal were filled with parades of "brave, earnest young faces" as men marched off amid flags and handkerchiefs unwittingly waving them to the slaughter. "Be Christian!" they were urged. "Be British!"[34]

Marguerite threw herself into the war effort. As honorary president of the Daughters of the British Empire in Montreal, she organized collection drives, solicited funds to buy soldiers care packages, and presided over knitting parties to produce socks, mufflers, and caps to be sent to the front. She established a convalescent home for wounded Canadian soldiers, and opened the doors of exclusive Ravenscrag to a curious public, hosting charity teas and bridge parties to raise funds for relief efforts.[35] Her eldest daughter, Martha, most like her in independent spirit, trained as a Red Cross nurse, bought several ambulances, and followed them to France, where she worked along the front lines, driving the vehicles and rescuing wounded soldiers.[36] And Marguerite's only son, Hugh, joined the Black Watch Regiment of Canada and went to England; later, he transferred to the Royal Naval Air Service and earned his wings as a flight lieutenant, trained to fly runs over occupied Belgium.[37]

In 1915, H. Montague was appointed head of the Canadian Overseas Pension Board in London, and Marguerite decided to join him. After discussing it with Martha, she decided that together they would open and run an English hospital for wounded Canadian soldiers.[38] And so, in the spring of 1915, Marguerite

booked passage aboard *Lusitania*. Anticipating a happy family reunion, she took her youngest daughters with her: sixteen-year-old
Anna and fifteen-year-old Gwen, along with two maids, Annie
Walker and Emily Davis. The maids were given their own cabin,
while the family took the starboard Regal Suite.

Delighted to find so many of their friends and acquaintances
from Montreal aboard the liner, Marguerite and her daughters
enjoyed the voyage. They laughed with Robert Holt, and were
happy to see that family friend Frederick Orr-Lewis was traveling with his valet, George Slingsby. Slingsby knew the Allans very
well. Lady Allan and her family had often shared holidays with
Orr-Lewis at Villa Edelweiss on the Riviera, and Marguerite used
the cooperative young Slingsby to occasionally smuggle her prized
dog through customs, rewarding him with a diamond tie pin in
the shape of a horseshoe.[39] She also once asked him to secretly
transport some of her prized jewelry as well, to avoid paying duty
on pieces she already owned. Slingsby wore her diamond bandeau
tiara, matching necklace, brooches, and bracelets—some £40,000
of jewelry—in a padded belt wrapped around his waist and hidden
under his clothing when he passed through customs. As Slingsby
divested himself of this cache of jewels, Lady Allan declared,
"George, you are a treasure! If you were not such an excellent
valet, you could make a fortune as a smuggler!"[40] On *Lusitania*, Slingsby entertained Anna and Gwen throughout the voyage.
They made him join their deck games, dragged him off to take
lemonade, and generally kept the valet rushing from one end of
the liner to the other. Sitting in a deck chair and watching Slingsby
pulled away by her daughters, Lady Allan gave him a smile, saying,
"It's your own fault, George! You spoil them."[41]

One day, crewman Leslie Morton was standing on deck, armed
with a pot of gray paint known as "crab fat," which was to be
applied to the lifeboats. As he was working, he noticed two girls,

in white accordion pleated skirts and sailor suit blouses with big bows, approach. "I could not help thinking what lovely children they were, and how beautifully dressed," he recalled. He later insisted that they were Anna and Gwen Allan. They smiled and watched him work for a moment before the older asked, "What are you doing, sailor?"

"I'm painting the lifeboat," he told her.

"May we help you?" she offered.

"I don't think this is a job for little girls," Morton replied.

The girl Morton thought to be Anna, though, "did not take much notice of my refusal" and snatched the brush from Morton's hand. For a few moments she swabbed the gray coating over the boat, but soon enough it was also "all over her beautiful clothes." "I was horrified," Morton recalled. He looked up and saw a member of the deck crew approaching. The girls apparently saw him as well. Deciding that they were about to get into trouble, the older girl dropped the brush and ran off across the deck with her sister.[42]

Everyone aboard *Lusitania* seemed to notice Anna and Gwen. Harold Boulton thought that they were "most attractive to look at" as they roamed the ship.[43] George Kessler agreed, recalling that the "handsome" girls were "virtually the life and soul of the ship." In the midst of war, and on a liner traveling under threat of torpedo attack, he said, "it did one good to see their smiling faces."[44]

CHAPTER EIGHT

Lusitania boasted eighty-seven special suites, as well as Parlor Suites, each with sitting room and private bath. Paneled in mahogany, satinwood, and veneered walnut, and furnished with inlaid desks, wardrobes, and dressing tables, they represented the taste for historicism so prevalent at sea: styles ranged from Louis XVI to William and Mary, Empire to Georgian, and Sheraton to Adams. Their private, marble-walled bathrooms included white-enameled, cast-iron claw-foot tubs fitted with shower cages and silver-plated fixtures; washbasins ornamented with onyx—as well as toilets—were rimmed in gilt.[1] The "delicacy and refinement of detail are eminently suited for the purpose of ship decoration," promotional literature assured potential passengers.[2]

Costing roughly $1,500 each way, these suites came with a personal steward to cater to the needs and whims of their travelers.[3] Many occupants traveled with their own maids or valets, leaving the stewards to run errands, arrange favors, and meticulously see to the cabins in the hope of a generous tip. Now, five days into the voyage, Walter Wood, the steward assigned to Parlor Suite B 65-67, rapped on the door and handed over a curious telegram: "Hope you have a safe crossing. Look forward very much to seeing you soon."[4] Reading these lines from a British woman named Mary Barwell, Alfred Gwynne Vanderbilt seemed eager to reach England.[5]

No one knew if Barwell was the latest in Vanderbilt's string of beautiful mistresses; everyone knew that few women resisted his charms—and he, theirs. Heir to America's largest railway fortune, thirty-seven years old, Alfred Vanderbilt was nearly six feet tall, with clear blue eyes, wavy brown hair, a dashing little mustache, and refined features. He always cut a fine figure—"he is almost too perfectly dressed," a British journal once complained.[6] Albert Bilicke represented one aspect of the American saga: the hardworking, self-made man enjoying his riches. Vanderbilt was living proof that a fortunate accident of birth was no guarantee of personal fulfillment.

Alfred was born in 1877, into "the nearest thing to a royal family that has ever appeared on the American scene."[7] His great-grandfather Cornelius Vanderbilt, known as the Commodore, had come from Holland, earned a fortune in shipping, and consolidated small railway lines to form the New York Central Railroad. In financial terms, Alfred wanted for nothing: his father's $67 million estate annually earned some $3.6 million in interest alone.[8] He was brought up in gilded splendor: his father's French Renaissance château at 1 West 57th and Fifth Avenue was, at over 130 rooms, the largest house New York City had ever seen. It was an ugly, ungainly place, bristling with fussy carvings, tall chimneys, and ornate windows concealing cavernous, glacially cold rooms meant to impress "with grandeur" rather "than with beauty."[9]

At least summers in Newport offered some relief from this architectural oppression. The Breakers, the seventy-room Vanderbilt "cottage" designed in imitation of an Italian palazzo, wasn't lacking in grandeur: there was a fifty-foot-square arcaded hall; a silver and gold music room from Paris; and a forty-two-foot-high, marble-walled dining room fringed by immense columns of red alabaster, where the family ate at a sixteenth-century Italian table precariously perched below two twelve-foot-tall ormolu and Baccarat crystal chandeliers.[10] The Breakers had one thing the New York château lacked: twelve serene acres of gardens overlooking the Atlantic. Here Alfred and his siblings—older brothers William and Cornelius (known as Neily), sister Gertrude (who later married Harry Payne Whitney and founded the Whitney Museum of American Art), and the two youngest, Reginald (father of designer Gloria Vanderbilt) and Gladys—could enjoy ordinary pursuits—at least they were ordinary by Vanderbilt standards. They had a little playhouse, though it came with call bells for servants and its own monogrammed china for afternoon tea.[11] The boys had to care for their toys, even if, in this case, their toys included a yacht their father had given them. There was even a printing press, so that the industrious brothers could typeset and produce their own newspaper, *The Comet*—replete with paid advertisements from family railways, Wall Street bankers, and Tiffany and Company.[12]

Cornelius and Alice, Alfred's parents, were a severe, rather dour couple; the father, it was said, had never been known to smile.[13] Courteous and even-tempered in public, Cornelius took himself very seriously: there was something "stern" about his character, and he "expected to be obeyed, and instantly."[14] Alice, "glacial and forbidding," as one of her grandsons called her, was so arrogant that she refused to speak to servants except through her butler: she once spent hours being endlessly driven around New York City because she felt it beneath her dignity to give her chauffeur directions.[15]

"We cannot always control other people's desires," Alice warned her children. "Most certainly we can control our own."[16] The young boy and his siblings had been brought up "in the firm belief that they were American aristocracy, embodying in their lives and actions all that was fine, honorable, and Christian. Theirs was a sacred, God-given trust to maintain these standards."[17]

When he was eighteen, Alfred got a lesson in the brutal consequences of ignoring these standards. The 1892 death of his eldest brother, William, had left second son Neily as his father's heir. But in 1895, Neily took up with beautiful Grace Wilson. Her siblings had married well—into the English aristocracy, into Gilded Age fortunes, even into the pinnacle of society itself, the Astor family; "the marrying Wilsons" people called them.[18] With her disconcerting habit of pursuing—and then dropping—potential beaux when their fortunes fell, Grace carried more than a whiff of the adventuress about her; there were even stories that she had briefly enjoyed the favors of Alfred's father.[19]

Neily's parents were horrified; the usually reserved Cornelius even took to the pages of the *New York Times* to declare that any such union was against his "expressed wish."[20] A meeting between father and lovesick son reportedly ended in blows; when Cornelius suffered a debilitating stroke, the entire family blamed "inhuman, crazy" Neily.[21] Every bit as proud as his proud parents, Neily married Grace in a ceremony his family boycotted: Alice ordered that her other children must never attend a party, dinner, or ball at which her disgraced son and new daughter-in-law might be present.[22]

Alfred learned how deep parental disapproval stretched on the 1899 death of his father. The family sat in the Breakers' Library, with its Circassian walnut bookcases, hand-tooled Spanish leather walls embossed in gold, and sixteenth-century, $75,000 stone fireplace ironically inscribed, "Little Do I Care for Riches, and Do Not Miss Them, Since Only Cleverness Prevails in the End," as Cornelius's will was read.[23] Alfred received some $42 million; each of his siblings inherited $7 million; Neily got $500,000 in cash, and the income on a $1 million trust.[24] Although Alfred eventually gave Neily an extra $6.5 million, his older brother was furious, publicly complaining that he'd been cheated and even threatening to take the matter to court.[25]

After this unpleasantness, the two brothers rarely spoke. Neily was conspicuously absent when, in January 1901, Alfred married society beauty Ellen French; ten months later, she gave birth to a son, William Henry Vanderbilt II. For a time, Alfred settled into acceptable passions: he kept four yachts; traveled aboard a private Pullman carriage called *Wayfarer*, replete with marble bathroom and velvet-draped parlor; escaped to his Camp Sagamore in the Adirondacks, where he could create "an illusion of wilderness hardship at great expense"; and imported a $30,000 Fiat to race along the beaches of Florida.[26] His true interest, though, centered on horses.

Alfred kept an impressive stable at Oakland Farm, his country estate just outside Newport, which boasted the world's largest private riding ring.[27] He won prizes for his equestrian skill at the New York Horse Show but it was his love of coaching that won him international fame. He was, said Gilded Age heiress Elizabeth Drexel Lehr, "the last great promoter" of the sport.[28] It appealed to his vanity: handsomely attired in a long black coat, checked suit, tan apron, buckskin gloves, and top hat, he cut a dashing figure as he drove his coaches down Fifth Avenue.[29] Deciding that riding with him was a privilege, Alfred even charged his guests for their seats, with the highest fee demanded of the person nearest to him.[30]

Until 1905, Alfred's closest companion in coaching was tall, dashingly handsome James Hazen Hyde, president of the Equitable Life Assurance Society, an aesthetic Francophile who claimed to be the epitome of perfect taste.[31] In October 1901, the two friends drove from New York to Philadelphia in just over nine hours, using seventy-eight horses strategically placed along the route.[32] Hyde even spent thousands of dollars to have wayside inns along their regular routes redecorated in Tudor style so that they could imagine themselves as English squires, stopping to enjoy imported ales and steak and kidney pies.[33]

When this illusion wore thin, Alfred transferred his adventures to England, shipping up to a hundred of his prized horses, shining coaches, and teams of grooms smartly dressed in the maroon and gold Vanderbilt livery, across the Atlantic.[34] In 1908, he drove his coach *Venture* from London to Brighton; hundreds lined the route, unwilling to miss the novel sight of an American millionaire racing along the roadways. It was, Vanderbilt happily declared, the "greatest day of my life."[35]

Five years of marriage failed to temper Vanderbilt's restless, amorous character. There were unseemly stories about wild parties with teenaged girls procured by Charles Wilson, Vanderbilt's manager at Oakland Farms, and a true breach of social proprieties with rumors that Alfred had become intimately involved with Caroline Lorillard. Not only was Caroline married, but, inexcusably, she also moved in the same elite circles as Ellen Vanderbilt.
[36] Vanderbilt allegedly came up with a novel way to hide the affair, using his relationship with another woman to conceal the rumored liaison with Caroline. That other woman, beautiful Mary Agnes O'Brien Ruiz, was a former actress: as such, she could be relied upon to play her part. A string of aliases and stage names suggest that Ruiz may have been something of an adventuress herself, willing to indulge Vanderbilt in exchange for whatever financial benefits came her way. Marital fidelity wasn't Alfred's strong suit and these affairs were scarcely a secret, especially when Ruiz left her husband, Cuban diplomat Don Antonio Ruiz y Olivares.[37]

Thanks to his somewhat less than discreet valet, Alfred's wife soon learned of his affairs; humiliated, she sued her husband for divorce, citing his repeated adultery with Ruiz aboard his railway carriage *Wayfarer*. Alfred's money ensured that the case was heard before a closed court and that Ellen's $10 million settlement was sealed along with the proceedings.[38] No amount of money, though, could keep newspapers from reporting the scandal. Ruiz divorced his wife; she, in turn, seems to have fallen in love with Vanderbilt. Then, in March 1909, Caroline Lorillard killed herself—for reasons unknown but amid whispers of an affair with Alfred; if Ruiz had been a necessary smoke screen, she was necessary no longer, and Vanderbilt abandoned her. Increasingly depressed, and with her reputation in tatters, Mary Agnes O'Brien Ruiz killed herself with a dramatic gunshot through the heart in London in May 1909.[39] Charles Williamson, a member of Alfred's circle, moved to avert further scandal, seizing her belongings and firing any servants who might talk to the press. Representing himself as Ruiz's "Parisian counsel," he apparently paid off those who "might be in a position to reveal the true facts."[40] Williamson also arranged that details of the coroner's inquest be kept secret; rumor held that he had bribed numerous journalists and officials "by an outlay of a large sum of money," presumably from Alfred, to conceal the full story and render a quick verdict that Mary Agnes Ruiz had been of "unsound mind."[41]

Scandal was no stranger to Gilded Age society, but somehow the Vanderbilt divorce and Lorillard and Ruiz suicides seemed more egregious than other peccadilloes. Ellen had not only been very popular in smart society but was also the wronged party whose husband had publicly humiliated her. Alfred found himself ostracized.[42] Thinking that an extended stay in England would improve his reputation, Alfred quietly took up residence in London, only to learn that many in British society also condemned his actions.

The surest way to quiet the rumors was to marry again, yet the unhappy Alfred soon found himself at the center of another maelstrom. He'd met Margaret Emerson McKim—wealthy American heiress to the Bromo-Seltzer fortune—a few years earlier; now, she left her husband, Smith Hollis McKim, claiming that he was an alcoholic who regularly beat her. McKim fired back in the press. Not only had his wife deserted him, he insisted, but she was also having an adulterous affair with Vanderbilt. He sued Alfred for alienation of affection.[43] Alfred couldn't refute the charges; what he could do was again use Vanderbilt money, giving McKim some $150,000 to buy his compliant silence. Amid the scandal—a hasty Reno divorce, Margaret excommunicated by the Catholic Church, and gleeful newspaper stories—a very quiet British registry office ceremony united Alfred and his second wife in December 1911.[44]

Alfred found Margaret to be an understanding and sympathetic wife. They lived in a two-dozen-room apartment atop the new Vanderbilt Hotel he built at Park Avenue and 34th Street.[45] Two sons followed: Alfred Gwynne II in September of 1912, and George Washington Vanderbilt IV, born two years later. Perhaps because his eldest son, William, spent most of the year with Ellen, Alfred was a diligent, attentive father. Not only was the nursery stocked with expensive toys but Alfred also could often be found romping on the floor with his sons.[46] "I have no recollection of my father being anything but kind and pleasant with me," William later wrote. "He gave me wonderful toys and played with me."[47]

Settlements to his brother and his former wife, bribes, and hush money—not to mention Alfred's profligate manner of spending—rapidly depleted his coffers. By 1915, his initial $42 million fortune had dwindled to just over $26 million.[48] Ostensibly, Alfred boarded *Lusitania* that May to attend a meeting of the International Horse Show Association in London.[49] In reality, he wanted to use his money to support the Allied cause. He secretly hoped to offer both motorcars and his own services as chauffeur to the Red Cross, explaining that he felt that he was not doing enough for the war effort.[50] He'd blithely dismissed talk of possible danger; he was looking forward to the trip—and perhaps to whatever new diversions awaited him in London.

Traveling with Vanderbilt was forty-four-year-old Charles Williamson, the man who'd gone to London in 1909 to hush up details of Mary Agnes O'Brien Ruiz's suicide. Williamson was himself a figure of some mystery. He'd worked as private secretary to Vanderbilt's close friend James Hazen Hyde and apparently transacted his business with Gilded Age heir George Gould, son of infamous robber baron Jay Gould.[51] Then, in 1905, Hyde gave an extravagant costume ball at Sherry's in New York; rumors that he had drained money from his Equitable Life Assurance Society to foot the $200,000 bill drove a disgraced Hyde into Parisian exile, with Williamson in tow.[52]

Soon, Williamson opened a small gallery near the Place Vendôme in Paris, where he dealt in tapestries and antiques. No one knew where Williamson's money came from, but it had come suddenly, and in abundance. He had kept Hyde's secrets; owed a small fortune to Gould; and, even after his role concealing the Ruiz suicide, was said to be heavily in debt to Vanderbilt as well.[53] Blackmail was then a profitable business: American society lived in fear of William d'Alton Mann and his notorious magazine *Town Topics,* which invented that gossip staple, the blind item.[54] Williamson had resorted to blackmail and bribery to cover Vanderbilt's indiscretions; had he now done the same to these prominent men to finance his own extravagant way of life?

Williamson brought to *Lusitania* his own hint of scandal in the person of aspiring actress Amelia Baker. Born in Minnesota in 1887, she'd studied music under a Duluth voice coach, won acclaim in a number of amateur productions, and gone to New York to further her career. She joined Charles Frohman's repertory company, but her 1907 marriage to musician Alexander Oliver Lynch seemingly put an end to her dream. "Of course I love the stage," she told a reporter, but added that her new husband opposed her career.[55]

When the marriage collapsed, Amelia returned to the stage, studying in Europe and taking small roles on Broadway. Now she was traveling with Williamson aboard *Lusitania,* where they occupied adjacent cabins on B Deck. Anticipating her Parisian debut, Amelia traveled with nearly $15,000 worth of clothing and jewelry—a significant amount when she herself had never had a prominent role onstage or enjoyed financial success.[56] Perhaps it had all come from Williamson: there were rumors that they were secretly engaged. But perhaps George Kessler offered an unwitting insight into the situation when he described Amelia as "a lady known to us all."[57]

Some frequent travelers made their living aboard ship, gambling and scheming to separate unwitting millionaires from their money; a few other oceanic entrepreneurs played more dangerous games of sexual intrigue. All it took was a lovely young woman and her attendant male partner. The beautiful lady flitted about the ship, flirting with some naive gentleman traveling without his wife. Sometimes she complained that she was alone on the ship and desperate for sympathetic company; at others, she unraveled sad tales of a neglectful husband who spent his days gambling in the Smoking Room and his nights passed out in a drunken stupor. The goal was the same: to draw the unsuspecting victim belowdecks to her cabin, with promises of a passionate rendezvous that soon went horribly awry when her male partner indignantly burst into the room. Threats of ruined reputations, compromising situations, and worries over exposure were usually enough to guarantee that the victim promptly paid whatever was demanded to keep the whole ignominious affair secret.[58]

Of course, not all sexual encounters aboard ship took place under such dubious circumstances. A woman willing to cater to a select clientele could easily count on voluntary financial rewards. Kessler's description of Amelia in this respect is striking: "a lady known to us all" was a curious turn of phrase, suggestive in that era of a highly questionable reputation.[59] Perhaps Williamson and Amelia had come by their riches honestly—or at least as honestly as was possible given his past actions. Yet, given Williamson's involvement, it is difficult to entirely dismiss the possibility—however unlikely—that this pair, with a taste for the finer things in life, may have discovered a less conventional path to financial success.

Amelia and Williamson moved throughout the ship, but Vanderbilt largely kept to himself, even taking most of his meals in his suite. "He was always like that," Kessler said. It was there that Kessler found him one afternoon, musing on the future. Alfred was adamant when discussing the war. "I'm sorry," he told Kessler, "but to drive a coach in these times is out of the question." He also complained about Germany and the ominous warnings. "They have disgraced themselves, and never in our time will they be looked upon by any human being valuing his honor save with feelings of contempt," Alfred declared. Then he offered the gravest insult imaginable from a gentleman of his standing: "How can Germany, after what she has done, ever think of being classed as a country of sportsmen?"[60]

CHAPTER NINE

Keeping proper time while traveling aboard *Lusitania* demanded some work. Each afternoon, as she steamed ever closer to her destination, *Lusitania*'s clocks were gradually advanced to accord with Greenwich Mean Time. By the evening of a beautiful and sunny Wednesday, May 5, the ship had completed two thirds of its journey.[1] "Travelers' watches," advised a guidebook, "should be set accordingly, as the hours of meals are dependent entirely upon these clocks."[2]

In the hours following tea, many First Class passengers retreated to the comfort of their staterooms, both to relax and to prepare for the evening. Gentlemen kept appointments with the ship's barbers, Lott Gadd and Reg Nice, who presided over what had been the first installation of its kind on an ocean liner, a white-walled shop at the end of the Promenade Deck, complete with a spinning chair atop a black and white tiled floor.[3] Here they offered shaves, haircuts, and other grooming services, generally from early morning until seven at night. Although technically members of the crew, the barbers were considered private contractors, and all accounts were to be settled with them when service was rendered rather than placed on a bill.[4]

Despite some changes wrought by the Great War, dinners for *Lusitania*'s First Class passengers were still largely formal, ritualized affairs that demanded sartorial splendor. "I liked the idea of dressing for dinner," recalled *Mauretania* passenger Theodore Dreiser, "and seeing everything quite stately and formal."[5] Steamer trunks and wardrobes revealed a bounty carefully wrapped in tissue paper. Valets laid out trousers, shirts, white waistcoats, starched collars and cuffs, and dinner jackets; only waiters wore tailcoats aboard ship. Ladies' maids smoothed dresses that only awaited shimmering diamond brooches, necklaces, bandeaus, or feathery aigrettes to complete the impressive display. Emily Post warned travelers against overdressing on a liner. "People of position," she wrote, "never put on formal evening dress on a steamer." For a lady to wear a ball gown to dinner, she wrote, was a sure sign that she had "no other place" to show off her "finery."[6]

Extended breakfasts, luncheons, and dinners also offered a useful way of filling up time for many passengers, and were often the highlights of days at sea.[7]

"The Cunard Company," declared a promotional guide, "has always been famous for its high class cuisine." To produce the necessary three thousand meals a day took a staff of dozens. Etienne Pierre Seurre served as *Lusitania*'s French chef, assisted by additional cooks, bakers, butchers, a roasting cook, vegetable cooks, a soup cook, a confectioner, and a dozen other members of the crew assigned to the kitchens. First and Second Class shared one galley, while Third Class had its own kitchen. The First and Second Class Galley eclipsed "anything afloat," a publication insisted, with "every modern device for the preparation of food under the best conditions." Stretching nearly 130 feet and spanning the width of the ship, the facilities included pantries; a still room; a bakery; a pastry kitchen; a confectionary kitchen; a vegetable preparation room; a fruit room; and immense walk-in refrigeration rooms. The main range was over seventy feet long; fourteen ovens, roasting spits, and steam closets offered an array of working space.[8] These arrangements, wrote a contemporary, "are not equaled by many hotels ashore."[9]

Breakfasts tended to be informal, though the menu itself offered a rich variety of choices designed to appeal to both British and European travelers as well as passengers from America: fresh fruits, juices, cocoa, and tea or coffee, followed by cereals, oatmeal, smoked kippers, fried turbot, calf's liver, roasted lamb, baked apples, eggs cooked to order, bacon, pancakes with maple or golden syrup, and pastries, scones, marmalades, and jams. Luncheon was also generally informal: although one could order a variety of hot soups, ham, spring chicken, roast beef, salads, and vegetables from the menu, a cold buffet might offer roast game, turkey, figs, cheeses, bread, and pastries.[10]

Dinners, though, were intricate affairs, surrounded by all of the pomp that *Lusitania* could muster. As seven o'clock approached, the corridors and public rooms were awash with splendidly attired ladies and gentlemen slowly drifting toward the Dining Saloon. Dreiser especially remembered "the bugler who bugled for dinner. That was a most musical sound he made, trilling in the various quarters gaily, as much as to say, 'This is a very joyous event, ladies and gentlemen; we are all happy; come, come, it is a delightful feast!' It was like something out of an old medieval court or a play."[11]

Entering *Lusitania*'s Dining Saloon, after the sedate Georgian splendors of the Lounge, Smoking Room, and Reading and Writing Room, was to abandon the illusion of the English country house in favor of the glories of Versailles. The Dining Saloon was the grandest of *Lusitania*'s public rooms, and one of the finest spaces on any liner, measuring nearly ninety feet square, spanning the width of the ship, and rising over C and D Decks between the third and fourth funnels. Cunard prided itself on the room's height: White Star's *Olympic* and *Titanic* might have been larger, but their squat dining rooms seemed oppressive. "Low ceilings," an official for the rival French Line once sniffed, "don't aid the appetite."[12]

The Dining Saloon evoked the period of Louis XVI, with mahogany-paneled walls enameled white, set with mirrors, carved and gilded festoons, and pilasters with gilded Corinthian capitals and bases. A seventeen-foot-long mahogany sideboard with ormolu pulls stretched along one side of the room. At the center of the lower deck, carved Corinthian columns supported a wide, circular well open to the deck above. Over this stretched a twenty-nine-by-twenty-three-foot elliptical dome rimmed in gold, rising to a height of nearly thirty feet and divided into panels covered in frescoed cherubs depicting the *Four Seasons,* in the style of François Boucher. The lower level could seat 323 diners, with another 147 above; being smaller, the upper level was considered to be the more exclusive space in which to dine. Large windows on the port and starboard walls of both decks flooded the room with light. The result was an airy space, neoclassical in feel; only the crimson brocade chairs, bolted to the rose-colored floral Brussels carpet to steady them in rough seas, shattered the illusion that this was not an ocean liner but a fine hotel.[13]

At night, the Dining Saloon glowed with soft, diffuse light from gilded sconces on the walls, electric bulbs hidden behind glass screens drawn across the portholes to give the illusion of sunlight, and silk-shaded gilt bronze lamps that stood on tables.[14] Moving past ranks of potted palms, passengers found the white-damask-covered tables set with an array of crystal and silver: a delicate Arts and Crafts–inspired floral design in soft blues and reds edged the white Wedgwood china plates, bowls, cups, and saucers.[15] Roses and carnations offered bursts of color. It was still the era of the grand dinner, and anyone who could not distinguish between a fish fork, an oyster fork, and a salad fork was doomed to social censure. Creamy damask napkins stood in elaborate folds, next to embossed menu cards edged in gilt, with the Cunard logo and the ship's name against sinuous and colorful designs.[16]

Seating arrangements led to minor wars. A few scheming passengers, hoping to mix with aristocrats, celebrities, and millionaires, casually forced themselves on the unsuspecting, offering a place at their table with promises that it was the best situated or home to the most entertaining conversation. With a single name of note thus drawn into his orbit, the Arriviste would use his cornered star as a walking advertisement to others, gradually gathering a circle of prominent acquaintances "whom he could not possibly have gotten together without just such a maneuver," as Emily Post warned travelers. "The question of what he gets out of it is puzzling, since with each hour the really well-bred people dislike him more and more intensely, and at the end of a day or so, his table's company are all eating on deck to avoid him."[17]

Although the notoriously reclusive Captain Turner rarely presided, social battles still waged over seating at his exclusive table. It was often up to the chief steward to make these assignments; he would scan the passenger list and select the worthiest and most notable travelers for this honor. Hinting to the chief steward that you would "consider" dining at the Captain's Table was a sure sign of the Arriviste.[18] Other passengers were advised to request specific seating assignments on boarding to ensure prominent tables.[19] Being noticed was important to Rita Jolivet: she made sure that she had a table near the main entrance, where everyone who entered the Dining Saloon could not help but spot her.[20]

Passengers were not above bribing stewards for better seats. Always on the lookout for any irritation, Oliver Bernard found himself the apparent victim of one such social climber. Armed with his table number, he entered the Dining Saloon and went to take up his assigned seat only to find that an "abominably supercilious" steward had changed the arrangement "without warning or explanation for the benefit, it so appeared, of a more important passenger." Infuriated by this "social discrimination," Bernard cornered his steward and demanded, "Will you condescend to inform me why the genius of marine engineers, shipbuilding, and financiers who have built this ship must be depreciated because you think some passengers are entitled to more attention than others?"[21]

Then there was the problem of socializing with one's tablemates: thrown together by circumstance, many struggled to find diverting conversation that avoided politics or points of view. Emily Post warned travelers to adjust their speech accordingly. "People always speak to those next to them. None but the rudest snobs would sit through meal after meal without ever addressing a word to their table companions."[22]

On this voyage, passengers paired off and united, forming tables with friends, traveling companions, or likely new acquaintances. Charles Lauriat had "a jolly time" with his neighbor, Boston genealogist Lothrop Withington, and made plans to see him in London, without ever suspecting that his delightful companion was a bigamist.[23] Wealthy passengers from Montreal dominated one table: Lady Allan and her two daughters, along with Frances Stephens, Dorothy Braithwaite, Robert Holt, and Frederick Orr-Lewis. The Montreal table was a little more festive than usual that evening: on May 5, Dorothy celebrated her twenty-fifth birthday aboard *Lusitania*. James Houghton arranged to sit at the table of his old college friend Richard Freeman. "We had a fine time at meals," he recalled; although "the conversation was mostly on mining topics, I enjoyed it immensely and felt that I was acquiring a great deal of information on that subject."[24]

Throughout the meal Madeira, sherry, Chablis, Burgundy, and champagnes came in waves, followed by liqueurs and port. The culinary variety offered by a First Class dinner was staggering. Although simpler than the lavish twelve-course meals of the period served ashore, dinner generally followed the familiar pattern. The meal might begin with caviar, crab, oysters, or lobster mousse served on chilled plates, followed by a soup, either consommé or cream-based. Broiled salmon, turbot, or poached sole in cream sauce might come next. The principal meat course, or *relevé*, followed. This was generally some form of beef, accompanied by entrées of asparagus in hollandaise, sweetbreads, foie gras, browned potatoes, or vegetables in rich sauces. Roasted seasonal game included partridge, grouse, quail, pheasant, and duck, usually accompanied by a salad. After a selection of cheeses, passengers could choose from an array of cakes, puddings, tortes, petit fours, and ice cream.[25]

"A band played in this gallery during meals," a former passenger noted, "and the whole scene seemed more that of a gay restaurant than a ship at sea."[26] People chatted, made plans, and observed their fellow diners. George Kessler was particularly taken by a lively, fair-haired "charming little boy" who sat with his mother at an adjacent table. "This, of course, is not generally permitted," he noted.[27] It was true: Cunard liked to keep young children out of the saloon, providing them with their own dining room. Yet on this voyage, the boy's engaging mother, Trixie Witherbee, had somehow convinced a Dining Saloon steward to bend the rules in favor of nearly four-year-old Alfred Jr.[28]

But then, twenty-four-year-old Trixie was accustomed to doing things differently. In 1910 she'd eloped with wealthy Mexican Solid Petroleum Fuel Company president Alfred Witherbee; not only was he forty-nine to her twenty, but he also had two divorces behind him, and a daughter nearly as old as his new wife. They'd lived happily in Larchmont, keeping suites at the Waldorf-Astoria in New York and the Savoy in London to use on their frequent travels. *Lusitania* was a favorite ship: Trixie determinedly ignored her brother-in-law's last-minute efforts to persuade her not to travel aboard with her child and her mother, Mary Brown. Perhaps now, she secretly worried about being separated from her precious son. A fellow traveler, businessman Charles Hill, agreed to watch after them on the voyage, but Trixie—as Kessler saw—"was entirely wrapped up in her little boy, devoting herself in amusing him."[29]

At the end of these meals, passengers scattered. After dining with Richard Freeman, James Houghton joined him for tea or leisurely strolls around the deck, "talking of our friends and of the days when we were at Cambridge together."[30] Others might retreat to *Lusitania*'s Lounge. There were coffee and tea, relaxed conversation, and gentle games of whist with the ladies. Wealthy Angela Papadopoulos, traveling with her carpet merchant husband, Michael, not only got to dine at the Captain's Table on May 5 but also spent the evening playing cards with Lady Allan and Sir Hugh Lane. When she learned that he was traveling with a number of paintings, Angela insisted that Lane let her see them. He duly led Angela and her husband back to his cabin and revealed the canvases. "I had the chance," she recalled, "to see those works of art for the last time before they were lost forever."[31]

Melodic strains issuing from the Lounge's Broadwood grand piano gave way to serenades by the ship's five musicians.[32] The repertoire reflected the popular songs of the day, including such hits as "Alexander's Ragtime Band," "Oh, You Beautiful Doll," "Curse of an Aching Heart," and "Moonlight Bay." Selections from light operettas like *The Merry Widow* alternated with Strauss waltzes and, more ominously, "Songe d'Automne," the tune many recalled *Titanic*'s band playing just before she slipped beneath the Atlantic. There were also sentimental tunes like Carrie Jacobs Bond's "The End of a Perfect Day" and "Just a Wearyin' for You."[33]

The latter must have pleased passenger Elbert Hubbard, for Bond was his favorite composer. Bohemian to the core and a professional, unrepentant firebrand, Hubbard was as much a celebrity as Rita Jolivet, Alfred Vanderbilt, or Charles Frohman. He was "an opinion molder and popular philosopher," a "public tastemaker," and a thorn in the side of his many critics.[34] Hubbard was both perpetually enthusiastic and cynical: life, he once mused, "is just one damn thing after another."[35]

A tireless self-promoter, Hubbard had been born in 1856. As a young man he drifted from job to job; although his prospects seemed dubious, he married well, wedding Bertha Crawford, daughter of a prominent Illinois family, in 1881. Working for his brother-in-law's Larkin Soap Company, Hubbard traveled the country and eventually moved to New York State to establish a branch of the company in Buffalo. In 1892, he sold his substantial stock in the company and set out to enjoy his financial independence.[36] He applied to Harvard; although his educational background was lacking, he was provisionally admitted, but, disliking the routine, he soon left.[37] What Hubbard wanted to do was write, but he found dealing with "pesky editors" an unwelcome nuisance. To avoid such interference, he decided to publish his own work, and founded a magazine, *The Philistine: A Periodical of Protest,* as a vehicle to accommodate his disparate interests in art, music, philosophy, science, and religion.[38]

Hubbard greatly admired William Morris, the foremost English proponent of the Arts and Crafts Movement, and deliberately copied his efforts. In 1895, he established the Roycroft Colony in East Aurora, New York. In addition to producing Craftsman-style furniture, pottery, stained glass, woven rugs, leather goods, and household items, the organization also included its own printing arm, publishing expensive new editions of classic works. To *The Philistine*, Hubbard added a second magazine, *The Fra*, and quickly made a name for himself. At one time, *The Philistine* had a quarter million monthly subscribers, while Hubbard's philosophical, antiwar work, *A Message to Garcia*, sold a stunning 52 million copies.[39]

Hoping to distinguish himself, Hubbard cultivated a deliberately flamboyant appearance: he habitually wore sweeping, oversized coats, enormous cravats of velvet or silk, and a floppy hat perched atop his long hair.[40] In addition to stores, a stone chapel that served as a meeting place, and workshops, Hubbard built an inn to house the many guests who came to East Aurora to hear his views, among them a young architect named Frank Lloyd Wright.[41] One person not enamored with the idea of meeting Hubbard was William Morris's daughter, who dismissed the man known as "the Sage of East Aurora" as "that obnoxious imitator of my dear father."[42]

A friend later described Hubbard as "a bundle of contradictions, and he knew it; and his philosophy of life was subject to frequent and radical revisions. . . . He was not a fossil; he was a living thing that assimilates and grows. He was as variable as the weather-vane, it may be; but, like the weather-vane, he marked the direction of the currents of public opinion."[43] Hubbard variously described himself as a socialist, an anarchist, a spiritualist who denied formalized religion, a proponent of women's suffrage, a social reformer—anything and everything to go against the grain.[44] "I believe in the Motherhood of God," Hubbard once wrote, denouncing the Bible as "an atrocious book, false, obscene, and misleading." He added "social, economic, domestic, political, mental, and spiritual" freedoms to the list of his beliefs. Divorce, he insisted, "should be as free as marriage."[45]

With Bertha, Hubbard had four children, three sons and one daughter, but the marriage collapsed when Mrs. Hubbard, who served as a trustee for the East Aurora Academy, invited a young, independently minded teacher named Alice Moore to live with them. In 1894 Alice gave birth to Hubbard's daughter, Miriam.[46] By 1901, Bertha had had enough, and, citing his adultery, sued her husband for divorce. Hubbard, for his part, painted himself as the victim of an intellectually vapid, bourgeois spouse, saying, "Great men often marry commonplace wives."[47] Hubbard did his best to ignore the ensuing public scandal, but newspapers loudly denounced him as an unrepentant adulterer and seducer of young women. The *New York Sun,* calling him an "all around rogue," openly wondered if he had "sold his soul to the Devil."[48] Hubbard refused to make excuses or apologize. "Never explain," he advised. "Your friends do not need it, and your enemies will not believe you anyway."[49] As soon as his divorce was final, he married Alice in 1904. Defiantly, he had a new motto, "They Will Talk Anyway," carved over the door of the Roycroft Inn.[50]

Hubbard and his second wife dedicated themselves to the causes of women's rights and social improvement. Alice eagerly took on daily management of the Roycroft community, and many credited her organizational gifts for its improved business practices and fortunes, though her brisk efficiency also alienated some of the members.[51] By 1915, their personal fortune amounted to roughly $419,000.[52]

The *Titanic* tragedy in 1912 deeply affected Hubbard, who wrote of the disaster at length—words that, under the circumstances, would echo eerily over his own fate. He spoke of the "ominous" silence that fell over the doomed *Titanic*; of panic boarding lifeboats, "for there has never been a boat drill on this ship"; the "perceptible list to starboard" as the ship began to sink; the swirl of "angry, jealous, savage, relentless" water as the liner disappeared; and the "mass of wreckage, the dead, the struggles of the dying" when the ship had vanished. He was particularly taken with the story of Ida Straus refusing to leave her husband, Isidor, and choosing to die together with "calm courage."[53]

Hubbard was unapologetic about the stir he caused: in 1913 he was fined $100 for sending "pornographic material" through the postal system (the "pornographic material" turned out to be a racy joke about birth control) and temporarily lost his American citizenship.[54] He greeted the Great War with undisguised scorn, comparing the conflict to the feud between the Hatfields and the McCoys, as "all the crowned heads of Europe are related." He foresaw "no romance or heroism" in the war, warning that it "will progress from horror to horror, and with it the protest, disgust, and anger of the people will deepen."[55]

Hubbard freely indulged in anti-German propaganda in his magazines, including a hyperbolic attack called *Who Lifted the Lid off Hell?* Hubbard angrily denounced Kaiser Wilhelm II, insisting that he had "a shrunken soul and a mind that reeks of egomania," and was a "megalomaniac" suffering from "paranoia," and a man who compared unfavorably with Caligula.[56] Charles Lauriat, to whom Hubbard lent a copy of the article when the men were aboard *Lusitania,* found it a stunning "piece of vitriolic English."[57]

Despite these inflammatory words, Hubbard and his wife sailed on *Lusitania* believing that the Kaiser would be amenable to an interview. "I used to be on friendly terms with the Kaiser," Hubbard insisted, "but I don't know how I stand with him, for you know I have written some things he may not have liked."[58] Hubbard blithely ignored warnings that *Lusitania* might be in danger; indeed, he seemed to relish the idea of death. "Speaking from a strictly personal point of view, I would not mind if they did sink the ship," he told a reporter. "It might be a good thing for me. I would drown with her, and that's about the only way I could succeed in my ambition to get into the Hall of Fame. I'd be a regular hero and go right to the bottom."[59]

Aboard *Lusitania*, Hubbard befriended a young journalist from Toronto traveling in Second Class named Ernest Cowper, welcoming him to his cabin on B Deck and chatting with him in the ship's public rooms.[60] When Cowper quizzed Hubbard about the possibility of a German submarine sinking the vessel, "the Sage of East Aurora" dismissed the idea. "No," Hubbard insisted, "they will never torpedo the *Lusitania*. The Germans have done some bad things since the War started, but I don't think they are that bad. Moreover, if a man was going to slug you as you came around a corner, he would not advertise the fact in a newspaper."[61]

After an hour or two of conversation in the Lounge or Smoking Room, most of *Lusitania*'s First Class passengers slowly made their way to their staterooms. Ladies might stop at the impressive mahogany and brass Purser's Bureau on Promenade Deck, handing over to purser James McCubbin diamond necklaces, brooches, aigrettes, and bandeaus they deemed too valuable to leave in their rooms.[62] Stewards had already prepared the cabins, closing windows to prevent unwelcome drafts, and turning back eiderdowns to reveal the crisp linen sheets. Ladies' maids and valets laid out negligees, pajamas, and dressing robes for their illustrious masters, taking their evening clothing away for any needed cleaning or pressing. One by one, lights dimmed until the vast corridors were still, their solitude interrupted only by young men retrieving shoes and boots left outside cabin doors to be shined before magically reappearing in the morning.

CHAPTER TEN

Lusitania's First Class passengers passed their days in comfortable uniformity, enjoying games of cards, leisurely strolls on deck, and lengthy, indulgent meals. For her Second Class travelers, life aboard the ship offered echoes of this ordered social world of tradition without the pretense. The distinctions were subtle: while First Class rooms featured Corinthian columns, those in Second Class had simpler Doric capitals.[1]

It wasn't merely wealth or status that separated those traveling in First and Second Class aboard *Lusitania*. Cunard imposed a visible gap between the two, a constant reminder of their unequal positions. First Class decks cascaded from the rear of her main body, to her tall mast, only to meet a second superstructure dominating the last quarter of the ship. Here, as close to the stern as possible, Cunard lodged its Second Class passengers.

"Only in magnificence, and not in comfort," a contemporary announced, "does the First Class accommodation surpass the Second Class, the same care and attention having been exercised in the equipment of both. . . . Indeed, a passenger on first going on board might well be excused for mistaking the Second Class public rooms and staterooms for the First Class."[2] The boast was true enough: Second Class rooms aboard *Lusitania* were far more luxurious than on previous liners, and in many cases equal to First Class on other ships.

Hoping to reclaim some of the revenue inevitably lost owing to the downturn in wartime travel, Cunard had cut Second Class fares from $70 to $50. As a result, many who would otherwise have traveled in Third Class had booked passage in Second Class, and accommodations meant to house 460 passengers were now stretched thin with 601 souls.[3] Most Second Class passengers were solidly respectable and engaged in professions: teachers, lawyers, merchants, and doctors. Second Class passage, noted one author, was suggestive of "a quietly satisfactory business arrangement between equals," often preferred by frequent travelers for its informality and lack of social pretense.[4]

Second Class passengers tended to adhere to a more traditional segregation of the sexes than their counterparts in Saloon Class. The Writing Room was even known by the formal designation of the Ladies' Drawing Room. This was a suitably refined, feminine space in the Louis XVI style of light gray paneled walls, with a leaded dome over comfortable groupings of satinwood furniture, and a piano atop the rose-colored Brussels carpet.[5] As in First Class, men congregated in the adjacent Smoking Room, lined with carved mahogany paneling and topped with a white plasterwork ceiling pierced by a stained glass, barrel-vaulted skylight. Wide, blue-tinted windows opened onto the deck; one wall featured an intricate mosaic of a river scene in Brittany.[6]

Here, Professor Ian Bernard Stoughton Holbourn had spent much of the voyage, resting after his third lecture tour of America.[7] Born in 1872, Holbourn came from a well-to-do, eminently respectable family: his minister father had several times preached sermons before Queen Victoria.[8] After graduating with honors in mathematics from Merton College at Oxford, Holbourn decided to suddenly change course: now he wanted to focus on art and classical literature. He studied, wrote articles, and lectured on the classical world so successfully that Oxford even gave him a job as a visiting professor.[9] He again strayed from his newfound specialty in 1903, publishing a biography of the painter Tintoretto, though he continued to lecture on classical subjects. Holbourn was generally mild-mannered, but could work himself into a frenzy of enthusiasm over his favorite topics; he could be equally adamant in his denunciations, and was especially critical of modern architecture, deriding the idea that form should follow function.[10] He had just labored over his own theories in *The Need for Art,* a manuscript he'd finished between lectures in America.

Holbourn was a proud Scot, living in Edinburgh with his wife, Marion, and their three sons, Hylas, Alasdair, and Philistos. But he was most proud of his position as Laird of Foula, a small island off the coast of Scotland that he purchased in 1900. Lost amid the remote Shetland Islands, Foula was indeed a miniature—if somewhat barren—kingdom, some two miles wide and four miles long. Fewer than two hundred people lived along its rugged shores, working the peat bogs, fishing, raising sheep, and knitting sweaters. Holbourn liked the idea that, as Laird, he had joined the ranks of the landed aristocracy; he also enjoyed being master of the island and benevolent ruler of its superstitious people.[11]

One afternoon, Holbourn wandered into *Lusitania*'s Second Class Lounge, where a wide wooden staircase descended amidst comfortable groupings of sofas and chairs, and spotted a young girl forlornly sprawled on a sofa. Twelve-year-old Avis Dolphin, he decided, had an "air of superior breeding" and gradually she unraveled the details of her sad story.[12] Her father had fought in the Boer War, and in 1905 had taken Avis and her mother to Canada, where two more children were born. Tuberculosis claimed her father's life; to provide for her young family, Avis's mother took over the operation of a nursing home in St. Thomas, Ontario. It wasn't hard for Holbourn to be impressed with Avis: she was quiet, dignified, and obviously intelligent—so intelligent, in fact, that despite the war her mother had decided to send her back to England to live with her grandparents so that she could get a more refined education.[13]

A recent bout with measles had left Avis weak and tended to by nurse Hilda Ellis, who insisted that she rest as much as possible; this allowed Hilda to spend time aboard *Lusitania* with her friend Sarah Smith.[14] Avis was left to while away her days at sea. Although she marveled at *Lusitania*—"like a floating palace," she said—she was bored and lonely.[15] Holbourn fetched an extra pillow, made Avis more comfortable, and began chatting with her.[16] He told her about his own children; entertained her with tales of life on Foula; and even promised to make her an honorary citizen of the little island. When she learned that he was a writer, Avis complained that "girls' books were too tame." Most girls, she insisted, "preferred to read the more exciting books of their brothers." To rectify this, Holbourn promised Avis that he would write an adventure story just for her.[17] And, although she seemed unperturbed by the potential danger, he promised that—if anything happened to *Lusitania*—he would take care of Avis.[18]

Margaret Mackworth had been surprised to see so many children traveling aboard *Lusitania*. A pregnant Emily Anderson sailed with her nearly three-year-old daughter Barbara. Young Barbara had never seen her English relatives—certainly a frivolous reason for potentially dangerous travel. But this explanation actually concealed a more pressing concern: twenty-four-year-old Emily suffered from tuberculosis. Hopefully a specialist in her native England could successfully treat her disease. Emily left her husband behind: Rowland Anderson worked at a Winchester Repeating Arms factory in Connecticut as a draughtsman.[19] The factory could barely keep up with orders to provide Russia and France with rifles, and so Rowland had to make do with seeing his wife and daughter safely aboard *Lusitania*. "If my father had seen the warning from the Germans," Barbara later insisted, "he would not have let us sail." She had only the fleeting impressions of a child: standing at the ship's railing with her mother in New York City, looking for her father on the pier below; a crowded cabin with beds "one on top of the other"; and a little souvenir spoon marked *Lusitania* that someone gave to her aboard the liner.[20]

Belle Saunders Naish had her hands full on this voyage: her husband, Theodore, was confined to his cabin, suffering from an acute case of seasickness.[21] Born in 1865 in Michigan, Belle had spent most of her life as a spinster schoolteacher; not until 1911, when she was forty-five, did she marry the well-to-do Theodore, an engineering draughtsman from Kansas City, Missouri.[22] That spring, Theodore decided to visit his brothers in England and introduce them to his wife.[23] He seemed unperturbed by the idea that *Lusitania* faced potential danger: "Maybe I can help my adopted country and my native land," Theodore joked, "by dying than by staying here."[24]

Belle, though, was nervous. She saw the rack where lifebelts were stowed in their cabin, but found she couldn't open it. She poked her head out into the corridor and flagged down a passing steward, asking him to unlock the device. At first he refused: he was expected in the Dining Saloon, and couldn't be bothered. Refusing to be put off, Belle insisted that he open the rack and show them how to properly put on the lifebelts. From the looks he gave her, she remembered, it was obvious that the man thought this was "a wholly unnecessary waste of time."[25] Scarcely reassured by this attitude, Belle made it a practice to leave and return to their cabin using the same route, "so that in case of anything happening, I would not be confused."[26]

And with Theodore sick, Belle was often on the run. He spent most of the voyage in their cabin, with his wife bringing in meals on trays from the dining saloon so that they could eat together. There were no suites in Second Class: passengers were accommodated in two- or four-person berths. Luckily, the Naishes had a two-berth cabin, with deep Brussels carpeting and a mahogany washstand fitted with two porcelain basins adorned with the Cunard logo; thick cotton spreads covered the beds, unlike berths in Third Class where, in a nod to lingering suspicions surrounding the "lower classes," all the spreads were emblazoned with the Cunard logo to deter theft.[27]

Some Second Class passengers, like twenty-six-year-old William Meriheina, were traveling on business. When he was four, his parents emigrated from Finland to America, where the family—who abbreviated their last name to Heina for everyday use—eventually settled in New York. He was thirteen when his father died, and quit school, presumably to help his mother with his four siblings. An early job driving a taxi awakened a love of motorcars, and the handsome young man was soon racing along Brighton Beach in expensive vehicles provided by the Lozier Car Company. The company used Meriheina to promote their motorcars, shuffling him around to various events and races, including the inaugural run of what became the Indianapolis 500; more than once, Meriheina narrowly escaped serious injury during devastating collisions. He married, had a daughter, and, while continuing to race, also took an active interest in fledgling air travel—again to nearly disastrous results on at least one occasion. Soon Meriheina took a job with General Motors' New York City Buick division.[28]

In the spring of 1915, the General Motors Export Company asked Meriheina to travel to South Africa to demonstrate its new ignition systems, and he booked passage aboard *Lusitania,* keeping a running journal of his experiences.[29] Although he noted that the ocean was "quite rough" on Sunday and many aboard were seasick, he enjoyed himself with "a dandy saltwater bath" and "a grand breakfast." Over the next few days, Meriheina was "feeling great," enjoying "dandy meals" along with "games, races, a whist drive, and various other entertainments." On Monday he saw fog and thought that the ship was "rolling quite a little," though he was not affected. Surrounded by "Scotch, English, and Irish dialects" throughout the voyage, he mused that he might "talk funny" by the end of the journey. But the overall trip was pleasant, and Meriheina was sure that it "will do me good."[30]

Second Class passengers also included those who, like their First Class counterparts, were on their way to Europe to join in relief efforts or visit relatives involved in the conflict. Handsome, twenty-seven-year-old surgeon Carl Foss of Montana was one such volunteer. Nephritis had prevented Foss from enlisting, and so he had signed on with the English Red Cross, hoping to put his expertise on gunshot wounds to good use. Still, like many others aboard *Lusitania,* Foss worried about a submarine attack, remembering, "We had been pretty nervous all the way over."[31]

Sixty-five-year-old Phoebe Amory of Toronto was on her way to visit her four sons serving in the war, "probably for the last time on earth," she sadly mused.[32] Alfred, the eldest at twenty-nine, served in the Canadian Army Service Corps Battalion, while two of his brothers were training with the Canadian Expeditionary Force and the fourth was with the Imperial Forces.[33] She had also booked passage so that she could see her gravely ill mother; unfortunately, her mother died before Phoebe could reach her.[34] Phoebe had not seen the German warning in the newspapers; even had she done so, she insisted, "I should have made the voyage." She later recalled "the vague feeling that so many were experiencing regarding the safety of the *Lusitania* when she should enter the danger zone."[35]

Amory was impressed by *Lusitania*'s luxury, especially the Second Class Dining Saloon on D Deck. Although smaller than its Saloon Class counterpart, it repeated the same grandiose, Louis XVI design scheme, down to carved pilasters and columns supporting a second-floor balcony with a large, open well to the main room below.[36] "Such a sight it was!" Amory recalled. "It would have gladdened the heart of anyone to gaze upon such a scene as was then before me. Such a beautiful dining room I had never seen, either aboard ship, or in the magnificent hotels that I have visited on both sides of the ocean. The pillars, extending from floor to ceiling, were as snowy white as the linen that covered the long tables. The walls and ceilings were frescoed in delicate tints, and in the center there was a round, open balcony, which permitted one to stand above and gaze down upon a spectacle that I believe could not be duplicated elsewhere. . . . I had never seen such palms as those that were profusely distributed about the saloon. One of them, I remember, reached nearly to the ceiling."[37]

Just as the carved capitals of columns and decorative pilasters gradually became plainer as one moved from First to Second Class, so, too, did the simpler, heartier fare aboard *Lusitania* reinforce these distinctions. In Second Class, breakfast included apples, bananas, stewed prunes, figs, oatmeal, porridge, fried fish, omelets and eggs cooked to order, bacon, and sautéed potatoes, accompanied by an assortment of pastries and scones washed down with cocoa, coffee, and tea. Luncheons and dinners changed daily, and included such options as soups, salads, spaghetti, mutton, roast beef, brisket, steak, turkey, roasted chicken, veal cutlets, rice, vegetables, smoked haddock, flounder, salmon, and broiled cod in parsley sauce, with tarts, ice creams, custards, cheese, and fruits for dessert.[38]

Immersed in such surroundings, stomachs full of fine food, *Lusitania*'s Second Class passengers echoed many of the attitudes of their counterparts in First Class. They might not be enormously wealthy, but most were successful, and their money tended to cushion them from inconvenient realities. There was a sense of impervious defiance when it came to possible danger. To many, the war seemed far away, a distant reality that had not yet affected their lives. Although tensions inevitably heightened as *Lusitania* edged ever closer to the war zone, few could imagine even the dreaded "Hun" deliberately attacking an unarmed passenger liner filled with women and children.

Ian Holbourn, though, didn't view the situation in quite the same way. Like many others, he'd seen the less-than-reassuring boat drills; his practical mind couldn't comfortably dismiss the sense of impending danger. Like several of his counterparts in First Class, he went to see Captain Turner, complaining that passengers were being ignored. Turner listened and said that he would speak to one of his officers about it—apparently his attempt to avoid confrontation; Holbourn was sure that the terse captain actually resented the request. Holbourn had no better luck with his fellow travelers in Second Class. Several times, he urged that they should at least try on their lifejackets so that they would know how to work them if disaster struck. Rather than spurring them on to precautionary action, such pleas seemed only to upset many. One afternoon, a fellow passenger drew Holbourn aside. All of this talk about possible danger, he said, was disturbing the ladies. He advised Holbourn to drop the subject for fear of antagonizing others. Holbourn was stunned: he dubbed his obstinate travelers "the Ostrich Club."[39]

CHAPTER ELEVEN

Friday, April 30—the day before *Lusitania* sailed from New York and half a world away—another vessel slipped from its pier and set out for the sea. No newsreels captured the scene; there were no curious crowds, no bands playing patriotic songs, no flags waving in the early morning breeze. Orders had come down to the master and crew: "Large English troop transports expected starting from Liverpool, Dartmouth. Get to stations on fastest possible route around Scotland. Hold as long as supplies permit. Submarines to attack transport ships, merchant ships, and warships."[1] Quietly, without fanfare, U-20 left the German naval base at Emden on the North Sea. Her route took her around Scotland and south to Ireland. There, she turned east, to sail along the southern Irish coast, unknowingly bound for her tragic date with destiny.

Completed in 1913, the U-20 was a diesel-powered submarine some 219 feet long and capable of 15 knots on the surface; when submerged, two electric motors drove her at a top speed of 9 knots. She carried one 3.5-inch gun mounted on her deck near the conning tower and had four tubes, two forward and two aft, to fire torpedoes. On this particular voyage, she carried two types: the regulation bronze projectiles, and new gyro torpedoes, whose heads were fitted with charges containing some three hundred pounds of the explosive Trotyl. Between twelve and sixteen feet in length and each weighing roughly a ton, these missiles traveled at some 40 knots when fired.[2]

Commanding U-20 was thirty-year-old Kapitänleutnant Walther von Schwieger. Born in 1885 to an aristocratic family in Berlin, Schwieger was the very image of Teutonic pride: tall and handsome, with blond hair, piercing blue eyes, and fine features, he had a "distinguished bearing" in keeping with his ancestry; he hated the pretensions that went with the honorific "von" and quietly dropped it from his name.[3] Comrades remembered the unmarried Schwieger as very intelligent, with "gifts of poise and urbane courtesy," a man who adored music and whose "talk was full of gaiety and pointed wit."[4]

Schwieger had joined the Imperial Navy as an eighteen-year-old sea cadet in 1903, and gradually worked his way up the ranks: in 1911, after serving aboard torpedo boats, he transferred to the Imperial Navy's U-boat division. In 1914, he was promoted to Kapitänleutnant and received command of U-20.[5] It took a special kind of man to helm a submarine: they were still on the cutting edge of technology and largely unproven. An aura of danger surrounded their missions, one that offered not only excitement but also opportunity. Courage and ability led Schwieger to his post: one man called him "one of the ablest officers we had, and a recognized expert on submarine matters—one of the few commanders who were consulted by Grand Admiral von Tirpitz and on whose advice von Tirpitz relied."[6] On this point, everyone agreed: Schwieger was one of the most respected commanders in the service, known for his courtesy and courage.[7]

Under Schwieger, the U-20, said one crew member, was a "jolly boat . . . a kindly boat." With four officers and just over thirty men crowded into the submarine's cramped quarters, maintaining morale was a constant struggle. The men wore waterproofed leather suits that became unbearably hot.[8] Water was scarce, hygiene a luxury, and fresh air rare: the inside of the submarine habitually smelled of sweat, cooking oil, and food.[9] Men slept in shifts, in bunks, or hammocks strung perilously close to torpedoes. "At first I was kept awake a bit at the thought of having so much TNT in bed with me," a crewman recalled. "Then I got used to it."[10] The men morbidly jested with the torpedoes, giving them names like "Fat Bertha," "Shining Emma," and "Yellow Mary." At all times, "like all ladies," said an officer, they were treated with tender "care and courtesy."[11]

As much as was possible, a submarine rode the waves rather than remain submerged. This allowed the batteries to recharge, and fresh air to permeate the vessel. The crew could walk the slick gray surface of the U-boat, and play with the vessel's dogs, a pair of black dachshunds, one of whom had been rescued from a Portuguese ship the submarine had sunk. "A canine romance developed," recalled a sailor, and soon the submarine was filled with the sound of four little puppies, tended to by a grizzled old salt. Eventually the men gave three of the dogs to other submarines, and kept three for themselves, snuggling with them in their bunks at night.[12]

Above all, life aboard U-20 was filled with uncertainty. Schwieger had to be on nearly constant duty, and often went several days without sleep. Spotting an enemy ship was not merely a potential opportunity to attack, but also brought with it the very real danger that the submarine itself might be rammed, fired upon, or hit by depth charges. At such times, men stood silently in unspoken fear as "the noise is distinctly heard of the propellers of the enemy's ships, hunting for us overhead."[13]

There had been several attacks by British merchant vessels on U-boats. The British steamer *Thordis* had rammed and sunk a German submarine in February 1915; King George V decorated the captain for his actions and the crew was financially rewarded. Four other U-boats had also been lost to British ramming or gunfire by the time Schwieger left Emden, and several other submarines had suffered close calls.[14] With British vessels painting out their names and company colors and flying neutral flags, accurate identification was often difficult. Then there was the threat of an ambush: given Winston Churchill's continued boasts that British merchant vessels had been armed, a U-boat commander had no way of knowing if he would be fired upon. Schwieger was nothing if not a skilled and able commander, a man who put duty and the safety of his vessel and crew above all other considerations. In February 1915 he waged an unsuccessful attack on a clearly designated British hospital ship. He reasoned that as it was leaving England, it could not have been carrying wounded soldiers. His method of operation was remarkably consistent: if suspicious or in doubt about a vessel, he attacked.[15]

As circumstances permitted, Schwieger attempted to follow the Cruiser Rules, though only when it was clear that the encountered vessel didn't threaten his submarine. On Wednesday, May 5, Schwieger spotted a small schooner, *Earl of Lathom,* off the Irish coast near the Old Head of Kinsale. The 132-ton ship posed no threat to U-20, so Schwieger surfaced, fired a warning shot, and, speaking English in "a very gruff voice," demanded to see the ship's manifest.[16] Soon he ordered the five-man crew to abandon ship. He waited until they had safely disembarked, then fired his deck gun into the vessel until she sank. Later that same afternoon, he spotted a British steamer bearing the Norwegian flag. Schwieger was suspicious and fired a torpedo, but the projectile missed and the vessel escaped.[17]

Early the following day, Schwieger spotted *Candidate,* a six-thousand-ton British merchant vessel that flew no flag and whose name had been painted out. He surfaced and opened fire with his deck gun. As the ship listed, he stopped his fire and allowed the crew to safely abandon her, then launched a torpedo into the vessel's side. The ship seemed to right itself: rather than fire another torpedo, Schwieger used his deck gun to sink the vessel. Shortly after this, U-20 spotted *Candidate*'s sister ship, *Centurion*. She, too, flew no flag; after U-20's pilot, Rudolf Lanz, identified her as a British vessel, Schwieger fired a torpedo into her side. The crew had ample time to abandon ship: even after an hour, though, *Centurion* was still afloat. It took a second torpedo to send her to the bottom of the Irish Sea.[18]

According to his war diary, Schwieger now had only three torpedoes left; he was supposed to save either one or two for his return voyage.[19] Persistently foggy weather made it unlikely that he'd have another successful chance encounter. He also worried about meeting a troop transport or merchant vessel accompanied by armed escort. Schwieger decided to remain off the Irish coast for the next twelve hours, and then start back for Germany on the afternoon of May 7.[20]

The British Admiralty was unusually cognizant of the dangers awaiting *Lusitania* off Ireland. Unknown to the Kaiser's officials, Great Britain had captured all three codes used by the German navy and could thus follow their wireless transmissions and movements. Intercepted messages went through decryption in Room 40, the Admiralty's center of naval intelligence. Because of the delay in receiving, decoding, encrypting, and sending information from these German messages out to merchant vessels and warships, there was always a slight lag in time, and reported positions were often outdated. But the information allowed Room 40 to follow Schwieger's progress once he left Emden and to track his general movements. Yet for some reason, specific information about U-20 was not passed on to the major naval stations on Britain's western coast nor to those along the Irish Sea.[21]

Passengers aboard *Lusitania* knew nothing of these developments: torpedoing of ships in her path of travel was scarcely the sort of news printed in the *Cunard Daily Bulletin* each morning. The first hint that something had changed came early on the morning of Thursday, May 6. "Shouts and the scuffling of feet" awoke Theodate Pope; peering out her cabin window, she saw members of the crew swarming around the twenty-two wooden lifeboats.[22] Over the next few hours, they loosened lines and swung the boats out over the deck. They still hung some eight feet above the deck by their falls, and chains kept them attached to their davits, but the captain had ordered that they be made ready as *Lusitania* approached the war zone.[23]

Before leaving New York, Turner said that he had received "special instructions" about his ship's navigation through the declared submarine zone, though he consistently refused to say what they had been.[24] The British Admiralty was so diligent in its advice and instructions that Turner actually complained about the sheer volume of communiqués—"I could paper the walls with them!" was his gruff comment.[25] The remark suggests Turner's annoyance at what he viewed as unwelcome interference with navigation of his ship. It also suggests a man unwilling or unable to adjust to changing circumstances dictated by the war.

With her funnels painted gray and no flags flying, *Lusitania* was as disguised as anyone could reasonably expect.[26] High up on the bridge, Captain Turner spent that Thursday morning barking out additional orders: all bulkhead doors were to be kept closed unless in use; lookouts were doubled, and extra men were added to watch duty on the bridge; all portholes were to be closed. The engine room was to maintain the highest steam pressure possible, and be prepared for orders to go at top speed—21 knots—if danger threatened.[27]

Seeing the lifeboats being made ready as *Lusitania* approached the war zone renewed many passengers' gnawing anxieties. As might be expected, the liner's officers brushed the worries aside, as did Captain Turner. Having witnessed one of the perfunctory lifeboat drills, and feeling that the purser had dismissed his concerns, George Kessler went to see the captain that Thursday. Wouldn't it be a good idea to actually involve passengers in the drills? At the very least, Kessler suggested, passengers should be assigned to specific boats "in case anything untoward happened"; surely, he said, this could be done when they booked passage, with the number printed on their tickets. Turner seemed annoyed. After the sinking of *Titanic,* he explained, Cunard had considered and then rejected such an idea as impractical. Even if he wanted to change the existing methods, the captain said, he'd have to first obtain permission from the British Board of Trade, which regulated maritime law. But, Turner assured Kessler, they would "go at all speed and get over the war zone" when they entered it early the following morning.[28]

When Francis Jenkins, manager of wool importers Holland and Sherry in New York City, tried to discuss his concerns with several officers, they belittled and ignored him. They had, he said, "the utmost confidence, even to the point of boasting," that nothing would happen to *Lusitania.* Not yet willing to abandon hope, Jenkins also complained to Captain Turner. There was, he told Turner, "considerable talk" of a submarine attack among the passengers. Would it not be best if the passengers also participated in the boat drills, so that they would be prepared? Turner greeted the idea coolly, commenting, "A torpedo can't get the *Lusitania.* She runs too fast."[29] Yet unbelievably, even after worried confrontations with George Kessler, Ian Holbourn, Francis Jenkins, and others, Turner later lied, insisting that he had never heard any passengers express worries about the possible dangers.[30]

By that Thursday, passengers also began to talk about the ship's lack of progress. "The speed of the boat had not been what I had expected," recalled Charles Lauriat. On the first full day out, it covered only 501 miles; the following days were even lower. But, he thought, "when we sighted the Irish coast" the ship would "show a burst of top speed" and equal her rate of 25 knots.[31] Nor could Francis Jenkins understand the ship's slow progress as she neared the Irish coast. "Everyone knew that was the path of danger," he said, "and we fully expected the ship to be speeded to the utmost. Instead, she reduced her speed so much as to make the passengers talk of it. I spoke to one officer, and he replied that there was no chance of a submarine getting the *Lusitania,* and her speed didn't make any difference." This, Jenkins thought, was "a strange attitude to take."[32]

That Thursday afternoon, Charles Frohman abandoned his self-imposed seclusion and hosted a party in his suite, complete with canapés and champagne. Alfred Vanderbilt attended, along with Elbert Hubbard, Rita Jolivet, Josephine Brandell, Justus Forman, and Charles Klein. The egalitarian Frohman even invited Lott Gadd, *Lusitania*'s barber. For all the joviality, Gadd remembered, the atmosphere was tense. "I shall never forget that evening," he recalled, "being in Mr. Frohman's room when Mr. Hubbard came in, and we chatted about ships being sunk by submarines."[33] Captain Turner also stopped by, on his way to the Lounge to attend a benefit concert in aid of the Liverpool Sailors' Orphanage.

Angela Papadopoulos had found the voyage aboard *Lusitania* pleasant, though the unending worry of her husband, Michael, over being torpedoed, coupled with several migraine headaches, prevented her from socializing as much as she might have wished. That evening, she, too, asked a few people to join them for a small party in their cabin on B Deck. Albert and Gladys Bilicke came, along with Sir Hugh Lane, Lady Allan, and Alfred Vanderbilt. "I remember that we were joking about Mike's fear of the ship being torpedoed," she wrote. Captain Turner, making his hated social rounds, also dropped in briefly as the talk was under way. Turner, she recalled, "did little to calm him down" or ease Papadopoulos's fears.[34]

At the end of the gathering, Lane escorted Angela to the First Class Lounge for an evening concert. Ordinarily, the traditional charity concert, a fixture on most British transatlantic liners, would have taken place on the last night of the voyage. But with *Lusitania* scheduled for an early Saturday arrival at Liverpool, people would likely be busy on Friday evening packing their belongings, and so it was moved to Thursday night.[35] Second Class passengers were invited to the First Class Lounge to share the entertainment in aid of seamen's charities, and the spacious room was crowded as Ian Holbourn escorted Avis Dolphin to her seat.[36] Leslie and Stewart Mason attended, as did Lady Allan and her daughters, sitting with Frederick Orr-Lewis; Lady Mackworth and her father, David Thomas; Josephine Brandell; Oliver Bernard; Angela Papadopoulos; Sir Hugh Lane; and Rita Jolivet, sitting next to Albert Vanderbilt and Charles Frohman. Everyone, Rita recalled, was "in high spirits."[37] "Being a young man," Harold Boulton remembered, "my eyes picked up all the attractive girls I could see." He spotted Rita, who was "most attractive to look at," but couldn't work up the courage to introduce himself.[38]

"Everyone is willing to do his or her best," declared a guidebook. "Many professionals who have refused to take part in other entertainments have gladly come forward to give their services on these occasions."[39] Rita Jolivet and Josephine Brandell, though, politely declined to perform.[40] Occasionally members of the crew joined in these performances. Purser James McCubbin played the flute, and several times had entertained aboard his previous posting. One night, a mischievous fellow officer filled his flute with flour; when McCubbin blew into the instrument, a shower of fine white powder landed over the elegantly dressed lady accompanying him at the piano.[41]

McCubbin sat out this evening's festivities. Instead, the Royal Gwent Singers from Wales performed and there were a number of popular songs.[42] Orr-Lewis thought that it was a "splendid" concert.[43] Passenger William Broderick-Cloete made an impassioned plea for funds that brought in just over £100, and urged his fellow travelers to buy souvenir programs.[44] When Phoebe Amory offered one to Alfred Vanderbilt, he pulled out a $5 bill and handed it to her, saying he "could not resist my good-natured smile," even though he had already purchased a copy.[45]

Oliver Bernard, typically, viewed the entire enterprise with cynicism. People were split into little groups, none of which seemed to speak to the other. "A submarine," he wryly noted, "would have at least socialized the audience." He was particularly critical of "that guy Vanderbilt," with "nothing better to do than driving a four-in-hand to Brighton," and referred to him as one of "New York's Four Hundred Fools."[46] Vanderbilt was more prominent that evening; at one point, he partnered with Angela Papadopoulos in a dance as the musicians played.[47] Officer Albert Bestic remembered peering into the room, "where dancing and gaiety held sway," and immediately thought of "that famous dance given by the Duchess of Richmond in Brussels on the eve of Waterloo."[48]

Captain Turner thanked the performers and the audience for their contributions. Then his comments turned ominous as he told passengers that within the next few hours *Lusitania* would enter the war zone. He reminded them to keep their cabin windows and portholes covered at night, and asked them not to smoke on deck, in case the light was visible to any lurking German submarine.

Someone asked if there was any danger. "In wartime, there is always danger," Turner replied, "but I must repeat there is no cause for alarm." The following morning, he told the room, *Lusitania* would be at full speed, and "could run away from any submarine."[49] He added his assurances that the ship would "be securely in the care of the Royal Navy."[50]

These last words seemed to resolve something that had been nagging away at many passengers: belief that vessels of the Royal Navy would provide a military escort once the ship reached Irish waters. "We certainly had been led to expect" an escort, said George Kessler, "when we reached the war zone."[51] A Cunard official had assured Charles Lauriat of this when he had purchased his ticket.[52] "The general opinion," recalled Francis Jenkins, "was that torpedo-boat destroyers would accompany us through the danger zone."[53] Harold Boulton was sure "we'd be conveyed," saying people expected that they would "be met by British destroyers or cruisers."[54] Much to his annoyance, several American passengers repeatedly asked Oliver Bernard—as if, being British, he knew something about the ship's operation—why there were no accompanying warships as escorts. But Bernard had no answer.[55]

At the end of the concert, passengers scattered. "I was nervous during the whole trip," Josephine Brandell recalled, "so much so that I kept worrying my friends about fearing the submarine." The concert did nothing to distract her from a sense of foreboding: she was so worried that she asked passenger Mabel Crichton if she could sleep in her cabin so as not to be alone. Crichton "did all she could during that whole night to quiet my nerves," but Josephine got very little sleep.[56]

Henry and Annie Adams returned to their cabin. "My husband was still obsessed with the idea that something was going to happen," she remembered.[57] *Lusitania* was equipped with lifebelts known as Boddy's Patented Jackets, heavy and cumbersome vests stuffed with cork.[58] Henry Adams "went to the wardrobe to take down the lifebelts, which were stored there. He found them so tightly jammed against the ceiling that it took much time and work to get them loose. "After we practiced putting them on, we threw them under the lower berth."[59] It became a common theme. Worried about what to do in case of an emergency, Francis Jenkins vainly searched his cabin for instructions on how to put on the lifebelt and where to go if the lifeboats were lowered. He also failed to find any obvious cache of lifebelts available to passengers on the decks.[60] Charles Jeffery had brought his own lifebelt with him. "I had, when a couple of days out from New York," he remembered, "looked for a lifejacket in my cabin, but could not find one."[61] Michael Byrne was amazed that few passengers even knew where lifebelts could be found, much less how to properly put them on.[62] Despite hearing assurances while seated at the Captain's Table that *Lusitania* was in no danger, Jessie Taft Smith was worried enough that she, too, practiced putting on her lifebelt, just in case of an emergency.[63]

Some passengers were more worried than others: an officer had actually interrupted Angela Papadopoulos during the concert. Her husband, Michael, "crazily had slipped into one of the lifeboats to pass the night, convinced that the *Lusitania* a little while later would be torpedoed."[64] Officers and passengers gathered around the lifeboat: the whole thing seemed absurd to Robert Timmis: "We all laughed at him."[65] Soon Angela arrived, accompanied by Alfred Vanderbilt and Sir Hugh Lane. At first, no amount of pleas or ridicule could convince Michael Papadopoulos to leave the security of his boat; finally, Angela—along with Vanderbilt and Lane—managed to coax him down and back to his cabin.[66]

Harold Boulton saw that many passengers, anticipating the worst and thinking that "they didn't want to be drowned in their cabins," had decided to spend the night in *Lusitania*'s public rooms.

Stewards arranged blankets and pillows on sofas in the Lounge, Reading and Writing Room, and Smoking Room. Boulton decided "it didn't much matter if I drowned in the cabin or in the lounge," and went back to his stateroom.[67] Members of the crew covered skylights with black canvas and stewards drew heavy curtains to conceal the few remaining lights.[68] *Lusitania* steamed through the night: in a few hours, she would enter the war zone.

CHAPTER TWELVE

A beautiful sunrise greeted *Lusitania* as she approached the Irish coast on the morning of Friday, May 7. Within a few hours, though, heavy fog enveloped the ship, shrouding the coast from view. *Lusitania*'s foghorn interrupted what had, for Rita Jolivet, been a restless night. "I had not slept well," she recalled, and she decided to remain in bed until just before luncheon.[1] What annoyed some alarmed others. Oliver Bernard thought that the horn only heightened "general apprehensions now that they were so near the danger zone." To him, "the policy of announcing the liner's whereabouts to friend and foe alike" seemed like madness.[2] Theodore Naish agreed: early that morning, he complained to his wife, Belle, that the incessant siren "sounded too much like calling for trouble."[3]

The deep, booming horn woke Harold Boulton at half-past eight. After dressing, he wandered over the ship; here and there, he saw passengers begin to stir from their makeshift beds on sofas in *Lusitania*'s public rooms, "picking up rugs and pillows and going down to tidy up."[4] A few sipped coffee or tea and looked over the latest edition of the *Cunard Daily Bulletin*. It was a hoax, the publication told readers, that the Germans were emerging victorious in the war. There were reports from Africa and Europe of the latest military action, but nothing about any recent vessels being sunk by submarines.[5] Nevertheless, Boulton recalled, there was "a great deal of excitement at breakfast over the U-boat threats."[6]

Walking the deck, Boulton was dismayed by the lack of speed. He cornered an officer, asking if the ship was going so slowly because of the fog. It wasn't just the fog, came the reply: *Lusitania* had deliberately slowed to save coal and reserve steam, in case any of the lookouts spotted a submarine.[7] Shortly after ten the fog dissipated; an hour later, the distant coast of Ireland again came into hazy view, and people lined the ship's decks to take in the scene as gulls swooped and circled above. The day was now "exceptionally lovely . . . bathed in clear spring sunshine, and the sea was as smooth as a mirror," recalled one man.[8] Even when the fog cleared, *Lusitania* seemed to inch along the coast. As he strolled around the deck, Michael Byrne heard the same conversation, over and over again: "Why are we not making full speed?"[9] Carl Foss stood against the port railing, scanning the horizon. Even though the day was now clear and the ship was near the coast, he recalled, "*Lusitania*'s speed did not increase."[10]

The blare of the foghorn had also roused Charles Lauriat earlier that Friday. "I turned over and took another snooze," he recalled, "for there was no use in getting up if it was foggy and disagreeable." Finally, around noon, he dressed and took to the deck for a quick stroll. He noticed "that we were not going anywhere near top speed" and "wondered at our loafing along at this gentle pace." Scanning the horizon, he enjoyed the "light wind, a smooth sea, and bright sunshine"; in the distance, he could see "the good old Irish coast." "If a German submarine really meant business," he thought, "she would have to wait weeks for a more ideal chance than the present weather conditions. With a flat, unbroken sea, such as that around us, the periscope of a submarine could certainly carry a long distance."[11]

George Kessler had endured "a very sleepless night"; the siren interrupted any efforts to nap. Finally, he got up and retreated to the Smoking Room for an early game of bridge. While he was there, a steward announced that the numbers for the ship's daily Pool Auction were to be posted. "For the previous two days," he recalled, "the mileage was 506 and 501, and on Thursday the mileage was 488." He heard the steward announce twenty numbers, "from 480–499. I thought it would be a grand speculation to buy the lowest number as we were going so slow. I did buy it, and paid $100." The pot, he remembered, was between $300 and $350. Kessler's gambit paid off: when the steward announced the run, his low number won the sweeps.[12]

More people appeared as luncheon drew near. In her cabin, Dorothy Conner carefully dressed in a fawn-colored tweed suit and set out for the Dining Saloon.[13] Passengers spotted Alfred Vanderbilt, dressed in a pinstriped suit and looking dapper.[14] "Hot and sweaty" from a vigorous game of medicine ball on deck, Robert Timmis and his friend Ralph Moodie decided to cool down with "a couple of cocktails" before eating.[15] Kessler met Edgar Gorer on deck, and asked if he would join him for luncheon; saying he "wanted to take five minutes of exercise," the art dealer agreed to rendezvous with Kessler in the Dining Saloon.[16] But apprehension remained beneath this apparently pleasant surface: Elisabeth Lassetter entered the Dining Saloon clutching her jewelry box, afraid to leave it in her cabin should disaster strike.[17]

At one, the ship's bugler sounded the call to luncheon. It was a fine day; when he entered the Dining Saloon, Michael Byrne—along with many other passengers—saw that the "portholes were all open."[18] "A spirit of animated, intimate, spontaneously confidential sociability," said Oliver Bernard, seemed to permeate the room.[19] Theodate Pope and Edwin Friend entered just as Bernard was paying his wine bill; the amount of coins he received as change, he grimly joked, would give him something to "hang on to in the event of an explosion."[20] Theodate and Friend took their places and chatted with their tablemates. One man had just ordered ice cream for dessert; as a steward ran back to fetch a clean spoon, Theodate heard her fellow diner joke that he'd hate for the ship to be torpedoed before he could enjoy his dessert.[21]

Lusitania was due to arrive in Liverpool early the following morning. Everything would be in a frenetic rush, and officers asked passengers who had steamer trunks in their cabins to pack them so that they could all be taken up on deck by ten that evening. Howard Fisher decided he would rather "get it over with," and spent the morning sorting his belongings. As a result, he and Dorothy Conner were late to luncheon. Margaret Mackworth and her father were just finishing their meal, but lingered as Fisher and Dorothy ordered squab and chatted about the voyage.[22] All the worry over submarines and talk of attack now seemed ridiculous; in fact, Dorothy complained, the trip had been dull. In the few hours they had left before reaching Liverpool, she jokingly said, she still hoped that there might be "some sort of thrill going up the Channel."[23]

In her cabin, Belle Naish "started to put on a pretty frock for luncheon," decided to save the dress for later, and went to fetch a tray for her husband. On the way, she went out on deck. "The day was fine," she remembered. "It was more than fine. It was glorious, with air so warm women went without their wraps on deck." Standing in the Second Class Dining Saloon, she noticed that "everybody was happy because of the radiant weather, and the idea that they were nearing land and safety."[24] Down the corridor, Phoebe Amory enjoyed a bath, hoping "to increase my appetite." She did not have time to dress properly before the bell signaled the second luncheon service; not wanting to miss her meal, she hastily flung a raincoat over her negligee and raced to her place at the table.[25]

Passengers had been certain that the Admiralty would send an escort to safely shepherd *Lusitania* through the danger zone; Captain Turner had said as much at the previous night's concert, but it was another of his many obfuscations. He didn't expect an escort: "the Admiralty never troubles to send out to meet the *Lusitania*," he had told reporters before leaving New York. "They only look after the ships that are bringing the big guns over."[26] This wasn't quite correct: on at least two previous occasions the Admiralty *had* provided *Lusitania* with an escort. In November 1914, the Admiralty ordered the battleship *Princess Royal* to escort *Lusitania* when she sailed from Liverpool to New York. And, in March of 1915, they had ordered two destroyers dispatched from Milford Haven, on the west coast of Britain, to meet *Lusitania* as she approached the war zone. This attempt was less than successful: the destroyers failed to meet the liner, as her then master, Captain Dow, refused to acknowledge wireless messages for fear of exposing his location to lurking submarines.[27]

Turner seemed curiously uninterested in the question. He didn't request an escort and left it up to the Admiralty. "It's their business, not mine," he declared.[28] Albert Bestic, *Lusitania*'s junior third officer, thought that it was "a pity" that "no protecting escort was sent," saying, "Even one destroyer encircling the liner as she entered the danger zone would have minimized the danger."[29]

Providing an escort for a merchant vessel or passenger liner immediately stripped the ship of its protected status under the Cruiser Rules. Any vessel accompanied by such an armed escort could be freely, and legally, attacked under international law.[30]

Yet the Admiralty had done it before. The nearest destroyers that could match *Lusitania*'s speed were bottled up a hundred miles away at Milford Haven on the western coast of Wales. They had just returned to port and were now refueling to escort troop transports and freighters carrying valuable war matériel. Rear Admiral Horace Hood had a ramshackle collection of fishing smacks, torpedo boats, and obsolete cruisers in his Queenstown Coast Patrol; these were deemed too old and too slow to provide adequate protection.[31] In the end, and even in the face of the German notice and the sinking of three vessels in *Lusitania*'s direct navigational path, the Admiralty did nothing.

Without an escort, it was up to Captain Turner to employ all measures at his disposal to safeguard *Lusitania*; in this respect, he failed miserably. He pored over the latest messages from the Admiralty in London. He'd had two rather ominous warnings the previous evening, sent by the Admiralty to all British ships after the sinking of the *Earl of Lathom* off the Old Head of Kinsale. The first, received just before eight, read: "Submarines active off South Coast of Ireland." Turner acknowledged receipt. Just thirty minutes later, a second message arrived: "Between South Foreland and Folkestone keep within two miles of shore and pass between the two light vessels. Take Liverpool pilot at bar. Avoid headlands; pass harbors at full speed; steer mid-channel course. Submarines off Fastnet." Curiously, neither message mentioned the three British ships that had been sunk in the area within the last twenty-four hours.[32]

Cunard was not allowed to contact *Lusitania* directly, but on the morning of May 7, Alfred Booth, its chairman, asked an Admiralty official in Liverpool to warn Turner of the danger.[33] After a brief query from Vice Admiral Sir Charles Coke in Queenstown to ascertain which version of the Merchant Vessel Code *Lusitania* was using, Turner received two messages. The first, just before noon, read: "Submarines active in southern part of Irish Channel, last heard of twenty miles south of Coningbeg Light Vessel."[34] A second message followed at 12:40: "Submarines five miles south of Cape Clear, proceeding west when sighted at 10AM."[35]

Cape Clear was now behind him; if the submarine in this last message was indeed heading west, Turner believed that the danger was behind him. But Turner couldn't be sure of this, nor how many submarines might be lurking off the Irish coast. These warnings, coupled with the previous evening's messages, should have spurred him to alarmed action. Instead, he stumbled through that morning and early afternoon with a series of incredible, ultimately fatal decisions that ignored nearly every instruction he had received. The Admiralty had advised Turner to steer a mid-channel navigational course; instead, he steamed *Lusitania* less than fifteen miles off the Irish coast. Nor did he have a sense of urgency: even when the fog cleared, he kept *Lusitania* at a steady 18 knots—3 less than she was capable of doing with one boiler room shut down.[36] He later excused this lack of speed by saying that he had wanted to arrive outside Liverpool for early the following morning, at a time when darkness would lend him cover from any waiting submarine and the high tide would allow him to continue to port without having to stop and pick up a pilot.[37] Yet such diversionary tactics—had he followed other orders—would have proved unnecessary.

One of these other orders that Turner admitted to receiving and ignoring involved the tactic of steering his ship on an evasive course, or zigzagging, when traveling through waters known to be active with submarines.[38] Turner later professed confusion over the instructions, complaining that no one had explained the action to him.[39] While the maneuver wasn't yet routinely deployed by merchant vessels, it also wasn't unknown: six months earlier, the captain of *Olympic* had zigzagged to evade a submarine attack.[40] But Turner clearly didn't understand: he later insisted that he thought he should zigzag only *after* he spotted a submarine—by which time evasive action would be too late.[41] Zigzagging would have made it extremely difficult for a slower U-boat to get into position to launch a successful attack; it would also have allowed *Lusitania* to travel at full speed and still arrive in Liverpool when Turner wanted.

Inexplicably, Turner—the weathered old sea captain, who had plied this route at the helm of numerous Cunard vessels—had become lost earlier that morning. Fog obscured Fastnet Rock, a navigational landmark off the southwestern tip of Ireland, and Turner continually misidentified familiar headlands when they came into view. Only at 1:40 P.M., after spotting the banded lighthouse atop the Old Head of Kinsale, did he know exactly where he was—just outside the entrance track to Queenstown harbor.[42]

The Admiralty had advised Turner to avoid headlands; he ignored the warning. A few minutes after spotting the Old Head of Kinsale, Turner actually ordered *Lusitania* swung inland, toward the familiar headland: she was so close to shore that passengers came out on deck to get better looks at the houses and trees.[43] Many passengers noticed the sharp turn. Charles Jeffery "observed by the vessel's wake that she had made a sudden alteration in course."[44] Carl Foss had been standing on the port side of the deck, enjoying the sunshine, when he was sure that he spotted a submarine roughly a mile in the distance. "I called the attention of other passengers on deck to the submarine," he recalled, "got my glasses from the Smoking Room to look at her, and also handed them to one of the sailors to examine the war craft, after which it dived below." Within a few minutes, Foss noted, *Lusitania* turned: he was sure that "the Captain on the bridge had also seen the submarine and had altered his course to avoid risk of being torpedoed."[45]

No submarine, though, had been reported to the bridge. Turner now made two last, critically fatal decisions. The Admiralty had instructed him to pass harbors at full speed; as *Lusitania* steamed toward the approach to Queenstown harbor, Turner kept her at 18 knots.[46] And then, traveling through waters where submarines were reportedly lurking, he decided he wanted to take a four-point navigational bearing—an unnecessary and foolhardy measure that slowed *Lusitania* and kept her on a straight line as she steamed through the war zone.[47]

There was no Admiralty escort, but another vessel did shadow Turner as he edged *Lusitania* along the Irish coast. At 1:20 that Friday afternoon, Walther Schwieger was suddenly called to the conning tower of U-20 as she rode the blue waters off Ireland. With the earlier fog, he had abandoned hopes of catching and sinking any other vessels; now, something had been spotted some ten miles in the distance. Schwieger peered through binoculars and aimed at the mass of smoke against the blue sky. At first, he thought that the distant image on the horizon must belong to several vessels, for he saw "a forest of masts and stacks." As the image steamed closer and came into focus, he saw that it was "a great steamer."[48] At 1:25 he ordered U-20 to dive; hatches thudded shut and were sealed, the warning siren rang, and a hiss rumbled through the submarine as water filled her diving tanks. Within a few seconds, the sunshine of the surface had disappeared.[49]

Schwieger ordered his crew to make for the possible target at his top underwater speed of 9 knots as he followed her progress through the periscope. She flew no flags, and her funnels were painted a dark charcoal color. Schwieger called on his pilot, Rudolf Lanz, a man, he said, who knew "all English ships from their structure, and can also state at once at what speed they usually run."[50] They were still too far away to read any name, but a quick scan through his manuals would have revealed that the distant, four-stacked profile must belong to one of a handful of ships: *Lusitania, Mauretania, Aquitania,* or *Olympic.* All were British liners, and the first two were listed in official British registries as auxiliary cruisers of the Royal Navy. Yet only one, *Lusitania,* was known to be sailing through these waters, keeping to its announced route and timetable. Although Schwieger never admitted it, he must have realized that his target was the Cunard liner.

Walther Schwieger now faced a momentous decision as he watched this approaching prize. Such liners could be converted to troop transports to help the Allied war effort; they regularly carried munitions through the war zone meant to kill German soldiers. Surfacing and firing a warning shot from his deck gun risked his submarine and the lives of his crew. Schwieger knew that British merchant vessels had been ordered to ram any U-boats; according to Churchill's boasts in Parliament and various newspaper accounts, many of these vessels, including liners, were armed with large guns capable of destroying his submarine.[51] In the end, the Admiralty's slow erosion of the Cruiser Rules left an efficient and loyal officer of the German Imperial Navy like Schwieger with only one option: to strike without warning.

Still, the ship was steaming away from Schwieger, in a line parallel to the Irish coast. Although only two miles now separated the vessels, Schwieger thought that pursuit was futile. The steamer, he estimated, must be going some 22 knots. "I had no hope now, even if we hurried at our best speed, of getting near enough to attack her," he recalled. But then the liner made another turn, as Turner set her on a straight course to take his four-point bearing. "She was coming directly at us," Schwieger said. "She could not have steered a more perfect course if she had deliberately tried to give us a dead shot."[52]

Seconds ticked by as Schwieger waited until he was positioned to strike the vessel amidships. His war diary records the grim details: at 2:10 P.M., when he was some four hundred yards away, he gave the order to fire. U-20 shuddered as a gyroscopic torpedo, loaded with its lethal warhead of over three hundred pounds of explosive, burst out of its forward tube and flew at some 38 knots roughly ten feet below the surface. Now Schwieger could only watch as the trail of foam streaked toward the unsuspecting vessel's starboard side.[53]

CHAPTER THIRTEEN

"The sea," Oliver Bernard remembered, "was like an opaque sheet of polished indigo, absolutely still, and the horizon undisturbed by sail or smoke of any other vessels as far as the eye could reach." *Lusitania* was going so slow that he thought she had actually stopped. The idea irritated him; everything, he mused, seemed so futile. It wasn't just the ship's lack of progress but life in general. If only he could believe in God or an eternal life, he thought, he would feel better. But as he stood on deck, he couldn't shake the feeling that "life is not really worth living."[1]

"A flicker of sunlight" interrupted Bernard's ruminations: at first, he thought it was a porpoise.[2] For a few seconds, he watched "spellbound" as the "long, white streak of foam" cut through the dark water toward the ship.[3] It wasn't a porpoise: he instinctively knew what he had seen, and he closed his eyes in dread resignation. In a few seconds the torpedo struck. "The impact was terrific," he recalled, "I could feel the ship reel, as if struck by a huge hammer." Almost immediately, "a terrific explosion" threw "a great column of coal dust, water, and debris" over the deck. "It reminded me of the picture showing mine explosions in the trenches at the Front."[4] Looking forward, he saw black smoke near the first funnel mingled with steam from the ship's ventilators and coal "as if from a volcanic eruption."[5]

Just behind Bernard, Harold Boulton sat in the Veranda Café, enjoying coffee and a cigarette as he chatted with a friend. In 1907, the Veranda Café had been an innovation, designed to resemble "a particularly charming corner in your favorite country club, or an enclosed veranda in your Oyster Bay house."[6] Large windows to port and starboard gave views of the ocean, while the entire aft wall could be opened to the deck in warm weather. Wicker chairs and tables, potted palms, hanging plants, walls of white trellis covered in ivy, and a large skylight gave the room a pleasant, airy atmosphere.[7]

A skylight meant to wash the room with light now seemed a dangerously fragile barrier as "a huge quantity of dirty water and wreckage" came crashing down from the explosion. Boulton was thunderstruck: just a few seconds before, his companion had declared, "The Germans would not dare to torpedo us!" He had scarcely finished speaking when Boulton heard a "terrific explosion, followed almost simultaneously by another. The noise was deafening. The whole ship seemed to be lifted up." Another sound soon replaced that caused by the falling wreckage: Boulton heard "the screams of the Second Class passengers below."[8]

Angela and Michael Papadopoulos had also been enjoying coffee in the Veranda Café when the impact came. "Immediately" after the first explosion, Angela heard a second, "and debris began to rain down all around us." Her husband, already nervous, jumped up in panic as *Lusitania* took a dramatic lurch to the starboard side, but Angela had the presence of mind to rush to their cabin for lifebelts. "I cannot say how I dared to retrieve them," she wrote.[9]

"Like the boom of a cannon," was how passenger Isaac Lehmann remembered the explosion. "They have got us at last!" he shouted, and rushed from the Smoking Room out onto the deck. Peering over the water, he was sure that he saw the wake of another torpedo, heading for the ship.[10] In a few seconds, *Lusitania* again shuddered and rocked beneath his feet. He thought that the two explosions, separated by perhaps "less than a minute," sounded quite different, and differed in intensity; the second, he said, shook the liner "like a leaf."[11] Charles Jeffery likened the impact to how "a train might shake if the locomotive was suddenly stopped." He thought *Lusitania* had probably struck a mine or run aground: "It never occurred to me that something so horrible would be done as to torpedo this defenseless ship," he later mused.[12]

The last, long afternoon aboard *Lusitania* was playing itself out in genteel fashion for passengers gathered in her First Class Lounge when the explosions interrupted coffee and convivial conversation. It was, said Laura Ryerson, "a jarring noise, not loud"; the impact rattled the delicate china cups and saucers atop tables.[13] Frederick Orr-Lewis, drinking coffee with Lady Allan and her daughters, Frances Stephens, and Dorothy Braithwaite, remembered that the sound came "like a bolt from the blue."[14] Robert Holt, sitting nearby reading a novel, heard "a dull crash. Immediately the *Lusitania* leaned over on its right side." As people fled the Lounge for the decks, he said, there was "no panic, but a lot of confusion."[15]

Robinson Pirie, "stretched out on a couch in the Lounge," felt the ship "tremble, and the listing was so quick that I had to get out by grasping the arms of chairs and tables. The room was full, most of the inmates thrown down or stumbling to the low side."[16] Mary and Ogden Hammond, celebrating their eighth wedding anniversary, felt *Lusitania* tremble "violently" with two explosions, separated by perhaps thirty seconds.[17] Rushing out onto the deck, they heard an officer shouting, "Go back, no danger!"[18] The

Hammonds were sure he was wrong: the list was so bad that it was difficult to stand, and Ogden, at least, feared the worst. "I started to return to my stateroom on D Deck to get lifebelts," he recalled, "but my wife refused to let me leave her."[19]

William Adams, a nineteen-year-old First Class passenger hoping to join the fighting in Europe, said, "The ship shook very violently. For all I knew, she might have gone ashore, it was so violent." He heard debris crashing down above the Lounge, and ran out of the room. Like Lehmann, he, too, thought he saw the wake of another torpedo. In a few seconds, there was another "loud explosion" and a geyser of water raining down on the deck.[20]

Jessie Taft Smith had been composing a letter in *Lusitania's* Reading and Writing Room when the ship "seemed to lift" and shudder beneath her. She made her way into the corridor toward her cabin to fetch her lifebelt: "I was told not to hurry as there was no danger," she remembered.[21] Having practiced donning her lifebelt, she made quick work of it and set off for the deck—forgetting her husband's mechanical plans that had brought her to this voyage; passing down the corridors, she was sure that "many people were caught in their staterooms. Evidently they shared my feelings that if struck, the ship would stay up for a long time." The list made it difficult to walk; she fell against one man, who seemed more interested in berating her than in assisting her. With a quick apology, she got up and hurried to the deck.[22]

"We had all imagined that the attempt would be made in the Irish Sea during our last night," Margaret Mackworth recalled. As she walked out of the Dining Saloon with her father, David Thomas glibly commented, "I think we might stay up on deck tonight, to see if we get our thrill." Neither felt much like climbing four flights of the Grand Staircase and headed for one of the elevators; just as they approached, Margaret heard "a dull, thud-like, not very loud, but unmistakable explosion." Almost instinctively, they stepped away from the elevator; "somehow," she remembered, "the stairs seemed safer."[23]

Curious, David Thomas ran to look out of a porthole, but his daughter decided not to linger. "I had days before made up my mind," she recalled, "that if anything happened one's instinct would be to make straight for the boat deck." Instead, she went to her cabin to collect lifebelts. "As I ran up the stairs, the boat was already heeling over."[24] As she went, she thought to herself, "I wonder I'm not more frightened?" The journey to her B Deck cabin, clutching the rail to avoid falling and the increasing chaos she saw, changed her mind: "I'm beginning to get frightened," she mused, "but I mustn't let myself." In the corridor, she collided with a stewardess, and "wasted a minute or so making polite apologies" before the ridiculousness of the scene and a sense of panic set in. She managed to retrieve lifebelts but, by the time she came out on deck, Margaret's father had disappeared.[25]

Passengers had taken to the decks to enjoy the sunshine and views of the Irish coast. "Look, there's a torpedo!" Thomas Home heard someone shout. "I saw an amber colored streak heading straight toward us," he recalled, "and only turned to run when the water thrown by the force of the explosion was high overhead." He was too late: "water mixed with ashes and cinders and wreckage caught me. I was struck by it above the heel of my left foot, cutting through my boot and injuring the back tendons." In "considerable pain," he limped toward the port side of the ship.[26] Michael Byrne had been smoking one of his three hundred cigars as he strolled the deck; stopping just before the starboard wing bridge, he looked out over the water and spotted "what I thought was a porpoise, but not seeing the usual jump of the fish, I knew it was a submarine. It disappeared and in about two minutes I saw the torpedo coming towards our ship, leaving a streak of white foam in its wake." The noise of the impact, he said, was "like a million ton hammer hitting a steel boiler, a hundred feet high and a hundred yards in length." The subsequent explosion seemed to lift "the bows of the ship out of the water. Everything amidships seemed to part and give way up to the superstructure of the boat deck where I was standing."[27]

James Brooks of Bridgeport, Connecticut, was on his way to Europe as a representative of the Weed Chain Company.[28] To this point, he thought, the trip had been "as pleasant as one could hope."[29] Shortly after he sailed, a friend asked his wife, Ruth, in New York, "Is Jay crazy? Didn't he see the notice in the papers this morning?" She'd admitted they had not seen the German warning; immediately, her thoughts turned uneasily to their four young sons.[30]

Now on deck, the forty-one-year-old Brooks saw two friends, who called over and asked if he wanted to join them in a game of shuffleboard. "I offered to watch rather than break the twosome," he recalled. As he stood, he happened to look out and spotted a torpedo. He ran to the railing, "expecting to see the infernal machine strike near the front stack." He watched as it "cut through the bow of the starboard side, just like you push your finger through tissue paper. In a second, hell broke loose."[31] A "dull explosion" shuddered through the liner; a plume of debris, water, and coal mushroomed over the deck just behind the bridge; afraid of injury, Brooks rushed toward shelter but the water knocked him to the deck. As he got to his feet and ran along the deck, "almost immediately" there was a second, "rumbling" explosion, "entirely different from the first," and clouds of steam and dust erupted from the vents.[32]

James Houghton had been in his cabin when the explosions came. Rushing out onto the tilting deck, he heard an officer shout that they had been torpedoed.[33] He found Marie Depage standing with his Harvard friend Richard Freeman by the railing. Both,

Houghton recalled, were "covered with spray and soot." Freeman "was immensely pleased" at having seen the torpedo, "and was laughing and joking about it and recounting the experience to anybody who asked about it."[34] Seeing that Marie Depage had no lifebelt, Houghton took off his and placed it around her shoulders.[35]

After winning the ship's pool, George Kessler was enjoying a cigar as he waited for Edgar Gorer to finish his walk and join him for a late luncheon. To Kessler's "astonishment," he saw "the wash of a torpedo, indicated by a snake-like churn of the surface of the water," followed by a "thud" that shook the vessel. Within seconds, confused passengers swarmed over the deck in shock. Most, he thought, "were wondering what was the matter, few really believing what it proved to be."[36]

Further along the deck, Charles Lauriat was chatting with Elbert and Alice Hubbard. They spoke about the trip and about Hubbard's "unlikely" hopes of landing an interview with the Kaiser in *Who Lifted the Lid off Hell?*[37]

As soon as he said this, there was "a heavy, rather muffled sound" and the ship "trembled" beneath them. Lauriat saw "a shower of coal and steam and some debris hurled into the air between the second and third funnels." A second explosion quickly followed: "the sound was quite different," Lauriat recalled. As *Lusitania* listed toward starboard, Lauriat suggested that the Hubbards go to their staterooms to fetch lifebelts. But Hubbard "stayed by the rail, affectionately holding his arm around his wife's waist, and both seemed unable to act."[38] Lauriat peered over the side of the ship. "I don't like the looks of this," he told the couple. "She is listing too much. You stay right here until I get back in about five minutes. I am going down to my stateroom after some life preservers."[39]

Walking the deck with Edwin Friend, Theodate Pope noted that

Lusitania was going so slow that she thought the engines had stopped. Looking out across the water, "a marvelous blue and very dazzling in the sunlight," she said, "How could the officers ever see a periscope there?" Suddenly, the impact came; she likened the sound to "an arrow, entering the canvas and straw of a target, magnified a thousand times," rapidly followed by another "dull" explosion from somewhere below. "By Jove, they've got us!" Friend cried out, slamming his fist against his hand. They ran into a small corridor just outside the Smoking Room to escape the water and debris raining down on the deck; as they entered, *Lusitania* lurched to starboard, hurling them against the wall. Stepping back out into the sunlit afternoon, Theodate saw that "the deck suddenly looked very strange, crowded with people," including two women who "were crying in a pitifully weak way." As they made their way through "the crush of people coming and going," Theodate saw Marie Depage. Her eyes, she recalled, "were wide and startled, but brave." When Theodate finally found her maid, she could only say, "Oh, Robinson!"[40]

In the First Class Dining Saloon, after a program that included "The Blue Danube," *Lusitania*'s band had just ended a vigorous encore of "Tipperary" to entertain the diners.[41] Cellist Handel Hawkins immediately stopped; although passengers rushed toward the exits, he saw "no panic."[42] Most diners seemed stunned: the shock was so severe that glass in portholes—at least those that were closed—shattered and showered over the carpet.[43] "It all happened so quickly," Josephine Burnside said, "that I can hardly remember it."[44] "I had just finished making a collection for the musicians," Josephine Brandell recalled, "and sat down to finish my lunch." The explosion convulsed the ship, and everyone "rushed for the stairs. I heard someone shouting to be calm." But Josephine was "simply horrified with fright."[45] Francis Jenkins, sharing her table, recalled how she clung to him as they made their way to the deck. "This," he said, "took perhaps some five minutes, as the boat listed very badly."[46]

Robert Timmis, having enjoyed his cocktails with Ralph Moodie, was paying his bill when the torpedo hit. "It was not a severe blow," he remembered. "It was more a penetrating thrust, as though the torpedo must have gone through the ship."[47] "They have got us!" Moodie cried out. As they fled the room, a steward shouted, "Steady, gentlemen, steady!" The list made ascending the Grand Staircase difficult, and Timmis helped a lady climb to the deck, one hand on the railing and the other holding her tight against his side. On reaching A Deck, Timmis struggled to his cabin: he found a lifebelt—there had been two, but another passenger had opened the door and taken the second.[48]

Dorothy Conner and Howard Fisher had just finished their squab when they heard "a rather dull sound, like a soft blast, a slight shock," as he recalled. "What is that?" Dorothy cried out. "That," he told her, "is what we came after, a torpedo! We must go on deck!" To Fisher, it seemed as if "everyone" was "pouring forward" in an attempt to reach the deck. "Everything was confusion," and he didn't see any officers to direct passengers.[49] Soon, Margaret Mackworth ran up, asking if she could remain with them until she found her father.[50]

The second sitting in *Lusitania*'s Second Class Dining Saloon was just beginning when the explosions came. Phoebe Amory, clad in her raincoat, saw a steward put a bowl of soup before her; this didn't appeal to her. Instead, "It occurred to me that I would like a salad." She was just about to ask the steward to switch out the two dishes "when there came the most terrible crash, which seemed to tear everything to pieces, and to rend the ship asunder."[51]

Young Barbara Anderson remembered being with her mother, Emily, on the upper level of the Second Class Dining Saloon. "I got out of my chair," she recalled, "and stood next to my mother and looked down through the railing at all those people having lunch at the long tables."[52] Curiously she had no memory of the explosions, merely that "great chaos" erupted in the room; unaware of the danger, she still clutched her spoon engraved *Lusitania*. Apparently assistant purser William Harkness spotted Emily struggling to carry her daughter through the crowd; he hoisted the girl in his arms and led them up and out onto the deck near the stern.[53]

Carl Foss was trying to enjoy his lunch; after spotting what he took for a submarine earlier, though, he was "keyed up" and found it difficult to relax. Suddenly, he heard "a heavy, dull sound, which was followed by a violent trembling." He thought that the explosion had "a deadening effect" on his fellow travelers: they "seemed to be stunned by the shock."[54] Instinct kicked in and, "in a more or less orderly and calm way," passengers ran to their cabins to retrieve lifebelts or made their ways out onto the deck.[55] A few tables away, William Meriheina "felt a heavy explosion up forward, near the First Cabin section, a grinding and a ripping. The boat immediately lurched to the side." Passengers quickly left the room—he saw "very little panic; individuals moaned and cried," but there was "just the suggestion of a rush for the exits." Meriheina ran toward his cabin but abruptly stopped when he saw water flooding through open portholes; instead, he opened an adjacent cabin door, took out lifebelts, and headed for the deck.[56]

"There was a rush for the stairs," Phoebe Amory recalled, as the Second Class Dining Saloon suddenly emptied. She had to push her way through slower groups ascending the staircase as the cry went up, "We have been torpedoed!" "I realized for the first time that we were doomed," she said. An officer kept shouting, "Keep cool!" as passengers pushed and struggled up the tilting stairs; Phoebe fell three times before finally reaching the top. By this time, the list was so heavy "I feared that we were turning over."[57]

At the moment of impact, Ian Holbourn had quickly glanced across the Second Class Dining Saloon; young Avis Dolphin sat with nurse Hilda Ellis and Sarah Smith, looking on in bewilderment as plates, silver, and crystal slid from the tables and smashed against the carpet.[58] He struggled over to Avis and picked her up in his arms, saying, "Don't panic, come to my cabin. I'll find you some lifejackets."[59] Having found three lifebelts, Holbourn, Avis recalled, "put me in one, and put one on Hilda and tried to force Miss Smith to take one, but she wouldn't, because she said he had a wife and three children. So he put it on himself."[60] As they stood by the railing, Avis recalled, Holbourn pointed "out the distant land to me" and told her that it was Ireland.[61]

At her husband's prompting, Belle Naish had gone out onto the Second Class promenade to enjoy the view of Ireland when "the shock of the explosion shook the vessel."[62] "I saw a great volume of dirty water rise," she remembered. "It was filled with broken iron and splinters of wood." The first thing she noticed was "the deepest, most awful silence." Everyone seemed stunned. Then, as people began to realize what had happened, "the air was filled with curses. The Germans were damned in shrieks." Her one desperate thought was to reach her husband, but the rush of passengers up the stairs and out onto the decks slowed her progress. Finally, she got to the cabin, where Theodore tied a lifebelt over her shoulders and helped her back up to the deck; although she had practiced taking the same route through the ship, the list and panic were so confusing that Belle lost her way and finally came out on the port side of the Boat Deck.[63]

In her cabin, nurse Alice Lines was looking after baby Audrey and five-year-old Stuart, two of the four children of Warren and Amy Pearl. "While I was feeding her," she said, "there was a terrific bang—instinct told me what it was—I just picked up the shawl and the baby with it." Stuart immediately burst into tears, sobbing,

"I don't want to be drowned, I don't want to be drowned!"[64] "I had difficulty in standing," Alice recalled, as she tried to make her way through the liner, the baby in her arms and the little boy holding fast to her skirt.[65] "No matter what happens," she told Stuart, "hang on to me. If I fall down, hang on to me. Don't let go."[66] Holding Audrey, and with Stuart clutching her skirt, she made her way along the corridor and up the staircase, where she met Greta Lorenson, nanny to Amy and Susan Pearl. "What shall I do?" Greta cried out. Alice told her to watch after the children but the rushing crowd soon separated the two women.[67]

Young Virginia Loney had also been in her cabin. "I had no idea what had happened, but joined in the rush for the deck. There, everything was in confusion." She found her father, who "went down to get some lifebelts, and returned with a number, which he distributed around, but did not keep one himself."[68] The impact had hurled Rita Jolivet about her cabin on D Deck, amidst breaking glass and flying toiletries. "Well," she said to herself, "the Germans have got us this time!"[69] Although she had largely ignored worried talk about a possible submarine attack, Rita *had* thought ahead: she told Harold Boulton that she had packed a small, pearl-handled pistol with her belongings. If something happened and she found herself in the water, she would shoot herself rather than drown.[70] She quickly grabbed the pistol, pushed it into her purse, and peered into the corridor: a woman was hastily tying on a life-belt, and Rita grabbed one from her own cabin before making her perilous way up four flights of tilting stairs.[71] On deck, she found her brother-in-law, George Vernon, standing with Charles Frohman and Alfred Vanderbilt. "I didn't think they would do it!" Frohman muttered.[72] The impresario seemed unusually calm and "magnificently courageous" as he nursed a cigar. "Stay where you are," he warned them. "This is going to be a close call. We shall have more chances here than by rushing for the boats."[73]

Back at *Lusitania*'s Veranda Café, Harold Boulton saw "confusion everywhere" in the first minute following the explosions. The shock was overwhelming: even those passengers who had feared the worst seemed stunned now that it had actually come. Boulton wanted his lifebelt, and he wanted to find his friend Frederic Lassetter and his mother; finding their cabin empty, Boulton ran to his own stateroom only to find the door open: another panicked passenger had rifled through the room, taking his lifebelt. The list was so great that Boulton could only walk down the corridor with one foot on the floor and one on the wall; he found a steward at the end of the passage handing out lifebelts, took one, and made his way back to the deck. Once he stumbled and fell by the listing Grand Staircase, landing at the feet of several women. To cover his embarrassment, he asked if he could do anything to help. "Not a thing," came the reply. "We are not going to get excited, but remain calm and stay here. The Captain says the *Lusitania* cannot sink."[74]

Boulton wasn't convinced. At 2:14 P.M., *Lusitania*'s power suddenly failed: cabins and corridors were plunged into darkness as screams and cries for help echoed through the liner.[75] As Boulton ran past the Grand Staircase, he said he saw a horrific scene: passengers trapped between floors in one of the First Class elevators when the power failed.[76] The attendants had run off, and panicked travelers had apparently rushed into at least one of the lifts.[77] Gates designed to open only when the car was in place now trapped passengers in an ornate cage.[78] The gates rattled and shook as "the most distressing cries" for help filled the air, but no one could force open the grilles.[79] Boulton could do nothing; running past, he knew that these unfortunate passengers would be "drowned like rats."[80]

CHAPTER FOURTEEN

Leslie Morton had gone on duty at noon that Friday, taking up his place on the foredeck of *Lusitania*'s starboard bow as an extra lookout.[1] At 2:10, he spotted "a thin streak of foam making for the ship at a rapid speed" some five hundred yards in the distance, followed by the wake of what he took to be a second torpedo. "Torpedoes coming on the starboard side!" he shouted through his megaphone.[2] Morton was supposed to wait until his warning had been acknowledged; instead, he was racing across the deck to tell his brother John when he felt "a shock all over the ship. It shook me off my feet."[3] This "tremendous explosion," he recalled, was "followed instantly by a second one."[4]

No one heard Morton's warning: a critical thirty seconds passed before Thomas Quinn, high up in the crow's nest, grabbed his voice tube and reported to the bridge.[5] "There's a torpedo coming, Sir!" Captain Turner heard Second Officer Percy Hefford shout; almost immediately, *Lusitania* shuddered from the explosion.[6] As "smoke and steam" rose over the ship, Turner felt a second explosion; this, he thought, "may possibly have been internal."[7]

Watching through his periscope, Schwieger saw his torpedo hit the "starboard side, right behind the bridge."[8] With massive force, the projectile pierced the hull, buckling steel plates and loosening rivets as it exploded, leaving an ugly, yawning hole of perhaps ten feet by twenty feet and shooting a geyser of water and debris into the sky. As *Lusitania* moved forward, the debris rained back down with such force that it tore Lifeboat No. 5, hanging over the starboard side, from its davits and sent it crashing into the sea.[9]

Precisely where the torpedo hit has always been a subject of some controversy. From Schwieger's account, it seems to have struck *Lusitania* somewhere below the bridge, at a critical point where bulkheads separated Boiler Room No. 1 from a transverse forward cross bunker and a longitudinal bunker used for reserve coal along the ship's starboard side. The sea rapidly flooded through the hull; bunkers meant to shield the ship's machinery from possible damage now concentrated the flooding on the starboard side, causing an almost immediate list of some 15 degrees, a situation exacerbated by *Lusitania*'s great height. The sea streamed through open watertight doors, flooding into the forward bunker and cargo holds and pulling *Lusitania* down by the bow; it swept aft, almost immediately spilling into the forward boiler room. The ship's continued progress through the sea forced even more water into the breach and added to the rapid flooding, as did numerous portholes that had been left open.[10]

Schwieger clearly saw the two explosions, "rather a small detonation, and instantly afterward a much heavier one."[11] He described this as "unusually heavy," with a cloud of debris reaching back "far beyond the first funnel." Steam, coal dust, and more debris shot through the ship's ventilators and over the decks; Schwieger thought that coal or a boiler might have exploded. The ship, he recorded, "heels over to starboard very quickly." The list was so bad that Schwieger thought the vessel might capsize at any moment.[12]

The second explosion only added to an already fatal situation. Whatever the cause, it likely opened even more of the hull to the sea. In eighteen minutes *Lusitania* would be gone, as water flooded through the forward part of the ship and began to pull her down by the bow. It also left *Lusitania*'s steam lines, which controlled her rudder and regulated pressure from the boiler rooms to the turbines, fatally compromised.[13]

This Captain Turner learned soon enough. "Come at once, big list off south head, Old Kinsale," read the emergency signal tapped out in *Lusitania*'s Marconi Room at 2:11 P.M. Stations all along the Irish coast immediately picked up the SOS, as the plea was repeated again and again.[14] Queenstown was some twenty miles away, past the Old Head of Kinsale and around a headland; it was unlikely that the ship could survive such a journey. The Irish coast, though, was close; hoping to beach the ship, Turner ordered Quartermaster Hugh Johnston to swing *Lusitania* toward land. Johnston put the wheel hard over, and *Lusitania* began to turn, but within seconds the hydraulic steering gear suddenly seized up.[15]

Turner then ordered the engines reversed, but this proved impossible: with the explosions, *Lusitania*'s steam pressure fell from 190 to 50 pounds per square inch.[16] Moving inexorably forward, unable to stop or turn, *Lusitania* now began to trace a slow, ever-widening arc through the serene water as passengers swarmed her decks.

Lusitania had no public address system, and the shouted instructions from a few officers could barely be heard above the roar of escaping steam and panicked cries. Oliver Bernard saw a "frantic rush" of stricken passengers. "Where is my husband?" someone shouted, "Where is my child?"[17] Almost immediately, "the noise of hundreds of trampling and rushing feet" drowned out the cries.[18] Coming out on deck, Thomas Slidell noticed "how few Saloon passengers" he saw there. "Somehow, it seemed that when it came to the rough and tumble flight, they were too slow to realize the danger."[19]

George Kessler found the Boat Deck "crowded with passengers, milling about and wondering what was the matter" in the first minute after the attack.[20] After initial confusion, the passengers, according to Captain Turner, seemed "almost calm."[21] People, Michael Byrne thought, "seemed transfixed where they stood."[22] "There was no great excitement, in the real sense of the word," Oliver Bernard recalled. "Most of the women tried hard to keep cool."[23] James Brooks spotted "a few isolated cases" of "hysteria on the part of the women," but otherwise thought that there was little sense of panic.[24] Cellist Handel Hawkins also noticed that "some of the women and children were crying and screaming. But there was no panic. I do not think that the people realized that the ship was going down."[25]

Most people were too shocked to panic. For all the talk of submarines, no one had really imagined that *Lusitania* would be attacked, at least not without any warning. A "strange silence," Albert Bestic said, seemed to hover over the deck. "Small, insignificant sounds, such as the whimper of a child, the cry of a seagull, or the bang of a door assumed alarming proportions."[26] Charles Lauriat saw the "infinite confusion," as "there seemed no one to take command of any one boat."[27] "Surely she cannot sink," passengers assured each other as Leslie Morton ran past them on the deck. He said nothing, but feeling the slant of the deck beneath his feet, he thought *Lusitania* "was doomed."[28] Frederick Orr-Lewis, meanwhile, had marshaled Lady Allan and her daughters, Frances Stephens, and Dorothy Braithwaite out onto the port side of the deck.[29] Slingsby quickly found his master, bringing with him Lady Allan's two maids, Annie Walker and Emily Davis. Marguerite Allan seemed acutely aware of the peril: Slingsby saw her standing at the railing, crying and tightly hugging her daughters. "Don't cry Mama!" one of them shouted. "It's all right now, George has found us and he will know what to do!" Seeing that Lady Allan had no lifebelt, Slingsby placed his own around her shoulders and ran off to find more.[30] Robert Holt soon joined them; Anna Allan, he saw, "gave a woman her lifebelt, and I tied it upon her." Then, realizing that Anna needed one, Holt ran off to find another lifebelt.[31] Things along the port side deck looked bleak: gazing down the ship, Orr-Lewis saw no lifeboats being launched and decided to run across to starboard; as he set off, the ship "gave such a terrible lurch that I came back."[32]

Oliver Bernard found Leslie Mason "panic stricken" standing outside the Veranda Café and assured her, "It's all right now, we go ashore directly so don't worry." But Leslie could not find her husband, Stewart. "Where's my husband?" she cried out over and over again, until Bernard thought that she was hysterical. He grabbed her by the shoulders and roughly shook her. "Pull yourself together and listen to what I'm saying now!" he demanded. "Stay right here, don't move from this spot, and your husband will find you here, surely, as they will be lowering the boats from this side. Do you hear?" When she nodded, he continued: "I'll find some lifebelts in case we need them." Bernard ran below to his cabin, falling as he descended the listing staircase; by the time he returned with lifebelts, Leslie had disappeared.[33]

Lifebelts, in fact, became a prized commodity. Unable or unwilling to retrieve them from their own cabins, many passengers simply pilfered lifebelts from other staterooms; those who did reach their cabins often found the doors open and their own lifebelts gone. With the ship listing so perilously, Carl Foss "did not dare" go below to his cabin for a lifebelt. Yet he saw "stewards and crew, busy putting on lifebelts." According to Foss, they "seemed to be more interested in caring for themselves," and made "no effort to assist the passengers who were frantically looking for lifebelts."[34] James Brooks spotted "about fifteen" members of the crew standing idly by, arms folded, and all wearing lifebelts. Brooks didn't have a lifebelt and wanted one: the seaman he spoke with said he didn't know if there were any more to be had, nor did he offer his. "There had been no effort by the crew," Brooks said, "to distribute life preservers," and he could find none on deck.[35] Witnessing such scenes, Annie Adams later insisted that the behavior of the seamen and stokers "was too terrible for words. I myself saw many instances of their bestiality."[36]

Oliver Bernard came up on deck wearing a lifebelt only to be accosted by a hysterical woman. "Where did you get that, where did you get that?" she screamed at him. Rather than explain, he simply took off his own lifebelt and gave it to her.[37] Even those passengers who managed to find lifebelts, Charles Lauriat saw, had often put them on incorrectly. Never having been shown how to use them, and with the crew offering no help, they had thrust heads through armholes, put them on upside down, or tried to wear them around their waists rather than their shoulders. Lauriat calmly tried to straighten out as many as he could.[38]

Robert Timmis reached the deck with his friend Ralph Moodie; as he looked out over the railing, he saw that the ship was "still moving forward." A woman from Second Class spotted his lifebelt and pleaded with him for it; "I was a strong swimmer in those days," Timmis recalled, "so I gave her mine." Another woman, without a lifebelt, held a baby in her arms; Moodie took his off and adjusted it around them.[39] Thomas Home found himself comforting hysterical mothers separated from their children and wives separated from their husbands. One woman, without a lifebelt, could not find her baby; "I told her it would be all right, and gave her my belt," telling her, "You are all right, go and look for your baby."[40]

Lauriat had struggled to reach his stateroom. Making his way down the corridor, he "realized how acute was the list of the ship," he recalled later. Lauriat had an inside stateroom; with the electricity out, he found the cabin in complete darkness. He groped through the inky space, finding a box of matches and managing to put on a lifebelt; he also retrieved some papers and photographs of his baby—"they were my mascot," he later wrote.[41] As he went, he saw numerous portholes open, threatening to spill water into the ship. By the time he returned to the Boat Deck, walking with one foot against the floor and the other against the wall owing to the list, Elbert and Alice Hubbard had disappeared.[42] Several passengers saw them standing calmly on deck, holding hands, before walking, almost casually, toward the Grand Staircase. After that, no one ever saw them again. Many thought that they had gone into a nearby cabin to die together, rather than be separated in the water when the ship sank.[43] As he roamed the decks, Lauriat spotted an elderly woman, her daughter, and three children— foreign passengers from Third Class—sitting calmly on a collapsible boat, awaiting instructions. They begged for his help in a language Lauriat took for Italian; Lauriat put two lifebelts on the women, and another on a child. It was, Lauriat said, "one of the most pathetic things I remember."[44]

Henry and Annie Adams had managed to retrieve lifebelts from their cabin; she was convinced that the ship would not survive "but my husband was just as sure she could not sink." Their journey to the Boat Deck was harrowing: twice the rushing crowd knocked Henry Adams over. Annie helped him to his feet and dragged him to the port side, climbing "the sloping deck" to reach the railing. Having been pushed, pummeled, and trodden over, Henry "seemed dazed and almost unconscious." Annie put a lifebelt on him, refusing to enter a nearby lifeboat so that she could remain at his side.[45]

GREG KING and PENNY WILSON

From the bridge, Captain Turner ordered that the lifeboats should not be lowered until the ship had at least lost some of its steam and slowed its progress through the water.[46] This took nearly ten minutes, during which time passengers clambered aboard many of the lifeboats and awaited lowering. *Lusitania's* sharp list to starboard now created problems. The previous day, Turner had ordered the lifeboats swung out over the railing. Those on the starboard side, given odd numbers, now hung at an angle from their davits some sixty feet above the water and were separated from the deck by gaps of six or more feet. At five tons each, they were too heavy to be pulled back in and boarding was difficult.[47] Passengers were forced to inch their ways over planks or deck chairs laid between the railing and the rims of the boats, trying to avoid a plunge into the sea below; a few of the more athletic passengers actually jumped the gap to reach the starboard boats.[48] On the port side, the immediate problem was worse, as lifeboats had swung inward and now hung over the deck. It was nearly impossible, as Albert Bestic found, to push them back into position for lowering. Even when this could be done, the boats lay against the ship's hull and were dragged over rivets peppering the steel plating, risking further damage.[49]

Two snubbing chains held the boats steady in rough seas; before launching, the bolt holding the chain to a deck chock had to be knocked out with a mallet. Then the falls, or ropes holding the boat to the davits, could be lowered manually until the boat was flush with the sea. The falls at the bow and stern worked independently from each other, requiring the men lowering the lifeboats to work in tandem to keep them even.[50] But most of *Lusitania's* crew had no experience working the falls and lowering lifeboats. Charles Lauriat saw "no discipline or order" along the port Boat Deck, and "no officer taking charge of the lowering of any one lifeboat."[51] James Brooks complained of the "lack of competent seamen on board," while David Thomas thought that the crew had largely "looked after themselves first."[52] "There was no order maintained," Michael Byrne summarized. "There was no one to tell you to get into this boat or that. It was everybody for himself."[53]

Passengers who got away safely were fortunate—and rare. Alice Lines reached the deck with Stuart still clinging to her skirt and baby Audrey in her arms. She struggled toward a lifeboat and, assisted by several passengers, managed to take a seat; she saw no seamen nearby. The boat was lowered and began to pull away from the side of the ship.[54] A steward literally hurled Jessie Taft Smith into Lifeboat No. 13 on the starboard side as it was being lowered. As it reached the water, she saw that "two thirds of the people in the boat were men."[55] Among the few women were Emily Anderson and her young daughter, Barbara. Having safely brought her to the deck, assistant purser William Harkness had continued to watch over Barbara as she stood, still clutching her engraved spoon, near her mother. "He scooped me up and we both fell together into a boat which was lowering," Barbara remembered. Luckily neither was injured, and Emily Anderson quickly climbed in alongside them.[56]

More often, though, the efforts proved disastrous. Lifeboat No. 1 was successfully lowered, but reached the water as *Lusitania* continued to steam ahead; drifting back along the side of the ship, it found itself directly in the path of No. 3, which landed atop it, crushing its passengers and capsizing both lifeboats.[57] Two more lifeboats, Nos. 10 and 12, also spilled their passengers into the water when seamen lost control of the falls. Lifeboat No. 12 finally fell atop those still alive and struggling in the water.[58]

Many passengers, like George Kessler, valiantly tried to help others into boats and assist in lowering them.[59] They were shocked to find many of the boats in poor condition. "The tackle was utterly stiff from paint and want of use," Oliver Bernard remembered, "and also so complicated that only capable seamen could have handled the boats. I regarded only a few of the men I saw as able seamen."[60] Some lifeboats lacked plugs; oarlocks were rusted, oars were missing, and ropes were frayed.[61] Nor were all of the twenty-six collapsible boats, stowed beneath the regular lifeboats, of much use. These had wooden keels over watertight tanks and canvas sides that would be raised for use.[62] One passenger tried to lift a collapsible boat near the Grand Entrance, but found that it was stuck to its cradle by a thick layer of paint.[63] Even when they were freed, many of the collapsible boats were useless. The metal ribs on many had rusted so badly that the canvas sides could not be pulled up.[64]

Thomas Home watched as a sailor insisted that one lifeboat be lowered without releasing the snubbing chain; a passenger had to stop him before it capsized into the sea. From this, Home thought that the passengers were "more capable than the ship's company."[65] Frightening scenes were repeated all along the deck. William Adams found his father and watched as a lifeboat, loaded mainly with women, fell "sixty or seventy feet into the water," spilling its occupants because "the crew could not work the davits and falls properly, so let them slip out of their hands."[66] Isaac Lehmann saw a cluster of seamen try to lower another boat as a sailor armed with an ax chopped away at the falls. Men on one side lowered away, while those on the other did nothing; the boat slanted at a terrifying angle. Apparently thinking the situation could not be saved, the seamen let go, and the boat and its passengers toppled into the sea.[67]

Albert and Gladys Bilicke had been resting in their Regal Suite after luncheon when "the first torpedo struck," Gladys recalled. "We rushed upon the deck," and saw that lifeboats were being lowered into the water. Albert and Gladys took their seats in a starboard boat with "about fifty other persons" and watched as it inched its way away from the deck down the ship's hull. "Before it reached the water," Gladys said, "it shot down suddenly and plunged beneath the water carrying us with it." Gladys never saw Albert again.[68] Josephine Brandell, too, found herself hurled into the sea when her lifeboat overturned on hitting the water. It was, she said, "too awful. Words cannot describe it." Luckily, Edgar Gorer had "rushed over" to her on deck a few minutes earlier, put a lifebelt around her, and "told me to be brave."[69] Now the lifebelt kept her afloat.

Angela Papadopoulos had fought her way back to the deck from her cabin. "I remember that on leaving the cabin in the darkest gloom," she wrote, "I was forced to move along on all fours until I could find my balance." Someone "pushed" Angela and her husband toward Lifeboat No. 17. Michael boarded first, and an officer "advised me to remove my skirt in case I had to swim." She did so: "At times like this," Angela said, "one must overcome modesty, and so I got into the lifeboat wearing only my petticoat."[70] Ian Holbourn helped Avis Dolphin, her nurse, Hilda Ellis, and the nurse's friend, Sarah Smith, into the same boat; as he let go of her, Holbourn kissed Avis good-bye.[71] "A lot of men jumped in on top of us," Avis recalled, and the falls could not take the added strain.[72] "We heard a noise like a branch snapping coming from above the bridge," Angela said, "and we found ourselves first of all thrown onto the steel of the ship and then into the sea." She caught a last glimpse of her husband before the suction dragged her beneath the surface.[73] Holbourn jumped over the railing, but it was impossible to reach Avis through the wreckage and struggling passengers.[74]

Margaret Mackworth stood with Dorothy Conner and Howard Fisher on the starboard deck, watching as lifeboats spilled their passengers into the sea. Fisher saw a stampede toward a boat:

"men jumped on women and children, trying to get into it." He decided that it was too dangerous to try to enter the lifeboats, and within seconds the group saw the crowded boat fall and spill its unlucky passengers into the sea below.[75] Soon, "a stream of steerage passengers came rushing up from below, and fought their way into the boat nearest us," she recalled. They were, she saw, "white-faced and terrified." People pushed toward the boats; an officer tried to prevent their entry, but "there was no real attempt at order or discipline."[76] Anxiously scanning the deck for any sign of her father, Margaret saw that "the strongest got there first" when it came to the lifeboats, and "the weak were pushed aside. Here and there, a man had his arm round a woman's waist and bore her along with him; but there were no children to be seen—no children could have lived in that throng."[77] As Fisher ran off to find more lifebelts, Margaret turned to Dorothy, saying, "I always thought a shipwreck was a well-organized affair!" Dorothy shot back, "So did I, but I've learnt a devil of a lot in the last five minutes!" Margaret saw one lifeboat capsize while being lowered, spilling the occupants into the water. "We turned away and did not look," she said. "It was not safe to look at horrible things just then." Even though the ship continued sinking, the group made no attempt to enter a lifeboat. "Death," Margaret decided, "would have seemed better than to make part of that terror-infected crowd."[78]

Theodate Pope agreed. She thought that *Lusitania*'s decks "suddenly looked very strange, crowded with people." Several nearby women "were crying in a pitifully weak way." She and Friend watched as a lifeboat filled with passengers was upset and spilled its unfortunate occupants into the water. "We looked at each other," she recalled, "sickened by the sight." *Lusitania* was sinking so quickly that she "feared it would fall on and capsize the small boats." Edwin Friend tried to convince Theodate to enter a boat, though he refused to board as long as any women or children remained on the ship. Neither would leave the other, and so, arms around each other's waists, they made their way toward the stern, "through the crush of people coming and going." If they remained on the ship, Friend decided, they needed lifebelts, and he led Theodate to a nearby cabin, where they managed to retrieve three. Back on deck, Friend tied them around Theodate and her maid, "in hard knots." Then the trio stood in silence, watching the clouds moving against the funnels and trying to guess how many more minutes *Lusitania* might live.[79]

After watching such scenes, Isaac Lehmann ran back to his cabin. Someone, he found, had already been in there and taken his lifebelt.[80] Passengers raiding cabins, lifeboats spilling helpless occupants into the sea, seamen refusing to give up lifebelts— the situation aboard *Lusitania* threatened to spiral into chaos: at any moment, Lehmann was sure, a true panic might erupt. "I don't know what possessed me," he later said, "but I looked in my dress suitcase and got hold of my revolver." Thus armed against the worst, he returned to the deck.[81]

And the worst was playing out. From his periscope aboard U-20, Schwieger could see that he'd inflicted devastatingly fatal damage. He called Rudolf Lanz, his pilot, over to look through the periscope. Until this moment, supposedly, no one aboard the U-20 conclusively knew the identity of the ship they had torpedoed. Lanz peered into the tube, gazed on the scene, and pulled back. "My God," he allegedly shouted, "it's the *Lusitania*!"[82] For a few minutes, Schwieger seemed transfixed. "Great confusion ensues on board," the entry in his war diary read. "The boats are made clear, and some of them are lowered to the water. In doing so, great confusion must have reigned; some boats, full to capacity, are lowered, rushed from above, touch the water with either stem or stern first, and founder immediately."[83]

What went through Schwieger's mind as he watched the tragic scene he had caused? He supposedly once commented that seeing the people struggling in the water "had no more effect on him than if they were a lot of sheep."[84] More sympathetically, he is said to have told a fellow U-boat commander, "It was the most terrible sight I have ever seen." Schwieger was stunned at how rapidly the ship was sinking. He spoke of the "terrible panic" as "desperate people ran helplessly up and down the decks." It "was too horrible to watch." There was nothing he could do: if he surfaced and made for the survivors, he could only pick up a few, and he still had no idea if the vessel was armed and would fire on him. He was also sure that at any moment rescue ships would appear— ships that would not hesitate to attack him.[85] "It would have been impossible for me, anyhow," his log tersely noted, "to fire a second torpedo into this crowd of people struggling to save their lives."[86]

CHAPTER FIFTEEN

Some five minutes after the torpedo struck, *Lusitania* suddenly righted herself: water flooding through her hull had finally reached compartments along the port side, and she began to settle back from her starboard list.[1] People thought that the worst was over: word passed along the crowded decks that the ship was safe. Staff Captain Anderson, Ogden Hammond recalled, "advised us not to be alarmed."[2] A murmur of relief swept through the crowd: disaster had been avoided.

"Don't lower the boats!" Harold Boulton heard Captain Turner shout. "Don't lower the boats! The ship cannot sink, she's all right, she cannot sink! Will the gentlemen kindly assist me in getting the women out of the boats and off the upper deck?"[3] Boulton had just helped Frederic Lassetter's mother, Elisabeth, into a boat; now, he steadied her as she climbed back out.[4]

"What do you wish us to do?" a woman called up to Turner.

"Stay where you are, Madame," Turner answered, "she's all right."

"Where do you get your information?" she asked.

"From the engine room, Madame," Turner shot back in "a rather severe and commanding voice."[5]

A seaman assured Annie Adams, "We're resting on the bottom. We cannot sink."[6] Ogden Hammond heard an officer yell, "There is no danger! Go back! Keep off the deck!"[7] Margaret Mackworth, still waiting with Dorothy Conner for Howard Fisher to return with lifebelts, greeted the news with a relieved sigh. "Well, you've had your thrill all right!" she joked to Dorothy. "I never want another," Dorothy answered.[8]

A woman on deck, Belle Naish saw, had on "a heavy fur coat that reached to the floor. She had put her life preserver over this." "Madame, you must get out of that coat," Theodore warned her. "The fur will sink you." She did so, and he helped her with the lifebelt; another woman, "glassy-eyed, mouth hanging open, and emitting queer sounds," dragged her lifebelt behind her along the deck. "The ship had tipped so far we couldn't keep our footing without taking hold of something," Belle recalled. They watched in horror as a lifeboat spilled passengers into the sea. "I turned faint," Belle said, "and asked Mr. Naish to pinch me, to help me back to consciousness." They made no attempt to board a lifeboat after what they had seen; Theodore promised Belle that he would not force her into one unless there was also room for him. Soon, a seaman came by, assuring them, "She's steady, she'll float for an hour." A few nearby passengers, relieved, sat down on some deck chairs and started to whistle and cheer. Looking down the sloping deck at the ever-rising water, though, Belle knew that *Lusitania* would sink.[9]

Soon enough, *Lusitania* began to list again starboard, now at an even more acute angle, and Annie and Henry Adams had to hold on to the railing to avoid plunging down the length of the deck.[10] The situation grew worse with each passing minute. By now, Oliver Bernard saw, the deck "was crowded with people frantic to get away." A stoker "was reeling about as if drunk, his face a black and scarlet smear, the crown of his head torn open like a spongy, bloody pudding."[11] A sailor turned his ax on a nervous passenger, hacking away at the unfortunate man's back when he tried to enter a lifeboat.[12] And now, from somewhere within the ship, smoke began billowing along corridors as a fire raged below.

❦

Ten minutes after the torpedo's impact, the sea was already lapping around *Lusitania*'s bow and whatever calm had once prevailed on the decks had given way to panic as the situation began to fall apart. Phoebe Amory said, "The screams of the women and children were terrible to hear" as she jumped across the gap between railing and lifeboat. She saw wives "torn from their husbands," and children "separated from their parents," being "handed from man to man and on into the boats." Women, Phoebe insisted, were "fainting and falling to the deck, only to be carried overboard by their own weight." Hurled against the liner's side, her lifeboat overturned its occupants into the water.[13] "By this time," Michael Byrne recalled, "the people were nearly stark mad, and screaming at the top of their lungs."[14]

Passengers continued to rove over the deck in confusion, reminding Margaret Mackworth of "a swarm of bees, who do not know where the queen has gone."[15] Her father, unable to find her, described the last few minutes aboard *Lusitania* as ones of "panic and tumult. Excited men and terrified women ran shouting about the decks. Lost children cried shrilly. Officers and seamen rushed among the panic-stricken passengers, shouting orders and helping the women and children into lifeboats. Women clung desperately to their husbands or knelt on the deck and prayed."[16] "The atmosphere was electric," Albert Bestic said. "Prayers and increasing cries of terror now took the place of that fearsome stillness."[17] As he tried to lower the lifeboats, Leslie Morton heard cries, turmoil, shouts, and sobs—"a horrible and bizarre orchestra of death."[18]

Ogden and Mary Hammond, having failed to find any lifebelts, wandered aft and entered Lifeboat No. 20 on the port side; it wasn't even half full. Just as it was being lowered, one of the sailors "lost his head" and let the falls slip from his hands.[19] The bow plunged forward; Hammond grabbed for the rope and tried to stop the downward momentum, but it tore his hands "to shreds." The boat plummeted sideways, spilling the passengers some sixty feet into the water below.[20] Trixie Witherbee made it into a lifeboat with her young son, Alfred Jr., but it, too, overturned while being lowered, separating mother and son in the sea.

Armed with his revolver, Isaac Lehmann came back up on deck. He saw James McCubbin, *Lusitania*'s purser, who assured him "there was not a chance" that the liner would sink. Although Lehmann now had one of the prized lifebelts, McCubbin ridiculed him for having it on, and insisted that he should remain calm. Lehmann saw fifty or more worried passengers sitting in Lifeboat No. 18 on the port side near the First Class Smoking Room. Several seamen stood idly by, making no effort to lower the boat. Lehmann glanced down the deck; even from here, he could see water just beginning to spill over *Lusitania*'s bow. Convinced that the end was near, he shouted, "Who has got charge of this boat?" A seaman armed with an ax pushed forward, saying that the captain had ordered that no more boats should be lowered. Lehmann waved his gun in the air, shouting, "To hell with the Captain! Don't you see the boat is sinking? And the first man that disobeys my orders to launch the boat I shoot to kill!" No one challenged him, and the boat was loaded with some sixty people. Just at that moment, *Lusitania* "gave an awful lurch, as if foundering," and the lifeboat swung inward when the lines were slack.[21] Robinson Pirie saw the grotesque scene; according to Lehmann, between thirty and forty people, standing on the deck, were crushed against the Smoking Room wall, injured "so badly that they could not move."[22]

It was now difficult to stand; George Kessler saw groups of people stumble and fall against the railings.[23] Oliver Bernard spotted Alfred Vanderbilt idly standing near the entrance to the First Class Lounge, "as if waiting for the next race at Ascot."

Vanderbilt grinned, "as if amused by the excitement."[24] Bernard described him as "absolutely unperturbed. He stood there, the personification of sportsmanlike coolness."[25] Vanderbilt could not swim, yet he made no effort to save himself. Thomas Slidell saw him place his own lifebelt around an elderly woman just before the ship sank.[26] "He forgot everything in the fact that he could be of service to this old woman," Slidell said later. "His own life, position, and wealth did not count. He did what he knew to be his duty."[27] "Did he wish to give it up," pondered one of Vanderbilt's society friends, "to someone else, or was he glad that fate had taken out of his hands the predicament of living, that daily, self-made fabrication of occupations and pleasures, that dreary, desperate difficulty of touching reality at any point, which has wearied so many of the very rich into forms of unconsciousness a good deal less clean than death?"[28]

Oliver Bernard wandered amidships and found himself at the Marconi House near the third funnel; here, he quietly began taking off his clothing in anticipation of jumping. Removing his jacket, waistcoat, collar, and tie, he carefully folded them and put them in a neat stack at the base of the funnel. "So this is the end," he thought to himself. All of life's "struggles, petty attainments, the substance of things hoped for," now seemed "insignificant." His entire life, he mused, had "amounted to just nothing." He looked in on the Marconi operators as they pounded out their frantic calls for help. One of *Lusitania*'s crew tried to assure Bernard that the ship would not sink, but it was obvious that the liner was doomed.

He was offered a chair on which to try to float off the liner. "That doesn't interest me much," Bernard said. "I can't swim a yard, and that's not enough." He let go of the chair: it went hurtling down the sloping starboard deck and splashed into the sea.[29]

Marie Depage stood with James Houghton and his friend Richard Freeman. She was, Houghton recalled, an example of "superb coolness" as the liner sank.[30] The surrounding passengers, though, were now panicked: "Women were terror-stricken," Houghton said, "and commenced to cry piteously," and "children were clinging to their parents."[31] Houghton saw Freeman "dash away every few minutes when he saw some place where he could be useful. I saw him helping lower one of the boats, and later I saw him upon the top deck disentangling ropes." Spotting a woman nearby standing as if in a daze, Freeman walked up to her and asked, "Haven't you a lifebelt?" When she answered no, he took off his and tied it around her neck; when she objected, Freeman laughed her concerns off, as Houghton recalled, "saying that he was a good swimmer and the belt was in his way." The two old college chums "joked for a moment or two" as they stood on deck, a way, Houghton recalled, to "cheer up those about us and relieve our own feelings." As they stood together, Marie noticed that Freeman had a handkerchief wrapped around his palm, covering a small wound he had received when debris had rained down on the deck. Although he protested, she examined the little injury and bound her own handkerchief around his hand, "scolding him all the while for being so careless." "I suppose," Houghton recalled, "under ordinary circumstances, nobody would have paid any attention to it, but as it was, it gave us all something else to think about." Freeman soon wandered off to assist others, leaving Houghton and Depage at the railing, watching as *Lusitania* increased her list and the final moments approached. When the water was nearly level with her deck, Houghton and Depage jumped into the sea.[32]

The foamy green water swirling around *Lusitania* was now awash with slicks of engine oil bubbling up from deep within her hull; debris, deck chairs, and pieces of wrecked lifeboats bobbed in the surf—a potentially lethal obstacle course for those jumping from her decks. Theodate Pope, her maid, Emily Robinson, and Edwin Friend, armed with lifebelts, waited along the railing. Friend, Theodate saw, "was standing very straight," watching the last few minutes of *Lusitania*'s life.

As the ship sank lower and lower, she looked over the railing. "We could now see the gray hull, and knew it was time to jump," she recalled. She asked Friend to go first. He stepped over the barrier, eased his way down a rope to the deck below, and leapt into the water. Once she saw him safely surface, Theodate stepped to the edge. "Come, Robinson," she said, and she, too, slipped over the side.[33]

Harold Boulton looked forward and saw water spilling over the bow. "This ship is going to sink," he told the Lassetters. "The only thing to do is to jump." Just before the end came, Boulton advised Elisabeth to remove her skirt, to avoid getting entangled in any wreckage or impeding her ability to swim. She did so; holding hands, and trying to push the "nightmare of being sucked in" to the back of his mind, Boulton led the trio as they jumped into the sea.[34]

Further along the deck, Marguerite Allan saw Sir Hugh Lane. He was "pale, but quite calm," and seemed to be searching for someone. She saw that he did not have a lifebelt on. When she approached, he smiled and said quietly, "This is a sad end for us all."[35] Frederick Orr-Lewis wanted to get Lady Allan and her daughters into a lifeboat on the port side; as he was leading them toward the edge of the deck, he saw first one, and then another, lifeboat filled with passengers sway and fall into the sea below, spilling their occupants. All this time, the water was rising. "I had Gwen's hand," Orr-Lewis remembered, "and Lady Allan had Anna." They all jumped into the sea.[36]

Robert Holt, "seeing rescue would be difficult by means of lifeboats," decided to "clamber down the side of the ship and jump into the sea." He "swam away as hard as possible," perhaps able to navigate better than others as he had given his lifebelt away and his arms were not constrained.[37] Thomas Home, too, slid down into the water, only to find himself caught "in a seething mass drawn down by suction" as the ship sank.[38]

Carl Foss finally managed to find a lifebelt and, with the end approaching, jumped over the starboard railing near the stern. "I had hardly hit the water," he remembered, "when a lifeboat crashed down beside me, narrowly missing my head." The occupants, flung into the water, were caught in the wash along the hull, and carried back. Foss saw a man drift into one of the bronze propellers; both of his legs, Foss recalled, were "almost severed." Foss tossed him a rope. "The poor fellow was bleeding terribly, and could not have lasted much longer."[39]

In the last few minutes of her life, *Lusitania*'s passengers made desperate efforts to fill and lower her remaining lifeboats. Josephine Burnside apparently found her daughter, Iris, amidst the confusion. Finally, at the last minute, Josephine, knowing that she could not swim, boarded a lifeboat; she was still holding on to Iris's hand as *Lusitania* sank before it could safely be launched, and a wave sent its passengers into the sea.[40]

Mary and Laura Ryerson climbed into Lifeboat No. 14 just outside the Smoking Room; Allen Loney saw that a place remained. "He ordered me to get in," his daughter, Virginia, remembered. "I protested, but finally obeyed."[41] Lott Gadd,

Lusitania's barber, helped lower the boat: no one seemed to know how to work the falls, and so Gadd jumped in and, with another man, began to let the lines out. When the boat reached the water, Gadd let go of the lines on his side but his comrade did not, and the falls jammed. When the lines were fixed and the boat finally touched the sea, it began to spin around and fill with water. Gadd shouted that the passengers should start bailing with their caps and hats; in the panic, he recalled, "I either slipped or was pushed, and was in the water." He found a buoy nearby and swam away from the ship.[42] *Lusitania* began to go under: suction from the vessel capsized Lifeboat No. 14, spilling its occupants into the sea. "With other passengers in the boat," Virginia recalled, "I was drawn ever so far down in the water." She finally rose to a surface crowded with panicked passengers.[43] "I am a good swimmer," Laura Ryerson said, "and although there was a crowd struggling together, I got clear."[44]

The end, Bestic recalled, "came with dramatic swiftness. A peculiar lurching movement made me look round." An "all-swallowing wave" swept up the Boat Deck and crashed over the superstructure, "enveloping passengers, boats, and everything that lay in its path. A heart-rending wail rent the air." For a few seconds, he eyed the scene. "I knew that should the wave reach me, it would be my end. Fully clothed and without waiting to even grab a lifejacket, I hurled myself over the side."[45]

Leslie Morton and his brother, John, jumped from the ship and swam away, through the "turmoil of bodies, women and children, deck chairs, lifebelts, lifeboats and every describable thing."[46] By now, the list to starboard had reached 25 degrees. On the nearly deserted bridge, Captain Turner knew it was hopeless. "Save yourself!" he told Quartermaster Hugh Johnston.[47] Morton, looking back, "saw Captain Turner quite clearly, standing outside the wheelhouse on the starboard side," as the ship began to slip beneath the water.[48]

James Brooks had spotted a number of women standing along the railing near a lifeboat, too afraid to enter. "I'll help you!" he had shouted, and assisted them in jumping from the starboard deck across the yawning void and into the boat. A seaman had appeared, waving a gun in the air and threatening him if he joined those already in the boat.

"Who the hell is trying to?" Brooks angrily shouted back.[49] Finally, though, Brooks joined them and, working with two sailors, tried to loosen the boat lest it be sucked down with *Lusitania*. They could find no tools or hammers to knock the pegs out and release the snubbing chains. Water rushed up to the boat and threatened to crush it beneath the davits. "There was no time to cast loose," Brooks recalled. "It became a mad race, every man for his life. We all leaped."[50]

By now Howard Fisher had returned to Lady Mackworth and Dorothy Conner with lifebelts. He'd been "rushing here and there in the dark," from cabin to cabin "for a chance lifebelt left behind by its owner," as he could not reach his own room: rising water made it impossible. Having finally got hold of two lifebelts, he struggled up the sloping staircase only to be accosted by "some devil who tried to snatch one of my belts. He did not get it."[51] He told Margaret Mackworth and Dorothy that water was rapidly flooding the ship.[52] Knowing that the end was near, Fisher suggested that the trio jump into the sea "rather than await the terrific rush and impact of water that would follow as the ship plunged headlong to the depths."[53] Margaret Mackworth unhooked her skirt so that she could easily remove it in the water.[54] She paused as she stood at the edge: the water, she thought, was so far down. Finally, she told herself "how ridiculous I was to have a physical fear of the jump when we stood in such grave danger." The ship threatened to take her with it when it sank beneath the waves. She looked again over the edge. "We were not, as I had thought, sixty feet above the sea; we were already under the sea." She had waited too long: a great wave circled the deck, swirling around her feet, her legs, and then abruptly subsuming her in its dark, boiling wake as *Lusitania* plunged beneath the surface.[55]

Robert Timmis didn't have time to jump: he glanced down the liner's deck as water rushed toward him, like "the rapids below Niagara Falls."[56] "How about it, old man?" his friend Ralph Moodie asked. Timmis merely shook his head.[57] The rising wall of water "struck me, and I went down, to be washed back and caught under a piece of superstructure."[58] Michael Byrne, standing on deck, "felt a chill, clammy feeling around my ankles." He looked down and saw that water was flooding over the deck, "so in the name of God I dived off and swam as fast as I could away from the ship, with the terrible thought of being pulled down by the suction."[59]

Still holding the hand of her husband, Henry, Annie Adams saw "a wave engulf the bow of the boat, and before I could turn my head toward my husband I found myself swept off the boat into the water."[60] Belle Naish and her husband, Theodore, "could feel the boat going down under us, like a slowly moving elevator." As the bow plunged further beneath the waves, people lost their footing; Belle saw a woman slide down the deck and land hard against a wall. Within seconds, "a bundle of chains slid against her, pinning her fast." She cried out for help but Belle could do nothing but shout, "it would not be much longer."[61] As water swirled over the deck, Belle let go of her husband's hand, "as I didn't want to drag him down." *Lusitania* lurched suddenly; Belle felt an explosion shudder through the liner, which she took for another torpedo. A lifeboat, swinging wildly from its davits, struck her in the head; without warning, she was "shot up into the air. As I rose, I looked for my husband, and saw his head about a yard from mine, but lower, although he was taller than I. The next thing I knew, I was twenty or thirty feet below the surface of the sea."[62]

Charles Frohman was standing on deck with Rita Jolivet and her brother-in-law, calmly smoking a cigar. Warren Pearl spotted him handing out lifebelts to other passengers.[63] "Don't bother about me," he said. "What I don't like about this is the water is so cold."[64] Although Rita helped Frohman put on a lifebelt, he soon gave it away. With the chaotic scenes on deck, no one was willing to enter a lifeboat. As *Lusitania*'s bow finally plunged beneath the waves, Frohman smiled and said calmly, "Why fear death? It is the most beautiful adventure in life," referring to a line in Barrie's *Peter Pan*, "To die would be an awfully big adventure."[65] Just as he finished speaking, there was "a tremendous roar" and "a great wave swept along the deck."[66] It was so strong, Rita remembered, that "my buttoned boots were swept off my feet" as she disappeared into the sea.[67]

George Kessler saw "a great wave of water" sweep along the deck. He later remembered falling, apparently into a descending lifeboat on the port side. As they tried to draw away, Kessler looked up. *Lusitania* seemed to right herself, then again lurched over to starboard; some wreckage caught on Kessler's boat and overturned it.[68] George Slingsby, separated from Frederick Orr-Lewis and his group, was swept off the deck into the sea without warning.[69]

Warren and Amy Pearl had no idea that their two youngest children had left the ship, and had spent the last ten minutes roaming the decks, desperately searching for Stuart and Audrey and their nurse. They found Greta Lorenson with their daughter Amy near a lifeboat, but daughter Susan was missing. Pearl asked Lindon Bates to look after his wife as he went below to their stateroom.[70] Finally it was obvious that the end was near as the ship "made a forward plunge to starboard." As the sea came rushing over the decks, Pearl grabbed several planks for his wife, children, and remaining nurse, but the surge swept them off the ship.[71]

Bates, Amy Pearl saw, was wearing "a heavy overcoat" as he raced back and forth across the deck, hurling chairs into the water for people struggling below.[72] A few years earlier, traveling in Central America, he'd faced a similar crisis when his boat threatened to sink. "One does a lot of quick thinking at such a time," he wrote. Thoughts had raced through his head: "The main emotion you have is of utter disgust at the whole proceeding."[73] Now, as waves washed over *Lusitania*'s decks, Amy Pearl saw him caught in the swirling water; as he twisted and turned, his foot caught in a rope, and she watched as he was dragged beneath the surface.[74]

"We shall have to swim for it," William Adams said to his father. He had tried to go below to their cabin for lifebelts but found water rushing around the staircase and pouring in through open portholes. On the ship's starboard side, father and son helped load Lifeboat No. 17 and joined its occupants as it was lowered from *Lusitania*'s side. The boat was about twelve feet from the water when the seaman at the front let go of the rope; the boat's bow fell, spilling most of the passengers into the sea. No effort could free the lifeboat of its falls as the *Lusitania* plunged lower and lower. With the Boat Deck now level with the sea, and fearing they would be pulled under when the ship sank, father and son jumped into the water. They swam for a short distance but were soon separated.[75]

Charles Lauriat had climbed into the stern of Lifeboat No. 7 and worked desperately to free it from its davits without success; it was still attached as water lapped at the deck. As the sea surged around the boat, the davits threatened to push it beneath the waves and crush it. Lauriat somehow managed to free the stern falls, but those at the bow still held it to the davits. Despite shouted instructions, he said, he could not make anyone "understand what to do or how to do it." A lone steward stood at the bow, trying to slice through the thick falls with a pocketknife. Lauriat tried to clamber forward but found his progress impeded by people, oars, kegs of water, "and God knows what." Glancing up, he saw a funnel "hanging over us," much to "the terror of the people in the boat." Knowing all was lost, Lauriat pleaded with the passengers to jump overboard, but "they were petrified" and could not or would not move. Finally, he dove over the side.[76]

Oliver Bernard found David Thomas and his secretary, Arnold Rhys-Evans, at Lifeboat No. 11 on the starboard side. Thomas had lost his daughter, Lady Mackworth, in the first few minutes after the impact, when she went to her cabin to fetch lifebelts, and he had no idea where she was. Bernard saw the "rather worried and puzzled expression on his face" as Thomas scanned the decks for her.[77] By now, the list was severe and the water was nearly level with the deck. Thomas helped several "hysterical" passengers jump in before he followed but the boat was still attached to its davits.[78] Bernard joined Thomas and his secretary in the boat, and watched as efforts to cut the falls seemed futile.

The ship's heavy list to starboard was now so great that the funnels loomed almost overheard, threatening to "smash them like flies" if *Lusitania* rolled any further. At the last moment, the lifeboat cleared the ship just as she began her final plunge.[79] But Bernard saw that one of the guy wires from the funnel, like "a huge, tight banjo string," was descending on them. "We managed to push the boat from under it," he said, as "water boiled up in great masses" all around them.[80]

Isaac Lehmann, injured when Lifeboat No. 18 smashed back over the deck, had just managed to crawl to the rails when there was "a terrific explosion" toward the front of the ship and he was thrown into the water. He was twice pulled under by the suction as the vessel sank, but finally managed to swim clear.[81] William Meriheina hadn't really believed *Lusitania* would sink, and remained aboard until the last few moments; near him on the aft docking bridge stood Charles Jeffery, the race car driver and the motorcar manufacturer, and together awaited the end. Finally, *Lusitania* gently eased itself beneath the surface and a torrent of water washed them into the sea.[82]

Charles Lauriat swam away as fast as he could; when he had reached what he deemed to be a safe distance, he turned to watch *Lusitania* go under. "I could still see the people on Deck B," he recalled, "clinging to the rail that ran along the side. . . . It was impossible to stand on the deck unless one had hold of some stationary object. People were clinging to one another, so that it seemed as if they were standing three or four abreast by the rail."[83] James Brooks saw "a crowd still on her decks, and boats filled with helpless women and children glued to her side. I was sickened with horror at the sight."[84] Cellist Handel Hawkins also looked back at the liner after having jumped over the side. "Hundreds of horror-stricken passengers were huddled together on the slanting decks," he said. "Women and children were crying for help that could not be given." As *Lusitania* sank, he saw dozens of people jump or fall into the sea. "The sight of so many helpless people going to their doom was sickening, and I had to turn away before the boat went down altogether."[85]

The weight of water flooding the bow pulled *Lusitania* deeper into the sea. Steam and cinders shot from the funnels as air pockets burst; boilers, machinery, and fittings tore loose and pummeled through the ship in a monstrous cacophony.[86] William Meriheina heard explosions from within the hull, and saw portholes blown out of the ship's sides.[87] Staterooms were flooded, engulfing elegant wardrobes packed into steamer trunks for arrival the following morning; the sea swept through her First Class Reading and Writing Room, swirling around the brocaded walls and plush chairs; it surged through the Grand Entrance, cascading down the crimson-carpeted staircase; it flowed through her First Class Lounge, enveloping the mahogany walls in a grip of death; it filled the Dining Saloon, washing over the plaster dome adorned with the *Four Seasons* and floating linens, china, menus, and flowers from the luncheon just served; it exploded through bulkheads, destroying the First Class Smoking Room, and continued its destructive path to the Veranda Café. Etched windows imploded under the pressure.

As she settled, *Lusitania* slightly righted herself, and seemed to sink deck by deck at a shallow angle, her entire length submerging until only her masts and funnels remained above water.[88] From her lifeboat, Alice Lines saw *Lusitania* go down. "There was this huge, lovely liner," she later said, "and as I watched one funnel went, and then the other, and the other, until the ship was gone."[89] At the last minute, when all but her funnels had disappeared, *Lusitania* again rolled to starboard. Her funnels raked over, crashing down into the sea at an angle. James Brooks saw water "rush into the smoke stacks, sucking in everything in its path. I could hear people screaming as they were pulled in."[90] There was, he said, "a thunderous roar, as of the collapse of a great building on fire" as *Lusitania* slipped beneath a sea that "rapidly grew black with the figures of struggling men, women, and children." Brooks "swam as hard as I could" as the funnels "loomed over my head. I expected them momentarily to fall and crush me," but he managed to get clear, grabbing hold of the wires and pushing himself away as he sliced his hands open.[91] Robert Holt turned and saw the ship listing over perilously close. "I dived under the water, and while there came into contact with one funnel," he remembered. "I put my hand alongside it, and felt the rivets."[92] Charles Lauriat, swimming hard to escape the vortex, was pulled under when one of the ship's aerials caught on the shoulders of his lifebelt. He had to furiously kick to reach the surface, grateful for his childhood days at camp when older boys had relentlessly dunked him beneath the water. "They proved mighty good training!" he now thought.[93]

Eighteen minutes after Schwieger's torpedo hit her, *Lusitania* disappeared, "sucking down with it a mass of bodies and wreckage which gradually rose to the surface again in an indescribably hideous manner," recalled Carl Foss.[94] "She was just swallowed up," said Oliver Bernard, "swallowed up in a gorgeous sea."[95] George Kessler turned to look back. "My God," he cried out, "the *Lusitania* is gone!"[96]

CHAPTER SIXTEEN

The scene was surreal: gulls loudly circling a beautiful, clear blue sky, a "wonderfully smooth" ocean, and a sea filled with screaming, struggling, pleading survivors left when *Lusitania* plunged beneath the waves.[1] The water, recalled James Brooks, "rapidly grew black with the figures of struggling men, women, and children."[2] A circle of wreckage marked the site of her final plunge: cushions, clothing, papers, deck chairs, and lifebelts floated aimlessly on green water slick with oil. The few lifeboats that had managed to safely get away bobbed restlessly against the horizon; a few others, washed loose from *Lusitania* in the last moments and turned upside down, rocked back and forth near collapsible boats that had floated off the ship. As soon as the ship disappeared, said Charles Lauriat, the air was filled with "a long, lingering moan" as people struggled in the water.[3] Albert Bestic would never forget "all the despair, terror, and anguish of hundreds of souls passing into eternity" as he saw "waving hands and arms belonging to struggling men, women, and children endeavoring to keep afloat."[4]

Within a few minutes, said numerous survivors, a submarine surfaced in the middle of this wreckage.[5] Harold Boulton spotted a submarine rise out of the water, and several crew members peering over the scene.[6] Michael Byrne, too, saw "a conning tower, followed by the hull" as it broke the surface. "The head and shoulders of a man appeared," he recalled. "He looked about the water in the neighborhood, and then went back, and the submarine dropped out of sight."[7]

Someone thought that he spotted Elbert Hubbard, holding fast to a steel drum bobbing in the water. Each time he tried to climb up, it slowly revolved and spilled him back into the sea. After several unsuccessful efforts, he apparently lost consciousness and sank beneath the surface.[8] An electrician from *Lusitania*'s crew saw Alfred Vanderbilt floating near the whirl of wreckage. At the last minute, he had grabbed a lifebelt and flung it around his shoulders without tying it properly. "I am Vanderbilt!" he cried out as the man unsuccessfully attempted to adjust the lifebelt. "He did his best to keep afloat," the electrician recalled, but they drifted apart and, when he looked back, Vanderbilt was gone.[9]

"The cries for mercy, the people drowning and coming up again," recalled Josephine Brandell as she floated on a deck chair, were "too terrible."[10] Others bobbed lifelessly in this sea of misery. Oliver Bernard saw "hundreds of heads and arms of struggling victims on barrels, deck chairs, and all the flotsam and jetsam that had remained." A woman floated by, "a frothy mucous on her lips," her eyes "peering blindly."[11] "Entangled in wreckage," Bernard said, "one by one" these survivors "seemed to fall off and give themselves up."[12] Another passenger was horrified to see a woman go into premature labor as corpses floated around her.[13]

"Oh God! Save me!" someone cried before sinking beneath the waves.[14] When Virginia Loney rose again to the surface after her lifeboat capsized, she saw that *Lusitania* had disappeared. "People were struggling in the water all around me," she remembered. Young and healthy, Virginia had learned to swim at her parents' estate in New York, and now kicked her way across the water, to be pulled aboard another lifeboat.[15] Laura Ryerson, too, escaped the suction when Lifeboat No. 14 capsized, and managed to clear the crowd of struggling survivors to reach another boat. A hole in one end, Laura recalled, continually filled it with water, forcing her and a few others back into the sea, where they clung desperately to the side.[16]

"As I sank," said James Houghton, "I was struck by some wreckage, but came to almost immediately. As I was whirled about in the whirlpool created by the sinking ship, I escaped death by an inch at least a dozen times."[17] After being struck by wreckage, and "weak from loss of blood," he managed to pull himself aboard a nearby raft; he looked around but he could find no trace of Marie Depage or Richard Freeman.[18] George Vernon, Houghton said, "lost his reason altogether" in the wake of the sinking; before anyone could stop him, Houghton remembered, Vernon plunged into the water and drowned himself before their horrified eyes.[19]

"I went down, and thought the world had come to an end," Josephine Eaton Burnside said. "Soon, I found myself on the surface again, clinging to a rope. I cannot swim, and I was only partly conscious. Finally, I grasped the side of a capsized boat."[20] Isaac Lehmann surfaced amid "hundreds of people struggling in the water, praying and crying for help. There was wreckage all around." The sights, he said, "defy description."[21] He finally caught hold of an oar, and managed to stay afloat.[22] Robinson Pirie was pulled below so many times that he "thought I would never get up." When he finally surfaced, he made his way toward a small box floating in the distance: a teenaged boy lay sprawled across it, and he helped an elderly man with a child in his arms also grab hold as it rolled and bobbed in the waves. For more than an hour, Pirie tried to keep them all balanced, but finally "the man with the child slipped away." Eventually, he swam to a collapsible boat, waiting for the rescue vessels he prayed would soon appear.[23]

Following his leap into the water, Robert Holt surfaced and clung to an oar. Fearing suction and being a good swimmer, he raced away from the ship only to have another man desperately grab at him. "Seeing he had a belt, I pushed him off," Holt recalled. He found an air tank floating nearby, but too many people were trying to crowd around it and so Holt swam toward a half-opened collapsible boat, where he saw Dorothy Braithwaite. "It was partly under water, and at any moment seemed as if it would sink."[24] "I saw Herbert Holt's boy," Frederick Orr-Lewis remembered, "and swam to him," helping pull him into another nearby collapsible boat.[25] Robert found not only Orr-Lewis but also Lady Allan aboard. "There was a slight swell, and any moment we thought the slender craft would go over," Holt remembered.[26] Marguerite Allan had been injured in the sinking: William Adams thought that she had been struck by a mast as the ship sank. She was now in agony, her spine injured and her collarbone broken.[27]

There was no trace of Anna and Gwendolyn Allan. Swimming away from the wreckage, Harold Boulton was sure that he spotted them in the water. He knew them by sight: he swam close enough to see that they were "very badly mutilated." Neither, he thought, had drowned, but instead they had been killed when struck by wreckage.[28]

George Slingsby, Orr-Lewis's valet, had struggled to the surface after being sucked down with the ship and swam toward a nearby boat. "I suddenly began to sink, and I was still on the raft with my head just out of the water when it disappeared," he wrote, "and I was left struggling in the water." He grabbed a floating tank, which he shared with one of *Lusitania*'s stewardesses. They balanced on either side of it, with Slingsby holding her hand at the top. After an hour, she let go: "I think the shock killed her, as the water was so cold." A frightened man swam up to Slingsby and grabbed at his left foot, ripping off his pant leg and pulling him under. He somehow managed to kick him off before drifting into semiconsciousness.[29]

Harold Boulton "went under a long way" when *Lusitania* sank, but quickly rose again to the surface. The lifebelt prevented him from swimming, so he floated on his back in this "struggling mass of humanity fighting for places on bits of wreckage, throwing each other off timber they had struggled to get on, pushing people under water to get out of it themselves like so many wild animals fighting for life, forgetting all chivalry."[30] The wreckage was unbelievable: "boats smashed to pieces, utter chaos," with bodies swirling around in what "looked like a tidal wave."[31] He reached a collapsible boat and helped pull in other survivors but all too quickly it was overloaded and threatened to sink. Boulton swam to a large box nearby. Soon, Dorothy Braithwaite floated by. "She had been so badly injured that I wondered if she was still alive," he remembered; she was bleeding and seemed "very weak." Sensing that she could not last, Dorothy gave him her name, slipped a small gold ring set with a green stone from her finger, and asked Boulton to give it to her family's lawyer, saying that she "had tried to die like a brave Canadian girl." Boulton held her hand; in a few minutes, she gasped for breath and then fell silent. Knowing she was gone, Boulton let go and "a wave carried her away." He was plagued with guilt that he had "been able to do nothing for her." Frustrated and overcome with emotion, he took the ring she had given to him and tossed it into the sea—an action that haunted him for the rest of his life.[32]

Soon, Boulton spotted Frederic Lassetter and his mother floating nearby, and called them to his makeshift raft. It was difficult to climb aboard the swaying box, but finally the two young men managed to sit Elisabeth at the center, protected in a cradle formed by their linked arms. It was all they could do to keep her from falling off as waves buffeted the box.[33] Just when they had worked out the equilibrium, a man bleeding from a gash on his head swam up, shouting, "God, you've got to make room for me on that box!" Boulton felt that he was too exhausted to last if he got back into the water, and doing so threatened to upset the entire box. He shouted at Lassetter to grab a nearby oar and drive the man away; the nameless survivor tried several times to grab the box, but Lassetter struck him repeatedly over the head and finally, cursing the group, the man sank beneath the water. "It sounds a cruel thing to have done," Boulton said, "but it meant three lives against one, and one of the three a woman's."[34]

Robert Timmis, caught in "the swirl of water," was pulled down with the ship as it sank beneath him. "The water was as black as the inside of a cow," he remembered. One piece of wreckage hit him on the head, and another struck his good eye, leaving him dazed. He managed to swim to the surface—"thirty-one strokes," he remembered—and made for a large piece of nearby wreckage. The survivors clutching their makeshift raft ordered him away: "I just wasn't welcome," Timmis said; finally, after being turned back several more times, he found his own bit of flotsam on which to cling.[35]

Michael Byrne swam through "bodies of infants laid in lifejackets and floating around, their dead, innocent faces looking towards the sky."[36] He reached a lifeboat; the men working the oars didn't know how to row, and thankfully for Byrne, it kept circling in the water. They refused to take him aboard, insisting that the boat was overcrowded already, and so he clutched a rope along the side. Finally, a steward aboard recognized him: "Oh, Mr. Byrne, I'm glad to see you!" he cried out. "I asked him to please pull me in," Byrne said, "and three of them got me in." After resting for a few minutes, "I took one of the oars and pulled with the rest of them. The bottom of our boat was lined with unconscious women."[37]

Dazed, Phoebe Amory found herself floating in a circle of bodies, "their upturned faces white and ghastly." With her lifebelt on improperly, she found it impossible to swim or turn over, and had to float helplessly on her back as waves "would wash over my face and fill my mouth with water." She feared that she was "destined to float around until I could no longer survive, and then to die. I could see myself being washed ashore a lifeless corpse, and I believe that had such wild thoughts continued I should have died from the shock of them." When a lifeboat finally approached, it was so full that she could only be partially pulled in, "so that my head and arms hung into the boat." Although the lower half of her body was numb, she was, she remembered, "so thankful for having been rescued that I decided to stand the terrible pains that were shooting through my body, until they became absolutely unbearable, and then ask them to please drag me in farther."[38]

Husbands and wives, torn apart by suction and separated in the sinking, desperately searched the water. Gladys Bilicke was dragged down with the ship, and slightly injured. "I fought my way to the surface," she remembered. "It seemed hours before I came up." There was no sign of her husband, Albert. She found "a floating spar or piece of timber. Several men were clinging to it and one helped me obtain a hold. Hours passed, and with them one man after another muttered a goodbye and dropped into the water until not one remained. But I believe I was possessed of superhuman strength, and held on."[39]

Angela Papadopoulos saw her husband, Michael, disappear "into the waves in front of me, and I can still feel his hand slipping from mine." For hours, she was "at the mercy of the waves" as she swam through a sea clotted with "motionless bodies"; "the only thing I could think of was going home with my children," she remembered. Finally, she was pulled aboard a collapsible boat, where she spotted an injured Russian man. She'd been to Russia and knew some of the language, and so "tried to hearten him as best I could" while tearing strips from her waterlogged petticoat to help bandage his arm.[40]

Ogden Hammond "never thought I would come back" to the surface after being dragged down; when he finally made it, there was no sign of Mary. Hammond was so dazed that he immediately slipped back beneath the waves. He managed to come up again and was hauled into nearby Lifeboat No. 15; there were so many survivors aboard, he recalled, that the edge of the boat was barely six inches above the water.[41] Warren Pearl, after being pulled down by the suction, "floated with the greatest of ease" in his lifebelt.[42] He eventually found a place in a collapsible boat; his wife, Amy, having suffered a broken arm, had been pulled onto an overturned lifeboat.[43]

Suction from *Lusitania* had separated Belle Naish from her husband, Theodore, and dragged her beneath the surface. "Why, this is like being on grandmother's feather bed!" she thought as she floated beneath the water.[44] "I had never before realized how beautiful things were under the water. I could see the rays of the sun slanting through the water and the light was beautiful." When she finally came to the surface, "the first thing I noticed was the beautiful blue of the sky, and how bright the sun was shining."[45] As she surfaced, Belle struck her head on a piece of wreckage. "I got my arms around something, and when I came out of the water, I was clasping the bumper of overturned Lifeboat No. 22." A nearby man reached out for her, saying, "Give me your hand. My back's broken, but I'll do what I can for you." Although at first she refused, Belle finally allowed herself to be dragged aboard the keel. Nearby was a dead baby someone had plucked from the sea; another man, bleeding profusely from the head, died in front of her. There was also a young boy, Robert Kay, who had been traveling with his mother, now missing, to visit relatives in England. Over the next few hours, Belle tried to keep his spirits up as they drifted through the water.[46]

TOP: The *Lusitania* outside New York harbor, showing tugboats at her bow and a view of the city in the distance.

MIDDLE LEFT: A view of the *Lusitania* dockside, looking up at her lifeboats.

MIDDLE RIGHT: The *Lusitania* arriving at her pier; a view down the port-side bow.

BOTTOM: The arrival of the *Lusitania* in New York on April 24, 1915. This was her final trip westward.

(All images on this page, courtesy Michael Poirier Collection)

TOP LEFT: Captain William Turner, the *Lusitania*'s master, shown here on the bridge of the *Aquitania*. (Private Collection)

TOP RIGHT: Junior Third Officer Albert Bestic of the *Lusitania*. (Courtesy of the Bestic Family and the Michael Poirier Collection)

BOTTOM LEFT: Cunard Line Passenger List booklet cover from 1914. (Michael Poirier Collection)

BOTTOM RIGHT: 1914 studio portrait of the actress Rita Jolivet. (Michael Poirier Collection)

TOP LEFT: Charles Jeffery, automobile manufacturer of Kenosha, Wisconsin.
(Courtesy of Chris Anagnos and the Michael Poirier Collection)

TOP RIGHT: 1915 passport photograph of Dorothy Conner. (Courtesy of Peter Lordan/NARA)

BOTTOM LEFT: 1915 passport photograph of Dr. Howard Fisher. (Courtesy of Peter Lordan/NARA)

BOTTOM RIGHT: Dr. James Houghton of Saratoga Springs, New York. (Michael Poirier Collection/NARA)

TOP LEFT: Retired New York City merchant and deputy sheriff Michael Byrne. (Michael Poirier Collection/NARA)

TOP RIGHT: Talented architect and psychical researcher Theodate Pope. (Michael Poirier Collection/NARA)

MIDDLE: Passengers on a previous voyage enjoying their sheltered deck chairs. (Michael Poirier Collection)

BOTTOM: The *Lusitania*'s First Class Promenade, showing her lifeboats. This photograph was taken approximately two weeks prior to the sinking. (Michael Poirier Collection)

TOP LEFT: A view from the *Lusitania*'s stern mid-ocean during a previous voyage. (Michael Poirier Collection)

TOP RIGHT: First Class passenger Angela Papadopoulos. (Courtesy of Demetrio Baffa Trasci Amalfitani di Crucoli)

BOTTOM LEFT: First Class passenger and Los Angeles hotelier Albert Clay Bilicke of South Pasadena, California. (Courtesy of Mary Carpenter)

BOTTOM RIGHT: First Class passenger Gladys Huff Bilicke of South Pasadena, California. (Courtesy of Mary Carpenter)

TOP: Passengers enjoying the fresh air on the *Lusitania*'s Boat Deck during a previous voyage. (Michael Poirier Collection)

BOTTOM LEFT: First Class passenger Margaret, Lady Mackworth, circa 1915. (Private Collection)

BOTTOM RIGHT: A postcard view of the First Class Lounge on the *Lusitania*. (Michael Poirier Collection)

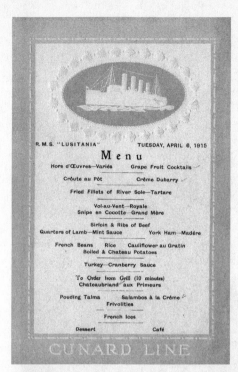

TOP LEFT: A First Class menu from April 6, 1915, almost exactly one month prior to the sinking. (Michael Poirier Collection)

TOP RIGHT: First Class passenger Robert J. Timmis, a British cotton broker living in Gainesville, Texas. Shown here with his children in 1913. (Courtesy of Rick Timmis)

MIDDLE RIGHT: First Class passenger Beatrice "Trixie" Witherbee and her son, Alfred, at the beach, circa 1914. (Courtesy of Mary Jolivet and the Michael Poirier Collection)

BOTTOM LEFT: Second Class passengers Barbara Anderson and her mother, Emily, at the beach, circa 1914. (Michael Poirier Collection)

BOTTOM RIGHT: Kapitänleutnant Walther von Schwieger, commander of the submarine U-20. He disliked the honorific "von" and seldom used it. (Private Collection)

TOP LEFT: Extremely wealthy philanthropist, sportsman, socialite, and ladies' man, First Class passenger Alfred Gwynne Vanderbilt. (Private Collection)

MIDDLE LEFT: Canadian Lady Allan with her younger daughters, Anna and Gwen, about 1905. (McCord Museum Collection)

TOP RIGHT: Showing her beautiful lines, the *Lusitania* in dock around 1907. (Private Collection)

BOTTOM: On November 4, 1916, the U-20 ran aground on the Danish coast with damaged engines; her crew destroyed her by blowing her up the next day. (Private Collection)

The suction had also twice pulled Rita Jolivet beneath the waves; when she finally rose to the surface, *Lusitania* had disappeared. She still had her pearl-handled pistol: looking around at the sea filled with wreckage and struggling survivors, she apparently decided that immediate death was better than losing consciousness and drowning.[47] She later told Harold Boulton that she managed to retrieve the pistol but when she pulled the trigger, immersion in the water caused the gun to fail.[48] She swam to a nearby boat, clinging to the sides with other passengers as she awaited rescue.[49]

"It got pitch black," Annie Adams remembered, as she was pulled beneath the surface when *Lusitania* sank. When she finally rose again, she saw sunshine but no trace of her husband, Henry. She spotted what was presumably an overturned collapsible boat nearby and begged to be picked up but the men refused; only when a woman aboard insisted did they stop and haul Annie out of the sea. But it was overcrowded and kept capsizing. "Each time," she said, "it was less buoyant, and almost every time it overturned one or more of the poor wretches would disappear. Finally the other woman went down." Annie managed to stay aboard by using "my gymnastic knowledge," crawling and twisting as the boat bobbed and turned. Finally, when only a handful of survivors were left, the boat sank beneath them and Annie drifted off into unconsciousness as she floated over the water.[50]

Ian Holbourn continued his desperate search for Avis Dolphin. He swam toward several people in the water but found that they were dead. As he made his way through wreckage and bodies, he could hear the "terrible" shouts for help all around him.[51] He swam to a nearby lifeboat; most of those aboard seemed dead; he asked to be hauled in, but those inside refused, nor would they attempt to save any of the dying passengers around them. After more than an hour of gripping lines at the side of the boat, Holbourn was exhausted, and asked if the officer in charge would hold on to his hand so that he would not sink. The officer refused, saying that holding another man's hand would make him "uncomfortable."[52]

Avis, meanwhile, had "lost sight of Hilda and Miss Smith" as she was dragged down with the ship. "I was under water for about a minute, then floated around for a few seconds." Finally, she spotted a nearby collapsible boat and swam to it. Several men took their knives and cut away the canvas top so that people could climb aboard. Now out of the water, but sitting in her drenched clothing, Avis shivered. To get warm, "I stood up and exercised a little," being careful not to tip the precariously balanced boat.[53]

Many of those aboard lifeboats found themselves in unexpectedly perilous positions. A survivor opened one of the kegs of water stowed aboard and found that it "was unfit for human consumption . . . a third full of a brown, stinking fluid."[54] Charles Lauriat swam to a nearby collapsible boat floating empty on the surface. Working with several other survivors including James Brooks, he managed to cut the covering loose and tried to raise the canvas sides. They found the wooden braces broken and the iron ribs so rusted that it was nearly impossible to make it seaworthy; there were not even any oars aboard.[55] Lauriat was "disgusted" that *Lusitania*'s captain and crew had deemed such a boat ready in case of emergency.[56]

George Kessler, hurled into the water when his lifeboat overturned, had been pulled under when *Lusitania* sank. "I thought I was a goner," he recalled, but he finally managed to kick his way back to the surface. He floated in his lifebelt to a collapsible boat and helped raise the canvas sides. Water filled the bilge. It was "all that human effort could do to keep her afloat," Kessler remembered. Soon the boat capsized, spilling its occupants back into the sea. They somehow managed to right it and climb back in, but

water continued to seep into the vessel. "Although we bailed fe-
verishly, we could not get the water out," and it capsized repeatedly, tearing Kessler's legs as he continually scraped against the
boat. Each time it was righted, fewer people climbed back in; the
"agony and suffering," Kessler said, were "indescribable." Within
a few hours, only three of those originally aboard remained. The
rest had perished in the water.[57]

Charles Jeffery "sank twice, but I had a chance in the mean-
time to get my lungs full of air." The second time he was pulled
under, he remembered, he "gave up hope," but somehow managed to swim back up to the surface and remain there, clinging
to a partially submerged collapsible boat.[58] Pulled down "again
and again," Thomas Home was exhausted by the time he finally
reached the surface; although he swam to a bit of wreckage, he
was so weak that he "felt I could not last." Finally, he spotted a
dead body nearby, kept afloat by a lifebelt. He swam over to the
corpse, unfastened the belt, and managed to pull it around his
shoulders just before he passed out.[59]

Carl Foss reached a half-filled collapsible boat but "didn't
like the look of things."[60] "There were several women on it," he
recalled, "screaming wildly and the raft was rocking heavily
because they would not keep still." Although he "shouted to
the women to keep quiet," they were, he said, "so hysterical that
they took no notice and the craft turned turtle, throwing them
all into the water."[61] He finally swam several hundred feet to
another collapsible. Foss was so exhausted that he could not
even clamber aboard, and had to be pulled from the water.[62]

Theodate Pope had been pulled down with the ship, "washed
and whirled up against wood"—one of Lusitania's lifeboats.
After swallowing the salty water, she closed her eyes. "This is, of
course, the end of life for me," she thought. She felt "no special
discomfort nor anguish of mind." She was happy that she had

made a will, and pondered the buildings she had designed as she "committed myself to God's care." A piece of wreckage knocked her unconscious, but she floated to the surface: "my stiff straw hat and my hair probably saved me," she later wrote. When she opened her eyes, she found herself surrounded by "hundreds of frantic, screaming, shouting humans in this gray and watery inferno." A desperate man, with "panic in his eyes" and without a lifebelt, grabbed at her. "Oh, please don't!" she cried as she was dragged down and again lost consciousness. Some minutes later, she awoke to find herself floating on her back, beneath "the brilliant sunshine." The water, she said, "felt warm," and she noticed that the gaps between clusters of survivors had grown wider. She reached for an oar, pushing one end toward an elderly man with a large gash on his forehead floating nearby. Her wet clothing continually threatened to drag Theodate down, and she was forced to throw one leg over the oar to stay afloat. Thinking her experience was "too horrible to be true," she again passed into unconsciousness.[63]

Dorothy Conner found herself entangled in ropes when she entered the sea with her brother-in-law, Howard Fisher, and quickly lost consciousness as she was sucked below. She was "quite calm under the water. The thought of God came to me," she recalled, "how at times like this, He was everyone's God, a living, warm, all pervading presence." She eventually floated up unconscious near an overturned boat and was pulled out of the water.[64] Fisher, too, had been pulled down. "It is just a question of how long you can hold your breath," he told himself. Finally, he surfaced and swam to a lifeboat, where he tended to the wounded. He was annoyed, though, at having "to share my pipe with two dirty sailors."[65]

William Meriheina awoke to find "bright sun shining in my eyes. It was cold, and I felt stunned, but I struck out for an overturned lifeboat." When he reached the craft, another survivor grabbed him around the neck and pushed him away, pulling them both under. Finally, Meriheina managed to clamber up on the overturned keel and helped his assailant aboard. While awaiting rescue, Meriheina pulled out his fountain pen and, using waterlogged postcards in his pocket, wrote two brief messages: "Ship sunk," read the first. "Seventy of us on a raft. Believe the lost will amount to half our passengers. May we all be happy in our destiny." His second was more philosophical, ending with the hope that "the lives of the lost ones will pay the score."[66]

Margaret Mackworth's wrist had been caught on a rope attached to the sinking ship, leaving a scar that she bore for the rest of her life. "It was very dark," she recalled, "nearly black." This, she said, was "the worst moment of terror, the only moment of acute terror that I knew." She struggled toward the surface and found a board several feet long that, together with her lifebelt, helped her float. "Slightly stupefied," she saw that she was part of "a large, round floating island composed of people and debris" so immense that she could scarcely see the water between them. A white-faced man grabbed the other end of her board; although sure it could not support both of them, she "did not feel justified in objecting." Every few minutes, his hands inched toward her; although it was an effort to speak, a frightened Margaret repeatedly warned him away. Soon, he drifted off into the sea. As she floated, she heard prayers over the water in "a curious, unemotional monotone." She tried to swim to one of the distant lifeboats but her legs were numb and she refused to let go of the board. "There was," she remembered, "no acute feeling of fear while one was floating in the water. I can remember feeling thankful that I had not been drowned underneath but had reached the surface safely, and thinking that even if the worst happened there could be nothing unbearable to go through now that my head was above the water." Except for the cold, she felt almost comfortable; once, she looked up at the "sun and pale blue sky" and wondered "whether I had reached Heaven without knowing it." Dazed and exhausted, she faded into unconsciousness.[67]

Captain William Turner had remained with his ship until it sank beneath him. Washed from *Lusitania* by the surging sea, he saw his vessel disappear into a swirl of wreckage. While fighting to stay afloat, Turner also battled seagulls. In horrific scenes, he saw the birds swoop down on helpless survivors, attacking and pecking out their eyes.[68] He finally managed to climb aboard an overturned boat with several others. "Some of you men will have to get off here," Turner told them. Several passengers went over the side; Turner "stayed on, and made no attempt to leave."[69]

Once the cries for help waned, the sound of singing filled the air. Floating beneath the expansive blue sky, survivors tried to keep spirits up with renditions of "Tipperary," "Abide with Me, Lord," and, more ominously, "Nearer My God to Thee."[70] Soon, unconsciousness and death took hold. The water was fifty-five degrees, and hypothermia soon set in.[71] Those fortunate enough to be in the six lifeboats that cleared the ship fared better than their fellow passengers drifting with the tide, soaked to the skin and clinging desperately to any floating object. After an hour or two, many of those struggling in the sea lost feeling in their arms and legs; disoriented and exhausted, they faded into unconsciousness and slipped beneath the surface. Carl Foss saw a woman float up, holding her dead infant, as he helped her onto his collapsible boat. She stared at her child's face for a long time, and finally said quietly, "Let me bury my baby." She gently placed it in the water and watched as the tiny body sank beneath the waves.[72]

A few of the lifeboats transferred their occupants to those only half full and returned to rescue survivors. By the time Josephine Brandell was pulled into a boat, she was so cold and unresponsive that the men thought she was dead.[73] The men who rescued Josephine Burnside from the water at first thought that she must have been a member of the crew, so soaked in oil and soot was she—at least until they saw her jewelry shining in the sunlight.[74] Lott Gadd took charge of one boat and rowed back to the debris field, as did George Kessler, Albert Bestic, and Leslie Morton.[75] Many times, though, the boats rowed to clusters of people bobbing in the water only to find them dead. One man spotted something flashing in the distance and rowed toward it: it was an immense diamond ring on the stiff fingers of a dead American passenger.[76]

Lauriat and Brooks finally managed to pull some oars from the flotsam before returning to rescue survivors. It was, Lauriat remembered, "simply awful" as they approached the scene. Many kept afloat by their lifebelts were already dead. One woman pulled in, he recalled, was "placidly chewing gum" and smilingly asked to be taken aboard as she couldn't swim. Lauriat wondered how they could possibly take in another person, but the woman solved his dilemma by simply offering to float alongside holding an oar. No one knew if *Lusitania* had managed to send out a distress call, but everyone could see the Irish coast in the distance, and Lauriat thought that they should aim their boat toward the lighthouse atop the Old Head of Kinsale.[77]

It seemed so close, just eleven miles away, yet the banded lighthouse was, for the desperate and freezing survivors, so far away. Beyond the tall cliffs and green hills, out of sight around a bluff, lay Queenstown, its picturesque shops and quaint houses standing in clusters on a hillside rising from the harbor. That placid, sunny afternoon, *Lusitania*'s distress signal sent shockwaves over the little town. Vice Admiral Sir Charles Coke, in charge of a small fleet of cruisers and patrol boats, ordered them out. At first, he included the cruiser HMS *Juno*, which could make 18 knots and thus reach any survivors quickly; then, worried that it might fall victim to a submarine, Coke ordered it back into port.[78] Instead, a ramshackle collection of slower vessels—fishing trawlers, steamers, tugboats, and tenders—sailed away toward *Lusitania*'s last known position.

It took several hours for this flotilla to reach the band of survivors. "Gradually," recalled Oliver Bernard, "smoke appeared on the horizon" as vessels neared.[79] "We all shouted ourselves hoarse," wrote Phoebe Amory. Soon, she was aboard "a dirty, smelly, fishing craft, but never did a ship of any description look so good to me." Wearing only her nightgown, shoes, and raincoat, Phoebe's "teeth chattered and my limbs shook." She was given tea to warm her, and soon felt "in fairly good shape."[80]

Robert Holt waited on an overturned boat for several hours, scanning the horizon for signs of rescue. When he finally spotted a distant curl of steam, he "tied handkerchiefs to an oar and attracted their attention."[81] One by one, the cold and dazed passengers who had managed to survive their ordeal were plucked from lifeboats, collapsible boats, and the sea: Warren Pearl and, separately, his wife, Amy; Thomas Home; William Meriheina; Leslie Morton; Virginia Loney; Annie Adams; Robert Timmis; Charles Jeffery; Gladys Bilicke; Dorothy Conner; Josephine Brandell; William Adams; Frederick Orr-Lewis and his valet, George Slingsby; Josephine Burnside; Lott Gadd; Alice Lines and the two youngest Pearl children; James Houghton; Carl Foss; Robert Holt; and Laura Ryerson.[82] Rescued by the trawler *Julia*, Belle Naish found herself called below to look after young Robert Kay, who had developed a high fever and was suffering from measles.[83] The already hefty Isaac Lehmann wore clothing so waterlogged that it took six men to haul him into a rescue boat.[84]

"The first thing I did was to make for the fire room," remembered Michael Byrne when he was hauled aboard the *Flying Fish*. He "stripped off and hung my clothing on the furnace doors, and helped to fire the boat so as to keep my blood in circulation." The man who had brought three hundred cigars and eleven pounds of tobacco on his voyage most wanted a smoke; when he put his hand into his coat pocket he pulled out damp tobacco.[85] While some survivors fled to the warmth of cabins and shed their waterlogged clothing, others stubbornly stood on deck clad in their wet garments and lifebelts, afraid that they would be torpedoed again.[86]

Pulled from her raft, Angela Papadopoulos drank a glass of sherry before following an officer to a cabin to change "my shabby, soaked clothes." A sailor handed her the only dry clothing at hand—his trousers and sweater—which she appreciatively donned.[87] Ian Holbourn long remembered the "heartrending" sobs of mothers crying for their lost children as his rescue boat steamed toward Queenstown.[88]

Jessie Taft Smith was aboard *Stormcock* when it cruised into the harbor at Queenstown a few minutes past eight; six hours had passed since *Lusitania* made her final plunge, and darkness was falling. There now began, as American consul in Queenstown Wesley Frost recalled, "a ghastly procession" of rescue ships. People armed with flaming torches lined the waterfront, watching as ship after ship came into view, discharging "bruised and shuddering women, crippled and half-clothed men, and a few wide-eyed children whose minds were still revolving blankly this new experience." Frost watched in horror as "piles of corpses" began to litter the quays as the hours passed.[89]

The fishing trawler *Julia* brought a barely conscious Theodate Pope into Queenstown. When the vessel encountered her floating in the sea, she was unresponsive, and sailors used grappling hooks to pull her aboard. Believing that she was dead, they cast her into a pile of corpses on the deck. Wandering the vessel, a shivering Belle Naish came upon this grim mound and knelt beside Theodate; the right side of face was covered with severe bruises and her body "felt like a sack of cement," so stiff was it from being immersed in the water. Belle thought she detected breathing, and quickly called over two sailors, begging them to perform artificial respiration on her. The men sliced off Theodate's wet clothing with an old carving knife and set to work; Belle insisted that they continue their efforts.

After two hours, Theodate's breathing became steady, and she was wrapped in a blanket and carried to the captain's cabin. Although she was "shaking from head to foot in a very violent chill," Theodate was alive.[90]

There were equally dramatic scenes aboard other vessels that Friday evening. British steamer *Westborough,* flying the Greek flag and disguised with the name *Katrina,* plucked numerous survivors from the water, including Harold Boulton, the Lassetters, Rita Jolivet, and Howard Fisher. Fireman John O'Connell gingerly helped the injured Lady Allan.[91] As she came aboard, a shivering Marguerite Allan looked at O'Connell and said, "I like you. What for, I don't know," before lapsing back into semiconsciousness.[92] Howard Fisher tried to assist as many of the injured as he could. One member of *Lusitania*'s crew was pulled aboard with his arm nearly severed by the explosions. Fisher watched as a doctor performed an emergency amputation.[93]

An old side-wheel paddle steamer formerly used to ferry passengers from Queenstown to ships waiting at anchor in the harbor, *Flying Fish* came in shortly after nine that evening. Many of those aboard, like Charles Lauriat, James Brooks, and Ogden Hammond, had been transferred from smaller rescue boats. Before abandoning his waterlogged collapsible, Lauriat had pulled an oarlock off as a souvenir of the sinking.[94]

Flying Fish, Lauriat remembered, "was positively slippery with fish scales and the usual dirt of fishermen, but the deck of that boat, under our feet, felt as good as the front halls of our own homes." Seeing that many people had removed outer garments before jumping from *Lusitania* and now were shivering in the twilight, he took off his sweater and handed it to a man clad in trousers and an undershirt, while his coat went to a lady who sat numbly on deck. Although they were safe, *Flying Fish*'s passengers faced another ordeal: when the vessel reached the harbor, the captain refused to disembark any passengers until he had made a report.

Lauriat led his fellow survivors to the side of the boat and lowered the gangplank, but a sailor standing guard at the dock tried to halt the operation.[95] Lauriat pulled out a revolver and waved it in the air. In "language decidedly to the point," fellow survivor Oliver Bernard recalled, Lauriat ordered the man to let the passengers off the boat.[96] The sailor complied.[97]

Survivors crowded the quays, watching, waiting, hoping, and praying to see the faces of loved ones each time a new vessel drew up alongside. David Thomas had not seen his daughter, Margaret, since the explosion. Now safely ashore, the agnostic Thomas found himself looked after by a Catholic priest, who took him off to dinner and, against the crusty Welshman's protests, made him drink several snifters of brandy. Thomas wanted to wire his wife, but he had still had no news of Margaret. Finally, he dispatched a telegram: "Landed safely, Margaret not yet, but several boats still to come." Then he wandered back to the quay and waited in the darkness enveloping Queenstown.[98]

Margaret was safe, carried with George Kessler, Albert Bestic, and Captain Turner aboard the steamer *Bluebell* toward Queenstown. One survivor had looked out over the horizon and seen "a young woman, sitting in a wicker chair, serenely riding the waves."[99] Somehow, in her unconscious state, her body had floated into the chair, which kept her above the water and made her visible to rescuers. She was so cold and unresponsive when pulled from the sea that the sailors assumed she was dead and laid her on deck with a pile of bodies. One sailor, though, looked her over, declaring, "I rather think there's some life in this woman.

You'd better try and see." When she finally came to, her clothing was so heavy with water that three men were needed to help her below to the captain's cabin. She was still in a daze.[100]

"You are better now," a sailor whispered as Margaret struggled to understand what had happened and where she now was.[101] "I had a vague idea that something had happened," she recalled, "but I thought that I was still on the deck of the *Lusitania,* and I was vaguely annoyed that my own stewardess should not be attending to me instead of some unknown sailor." Her entire body "was shaking violently" and her teeth "were chattering like castanets." In the "delicious" warmth of the cabin, she gradually remembered what had happened. Several other survivors filled the cabin. "Almost all of us down there," Margaret said, "were a little drunk with the heat and the light and the joy of knowing ourselves to be alive."[102]

"The reporters will be after me to get information," Captain Turner had confided to Kessler aboard *Bluebell,* "but I shall tell them nothing."[103] He now sat in stony silence as one survivor, thought to be Trixie Witherbee, described how she had lost her child when a boat capsized. His death, she insisted, had been due to the lack of discipline and organization on the ship, and she told Turner that she meant to say so publicly. A sailor tending to Lady Mackworth whispered that the woman was hysterical, but Margaret, "fresh from the incompetent muddle on the *Lusitania's* deck," thought that she was "the one person on board who was not." It was after eleven that night when *Bluebell* steamed into the harbor at Queenstown. Margaret was naked but for a blanket wrapped around her and the captain's slippers, and borrowed a long coat when they landed. "I must have been pretty weak," she recalled as she reached the gangway, "for I had to get down on my hands and knees and crawl on to it. At the other end of the gangway, my father was waiting."[104]

CHAPTER SEVENTEEN

Rising along the steep, cobblestone streets ringing its harbor, Queenstown was a quiet, almost serene little town. In 1849, Queen Victoria had visited the town then known as Cove; it was the first time a British monarch had ever set foot on Irish soil, and Cove was renamed Queenstown to mark the occasion. American consul Wesley Frost thought it was a "beautiful little city," its streets filled with rustic laborers, women in shawls, and picturesque donkey carts.[1]

Queenstown had long been a point of embarkation for many, principally steerage passengers leaving their homeland in the hope of better lives in America. *Titanic* had called here on her maiden voyage, collecting hundreds of émigrés before sailing to oblivion. Now, shocked survivors of another doomed liner slowly shuffled into the city as the night wore on, shaking, dazed, eyes downcast, clothing wet and torn. As James Brooks came ashore, he thrust his hand into his trouser pocket and found that he had only four cents.[2] Another passenger, too, searched in his pocket and pulled out a crumpled, damp piece of paper: it was a New York City newspaper, carrying the German notice bolded in black.[3] An exhausted Harold Boulton had promptly downed six whiskey and sodas at his hotel; "I was not a drinking man," he later said, but "I gulped them down." He was sure that the alcohol saved his life.[4]

A fortunate few, like Amy Pearl, Rita Jolivet, and Laura Ryerson, stayed with Vice Admiral Coke at his private residence; others found beds at the Imperial Hotel or cheap lodging houses. The largest number, though, went to the forty-three-room Queen's Hotel, owned ironically by a German immigrant who wisely hid in his cellar that night for fear of retribution.[5] It was, thought Margaret Mackworth, "by far the dirtiest place I have ever seen," while her father bluntly told the proprietor that it was a "damned dog kennel."[6] It was now crowded with the displaced and distressed. Dorothy Conner calmly walked up to the front desk and asked for a private room and a bath. The attendant stared at her in disbelief. If she wanted a room, she could stay, but she would have to share with other survivors. Along with a small bowl of lukewarm water in which to wash and a bottle of cold lemon soda came a lecture on her selfishness.[7]

People crowded in as best as they could, "a curious, heterogeneous party of complete strangers," recalled Margaret Mackworth, "whom this great catastrophe had shaken into a temporarily close intimacy."[8] At the Imperial Hotel, Belle Naish looked after Robert Kay. Still uncertain about her husband's fate, she could only wait. To help take her mind off her anxiety, she sat with Robert and taught him the Lord's Prayer.[9]

"All night," said Michael Byrne, "delirious survivors were moaning in their sleep and crying, 'Captain, save us!'" Carl Foss had collapsed from shock and exposure, and was carried to his temporary lodgings.[10] "You're badly hurt," an officer told Robert Timmis, "your head is bashed in." Timmis would eventually lose the sight in his other eye from injuries sustained in the sinking.[11] Robinson Pirie couldn't understand why he was covered "by a coat of black tar," the mixture of coal and oil that had swirled around the sinking ship. Though he scrubbed and scrubbed at his Queenstown hotel, he thought he would never again get clean. Like many other survivors, his actions were almost mechanical: shock and exposure left them unable to do much more than simply follow routine motions.[12]

Isaac Lehmann complained not only of the arrival at Queenstown—"the arrangement for the reception of the survivors was just as hard and difficult as it was to get saved from the *Lusitania*"—but also grumbled that he received "no attention at all" at the Queen's Hotel.[13] David Thomas and Howard Fisher, wrapped in blankets at the hotel, were trying to sleep in the lounge when a boisterous fellow survivor burst in. Not only had he survived, but so had his wife and child, and he insisted that everyone celebrate his good fortune by singing and drinking the night away. When the men refused, he shouted, "Drink with me, and I'll shut up!" Fisher just wanted him to go away, but finally Thomas reached across the table, grabbed the bottle of whiskey, and toasted the man. Seemingly satisfied, he calmed down and allowed the men to sleep. "It was the one humorous incident of that tragic day," Fisher recalled.[14]

Early reports of survivors were garbled and often wrong. Lady Mackworth, one newspaper reported, "is hovering between life and death."[15] Many survivors sent short, reassuring cables to friends and relatives. "Safe and well," Timmis cabled to his wife in Texas.[16] Charles Lauriat reported that he was "safe and sound, and suffering from no after shock."[17] "Saved," ran the terse telegram from George Kessler to his brother-in-law. "Unharmed. In water three hours."[18] The champagne merchant seemed stunned; when cornered by a reporter, Kessler rubbed his forehead thoughtfully and slowly said, "How I escaped, why I escaped—is a miracle. It's God's mercy. I cannot believe it happened. It is more like a nightmare."[19]

Saturday, May 8, was "a beautiful morning," remembered Charles Lauriat. The sun "was shining warmly, and hardly a breath of air was stirring."[20] Dawn revealed a sickly sight: a cluster of white lifeboats, bobbing quietly in the harbor. Curious crowds gathered around them. A few smiled and posed for photographs with the macabre debris of disaster; adventuresome young boys scampered over their hulls at play.[21] Six lifeboats: all that remained of the mighty *Lusitania*.

For most, it had been a long, unnerving night. Charles Lauriat had secured a room at the Imperial, but restlessly wandered the streets of Queenstown until passing into "a dead, dreamless sleep." His landlady dried his clothing and shoes, served him whiskey made by her grandfather, and fed him breakfast before Lauriat set off through the town. Knowing that many survivors were "practically destitute," he went to the local bank and presented a waterlogged check for £40 to a rather startled cashier. "He told me he didn't know me," Lauriat recalled, "and I told him that didn't make any difference, I didn't know him. He said he couldn't guarantee my signature, but I told him that I thought my signature was as good as his money. I produced my soaked passport and showed him my autograph." Lauriat explained that he needed the money for "twelve half-starved, half-naked Americans that had to be fed and clothed." The clerk remained unmoved. Finally, Lauriat told him that he would not leave the bank until he had his funds. Although the man grumbled that he would "probably lose his job," he eventually gave Lauriat his money and the Boston bookseller promptly distributed it among his fellow survivors, divided "into as small fractions as possible" to help as many as he could.[22]

Unknown to Lauriat, orders from American Secretary of State William Jennings Bryan had come instructing consul Wesley Frost to "care for bodies of the dead, to give all help to the sick, and to aid the survivors who lost all cash."[23] Frost went to the local bank, retrieved several hundred pounds, and spent the next few days loaning it out to American survivors.[24] Even so, Isaac Lehmann was still disgruntled. Feeling that he was receiving "very little" attention from authorities, "I decided the best thing to do was to get out of Queenstown as quick as possible."[25]

Survivors, clad in borrowed clothing, wandered the streets in a daze from hospital to hospital, searching for missing friends and relatives. Hearing that a woman identified as Mrs. Hammond was in a hospital, Ogden Hammond rushed to see her. Instead of his wife, Mary, he found a stranger, Canadian passenger Kathleen Hammond, who had lost her husband in the sinking. Not knowing what else to do, Hammond generously gave Kathleen money for clothing and her return passage.[26] Warren Pearl found his wife, Amy, along with nurse Alice Lines and his two youngest children, Stuart and Audrey. There was, though, no trace of the other two children, Amy and Susan. "Two were gone," he commented philosophically, "but I thank God that so many of my family were saved, especially when I recall that whole families have perished."[27]

Josephine Burnside spent that Saturday in the Queenstown Cunard office, sobbing. "I fear my daughter is lost!" she cried. "I have not seen her since the torpedo struck the *Lusitania*. I know she must have gone. The Lord alone can tell how I was saved." A reporter noted that she was "almost fainting" as she persisted in a "futile effort to obtain reassuring information."[28] Avis Dolphin had been put into a bed at the Queen's Hotel with a glass of hot milk the previous evening: "it was lovely," she remembered. Ian Holbourn found her the next morning, and soon she had new shoes and a hat to replace those she had lost. Even after taking a bath, she couldn't get the engine oil and grime that had covered the sea when *Lusitania* went down out of her hair. But, she wrote to her mother, she thought that she had "escaped very nicely. A few bruises is all I have, and I can't feel those unless I press them very hard. I haven't got a cold or anything."[29]

Theodate Pope had been so weak that sailors carried her from the quay to a motorcar, which took her to "a third-rate hotel." There, she spent a restless night. "All night long, men kept coming into our room, snapping on the lights, bringing children for us to identify, taking telegrams, getting our names for the list of survivors," and making any number of requests. "I kept expecting Mr. Friend to appear, looking for me," she recalled, but he had been lost.[30] Late that Saturday morning, Dorothy Conner came to see Margaret Mackworth at the Queen's Hotel. Dorothy still wore the same fawn-colored tweed suit she had dressed in the previous day; it looked, Margaret recalled, "as smart and well-tailored as if it had just come out of the shop." Later, a woman asked Lady Mackworth and other ladies what they needed in the way of underclothing and personal items, and soon returned from Cork with the gifts.[31]

Most often, hospital and hotel searches failed. Queenstown, the *New York Times* reported, was "now a vast morgue."[32] Survivors fearfully took to the three temporary morgues at the City Hall, a shed at the Cunard Quay, and a disused chandlery on the harbor. All night long and into morning, bodies continued to wash up along the Irish coast. "The scenes among the debris cast up from the wreck were so excruciating as to defy description," recalled Wesley Frost. "Drowned bodies of women and children were numerous, and many had been mangled or disfigured in the surge and grinding of the wreckage so as to stain the ocean with blood."[33]

Shattered survivors passed down these grim rows of corpses, the eerie silence broken only by an occasional cry or sob. Dim lights revealed mangled, bloated bodies, limbs twisted and mouths contorted in silent screams; some women still clutched the life-less bodies of infants in their arms.[34] Many corpses lacked shoes, "evidence of a hurried attempt to free themselves of impeding attire," the *New York Times* reported.[35] Attendants had gone through pockets looking for papers; watches and jewelry lay in little piles atop each of the bodies, in the hope that someone would be able to identify a friend or relative.[36] To Oliver Bernard, the victims "looked like battered, bruised, broken dolls" resembling some macabre illustration by Gustave Doré. Body after body, the "trophies of war" took on a "horrible, lifeless uniformity."[37] He saw "a heap, literally a heap, of babies" on the floor. "They were almost naked, and their poor little bodies were bruised and cut. Some of them were purple, while some were almost black and others were yellow. It was a terrible sight."[38]

Here lay Charles Frohman, with a "most beautiful and peaceful smile" on his face.[39] Paul and Gladys Crompton, along with their six children and nursemaid, Dorothy Allen, all perished in the sinking. Only the bodies of nine-month-old Peter, six-year-old John, and seventeen-year-old Stephen were recovered. Frederick Orr-Lewis identified Frances Stephens, who still wore her rope of magnificent pearls around her neck, but there was no trace of her young grandson, John.

Annie Adams searched for her husband, Henry, but to no avail; honeymooners Leslie and Stewart Mason were found in one of the morgues. "I made the trip through the morgues for several days," Belle Naish recalled, "in search of my husband's body. I never saw him again after I turned toward him following the last explosion. The sights I saw in the morgue are the most terrible recollections that I can ever have. They will remain with me until my dying day."[40] Only Leslie Morton had an unexpectedly pleasant experience. Searching up and down the rows for his brother, he happened to look up and see him across the room, walking slowly between piles of corpses. "It was quite a meeting!" Morton later wrote.[41]

Sunday, May 9, was Mothers' Day. In great pain from her broken collarbone, Marguerite, Lady Allan waited in a local hospital for word of her daughters Anna and Gwendolyn. She held on to hope: *Spero* ("I Hope") was the Allan family motto, carved into stone above Ravenscrag's proud doorway.[42] Such was her social importance that even the prime minister of Canada received a report that Lady Allan was "considered to be holding her own splendidly." In these days, Queenstown was a city of rumors, and there were early reports that both Anna and Gwendolyn were safe.[43] Still, they failed to appear. Finally, George Slingsby volunteered to search for them in the morgues. It was an emotional ordeal: Slingsby knew Anna and Gwendolyn quite well, but he was so traumatized by the rows of corpses that he mistakenly identified "two girls, bloated and mottled and wearing vests," as the Allan daughters. Disheartened, he could not bring himself to tell Lady Allan; instead, a doctor informed her that her daughters were dead.[44] "I am much too upset to talk," Marguerite told a reporter. "It is a most terrible thing to look back on those scenes." The Germans, she added, "must have intended to drown us all."[45] Finally, on May 12, Marguerite Allan left Queenstown for a hospital in Dublin; a few days after, Gwendolyn's body washed ashore, but Anna was never found.[46]

Tending to the recovered bodies became a problem. The corpses of "important Americans," wrote Wesley Frost, needed to be embalmed for shipping back to the United States. Apparently, though, no one in Queenstown knew how to do this. Finally, Frost hired a surgeon from the University College Medical School in Cork to do the work, for the astronomical fee of £80 per body.[47]

The first funerals took place on Monday; even with reinforcements sent from Dublin, the supply of caskets ran out, and officials set soldiers to work hastily building pine boxes. Shops closed out of respect while the long, grim cortege of coffin after coffin, borne by hearses, wagons, carts, and trucks, made its way over Queenstown's cobbled streets as crowds stood with hats off and heads bowed and church bells tolled. A major in the Royal Irish Infantry walked at the head of the procession, followed by Protestant and Catholic clergy, representatives from Cunard and the Admiralty, local officials, and soldiers as a band played the mournful dirge of Chopin's "Funeral March." After a requiem service at St. Coleman's Cathedral, the procession made its way some two miles to the Old Church Cemetery, where mass graves had been dug the previous day. One by one, the coffins were lowered; there were so many that they were stacked atop each other.[48]

There were other noises amidst the sobs and funeral dirges clinging to Queenstown: voices loudly condemning Cunard, *Lusitania*'s crew, the British Admiralty, and Captain Turner. Cunard took a carefully measured response. Accounts were opened at some shops in Queenstown so that survivors could buy clothing, and temporary housing was commandeered for them. Representatives took names of survivors, contacted relatives, and made arrangements for passengers to continue on to Great Britain.[49] Yet when it came to practicalities, Cunard offended more than they comforted.

Wesley Frost complained that "the search for floating bodies has been wretchedly managed." Neither Admiralty representatives nor Cunard made any effort to search after Friday midnight. A full twenty-four hours elapsed before Cunard dispatched a tug late Saturday night; it returned within a few hours, never having reached the scene of the disaster. Infuriated, Frost finally told a Cunard agent that continued failure to act would result in serious "diplomatic intervention." Finally, late Monday—some seventy-four hours after the tragedy—a more thorough search began.

Cunard and the Admiralty, Frost noted, "each appear willing to shift responsibility to the other."[50] When Michael Byrne asked "the Cunard Company about compensation for my personal effects, they said to file a claim with the Admiralty and at the termination of war, they would collect it for me. In answer, I said I bought my ticket from the Cunard Company, and not from the Admiralty."[51] This dismissive attitude was made more infuriating as, over the next few weeks, officials in Queenstown sold off *Lusitania*'s six lifeboats, and Cunard billed them, demanding immediate compensation.[52]

After landing in Queenstown, Cunard officials had quickly shuffled a stunned Captain Turner off to a secluded room above the main bank. He tried to remain hidden, though one enterprising journalist managed to corner him on the street and ask what had happened. "It is the fortune of war!" was all the captain said before rushing away.[53] One local official described him as "a broken man," clad in a "badly-fitting old suit," dazed and traumatized by his experiences.[54] The sense of anger was palpable. Captain Turner got an early taste of it when he dared venture out of his temporary lodgings and into the town. One survivor, seeing him shopping, accosted the beleaguered captain. "You should be worrying about a hat, when so many of us have lost everything we own!" she shouted. "Why, you ought to be ashamed of yourself!"[55]

Majority opinion, reported the *New York Tribune*, was "avowedly hostile to Captain Turner, the Cunard Company, and the authorities." Many people declared that Turner "had no business" sailing his ship so close to the shore, and at such a slow speed. He and his crew had "insisted that there was no danger" and prevented the lifeboats from being quickly and safely launched. Nor had the Admiralty provided "an adequate escort."[56]

In those first days, frustrated and mourning survivors did not shy away from voicing such bleakly disturbing views of the disaster. "The standard of human efficiency is far below what we are entitled to expect!" David Thomas thundered at Queenstown. What had happened aboard *Lusitania,* he said, was "outrageous, simply outrageous."[57] His daughter agreed, thinking that "the accident could very possibly have been avoided and that in any event, the loss of life had been pretty well doubled by lack of organization on board." Margaret Mackworth railed against "the intolerable British stupidity, which had made the catastrophe so much worse than it need have been."[58] Privately, Vice Admiral Coke complained to Wesley Frost that "Turner should have kept further out," though the American consul also thought that "the Admiralty had by no means done their full duty by him."[59]

"It was outrageous that the *Lusitania* pushed ahead right into the path of danger," one survivor said in Queenstown.[60] "I cannot condemn too strongly the sacrifice of human life," Carl Foss declared, "mainly through the reduced speed at which *Lusitania* was going at the time."[61] "We lived in a fool's paradise of disbelief that anything like torpedoes could vitally injure our ship," George Kessler mused.[62] He believed that *Lusitania*'s slow speed contributed to "our risk of being torpedoed," and he could not understand "why there were no destroyers or patrol boats about."[63] Noting that he spoke with "considerable bitterness," a reporter quoted Howard Fisher as saying that neither "discipline or precautions were up to the standard." He did not understand "how the Cunard Company or the Admiralty can hold themselves free from blame for this tragedy. The authorities allowed a great ship, loaded with valuable cargo, to proceed through known dangerous waters without a single torpedo boat as a convoy."[64] Michael Byrne thought that passengers had been "led to the slaughter," adding, "the slightest precautions were not taken. Either the Cunard Company or the British Admiralty should be held strictly to account."[65] Ogden Hammond railed against Staff Captain Anderson and his orders "not to be alarmed," which he believed had led many aboard the ship to their deaths.[66]

Annie Adams, while "not wishing to do anything that might minimize this hideous crime of the Germans," decided that it was her "duty to my fellow beings to emphasize the lack of provisions for safety and the negligence on the part of the men responsible for our safety in this crisis." Something, she insisted, "must be done to make a repetition of this unnecessary loss of life impossible."[67] Another survivor was "dumbfounded" on reaching Queenstown and finding boats of the Irish Coastal Patrol "secure and snug in the harbor, with their crews lolling about the decks, while German submarines were blowing up English ships a few hours away."[68]

Oliver Bernard's blood boiled when, walking through Queenstown, he spotted "officers in gold braid" from *Lusitania*. They had, he said, "let all those poor things drown like rats." His "contempt for the seamanship displayed on that memorable voyage" led him to ponder "deliberate treachery on the part of all who were responsible for the safety of the passengers, to say nothing of the crew." Yet he was also certain that "whatever happened to *Lusitania*, however the war might end," British officials, "admirals, generals and the like," would continue to insist that they were "never in the wrong about anything."[69]

❦

Yet while decrying the sinking, few of the American survivors thought that their country should take action. "We were warned by the German Government," Fisher commented, "and I, for one, do not want any official action by my country."[70] George Kessler thought that the United States must act "in a prompt and manly manner as becomes the dignity of our country," insisting that something had to be done to protect American honor. But he was also philosophical: "What can America do?" he asked. "Nothing will bring back these people to life. It was cold-blooded, deliberate murder, and nothing else—the greatest murder the world has ever known. How will going to war mend that?"[71]

As the days passed, distraught, disillusioned survivors finally left the little town, making their ways across the globe. The tragedy continued to hang over Queenstown as remaining survivors haunted hospitals, awaited ships searching for bodies, and repeated harrowing tours of morgues.

"There is no hope of finding him alive now," Hugh Lane's sister wrote to a friend. "It is not even certain his dear body can be found."[72] Lane was never recovered, nor were Edgar Gorer, Henry Sonneborn, and Leo Schwabacher. The Vanderbilt family dispatched a lawyer to Queenstown, and offered $1,000 for recovery of Alfred's body, a sum, said Wesley Frost, "potent to the minds of the fishers."[73] Searchers pulled Marie Depage's corpse from the sea; on May 12, sailors loaded her coffin, draped in a Belgian flag, aboard a ship to return her to her homeland.[74] A week after the disaster, Angela Papadopoulos learned that her husband's body had been found. There was no sign of Trixie Witherbee's mother, Mary Brown, and not until June did Trixie learn that the body of a young boy had washed ashore. By this time, his face was unrecognizable, but from a description of the clothing she believed that it was her son, Alfred. An almost unbearably painful ordeal followed, when the father of a *Lusitania* victim claimed that the body was actually that of his son. In the end, Alfred Witherbee prevailed, and the body was buried under his son's name in the cemetery at Queenstown.[75]

Lindell Bates came to look for his brother, Lindon; officials in Queenstown took him for a spy and imprisoned him briefly; finally, he was released and he identified the body of Lindon when it washed up on the Irish coast on May 10.[76] Gladys Bilicke, too, had desperately looked for her husband, Albert, wandering from morgue to morgue without result.[77] Finally, certain that he hadn't survived, she said his body could be identified by the two abdominal scars from his recent surgery; his monogrammed gold and platinum watch; his sapphire cuff links; his diamond and turquoise ring; and his diamond tiepin.[78]

Over the weeks and even months that followed, bodies continued to wash up on the Irish coast. The first bodies recovered, Wesley Frost wrote, "made a very strong appeal through their likeness—a sort of unearthly aura of personality." With the passing days, the bodies were in "revolting condition," their "rigidity relaxed into an inebriate flabbiness, and the features broke down into a preposterously animal-like repulsiveness." What remained of faces was "grotesque and hideous. The lips and noses were eaten away by sea birds, and the eyes gouged out into staring pools of blood. It was almost a relief when the faces became indistinguishable."[79]

Only 768 people—passengers and crew—had survived; four of those died of their injuries in the next months. Some 1,198 had perished, including 128 Americans. Over 800 of *Lusitania*'s victims were never recovered.[80]

CHAPTER EIGHTEEN

News of *Lusitania*'s sinking sent shockwaves around the world. Great Britain was both numb with horror and pulsing with a desire for revenge as newspapers battled each other in hyperbolic headlines. "The Huns Carry Out Their Threat to Murder!" ran one; another deemed the tragedy the "latest achievement of German frightfulness."[1] Even the staid *Times* denounced "the diabolic character of Germany's action" and the "wholesale massacre of those on board."[2] It had been, the newspaper declared, "wholesale murder, and nothing else."[3]

The disaster became a powerful weapon in the ongoing propaganda war. Shopkeepers of German ancestry found their store windows broken and their goods looted; German nationals were attacked on the streets. Six days after the sinking, Prime Minister Asquith declared that all German males between seventeen and forty-five would be interned as enemy aliens; others would simply be deported.[4] The tragedy needed no distortion to arouse indignation, yet newspapers eagerly published photographs of the dead and offered up salacious stories that the U-boat had machine-gunned desperate survivors and its crew laughed as they watched babies drown.[5]

American reaction was slightly more subdued. The sinking, wrote the *New York Tribune,* was "in defiance not alone of every principle of international law, but of every dictate of common humanity. American men, women and children, citizens of this neutral nation, have been exposed to death, have, perhaps, been actually murdered by German war craft. For this murder there is no justification."[6] "The civilized world stands appalled," declared the *New York Herald,* adding, "if ever wholesale murder was premeditated, this slaughter on the high seas was."[7] The *New York World* summed up what must have been on many minds when it wrote: "What Germany expects to gain by her policy is something we cannot guess: what advantage will it be to her to be left without a friend or a well-wisher in the world?"[8] Editorials condemned, anger poured out in column after column, and cartoons depicted the Kaiser surrounded by a sea of dead children. Only the *New York Times* looked beyond the emotion of the moment to directly address what it termed "the Admiralty's neglect," writing that the lack of a convoy was "unaccountable" and that the Admiralty had failed in its "plain duty."[9]

While a few German newspapers decried the sinking, most described it as a great patriotic victory in the ongoing war. "We rejoice over this new success of the Germany Navy," declared the *Neue Freie Presse.*[10] The *Kölnische Volkszeitung* wrote that the *Lusitania* disaster was "a success of moral significance," explaining, "the English wish to abandon the German people to death by starvation. We are more humane. We simply sank an English ship with passengers, who at their own risk and responsibility entered zone of operations."[11]

Kaiser Wilhelm II was outraged over the sinking, telling American ambassador to Berlin James Gerard that "no gentleman would kill so many women and children."[12] Apocryphal stories that the Kaiser gave German schoolchildren a holiday in celebration were widely circulated.[13] Germany might have fended off much of the international criticism had she simply apologized and expressed regret: instead, she justified the sinking. It was, wrote Grand Admiral Alfred von Tirpitz, sad that many Americans, "in wanton recklessness, and in spite of the warnings of our Ambassador, had embarked in this armed cruiser, heavily laden with munitions," and had lost their lives, but Germany had been within her rights to torpedo the liner.[14] German propagandist Bernard Dernberg, who had been posted to New York City, only exacerbated and aroused American opinion. He not only insisted that *Lusitania* had been carrying contraband and munitions and was therefore a legitimate target, but added that the Americans who had perished had "committed suicide" by sailing on the liner.[15] Count Johann von Bernstorff, Germany's ambassador to America, was shocked by Dernberg's callous remarks, and quickly sent him packing back to Germany.[16]

A more formal statement came from Berlin on May 10, three days after the sinking. While the Foreign Office in Berlin expressed "its deepest sympathy at the loss of American lives" aboard the liner, it insisted that responsibility rested "entirely with the British Government, which, through its plan of starving the civilian population of Germany, has forced Germany to resort to retaliatory measures." The statement pointed out that many British merchant vessels were armed with heavy guns and had previously tried to ram German submarines when they surfaced to give warning. It also declared that *Lusitania* had regularly carried large amounts of arms and ammunition. Such actions effectively turned the liner into a blockade-runner, carrying materials even the British government had deemed to be contraband.[17]

How would the United States respond? American ambassador Walter Page wrote from his post in London of the widespread feeling that his country "must declare war, or forfeit European respect."[18] Former president Theodore Roosevelt loudly denounced the sinking as "piracy on a vaster scale of murder than any old time pirate ever practiced," adding, "it seems inconceivable that we can refrain from taking action in this matter for we owe it not only to humanity but to our own national self-respect."[19] Yet President Wilson was cautious. Three days after the disaster, he gave a speech in which he declared, "The example of America must be a special example." The country, he said, would "not fight" but instead seek peace "because peace is the healing and elevating influence of the world." He ended, "There is such a thing as a man being too proud to fight. There is such a thing as a nation being so right that it does not need to convince others that it is right."[20]

Six days after the sinking, Wilson's State Department dispatched a formal note to Berlin. The president expected "that the Imperial German Government will disavow the acts of which the government of the United States complains, that they will make reparation so far as reparation is possible for injuries which are without measure, and that they will take immediate steps to prevent the recurrence of anything so obviously subversive of the principles of warfare for which the Imperial German Government have in the past so wisely and so firmly contended."[21] While decrying the loss of life, Secretary of State William Jennings Bryan believed that Germany was fully within her rights to sink the liner. The most vocal public opinion supported a strong American response; Bryan soon resigned in protest over the president's insistence that "England's violation of neutral rights is different from Germany's violation of the rights of humanity."[22]

Throughout that long summer of 1915, governments warred in diplomatically polite notes. That the sinking had transcended disaster into the realm of propaganda soon became apparent. Victims were quickly forgotten in the nationalistic rush on all sides to exploit the tragedy. British recruiting posters depicted the last minutes of the liner in horrific exaggeration, or carried provocative images of drowned women clutching dead babies. Then there was the infamous "Medal of Death," created in Munich by sculptor Karl Goetz. One side depicted the sinking ship; the other showed a Cunard window manned by the skeletal figure of Death, dispensing tickets to waiting passengers beneath a sign that read, "Business Above All." Goetz mistakenly dated the sinking as having taken place on May 5; the British insisted that this thus revealed a premeditated plot to sink the ship.[23]

Although Goetz manufactured the image as a private souvenir, to mark what he viewed as Cunard's lethal business practices, British authorities were quick to realize the propaganda benefit of a medal they insisted celebrated the sinking, and commissioned Selfridge's Department Store in London to make and sell some 300,000 duplicates to further arouse public indignation, falsely claiming it had been awarded to U-boat crews.[24]

On Monday, May 10—the same day on which the funerals took place in Queenstown—Kinsale coroner John Horgan summoned Captain Turner to appear at the first inquest into the disaster. Turner seemed to be "a broken man" as he testified before a jury of shopkeepers and fishermen in the Old Market at Kinsale. The captain admitted that he was aware of the submarine danger and had received warnings from the Admiralty; he had, he insisted, carried out his orders "to the best of my ability." Turner believed only one torpedo had struck the ship. The captain seemed so overwhelmed that Horgan interrupted the proceedings, saying, "We all sympathize with you very much in the terrible crime which has been committed against your vessel." At these words, Turner lowered his head and burst into tears.[25] There was also a fair amount of revisionism: even after the worried confrontations aboard ship with George Kessler, Ian Holbourn, Francis Jenkins, and others, Turner lied, saying that he had never heard any passengers express worries about possible danger.[26] Just as Horgan concluded his proceedings, a telegram arrived from the Admiralty in London, ordering Captain Turner to remain silent. The Admiralty were, Horgan commented, "as belated on this occasion as they had been in protecting the *Lusitania* against attack." The humble jury duly rendered its verdict. The "appalling crime" had been committed "contrary to international law," it read. Not only the crew of the submarine but also "the Emperor and the Government of Germany" were guilty of "willful and wholesale murder."[27]

Lusitania's surviving passengers and crew continued to be pawns in the ongoing propaganda efforts that followed the sinking. The British government's official inquiry conducted by the Board of Trade into the tragedy began on June 15, 1915, in London, just a month after the disaster. Of the 768 survivors—passengers and crew—only 36 were called upon to give evidence. Some passengers, like Oliver Bernard, were willing to testify but were refused when officials suspected they might be openly critical.[28] From its inception, the British inquest was meant to absolve the Admiralty and Cunard of any responsibility. The surviving officers and crew, as historians Thomas A. Bailey and Paul B. Ryan noted, "were no doubt aware that the way to promotion and pay was to say no more than they had to and to avoid giving unduly damaging testimony against their employer."[29]

The Board of Trade inquiry into the sinking lasted a mere three days, with two additional sessions a few weeks later. The first session began at Westminster Central Hall in London, under the direction of John Bigham, Lord Mersey. Three years earlier, Mersey had conducted the Board of Trade investigation into the sinking of *Titanic*. He had found that neither Captain Smith, who had raced his ship through a dark night despite ice warnings, nor the

White Star Line was in any way responsible for the tragedy. Mersey could now be relied upon to be similarly sympathetic to Cunard and the Admiralty, especially during a time of war. The implicit goal was to conceal unfavorable evidence while absolving officials of any responsibility and assigning the entire blame to Germany. As such, the outcome was cynically predetermined.

No one knew what had caused the massive second explosion; persistent fears that arms and ammunition aboard *Lusitania* were responsible meant that any such hint had to be strenuously denied. There was, Mersey emphatically declared, "no explosion of any part of the cargo."[30] But how to account for the second explosion? Five days after the sinking, Admiralty intelligence intercepted a wireless message in which Schwieger reported having used only one torpedo; this information was passed on to First Sea Lord Fisher, First Lord Winston Churchill, Chief of War Staff Rear Admiral James Harrison Oliver, and Director of Intelligence Captain Reginald Hall, who promptly suppressed it.[31] Numerous people aboard *Lusitania* spoke of a second torpedo; the inquiry seized on their accounts, insisting that this had caused the second explosion. Those who insisted otherwise were ignored; in at least one instance, Cunard and the Admiralty briefed a witness before testimony, insisting that he refer to two torpedoes.[32] Even Captain Turner played along. At the Kinsale inquest, he had said that a single torpedo struck the ship; now he added a second for his appearance before Lord Mersey.[33]

Two of the sessions were held behind closed doors, during which Captain Turner was relentlessly grilled over his actions. The Admiralty clearly believed that he had been negligent, ignoring warnings and instructions to zigzag; to keep *Lusitania* away from headlands; and to maintain full speed. In advance of the hearing, Captain Richard Webb, director of the Admiralty's Trade Division, prepared a memorandum in which he outlined Turner's failures. Turner, Webb reported, had "acted directly contrary to the written general instructions received from the Admiralty." In disregarding warnings and orders, Turner had displayed "an almost inconceivable negligence" in operating his ship.[34] At the Admiralty, both Lord Fisher and Winston Churchill heartily agreed that Turner should be made an example of and arrested no matter the outcome of the Mersey Inquiry.[35]

The captain, as his own lawyer reluctantly admitted, was "undoubtedly a bad witness" during the inquiry, unable to explain or justify his actions.[36] Yet the Admiralty was pursuing a foolish policy: if Turner was indeed found negligent, then survivors could sue Cunard for having employed him. Mersey, aware of the precariously balanced situation—and not wanting to weaken the propaganda case against Germany—finally shut down this line of investigation. It was, wrote historians Bailey and Ryan, "war, and no time for Britons to be bickering with one another when the real culprit, as seemed obvious, was a ruthless Germany. The British could hardly strengthen their case before the world against Hunnish barbarity and win the maximum sympathy of neutral nations if they blamed themselves."[37]

Mersey's eventual verdict was indeed a whitewash and almost unbelievable in its assertions. Only 39 percent of the passengers had survived, compared to 42 percent of the crew.[38] Yet Mersey ignored this uncomfortable fact, transforming inept members of the crew into heroic figures of self-sacrifice. They had, he declared, "behaved well throughout and worked with skill and judgment."[39] Instead, Mersey blamed "the well-meant but probably disastrous attempts of the frightened passengers" in loading and assisting in lowering the lifeboats, declaring that they "did more harm than good."[40] Incredibly, he insisted that *Lusitania*'s slow speed had absolutely nothing to do with her having been torpedoed; that all of the portholes had been closed, contrary to what numerous passengers recalled; that lifebelts had been plentiful, again contrary to what many passengers saw; and that the evacuation had been calm and orderly. With a fair dose of class bias, he blamed Third Class passengers for the final moments of panic.[41] He also dismissed accounts of faulty lifeboats with rusty oarlocks and ribs, insisting that any such damage had occurred during the eighteen minutes of the sinking. Turner, Cunard, and the Admiralty were absolved of any negligence. Instead, Mersey declared, "the whole blame for the cruel destruction of life in this catastrophe must rest solely with those who plotted and those who committed the crime," the U-boat captain and his German masters.[42] This political charade so upset Mersey that he supposedly later referred to it as "a damned, dirty business."[43]

When the report was published, an angry Charles Lauriat protested, "with every spark of manhood," assertions that the crew had been disciplined and that it had been panicked passengers who caused lifeboats to upend and crash into the sea. It was the passengers, thought Charles Lauriat, who made "heroic efforts" to load and launch the lifeboats, while most of the crew didn't know how to operate them. "It doesn't seem to me," he wrote, "that this Court of Inquiry has stood up to its business like the historic Briton who isn't afraid to take his medicine, and place blame where it should be placed; rather, it has hidden behind the act itself."[44]

Three years after the sinking, a group of American survivors lodged suit against Cunard for negligence, seeking compensation for lost possessions, medical expenses, and injuries.[45] Captain Turner was deposed in London, and again altered parts of his earlier testimony. The case was heard in the U.S. District Court for the Southern District of New York before Judge Julius Mayer; in 1912, Mayer—like Mersey—had presided over American claims of negligence lodged against the White Star Line in the *Titanic* disaster. And, like Mersey, he had ignored evidence of Captain

Smith's recklessness that fatal night, finding that there was no legal basis for any lawsuits alleging negligence. This amenable attitude appealed to Cunard, and Mayer soon proved them correct in their choice to let a judge, rather than a jury, litigate the issue. Mayer deemed any discussion of *Lusitania*'s lethal cargo irrelevant and refused to hear evidence on the question. He lifted most of his opinions on Captain Turner, the crew, the Admiralty, and Cunard straight from Mersey's published report. No official in charge of the ship would ever be made to answer for what had happened to *Lusitania*.[46]

❧

Shipwrecks have an undeniable allure, embodying tragedy and human drama played out upon an artful and artificial stage.

Some, like *Titanic,* have come to represent the passing of an age or been portrayed as grand morality tales, replete with virtuous heroes and selfless survivors. Others linger in the collective imagination because of misconception and myth. People still harbor the erroneous belief that *Lusitania*'s sinking directly drew America into World War I: in fact, nearly two years passed before President Wilson finally asked Congress to declare war on Germany.

The most persistent of all *Lusitania* lore, though, speaks to a cynical darkness, embracing tales of conspiracy and cover-up in an effort to explain the tragedy, to shroud her last voyage in an air of political pretense and Machiavellian machination that led to her deliberate sacrifice off the Irish coast. Within days of the tragedy, people wondered whether something more nefarious than German torpedoes had been at work that fateful day; even after a century, the question lingers: did the British Admiralty deliberately expose *Lusitania* to danger in the hope of embroiling America in the ongoing war?

❧

The circumstantial case seems uncomfortably strong. In September of 1914, First Lord of the Admiralty Winston Churchill supposedly referred to *Lusitania* as "live bait."[47] More specifically, three months before the tragedy, he wrote: "It is most important to attract neutral shipping to our shores, in the hope especially of embroiling the United States with Germany. . . . For our part, we want the traffic—the more the better, and if some of it gets into trouble, better still."[48]

An unusually strong aura of potential danger surrounded this particular voyage. Numerous passengers received warnings not to sail aboard *Lusitania*; the German embassy placed its notice in New York newspapers, practically signaling intent if the opportunity came. Room 40, the Admiralty's naval intelligence division, knew that at least one U-boat was active off the Irish coast, operating along the same route *Lusitania* would travel; three British vessels had been torpedoed in these waters in the space of twenty-four hours.[49] Yet when it came to protecting *Lusitania*, little was done. There was no escort; the Admiralty's warnings to Turner that submarines were active along his route seem to have been the extent of their precautionary measures. Adding to the intrigue, certain official files on *Lusitania* and her last voyage remain classified; others appear to have been lost.[50]

Author Colin Simpson posited a rather contradictory, two-pronged hypothesis of deliberate destruction in his 1972 book on the sinking. On the one hand, he insisted that *Lusitania* was likely loaded with disguised munitions desperately needed in the British war effort. On the other hand, he then suggested that Churchill and the Admiralty deliberately placed the ship—and its important cargo—in harm's way, in the hope that her torpedoing would draw America into the war.[51] Historian Patrick Beesly, himself a former Royal Navy intelligence officer, seemed to agree in large part with Simpson's general theory. "I am reluctantly driven to the conclusion," Beesly wrote, "that there was a conspiracy deliberately to put the *Lusitania* at risk, in the hopes that even an abortive attack on her would bring the United States into the war."[52]

Without question, an attack on *Lusitania* would provoke sentiment and arouse indignation; it would also offer Great Britain a valuable propaganda tool in the ongoing war—one that might help sway American opinion. A direct conspiracy, in which Churchill somehow engineered a deadly encounter between *Lusitania* and U-20, though, would have relied on a set of variables beyond the Admiralty's control. By the time intercepted transmissions from U-20 were decoded, they were already hours out of date: steering *Lusitania* into her path with any degree of certainty would have been impossible. Nor could the Admiralty know that Turner would ignore his orders about speed, his navigational course, and zigzagging the *Lusitania*. In short, the logistics of such an operation are staggeringly unlikely.

It is equally difficult to believe that Churchill was so naive as to think the automatic American response to any such sinking would be a declaration of war against Germany. He certainly wrote of attracting "neutral shipping" to Britain's shores and using any attendant incidents to diplomatic advantage; but *Lusitania* wasn't "neutral shipping"—she was a British ship, under control of the Admiralty. More to the point, Churchill must have realized that American entrance into the war in the late spring of 1915 would have proved disastrous for Great Britain. Suffering from shortages, Britain was heavily reliant on the purchase of munitions from friendly American companies: had America gone to war over the sinking of *Lusitania,* those munitions would have gone to American, not British, troops.

❧

If there wasn't a conspiracy of commission, what of a conspiracy of omission? Is it possible that the Admiralty, aware of the possible danger, simply left *Lusitania* to chance her fate on what turned out to be her final voyage? Such a theory isn't entirely out of the realm of possibility; perhaps someone envisioned a chance encounter, a terrible meeting at sea during which *Lusitania* might be torpedoed and badly damaged. But even this lacks compelling evidence. What can be said is that, once *Lusitania* sank, embarrassed bureaucrats who had done nothing moved swiftly to conceal the incompetence of an Admiralty that neglected to provide an escort and a captain who ignored warnings and steered his ship into a U-boat's path. Churchill had paid little attention to *Lusitania,* consumed as he was with the ongoing Dardanelles campaign; the Admiralty had been remiss in diligently safeguarding the liner; and perhaps more important, no one knew what had caused the second explosion. The Germans claimed that an immense cache of contraband munitions had led to *Lusitania*'s quick end: even the suggestion that this might be true could alter public opinion. And so evidence was suppressed—not to conceal a conspiracy but rather to hide an astonishingly lethal lack of diligence on officialdom's part when it came to the lives of those aboard *Lusitania.*

Such a scenario also casts doubt on the persistent myth that *Lusitania*'s munitions exploded, which has fueled the fires of conspiracy for years.

That she was carrying munitions is beyond doubt: they are carefully detailed in her longer manifest, filed with the Port of New York a few days after she sailed—ammunition, shrapnel shells, fuses, and aluminum powder. This cargo wasn't a secret: New York newspapers published both manifests the day after the disaster.[53] Colin Simpson wrote mysteriously of "a strange and possibly sinister mixture of goods" aboard *Lusitania,* suggesting that she carried gun cotton and other explosives disguised as furs, tubs of butter, and several thousand boxes of cheese.[54] A 2008 expedition to the ship revealed that rifle ammunition was located in an area where no munitions were supposedly stored on the last voyage.[55]

Allegations about additional concealed munitions, never substantiated, matter only if they caused a second explosion that lethally damaged the ship and significantly added to her rapid sinking. The ruins of *Lusitania* herself help resolve the issue. As with tales of conspiracy and cover-up, rumors of secret explorations of the wreck have contributed to the aura of mysterious intrigue. Stories that the Admiralty dove on the ship to retrieve, or conceal, munitions or guns on the liner have persisted for decades.[56] In the 1960s, American Navy diver John Light began visiting the wreck. Although conditions were difficult and visibility was poor, Light thought that, contrary to accounts by survivors, the second, internal explosion had blown off the bow; he also believed that he saw a gun still mounted on the deck. He attributed steel cables across the wreck to remnants of an earlier salvage operation; a large, rectangular hole cut into the hull, he theorized, had been made when a mounted gun had been retrieved.[57]

Light had the good fortune of diving a ship that was still in relatively good condition, recognizable and not yet disintegrated. Things had deteriorated badly by the summer of 1993, when Robert Ballard—the man who had located the wreck of *Titanic*—investigated *Lusitania.* The ship rests on her starboard side, thus concealing the location of the torpedo strike, as well as any other damage. But Ballard was sure of one thing: the second explosion hadn't come from munitions. He found that, contrary to what Light believed, *Lusitania*'s bow had not been blown off: in fact, it was the most recognizable part of the ruined ship. Had the munitions stored there exploded, the bow should have been all but obliterated.[58]

To account for the second explosion, Ballard proposed that the torpedo managed to spark loose coal dust in the bunkers.[59] Another historian has suggested that the torpedo might have ignited the aluminum powder *Lusitania* carried, to devastating effect.[60] Subsequent tests conducted at the Lawrence Livermore National Laboratory in California have challenged these theories: the coal dust would likely have been damp from contact with the steel hull, making ignition implausible. As for the aluminum powder, it indeed has highly explosive properties; had it ignited, though, the presumably devastating explosion should have significantly damaged *Lusitania*'s bow—damage no expedition to the wreck has yet found.[61] A century after the tragedy, a consensus of informed opinion favors a failure in *Lusitania*'s steam plant as the likely cause of the second explosion. On *Lusitania*, inflexible lines carried high-pressure steam from boilers to turbines. Cold water rushing in from the sea might well have caused them to fracture to devastating impact. The steam lines clearly failed, and failed quickly: less than a minute after the second explosion, *Lusitania*'s steam pressure dropped so much that she could no longer be steered, leaving her adrift in the Irish Sea.[62]

There is, though, one last, possible explanation for the second explosion. Leslie Morton was positive that he saw two torpedoes—and numerous survivors agreed. Human memory is fallibly fragile, especially at times of unexpected trauma. Yet several passengers like Isaac Lehmann, William Adams, and George Slingsby told remarkably consistent stories, independent of each other, revealing a telling sequence of events after the first explosion. Between thirty and sixty seconds elapsed; they rushed to portholes or to the railing in time to spot a second torpedo coming at the ship; only after this did they hear and feel the second explosion.[63] At the same time, glass in the First Class Dining Saloon's portholes shattered over tables, and heavy debris rained down on the roof of the Veranda Café—some four hundred feet aft of where Schwieger said his torpedo struck.[64]

Historians have largely dismissed the idea of a second torpedo based on Schwieger's war diary. This would indeed seemingly end the issue, yet the diary's integrity is not above suspicion: the original was destroyed, and only a typed copy survives.[65] The entry concerning *Lusitania*'s sinking contains a number of questionable claims and demonstrable errors: that the liner turned toward Queenstown before being hit, when in fact it turned in the opposite direction; that Schwieger had no idea as to the ship's identity before firing his torpedo; that *Lusitania* stopped immediately after the torpedo hit, when in fact she was unable to stop; and that her superstructure and bridge were "torn asunder."[66]

Then there is the claim that, before *Lusitania* sank, U-20 "dived to a depth of twenty-four meters and ran out to sea."[67] Many survivors recalled that a submarine surfaced after the sinking, and that several members of its crew surveyed the scene.[68] Finally, Schwieger wrote that it "would have been impossible for me, anyhow, to fire a second torpedo into this crowd of people struggling to save their lives."[69]

The sentiment, recorded historians Bailey and Ryan, is "quite out of keeping with the tone and substance of what preceded and followed. Nowhere else in his diary of this voyage do we find evidence of the slightest regard for humanity after he repeatedly fired torpedoes without warning."[70]

It is, of course, possible that Schwieger was traumatized by the chaos he had unleashed. Considerable evidence, though, suggests that German officials altered the diary sometime after Schwieger's death in 1917: not only is the formatting peculiar but the entry for May 7—when *Lusitania* was sunk—is the only page lacking

Schwieger's signature attesting to its accuracy.[71] Why would the diary have been altered? Germany faced international condemnation over the sinking: adding doubt about the torpedoed vessel's identity until it was too late and a declaration of sympathy for the victims may have been an attempt to alleviate moral guilt.[72] Yet if such alterations took place, what better reason could there be than to remove mention of a second torpedo fired at the unarmed passenger liner? Why else insert a line specifically refuting the idea?

The U-20 ordinarily carried six torpedoes: uniquely on this voyage—according to the diary—she carried seven. On May 5, Schwieger used four: one missed a passing Norwegian-flagged vessel; one hit *Candidate*; and it took two torpedoes to sink the *Centurion*.[73] According to a 1933 German source, Schwieger had orders to save two torpedoes for his return voyage; Bailey and Ryan asserted that the actual order was "to save one for the journey home." After firing at *Lusitania*, the diary records, torpedoes were left only in the rear tubes: the time needed to turn his submarine around to take another shot exceeds that between the first and second explosions. Yet if the diary was indeed rewritten, the integrity of the entire document is compromised. While not supporting the second-torpedo scenario, Bailey and Ryan suggested that Schwieger "could have failed to mention the use of a second torpedo, and then have accounted for this extra one by listing it among the several misses on this cruise, both earlier and later."[74]

To Schwieger, *Lusitania* was a large and prized target. On May 3, a torpedo had jammed in the tube when Schwieger tried to fire on a Danish vessel; on May 5, it had taken two torpedoes to sink the much smaller *Centurion*. Even a damaged *Lusitania*, if it was indeed armed, Schwieger may have thought, would pose a threat. He would also have known that roughly 60 percent of all torpedoes fired either failed to eject from their tubes, missed their target due to erratic steering mechanisms, or failed to explode on impact.[75] Given these circumstances, would Schwieger really have been so reluctant to fire a second torpedo? He had only one chance to take his shot: two torpedoes fired in quick succession would increase the odds that at least one made it to the target. The potential success far outweighed the risk.

If the diary was indeed altered, as historians have suggested, it would have been because Schwieger—and his superiors—had every reason to erase a second torpedo. After the fact, and in the face of universal condemnation, admission that Schwieger had fired a second torpedo would only have made him appear cold-blooded and bent on the deaths of all aboard. Covering up a second torpedo would also serve a dual purpose: to attribute the second explosion to illegal munitions aboard the ship and embarrass Great Britain in the ongoing propaganda war.

Of necessity, a second torpedo would demand that no one aboard U-20 that day ever admitted the truth: conspiracies are notoriously difficult to keep secret. Yet who would want to claim a second torpedo fired on an unarmed passenger liner that went to the bottom of the Irish Sea with such devastating loss of life? Perhaps the idea is implausible, but implausible is not the same as impossible, and the evidence suggesting a second torpedo as the cause of the second explosion cannot be entirely dismissed. *Lusitania* herself hides her secrets: if a second torpedo struck her, the proof has long since been buried beneath the wreckage of collapsed decks and in an impenetrable hull whose starboard side has not been seen since May 7, 1915.

Something certainly caused the second explosion aboard *Lusitania,* but the reason and the damage will always be matters of speculation. A massive explosion of some contraband that tore open the ship's hull lingers as such an attractive theory because it helps make sense of the apparently inexplicable speed at which

Lusitania sunk. Yet while the second explosion may have contributed to the ship's sinking, it probably only accelerated the inevitable. *Lusitania*'s swift end is not without parallel: in 1914, a collier rammed *Empress of Ireland* in the St. Lawrence River, causing the liner to sink in just fourteen minutes. The death of White Star's *Britannic,* operating as a hospital ship, was equally rapid: fifteen minutes after striking a German mine, she had disappeared beneath the Aegean Sea.[76] The irony is that Schwieger didn't need to fire a second torpedo: the first caused fatal damage to the ship. Hitting at the precise spot it did, coupled with the rapid asymmetrical flooding, *Lusitania*'s continued progress, which forced even more water into her hull, and the sea pouring through open portholes, was enough to send the liner to the bottom of the Irish Sea.[77]

The effect was lethal and catastrophic, resulting in the deaths of nearly 1,200 people; even Schwieger later professed shock at the destruction he had caused. The man who, recalled one of his friends, described the sinking of *Lusitania* as "the most terrible sight" he had ever witnessed, a scene "too horrible" for him to watch, only learned just how many had died when he arrived back in Germany. A friend said he was "appalled to discover the anger of outraged humanity that his act had aroused, and horrified at the thought that he was held up all over the world as an object of odium and loathing."[78]

With the world in an uproar, Schwieger found himself summoned to Berlin. Despite public pronouncements that the sinking had been justified, authorities in Berlin were now on the defensive; there were rumors that Kaiser Wilhelm II personally berated him, while Admiral Tirpitz recalled that he was treated "very ungraciously" by military officials.[79] After the sinking, Schwieger seemed "so haggard and so silent and so different," said his fiancée.[80] Yet soon he was back at sea aboard U-20, sinking more ships. In September, he torpedoed the Allan Line's *Hesperian* off the Irish coast, again without warning. Thirty-two of the 1,100 aboard died when one of the lifeboats overturned during evacuation. Also aboard was a coffin holding the remains of *Lusitania* passenger Frances Stephens, who now fell victim to Schwieger a second time when the vessel sank the following day.[81] This time, Schwieger was ordered to apologize for having violated German assurances that no further passenger liners would be attacked without warning. On May 8, 1916—one day after the first anniversary of *Lusitania*'s sinking—Schwieger's torpedoes struck another liner, White Star's *Cymric*. This time, the vessel was being used as a troop transport, and although five aboard perished, Schwieger suffered no serious repercussions.

In November 1916, U-20 ran aground off the Danish coast and had to be abandoned; today, its salvaged conning tower and deck gun are on display at the Strandingsmuseum in Thorsminde in West Jutland.[82] Schwieger was then given command of a larger boat, U-88. The following year, he received the ironically named *Pour le Mérite* in recognition of his gallantry and service in sinking nearly 200,000 tons of Allied shipping.[83] That fall, he took U-88 on a mission into the North Sea and, on September 5, 1917, Schwieger's luck ran out when he struck a mine. There were no survivors: Schwieger was just thirty-two.[84]

What might Schwieger have said had he survived? How would he justify his actions that sunny day in May? Popular sentiment at the time of the tragedy roundly condemned his actions. Even today, an apparently dispassionate historian can refer to his action as "willful murder."[85]

By law, Schwieger was expected to surface and fire a warning shot, demanding that *Lusitania* stop and allow her cargo to be searched. The commander knew that many British merchant vessels were armed with guns that could tear the hull of his submarine to pieces. Then there were the specific points under which *Lusitania* operated, which not only violated the Cruiser Rules but also made them obsolete that May 7. She was regularly transporting contraband, even by the British definition of the term; she operated under the sole control of the Admiralty; and she could also, should the need arise, be converted into an armed auxiliary cruiser to join the war. *Lusitania* was disguised, her funnels cloaked in gray, and she flew no flags. She was a non-neutral vessel in a declared war zone, with instructions to evade capture and even to ram a challenging submarine. Had Schwieger surfaced and fired a warning shot across *Lusitania*'s bow, does history really think that Captain Turner would have stopped the vessel and allowed a search, as demanded by the Cruiser Rules? The Admiralty's steady erosion of the established rules of naval warfare all but ensured that, sooner or later, some unarmed passenger vessel would be torpedoed with devastating loss of life. In creating the very set of circumstances that led to *Lusitania*'s destruction, the Admiralty, too, must share a significant portion of the blame.

This was the legal justification, but what of the moral case? Schwieger's responsibility was to his submarine and to his crew: surfacing and challenging *Lusitania,* he might reasonably have believed, would have put them in danger of being fired upon or rammed. Schwieger was under orders to sink troop transports, merchant ships, and warships. It was only chance that brought *Lusitania* into his path, but once the opportunity presented itself, the dutiful Schwieger had little recourse but to act; if he failed to do so, his inaction would certainly become known as soon as the submarine returned to its base.[86] He had no reason to think *Lusitania* would sink so quickly, and with such devastating loss of life. In his mind, he probably took the only action that he deemed available to him at the time: however callous the rationalizations might sound, the war made such an action almost inevitable.

Yet however legitimate Schwieger's actions, it is undeniable that in torpedoing *Lusitania* he made a grave mistake, if not from a legal perspective than certainly from humanitarian, political, and diplomatic ones. The attendant outcry over *Lusitania*'s sinking offered the world a vivid exhibition of the very worst excesses of German warfare, painting the dreaded "Huns" as barbaric murderers of innocent women and children. In this sense, as historians Bailey and Ryan wrote, Germany gained a temporary victory that was "worse than a defeat."[87]

Churchill aptly summed it up when he wrote, "The poor babies who perished in the ocean struck a blow at the German power more deadly than could have been achieved by the sacrifice of a hundred thousand fighting men."[88]

EPILOGUE

It was just after dawn when the first trains carrying *Lusitania* survivors began arriving in London on Sunday, May 9. "Bedraggled and weary," reported the *New York Times,* many still wore the "ill-fitting clothes" they had been given at Queenstown.[1] Crossing from Ireland to Wales had, for some, been yet another ordeal. "Every throb of the engines went through the pit of my stomach," recalled Charles Lauriat. He saw that nearly all of the dazed survivors kept their lifebelts on throughout the voyage.[2]

Stepping out of the train from Wales at London's Euston Station at seven that morning, Lauriat was "almost mobbed" by a mass of reporters. Even more upsetting was the rush of wide-eyed others, shouting, begging, pleading with Lauriat for word of friends and relatives who had been aboard *Lusitania*. Once safely whisked away to a friend's country house, Lauriat sat down and began to write a detailed account of his experiences, published later that year as *The Lusitania's Last Voyage*. Lauriat cast a critical eye over everyone involved with the disaster. "I did not think any human being with a drop of red blood in his veins, called a man, could issue an order to sink a passenger steamer without at least giving the women and children a chance to get away," he wrote.[3] Yet he also heaped scorn on *Lusitania*'s captain and crew, and on the efforts by the British government to absolve Turner and his men, as well as Cunard and the Admiralty, of any responsibility in the tragedy. Lauriat eventually returned to his family's book business in Boston, and died in 1937.

Lauriat recovered quickly from the disaster, but many other survivors faced long years of suspicion, guilt, anxiety, and pain from the injuries they had suffered. Those survivors who had boarded *Lusitania* to join the Great War, see loved ones before they went off to fight, visit wounded relatives, or throw themselves into relief work, had now personally experienced the horrors of the conflict. Mary Ryerson, declared one Toronto newspaper, "died as much for the British Empire as her noble son died fighting in Flanders." For several years after the disaster, her daughter, Laura, suffered from depression, nightmares, and anxiety—the after-effects of the sinking that modern psychology would term post-traumatic stress disorder.[4] She died in 1943. Nor was Jessie Taft Smith ever able to completely recover from the trauma: in 1916, she suffered a nervous breakdown and, although she recovered, was never again the same. She died in 1928.[5] James Dunsmuir's parents, too, suffered through the loss of their son. His father sat for hours in his baronial study, endlessly listening to a gramophone recording of "Oh, Where Is My Wandering Boy Tonight?" And recurring nightmares plagued his mother, Laura: her son, trapped behind a window, desperately pounding on the glass and attempting to escape as water overwhelmed him.[6]

As both of her parents had perished in the sinking, young Virginia Loney—who, said family friend Henry James, had "almost as tragically survived" the tragedy—inherited a substantial fortune.[7] After several weeks resting at her parents' country house in Northampton, she returned to New York aboard the American liner *St. Paul*. Standing on the liner's deck, passengers spotted a distant periscope. "No, no!" Virginia cried out. "I can't stand it again!" The danger passed, and Virginia landed in New York looking, said a newspaper, "none the worse for her experience."[8] In 1918, at the age of seventeen, she married a naval aviator; after five years of marriage and two children, the couple divorced. Virginia soon remarried, and spent much of life among the fashionable elements of café and jet-set society before her death in 1975.[9]

For months following the sinking, Ian Holbourn would wake up screaming, "shrieking that the boat had overturned," as his wife remembered.[10] The night before the disaster, Marion had what she took to be a strange vision: "a large vessel sinking, with a big list." She shook off the sense of impending doom, only to learn the following evening that Lusitania had been torpedoed. Not knowing what else to do, she packed a small suitcase with her husband's clothing, assuming that if he had survived he would be in need. Just after eight on Saturday morning, Marion finally received a cable from her husband and told their eldest sons. The sinking, she assured her eldest son, Hylas, would put the whole world in an uproar; the boy then ran up and down the streets, yelling, "The whole world is in an uproar! The Lusitania's down, and my Daddy's saved!"[11]

Having reunited with Avis Dolphin in Queenstown the morning after the sinking, Holbourn escorted her by ferry and train to her grandfather's house in Worcester.[12] Marion, clutching her carefully packed suitcase, met his train at Birmingham. Holbourn had Avis on one arm, and a pair of damp trousers folded over the other. "Oh, then you've been in the water!" his wife said cheerfully. "Where did you expect me to be?" he answered. They took Avis to her grandfather, a man "with a long white beard" who looked like "an Old Testament prophet," before finally returning to their own home.[13]

Holbourn and Avis would remain in close contact for the rest of his life. A year after the disaster, Holbourn kept his shipboard promise, writing *The Child of the Moat: A Book for Girls* and dedicating it to Avis. Set during the Reformation, it told of Aline, a young orphaned Scottish girl and her adventures, which included dressing as a boy to fight in a battle and marrying her love, a Scotsman named Ian.[14] After finishing her education, Avis moved to Edinburgh, where she frequently saw the Holbourns; it was at their house that she met correspondent Thomas Foley, whom she married in 1926. Ian Holbourn died in 1933. Avis survived him by sixty-three years, dying in 1996 in Wales at the age of ninety-two. "As a Quaker," she wrote, she denounced "all acts of war." The sinking of *Lusitania* had been a tragedy, but she thought that "the bombing of civilians" during World War II "was just as horrible."[15]

Ogden Hammond returned to his three children in New Jersey. He married again, and became the American ambassador to Spain under President Calvin Coolidge. He died in 1956 as his daughter Millicent was making a substantial name for herself. After having married and divorced, Millicent Fenwick threw herself into social causes, campaigning for the civil rights movement and becoming involved, like her father, in New Jersey state politics. An aristocratic, authoritarian figure deeply involved in the social struggles of the time, in 1975 she was elected to the United States Congress. Millicent Fenwick died in 1992.

The mother of Lindon Bates, hearing of his last minutes aboard *Lusitania* spent helping others, told a newspaper, "It is good to know that my son acted with courage and unselfishness."[16] James Houghton had desperately searched the water for Marie Depage after the ocean separated them when *Lusitania* sank. Her body, identified by her grief-stricken husband, was taken back to Belgium. King Albert and Queen Elisabeth attended her funeral, and she was buried near the hospital at La Panne. Houghton sent a long, anguished letter to the family of his friend Richard Freeman, excusing himself for the delay as "my nerves have been in such a condition since the catastrophe that I have actually been unable to write about it." He had known Freeman "since sophomore year in College, and he being the only person on board whom I had known for any length of time, I feel his loss more keenly than any of the others." Although acknowledging the "perfectly terrible blow," he thought "it must be a continual source of comfort to you to know that Dick went like a man, thinking only of others and giving his life that the women and children might be saved."[17] Houghton died in 1931.

Carl Foss had embarked on *Lusitania* as a humanitarian, hoping to offer his expertise in surgical wounds to the Red Cross, but his later life was shrouded in scandal. Returning to his home in Montana in 1916, he resumed his medical practice, but soon became involved in a land dispute with a neighbor that turned ugly. To resolve the problem before it reached the courtroom, Foss and several friends apparently murdered the neighbor, which earned the doctor a prison term at the federal penitentiary at Leavenworth, Kansas. He spent only a year in custody.[18] Suffering from the nephritis that had originally kept him out of the war, he was released and returned to Montana. He died in 1924 at the age of thirty-four, after an operation for a gangrenous appendix, lauded in the local newspaper as "one of the most prominent physicians and surgeons of Northern Montana."[19]

Young Barbara Anderson came through the ordeal with no ill effects and only vague recollections of the disaster. A few months after the sinking, her mother, Emily, gave birth to a son, who lived only five months; tuberculosis claimed Emily Anderson in 1917. When the Great War ended, Barbara returned to her father in America; unfortunately, the prized spoon engraved *Lusitania* that she had carried aboard the ship and into the lifeboat was lost. Back in Connecticut, she completed her education, married Milton McDermott, and had two children. In her later years, she appeared in a number of documentaries about the tragedy, a soft-spoken lady with dazzling blue eyes. Every night, she once said, she thanked God for having saved her from the *Lusitania*. Barbara Anderson McDermott died at the age of ninety-five in 2008.[20]

The vivacious Dorothy Conner, who had naively embarked on her Red Cross mission armed with evening gowns and fur pieces, spent several years working with her brother-in-law, Howard Fisher, at a relief hospital and canteen in France. In 1923, she married naval lieutenant Greene William Dugger, and had two children. Her husband predeceased her, dying in 1941, while Fisher died in 1946. Dorothy lived until 1967.[21]

Phoebe Amory returned to Canada, where in 1917 she published a booklet, *The Death of the Lusitania*. This mingled her experiences aboard the doomed liner with a fair dose of jingoistic nationalism and anti-German propaganda. "I hated the race that made war on women and war on children," she confessed, "and I would have given everything for revenge."[22] She died in 1942. Fellow Canadian Josephine Eaton Burnside lived until 1943. Isaac Lehmann died in 1947, Thomas Home in 1952, and Michael Byrne in 1953.[23]

Shortly after the *Lusitania* disaster, Harold Boulton was given a post as Equerry to Princess Louise, Marchioness of Lorne, Queen Victoria's daughter. Three years later, he married Louise McGowan and had three children. On his father's death in 1935, he became 3rd Baronet Boulton. During the Second World War, he served in the RAF Reserves as well as an infantry battalion. He lost his youngest son, Duncan, in fighting in 1944.[24] "The memory" of the *Lusitania*, Boulton wrote in 1939, "is with me as clearly now as in the first days following. Sometimes I can speak of it all quite calmly, as if I were a literary third person reporting it, and the next time, a sickening wave comes over me and I am living everything again all too vividly." He suffered frequent nightmares, and would awake to "find myself standing on my pillow, clinging to the bedpost, trying to get out of the water."[25] Boulton died in 1968. Elisabeth and Frederic Lassetter, with whom he had shared a floating box in the aftermath of the sinking, later gave testimony to the official British inquiry into the disaster. Elisabeth died in 1927; Frederic died in 1940.

The trio of wealthy Montreal survivors, Frederick Orr-Lewis, Robert Holt, and Lady Allan, all returned to Canada. Orr-Lewis died in 1921; George Slingsby, his faithful valet, died in 1967. Holt completed his education in England and joined the British Army. Having inherited his father's immense fortune, he became one of Canada's leading and most important financial figures before his death in 1947.

Despite her grief, the formidable Marguerite Allan proceeded with her plans to open a convalescent home for Canadian soldiers in England with her daughter Martha. But the Great War was not yet done with the illustrious Allans. On July 6, 1917, their only son Hugh, serving as flight sub-lieutenant in the Royal Navy, left on his first patrol over enemy lines in Belgium. German artillery caught his plane, and he was shot down and killed at the age of twenty. Rather than bring him back to Canada, his parents decided to bury him in Belgium.[26]

Born into the comfortable luxury of the Victorian world, and having presided over the splendor of Edwardian-era Montreal, Marguerite Allan now witnessed the raucous Jazz Age that followed in the wake of the Great War. Once stately Ravenscrag had brimmed with elegantly attired ladies and Strauss waltzes; now, its halls rang with the sound of clinking cocktail glasses as

Martha ushered in a new era of hospitality. She never married, instead devoting herself to the theater, and wrote and acted in a number of popular works at her parents' estate. The audiences grew so big that she finally took over Ravenscrag's stables, where the Montreal Repertory Theatre was born.[27]

Fate had one remaining cruel turn of events in store for Marguerite Allan: in 1942, Martha died unexpectedly in Vancouver. Lady Allan had given birth to four children; all had predeceased her. Occasionally she and her husband, Hugh, still spent summers at Montrose in Cacouna but the house was too large for the elderly couple; in 1941, they sold it to an order of Capuchin monks. Ravenscrag, too, had outlived the era in which it had been built: by World War II, it was too difficult to maintain, too expensive to heat, and too impractical as a private residence. With Martha's death, the couple moved permanently into a hotel suite, and gave the grand house to Montreal's McGill University Faculty of Medicine. Most of its once famously lavish interiors—columns, plaster reliefs, painted ceilings, and silk brocaded walls—were stripped, replaced with utilitarian enamel paint and institutional rubber tiling. Today, Ravenscrag still dominates the city from the foot of Mount Royal as the Allan Memorial Institute.[28] Sir Hugh Montague Allan died in 1951; Marguerite Allan lived for another six years, dying in September 1957 at the age of eighty-four. She is buried beside her husband, Gwendolyn, and Martha at Montreal's Mount Royal Cemetery.

Gladys Bilicke returned to America, remaining in New York City for several weeks to recuperate before continuing on to Los Angeles. She was, reported the *Los Angeles Times,* "still unnerved by her dreadful experience aboard the *Lusitania*"; not only did she refuse to speak about the disaster but she also refused to see any of her friends or her husband's business acquaintances.[29] Doctors treated her for shock and exposure immediately after the disaster, but the effects lingered and caused something approaching a nervous breakdown. "In all probability," a report noted, "she will never recover her former mental and nervous poise."[30] Living in the house she had shared with Albert apparently proved too disturbing, and she soon moved to a residence in Los Angeles; ironically, just down the street lived a couple who had lost a son in the sinking of *Titanic*.[31] In the 1920s, Gladys was among numerous *Lusitania* survivors and relatives who lodged lawsuits against the German government. A commission, established after the end of the Great War, heard evidence. Some $15.5 million in lost property, personal injury, and lost revenue was claimed; in the end, and some ten years after the disaster, the Mixed Claims Court awarded just $2.5 million versus the $15.5 million asked for in damages and compensation, money paid by the German government.[32] Gladys Bilicke received $50,000 in compensation from Germany, while her two children were granted an additional $90,000 in total.[33] Gladys disliked speaking of the *Lusitania* and its painful memories. She died in 1943.

Surviving the *Lusitania* forever changed George Kessler. The charming bon vivant and wine merchant became a philanthropist. Determined to help soldiers fighting Germany, he organized and became president of the Blind Relief War Fund, a training organization for soldiers who had lost their sight. This interest soon led him to Helen Keller, who encouraged the work and became—along with Kessler's wife, Cora—one of the initial trustees in his Blind Relief War Fund. Kessler spent the next few years raising funds for the organization. He died in Paris in 1920.[34]

Angela Papadopoulos felt that her experience on *Lusitania* "destroyed forever my poor nerves," writing, "I believe I will never be able to erase those moments from my memory." She kept in regular contact with several other survivors, including Lady Allan. She lost two of her children to the great influenza epidemic, and eventually moved to Paris, where in 1924 she married Russian émigré Count Alexander Bakeev; she died in 1936 at the age of fifty-three. "At my death, when and wherever it should be," she wrote, "I want to be buried wearing the uniform of a sailor" who had given her his clothing when she was pulled from the water and which "I still jealously guard."[35]

On hearing of the tragedy, Alfred Vanderbilt's wife, Margaret, had locked herself in their suite at the Vanderbilt Hotel in New York City. Her brother-in-law Reggie and sister-in-law Gertrude rushed to see her, and let it be known that she was "bearing up bravely."[36] Although the hotel lowered its flag in mourning, Margaret still held out hope that Alfred had somehow survived.[37] "I will not believe Alfred is dead until I see the body," she insisted. "I have a feeling that he has been picked up, perhaps unconscious and unable to give an account of himself and that his identity will be made known within a short time."[38] When, after a few days, it finally became apparent that he had perished, she was said to be suffering from a "severe strain" that caused her friends "great anxiety."[39]

Despite the immense reward offered, Alfred Vanderbilt's body was never recovered. On May 22, the family finally announced in the *New York Times* that Alfred had "died at sea on May 7." There was no mention of *Lusitania*.[40] Five days later, Alfred's icily regal mother, Alice, held a private family memorial at her New York City château; among the two hundred invited mourners who filled the immense stone hall were Alfred's outcast brother, Neily, and his scandalous wife, Grace, death finally healing the breach their marriage had caused. Again there was no mention of *Lusitania,* though the short service ended with an Episcopal prayer for burial of the dead at sea.[41]

On arriving in London, Oliver Bernard found his talents commandeered by the *Illustrated London News,* which wanted firsthand sketches showing how *Lusitania* had met her end. Bernard produced a series of drawings dramatically depicting the liner's last minutes, from the initial torpedo impact to the debris left in her wake after she had disappeared beneath the surface. Later, as he had hoped, he was allowed to join the army. During fighting on the Western Front he was wounded in the leg and forced from the fighting; thereafter he designed camouflage for British units, and was honored with the Order of the British Empire by King George V for his services.[42] Having divorced his first wife, Muriel, he married his second, opera singer Dora Hodges, in 1924 on learning that she was pregnant. Various theatrical and industrial design commissions kept him busy: in 1929 he was responsible for the striking art deco–style entrance to the Strand Palace Hotel in London, yet Bernard felt that he was not being allowed to fully use his talents. This, as his son recalled, left him somewhat embittered and sensitive.[43] Oliver Bernard died of peritonitis in 1939.

Robert Timmis returned to Texas, where he soon lost the sight in his good eye after having been struck in the face by wreckage during *Lusitania*'s sinking. He died in 1939.[44] Robinson Pirie died in 1920; Charles Jeffery returned to Wisconsin; in a strange twist of fate, he hired fellow *Lusitania* survivor William Meriheina to promote his line of cars. Jeffery eventually sold his automobile company to Charles Nash, and it later merged with American Motors Corporation. Jeffery died in 1935.[45] As for the inventive Meriheina, he left a legacy enjoyed around the world, having perfected—using the name William Heina—the car radio. He died in 1976.[46]

By a strange twist of fate, the *Lusitania* tragedy continued to bring survivors together in unexpected ways. Having lost not only her young son but her mother as well, Trixie Witherbee refused to discuss her experiences aboard *Lusitania*: the memories were simply too agonizing. Within a year, she suffered a nervous break-down; to recuperate, she stayed with the family of fellow survivor Rita Jolivet outside London. Here, she met and fell in love with Rita's brother Alfred. "That horrible Witherbee woman!" was Rita's verdict on learning of the romance between her brother and the still married Trixie.[47] After divorcing her husband, Trixie married Alfred Jolivet in 1919; a year later, Trixie gave birth to their son, Lawrence. In the 1920s, Trixie decided not to seek monetary damages from Germany for the loss of her son. "It is my deepest wish," she wrote, "that the tragic death of my little son is not turned into profit or made a matter of money consideration." Eventually, the Jolivets moved to Canada; Alfred died in 1958 but Trixie outlived her second husband by nearly two decades, dying in 1977 at the age of eighty-seven.[48]

A little more than two months after the sinking, Rita Jolivet's now widowed sister, Inez Vernon, dressed in an evening gown, put her jewelry on, knelt in prayer, and put a bullet through her head in despair.[49] As for Rita, she continued her theatrical career: in 1916, a visiting Harold Boulton went to see her in a Broadway production, recalling that her lifebelt from *Lusitania* had been hung outside the theater to advertise her presence.[50] Later that year, Rita married Italian aristocrat Count Giuseppe de Cippico, though the union soon ended in divorce.[51] Then, in the 1920s, Rita began visiting Lady Allan in Montreal, and Marguerite introduced her to her husband's cousin, Captain James Bryce Allan. In 1928, they married in Paris and moved to his Scottish castle. For the next forty years, Rita mingled with politicians and aristocrats, fully enjoying her privileged life.[52] She died in Nice in 1971 after attempting to prove her vigor by dancing a jig. "Oh well," Trixie commented of her sister-in-law's death, "she *would* go like that."[53]

Although Rita announced that she was retiring from films on

wedding Count de Cippico, the allure of the screen, coupled with her disintegrating marriage, proved too enticing. She made a number of motion pictures throughout the first half of the 1920s in America, France, and Italy, until finally abandoning acting in 1926. Many of those who had endured the *Lusitania* disaster used their survival to arouse public indignation against Germany and plead for relief funds. Some, like Phoebe Amory, wrote books and gave speeches. Being an actress, Rita recognized the propaganda value in such actions. She, too, joined in selling Liberty Bonds, but her principal contribution to public awareness of the dastardly Germans was a 1918 film called *Lest We Forget*. Said to have cost a quarter million dollars and with a cast of a thousand extras, it had been produced with the cooperation of the United States Navy and Army, the latter supplying some three hundred soldiers for one battle scene. Rita, naturally enough, starred as the heroine, a young French opera singer named Rita Heriot caught up in the dangers of the war. After narrowly escaping a German firing squad, Heriot sails aboard *Lusitania* and survives the sinking, to be reunited at the end with her lost love, a soldier she believed to have been killed in action. The American government allowed Rita to film the *Lusitania* scenes aboard the impounded German liner *Martha Washington* in Hoboken, New Jersey, lending a certain verisimilitude to the endeavor. The film, which the government endorsed for its "outstanding examples of patriotic ideals," proved a hit in a nation now at war with Germany. Sadly, this epic, starring one of *Lusitania*'s survivors, is now lost to history.[54]

Rita's fellow actress aboard *Lusitania*, Josephine Brandell, was left traumatized by the sinking and soon retired from the stage. In 1920 she married John Lawson-Johnston, whose nephew, in another of those twists of fate peculiar to *Lusitania*, later wed one of her youngest survivors, Audrey Pearl. Divorcing Lawson-Johnston in a few years, Josephine wed George Repton, a captain in the Irish Guards Regiment, in 1929. For fourteen years they were happily married, until Repton's unexpected death in 1943. Two years later, Josephine entered into another marriage, with Beresford Bingham, 8th Earl of Annesley, which made Josephine a countess. After his death in 1957, the countess returned to New York, where she died in 1977.[55]

Charles Frohman's death aboard *Lusitania* left the theatrical world stunned. "Expressions of sorrow were heard on all sides in the theatre district yesterday over the fate of Charles Frohman," the *New York Times* reported two days after the tragedy. His brother, Daniel, was reportedly in shock, while fellow impresario David Belasco lauded his "dear old friend" as the person who "did more for the theatre than any other man."[56] His body, washed ashore on the Irish coast, was embalmed and shipped back to New York City, where on May 25 a lavish funeral took place at Temple Emanu-El on Fifth Avenue that, said the *New York Times,* "assumed the proportions of a public demonstration" as the "tears flowed freely."[57] His coffin carried a bouquet of violets from his rumored love, actress Maude Adams. She had collapsed on hearing of the sinking, but bravely if tearfully carried on in a production of her latest play the same evening.[58]

Elaborate memorials also marked the passing of Elbert and Alice Hubbard. On learning of the sinking, his son had insisted, "My father's not dead, nor Alice Hubbard. The news they are is false. They must have been saved!" Yet soon enough the devastating confirmation arrived, and the flags at his Roycroft Colony in East Aurora were lowered in respect.[59] Their memorial in New York City opened with the mournful sounds of Chopin's "Funeral March"; ironically, the couple had enjoyed the same piece at a Roycroft concert just before sailing—a rather grim selection at a bon voyage party. The service in New York was filled with "applause and laughter," and ended with a call to action:

"We trust Uncle Sam," declared a speaker, "trust in the rightness of his purpose. Let us arm him so that he can enforce good behavior if need be, and so that no foreigners can use the Stars and Stripes as a carpet!"[60] Hubbard left an estate of $397,845—a sum substantial enough to continue his beloved colony to the present day.[61]

For *Lusitania*'s two most prominent surviving female bohemians, Margaret Mackworth and Theodate Pope, life was never to be the same. After years of unhappiness in her marriage and struggles for suffrage, Lady Mackworth emerged from the disaster confident and assured. Floating half-conscious amidst a sea of wreckage while awaiting rescue, she had pondered her life and felt as though "something" was caring for her.[62] This sense led her to fully embrace the Christian faith about which her skeptical father had seemed so ambivalent. It also strengthened her determination in life. "I had got through this test without disgracing myself," she wrote. "I had found that, when the moment came, I could control my fear." The sinking of the *Lusitania*, she said, "altered my view of myself."[63]

David Thomas, her father, went on to become minister of food control during the last years of the Great War, charged with introducing and supervising rationing. Although successful, the work left him tired, and in 1918 he died at the age of sixty-two.[64] The title of Baron Rhondda, which he had been given in 1917, now passed, through a previous special remainder, to his only daughter, Margaret, who became viscountess. Ever her father's daughter, Margaret easily assumed control of his companies and took over as chairman for a number of other endeavors. Her campaign for women's suffrage continued until 1918, when Great Britain finally agreed that women over thirty would be allowed the right to vote.

With one campaign won, Margaret embarked on another. In

1922, she divorced her husband, Humphrey, on the grounds of "statutory desertion and adultery," and tried to test this equalization of the sexes with a practical endeavor, attempting—as a member of the Peerage—to take a seat in the House of Lords.[65] The government refused to acquiesce, denying her a place in the chamber. Infuriated, she took to the pages of *Time and Tide,* a magazine she had founded to promote feminist and liberal ideals. Contributors included Nancy, Lady Astor—another dedicated feminist—as well as George Bernard Shaw, Emma Goldman, George Orwell, D. H. Lawrence, and Rebecca West, although with the passage of time it began to reflect Margaret's increasingly conservative political views. Its first editor, Helen Archdale, apparently also became Margaret's lover, and the two lived together for many years. In another peculiar twist Margaret became close friends with fellow activist Doris Stevens, whose husband, Dudley Field Malone, had actually approved *Lusitania*'s cargo on her last voyage as a Port of New York inspector.[66] Margaret, Viscountess Rhondda, lauded by the *Times* as "a truly exceptional woman," died of cancer in 1958 in a London hospital.[67]

Theodate Pope, too, emerged from the *Lusitania* tragedy a changed woman. After days of anxious waiting in Queenstown, there was no sign of her maid, Emily Robinson, or of Edwin Friend. Theodate finally admitted to herself that both had been lost and "cried my heart out." Novelist Henry James assured her of his "tenderest love and blessing," writing, "You have been through more than is knowable or conceivable."[68]

Theodate worried constantly about Friend's widow, Marjorie, who was then pregnant with her late husband's child. "I really think she should not hear the details," she warned her mother, adding, "it might have such a bad effect on her and the baby."[69] In September 1915, Marjorie gave birth to a daughter, who was mentally deficient and was later institutionalized. Theodate repeatedly attempted to contact Friend through séances, but her life was moving away from the esoteric. On the eve of the first anniversary of *Lusitania*'s sinking, she did something she had always pointedly avoided, marrying diplomat John Riddle, whose intelligence, breeding, and travels matched her own. Thereafter, she threw herself into her architectural work, designing Avon Old Farms School and working on restoration of Theodore Roosevelt's birthplace in New York City. She died in 1946. Hill-Stead, the house she had so carefully crafted and helped design for her parents, is today recognized as one of the most important and influential Colonial Revival structures in America.

Theodate never forgot *Lusitania* survivor Belle Naish, the woman who had spotted her crumpled in a cold heap after being pulled apparently lifeless from the sea and insisted that sailors attempt to revive her. After the sinking, Belle traveled on to England, staying with her husband's brothers. "She suffered so greatly from the shock and exposure," one newspaper in her home of Kansas City reported, "that she has been unable to send any definite particulars of her husband's death to relatives and friends in America."[70]

When she eventually did return to America, Belle threw herself into work. The *Kansas City Star* reported that she "perhaps put in a higher average of hours per day in Red Cross work than any other Kansas City woman." She tried to do as most other *Lusitania* survivors did despite the traumatic event and losses: get on with life. When her brothers-in-law raised a monument to her husband in Birmingham, Belle implored them to omit any reference to *Lusitania*, saying, "We'd better not perpetuate hate." By the end of the war, she was philosophical, though like many, she personally blamed the by then former Kaiser Wilhelm II for the disaster. A reporter who interviewed her, noting her sad face, quoted her as saying, "The worst punishment I could wish for the Kaiser is that he might know for just one hour the dread of being alone when he is eighty. I wouldn't have him killed, but I would have him put where he never again could have the power to accomplish evil." Theodate visited her in Kansas City, and Belle kept in touch with young Robert Kay, whom she had looked after in the hours and days following the sinking.[71] Pope was so grateful to the woman who had literally saved her life that she gave Belle a generous pension.[72] Belle, in turn, used this and money she was awarded in the wake of the sinking to establish a ninety-acre camp for Boy Scouts in memory of her lost husband, Theodore, outside Kansas City. She died in 1950 at the age of eighty-six.[73]

Nineteen-year-old William Adams had searched for his father, Arthur, in Queenstown, but to no avail. As he had wished, he joined the British Army to fight in the Great War, living until 1986. Annie Adams had the comfort of knowing that the body of her husband, Henry, was found two weeks after the disaster. Once identified, she brought him back to his village in England for burial. She died in 1923. James Brooks duly returned to America, eventually receiving some $6,000 in compensation for the sinking. [74] In the last year of his life, he assisted authors Adolph and Mary Hoehling in researching their book about the disaster. He mused about a possible motion picture of the tragedy, insisting that "no stars" were needed, "no glamour girls or actresses with legs and big busts. I like," he confided, "the latter two items, but not in a picture of the sinking!" Above all, he thought, there should be "no heroes" and no focus on Captain Turner, whom he continued to hold largely responsible for the tragedy.[75] Brooks died in 1956.

Fittingly, one of *Lusitania*'s youngest passengers aboard her final, fatal voyage was also the last survivor to die. Warren and Amy Pearl survived, as did their two youngest children, Stuart and

Audrey, but daughters Susan and Amy, along with their nanny, Greta Lorenson, were lost and their bodies were never found. Warren Pearl died in 1952, while his wife died in 1964. Audrey enjoyed something of an enchanted life, as if Fate was atoning for the misery the *Lusitania* tragedy had caused her family. She attended prestigious schools, was presented at Buckingham Palace as a debutante before Queen Mary, and enjoyed a mad rush of parties, balls, and skiing holidays at St. Moritz with American ambassador Joseph Kennedy's energetic and entertaining clan before World War II erupted. Audrey then devoted herself to charitable work with the Red Cross. She drove an ambulance before taking a position with the United States embassy, working in London for the governments in exile of several occupied European countries. In 1946, she married Hugh Lawson-Johnston, a wealthy aristocratic scion whose grandfather had invented Bovril, the meat extract, in a lavish society ceremony before a thousand guests at the exclusive St. Margaret's, Westminster. The couple had three daughters and, in time, ten grandchildren and two great-grandchildren. Throughout the years, Audrey maintained a close friendship with Alice Lines Drury (her married name), her former nurse and the woman who had held her small body to hers and, with five-year-old Stuart clinging to her skirt, fought her way up the slanting stairs to a lifeboat and thus saved their lives when *Lusitania* sank. They remained friends until Alice's death in 1997 at the age of one hundred. Although too young to remember her time aboard *Lusitania*, Audrey gave endless interviews about the disaster. She'd crossed the Atlantic many times since May 1915 but said, "The one voyage everyone wants to hear about is the one I don't remember."[76] In 2004, she returned to Kinsale, standing on the bluff above the beach where many victims had washed ashore.[77] "I never blamed the sea," Audrey once said of the *Lusitania* tragedy, "because it wasn't the sea's fault. It was the Germans' fault."[78] "I hope I'm living up to worth being saved," Audrey commented in her last years.[79] On January 11, 2011, Audrey Lawson-Johnston died at the age of ninety-five, the last of those who had been aboard *Lusitania* on her final, fatal voyage.

Captain William Turner never escaped the widespread perception that his actions had, in part, been responsible for *Lusitania*'s sinking and the attendant loss of life. He was, said his son Norman, "very bitter" about the experience, and especially about the British government's accusations of negligence.[80] After the tragedy, Turner returned to sea; the former captain of such magnificent liners as *Lusitania, Mauretania,* and *Aquitania* was now reduced to the helm of a small Cunard freighter. His next commission, the former Cunard liner *Ivernia,* had been requisitioned as a troop transport; in an almost unbelievable turn of events, it was torpedoed on New Year's Day 1917. Thirty-six people perished, but Turner again survived. In 1919, he finally retired from the sea.[81]

Turner spent his last days pottering about the garden of his home just outside Liverpool, habitually shooting at the seagulls he had grown to hate since his experience in the water after *Lusitania* was sunk.[82] In 1932, hearing that Turner was suffering from incurable cancer, *Lusitania*'s former junior third officer, Albert Bestic, visited him. He found Turner still bitter about his treatment; the former captain complained that he had not received "a fair deal."[83] Turner died in June of the following year at the age of seventy-seven.

Bestic survived another thirty years. He lived long enough to have the extraordinary experience of seeing the once beautiful *Lusitania* in documentary footage of the wreck taken by divers in 1962 before his death later that year.[84] Lott Gadd, *Lusitania*'s barber, moved to Detroit, where he operated a salon for many years. He hoped to write a book about his experiences at sea and aboard the *Lusitania,* but died in 1942 before he could finish the project.[85]

Leslie Morton, who had first spotted the torpedo coming at *Lusitania,* did write about his experiences, in a 1968 autobiography published just before his death. King George V decorated Morton with the Silver Board of Trade Medal for Gallantry in recognition of the many survivors he had helped pluck from the sea after the disaster.[86] "I rather feel that my youth," he confided, "with a lot of ready wit and impudence at the Inquiry, coupled with my having seen the torpedoes coming and a sympathetic press, earned this honor."[87] Morton remained at sea. Three months after the *Lusitania* disaster, he survived the sinking of his next ship, *City of Venice.* He married his wife, Constance, in 1920; having to "choose between my love of the sea" and that of his wife, he finally ended his days on the ocean.[88]

"I personally did not blame Captain Turner," Morton wrote, "except insomuch that a captain must accept full responsibility for anything and everything that happens to his command or persons thereon." Privately, he thought that blame for the tragedy "must be laid at the door of the authorities."[89] Yet the man who, after spotting the torpedo, had abandoned his post without waiting for acknowledgment from the bridge was sure that "had the ship been swung to starboard immediately upon my report, she would have turned inside the line of the torpedoes" and thus avoided disaster. To the end of his life, Morton was adamant that he had seen two torpedoes that fateful day.[90]

❧

The sinking of *Lusitania* underlined the brutality of war in a previously unthinkable way. For the first time in the conflict, a large number of civilians were sacrificed as if they were nameless soldiers: brutally and without consideration, underscoring the terrible tragedy of the war itself. And the sinking played out in an unexpected way. Life aboard *Lusitania* was still largely stratified by social class and financial worth, yet what happened in those pivotal eighteen minutes destroyed any illusions about privilege. A few passengers, like Alfred Vanderbilt, rigidly clung to traditional notions of a gentlemen's code; in doing so, he perished, just as the brightest generation of British and European young men, standing by similar conceptions of tradition, did in trenches across the continent. Death and survival were random: passengers assuming their lives would continue on as normal saw their world turned upside down. Those fortunate enough to get into lifeboats were hurled into the sea and killed; people who remained on deck survived. Lady Allan's two daughters perished; her two maids survived. The utter randomness of the disaster mocked expectation.

Nearly everyone aboard *Lusitania* knew that she would sail into a declared war zone; knew that German submarines had sunk a passenger liner just a month earlier; and many were also aware of the German notice in the New York newspapers. The possibility that *Lusitania* might be torpedoed was therefore not a surprise.[91] Yet most passengers dismissed the possible danger, as if such an event was not only impossible but also beyond the realm of imagination. The *Titanic* disaster was cast as a morality play, proof that man's technological advancements and the sense of security they gave were hollow against the forces of nature and the inexorable will of God. *Lusitania,* for all of its elements of tragedy, more closely resembled an almost unbelievably stunning example of hubris.

If the passengers aboard *Lusitania* were complacent, then so, too, were those charged with keeping them safe. Even without the nagging tendrils of a conspiracy, it is impossible to conclude that the Admiralty did all within its power to protect the liner and its passengers from danger. *Lusitania* was in their hands: their actions over the preceding months, by ignoring international convention, had created the very environment that led to the tragedy. Nor was the Admiralty diligent in guarding the ship. The warnings were clear, and just as clearly they were ignored. Why was there no escort on this particularly dangerous voyage? Cunard, too, proved to be irresponsible: while ensuring that *Lusitania* carried ample lifeboats, the line's officials refused to assign stations to passengers or even provide them with a drill. It was war, and a wartime crossing through a declared war zone known to be the hunting ground for German submarines certainly called for a higher degree of caution and some sense of heightened danger. Yet no one in charge of *Lusitania* seems to have given the ship and its safety much thought.

The Edwardian Era's mythology painted Edward Smith and his crew aboard *Titanic* as heroic figures. The captain went down with his ship, his death atoning for whatever navigational mistakes contributed to the disaster. And Smith's crew had lingered below in the sinking ship, stoking furnaces to keep the lights burning, aware that they would likely not escape. The contrast between the behavior of the crews of *Titanic* and *Lusitania* is stunning. Perhaps the war heightened sensitivities to looming death; then, too, *Lusitania*'s crew were largely a poorly trained, haphazardly drawn bunch with no loyalty to Cunard, the ship, or her captain. Refusing to give away their lifebelts to help passengers and, in at least one instance, actually turning an ax on a terrified passenger, these seamen revealed that their foremost thought was their own preservation.

And ultimately, the man at *Lusitania*'s helm failed miserably in his role. Captain William Turner loved the sea, but he also loved to play by his own rules, as evidenced by his refusal to socialize—as other captains were expected to do—with his passengers. Turner had complained about the condition of the lifeboats before this voyage, but apparently he never bothered to inspect them to see if they were in good condition—an inexcusable lapse considering the danger to which his ship and those on it were to be exposed. He knew that his crew was poorly trained and not proficient in handling the boats, yet he made no effort to provide them with additional instructions during the voyage. Numerous passengers came to Turner with worries about lifebelts and lifeboat drills; Turner dismissed them all, and later lied about it. Even twelve-year-old survivor Avis Dolphin couldn't believe the way Turner had acted. "The captain had signals three times not to take the usual course," she wrote, "but as he thought he knew most, he went his own way."[92]

In the last few decades, it has become fashionable to treat Turner as a victim, a good-natured, crusty old salt who did his best when faced with tragedy. Yet the same man who so eagerly condemned Captain Edward Smith in the case of *Titanic* likewise ignored warnings and advice, and abandoned common sense. He ran his ship at a lower speed, close to land, and in a straight line, despite instructions from the Admiralty. His negligence was astonishing. Schwieger fired the lethal torpedo; the Admiralty created the tragic conditions that made the disaster inevitable; but Turner, obstinate, convinced of his own judgment, and unwilling to adjust to changing circumstances, helped weave the terrible threads into an ultimately lethal tapestry.

❧

Battered and torn, *Lusitania* today rests on her starboard side some three hundred feet below the Irish Sea, wrapped for eternity in a grave of shifting dark green water and nestled in deep silt that conceals her remaining secrets. Fishing nets provide her burial shroud, weaving and waving gently in the current. Like carrion, maritime salvagers have picked apart her once graceful body: her whistle is now gone, along with three of her four immense bronze propellers; the telegraph from her bridge; the bell from her crow's nest; and two of her anchors. Her proud bow, pointing northeast toward the coast some eleven miles distant, rises from the silt, twisted at an angle from a hull broken amidships. Her tall funnels long ago disintegrated, their positions marked by steam pipes stretched across the ocean floor. Gashes, torn plating, and open wounds dot the length of her hull, the result of depth charges dropped by the Royal Navy in World War II. Why would the Royal Navy bomb what was, after all, a maritime war grave, still entombing hundreds of passengers and crew? To prevent German U-boats from lurking among the wreckage goes one explanation; to provide target practice on test runs asserts another.

Today the area around the wreck is littered with unexploded mines, a powerful deterrent to anyone intent on probing her ruins.[93]

A century beneath the Irish Sea has played havoc with *Lusitania*: her decks and superstructure long ago slid onto the ocean bed "as if a tall house of cards had collapsed."[94] Here and there, a piece of colorful decorative tile, a window filigree, a stretch of decking, the ghostly outline of her name—these images loom out of the ghostly, perpetual darkness, haunting reminders of her former glory. But the grand lady is rapidly fading, rusting away into her eternal maritime grave. Soon, the once proud *Lusitania* will crumble to unrecognizable oblivion.

NOTES

AUTHORS' NOTE

1. Layton, 44.
2. *Atlanta Constitution*, May 8, 1915; Hoehling and Hoehling, 47; *Chicago Tribune*, May 10, 1915, courtesy of Michael Poirier; Chidsey, 15–16; King, *Handbook*, 49, 212, 220–23; Friedman, 93.

PREFACE

1. Ellis, iii.

PROLOGUE

1. *New York Times*, August 2, 1914.
2. Wells, 40.
3. Clews, 448.
4. Vanderbilt, *Fortune's Children*, 264; Martin, 39; King, *Season*, 399.
5. King, *Season*, 19–21, 400–401; Lehr, 138.
6. Cowles, 235.
7. Dulles, 296; Hickey and Smith, 37.
8. *New York Evening Post*, May 8, 1915.
9. Fletcher, 86.
10. Ibid., 284.
11. Bailey and Ryan, 99.
12. Bernstorff, 77.
13. O'Sullivan, 71, 97–102; Simpson, 106–7; Ramsay, 56–57; Bailey and Ryan, 96; Lauriat, 132; *Daily Mail*, December 20, 2008; Ballard, 27; Hoehling and Hoehling, 27; Beesly, 113–14; Mayer Opinion, 6; Ellis, 245; *New York Times*, May 8, 1915. NARA, M580-197, holds a copy of the actual Report and

Manifest of the Cargo Laden at the Port of New York on board the SS *Lusitania*, filed May 5, 1915.

14. *New York Times*, May 10, 1915.
15. Layton, 76–80, 268, 270; *Ocean Liners of the Past*, 9, 89–100; *New York Times*, May 10, 1915; Peeke, Walsh-Johnson, and Jones, 8; Decies, 215; Sauder, *The Lusitania Disguised?*
16. Hoehling and Hoehling, 154.
17. Ibid., 33.
18. Amory, *Who Killed Society*, 9–10.
19. Snyder, 2–3; Bernstorff, 137.
20. Viereck, 64–65; Ramsay, 52–53; "Lusitania," *American Journal of International Law*, 868; Bernstorff, 137.
21. *New York Tribune*, May 2, 1915.
22. Hickey and Smith, 16–17; Hoehling and Hoehling, 69; Preston, 104.
23. Hickey and Smith, 16.
24. *The Times*, May 3, 1915.
25. Lauriat, 67.
26. Bernard, *Cock Sparrow*, 145.
27. Rhondda, *D. A. Thomas*, 195.
28. Hoehling and Hoehling, 30.
29. *New York Times*, May 16, 1915.
30. *The Times*, May 8, 1915; Jones, 193.
31. *New York Times*, May 16, 1915.
32. Marcosson and Frohman, 417.
33. Barrymore, 205.
34. Marcosson and Frohman, 383–84.
35. *New York Sun*, May 25, 1915; Ellis, 42.
36. Hoehling and Hoehling, 71; *New York Times*, May 8, 1915.
37. Poirier and Kalafus, "The Jolivet Family," 165; information from Michael Poirier to the authors.
38. Schapiro, 16–17.
39. Ogden Hammond testimony, Mayer Hearings, 30, in Bailey and Ryan Archive, Box 7.
40. Schapiro, 18.
41. *Pittsburgh Press*, August 11, 1935, courtesy of Michael Poirier.
42. Thomas Home, letter of May 1, 1915, courtesy of Michael Poirier.
43. *Toronto Star*, May 15, 1915, courtesy of Michael Poirier.
44. Thomas Home, letter of May 1, 1915, courtesy of Michael Poirier.
45. Hopkins, 95.
46. *New York Times*, May 2, 1915.
47. Michael Byrne, letter of June 8, 1915, in NARA: United States Department of State, 841.857 L97/72, courtesy of Michael Poirier.
48. Lauriat, 65.

49. Hoehling and Hoehling, 39.
50. *Washington Post,* May 8, 1915.
51. *Atlanta Constitution,* May 8, 1915, courtesy of Michael Poirier; *New York World,* May 2, 1915.
52. Hoehling and Hoehling, 35.
53. Ellis, 168.
54. *New York Times,* May 2, 1915.
55. Ellis, 169.
56. Hickey and Smith, 32.
57. Ramsay, 59.
58. Bailey and Ryan, 91.
59. Chidsey, 19–20; Lauriat, 130–31; Fletcher, 135.
60. Fletcher, 135.
61. Ibid.; Lauriat, 130–31; Chidsey, 19–20.
62. Lauriat, 130–31; Chidsey, 19–20.
63. Fletcher, 144–45; Maxtone-Graham, 177–78.
64. Frothingham, 5.
65. Williamson, 116; Brinnin, 395.
66. Pope, Theodate *And Then the Waters Closed Over Me,* 98, in Hoehling and Hoehling Archive, MS Collection 45, Box 2, Folder 1.
67. Rhondda, *Recalling,* 636, in Hoehling and Hoehling Archive, MS Collection 45, Box 2, Folder 1.
68. *The Sun,* Baltimore, undated clipping, courtesy of Michael Poirier.
69. Hoehling and Hoehling, 34; Preston, 132–33; *New York Times,* May 2, 1915.
70. Bernard, *Cock Sparrow,* 146.
71. Maxtone-Graham, 178–79.
72. Doubleday, 9804.
73. Dreiser, 6.
74. Amory, *Last Resorts,* 11.
75. Hoehling and Hoehling, 44–45.
76. Dreiser, 18.
77. Hoehling and Hoehling, 43–45.
78. Ibid.
79. Bernard, *Cock Sparrow,* 147–48; Dreiser, 7.
80. Bernard, *Cock Sparrow,* 147; Bailey and Ryan, 6; Miller, ix; Ramsay, 35.

CHAPTER ONE

1. Layton, 12–13, 24–25; Warren, 51, 59; *Ocean Liners of the Past,* 195.
2. Beebe, *Big Spenders,* 195.
3. Decies, 211, 213; Beebe, *Big Spenders,* 155.
4. Kludas.
5. Maxtone-Graham, 85–88; Bailey and Ryan, 4; Butler, *Cunard,* 132–36; Brinnin, 316–21; Miller, 2, 6, 9.

6. Butler, *Cunard,* 139–40; Brinnin 325–29; Huldermann, 51–56.

7. Ramsay, 12–17; Chamberlain, 537–40; Maxtone-Graham, 11; Warren, 13–14; Bailey and Ryan, 5.

8. Warren, 3.

9. Layton, 86–89; Warren, 3, 19, 36, 48–49, 55; Brinnin, 342; *Ocean Liners of the Past,* 9, 89–100; Ramsay, 30–31; Bailey and Ryan, 5; Peeke, Walsh-Johnson, and Jones, 7.

10. Warren 3, 19, 36, 48–49, 55; Brinnin, 342; Butler, *Cunard,* 162; Ramsay, 24, 30–31; Layton, 69; Ballard, 23; *Ocean Liners of the Past,* 9, 89–100, 196; *New York Times,* May 8, 1915.

11. Sauder and Marschall, 20.

12. Ramsay, 23–24; Peeke, Walsh-Johnson, and Jones, 25–28; Butler, *Cunard,* 169.

13. Warren 55; Brinnin, 342; Butler, *Cunard,* 162; Ramsay, 24, 27–29; Ballard, 23; *Ocean Liners of the Past,* 196.

14. Alec-Tweedie, 302.

15. Simpson, 72; Bailey and Ryan, 7; Ramsay, 36.

16. "Lusitania," *American Journal of International Law,* 863–64.

17. Ramsay, 49; Preston; 107; "Lusitania," *American Journal of International Law,* 864; Simpson, 61.

18. *New York Times,* May 8, 1915.

19. Michael Byrne, letter of June 8, 1915, in NARA: United States Department of State, 841.857 L97/72, courtesy of Michael Poirier.

20. *Atlanta Constitution,* May 8, 1915.

21. *New York American,* May 8, 1915.

22. Fisher, 30.

23. Bailey and Ryan, 40–41.

24. Butler, *Cunard,* 215.

25. *Papers Relating to the Foreign Relations,* 1915 Supplement, 653–54; *Papers Relating to the Foreign Relations,* 1916 Supplement, 196; "Lusitania," *American Journal of International Law,* 865; Beesly, 94; Bailey and Ryan, 47–52.

26. Bailey and Ryan, 29.

27. Ibid., 22, 43, 48.

28. Churchill, *World Crisis,* 724–25.

29. Beesly, 94; Bailey and Ryan, 47.

30. Bailey and Ryan, 27–29, 96; Read, 131.

31. *Papers Relating to the Foreign Relations,* 1915 Supplement, 96–97; "Lusitania," *American Journal of International Law,* 865.

32. *Papers Relating to the Foreign Relations,* 1915 Supplement, 98–100.

33. Ibid., 117–18.

34. Simpson, 49, 88; Bailey and Ryan, 65.

35. Norman Turner, letter of September 18, 1955, in Hoehling and Hoehling Archive, MS Collection 45, Box 1, Folder 55.

36. Ellis, 244; Hoehling and Hoehling, 64–67.
37. Hoehling and Hoehling, 67; Hickey and Smith, 59–60; Norman Turner, letter of September 18, 1955, in Hoehling and Hoehling Archive, MS Collection 45, Box 1, Folder 55.
38. Brinnin, 340–41.
39. Bailey and Ryan, 65.
40. Hoehling and Hoehling, 66–67.
41. Bernard, *Cock Sparrow,* 146.
42. Bisset, *Tramps and Ladies,* 213.
43. Hopkins, 169.
44. Bisset, *Tramps and Ladies,* 213.
45. Simpson, 89.
46. Ibid.; Layton, 182.
47. Bisset, *Tramps and Ladies,* 213; Hickey and Smith, 47.
48. Layton, 276; Molony, *Lusitania,* 76.
49. Bisset, *Tramps and Ladies,* 156.
50. Mersey Report, 5–6, in Bailey and Ryan Archive, Box 2.
51. Leslie Morton, letter of July 25, 1955, in Hoehling and Hoehling Archive, MS Collection 45, Box 1, Folder 43.
52. Ibid.; Morton, 98–99.
53. Leslie Morton, letter of July 25, 1955, in Hoehling and Hoehling Archive, MS Collection 45, Box 1, Folder 43.
54. Morton, 100.
55. Leslie Morton, letter of July 25, 1955, in Hoehling and Hoehling Archive, MS Collection 45, Box 1, Folder 43.
56. Morton, 98–100.
57. *New York Times,* May 14, 1915.

CHAPTER TWO

1. Maxtone-Graham, 112.
2. *Ocean Liners of the Past,* 22.
3. Doubleday, 9804–5.
4. Warren, 3, 23, 52–53; Maxtone-Graham, 37; *Ocean Liners of the Past,* 123, 127; Layton, 33; Sauder and Marschall, 50.
5. Alec-Tweedie, 308.
6. Layton, 102–3, 121; Warren, 3, 23, 52; Maxtone-Graham, 37; *Ocean Liners of the Past,* 123, 127.
7. Fletcher, 249.
8. Doubleday, 9805.
9. Ibid.
10. Hopkins, 99.
11. Chatterton, 300.
12. Fletcher, 255.

13. *Ocean Liners of the Past,* 144, 163; Warren, 22, 25–26, 52; Ramsay, 26.

14. Doubleday, 9805.

15. Maxtone-Graham, 34.

16. *Ocean Liners of the Past,* 162.

17. Ibid., 162–63; Maxtone-Graham, 37.

18. *Los Angeles Herald,* September 12, 1907.

19. *New York Times,* May 8, 1915; Ellis, 112–13; Browne and Koch, 270–71.

20. Hughes, 337–38; Eaton, 135–36.

21. Ellis, 112–13; Browne and Koch, 270–71.

22. Marshall, 14.

23. *Atlanta Constitution,* May 8, 1915; *New York Times,* May 8, 1915; Ellis, 111–12.

24. Marcosson and Frohman, 387–89.

25. Ibid., 150; Hickey and Smith, 20.

26. Marcosson and Frohman, 187; Browne and Koch, 183; Hughes, 238.

27. Marcosson and Frohman, 212, 284; Hughes, 238–39.

28. Hickey and Smith, 21.

29. Burke, 49.

30. Preston, 96.

31. Marcosson and Frohman, 168.

32. Browne and Koch, 183–84.

33. Burke, 54, 66.

34. Marcosson and Frohman, 366.

35. *New York Herald,* May 10, 1915.

36. Dressler, 171; Marcosson and Frohman, 154.

37. Marcosson and Frohman, 376, 381.

38. Burke, 57–58.

39. Ibid., 71.

40. Marcosson and Frohman, 363.

41. Burke, 109; Marcosson and Frohman, 366.

42. *New York Times,* May 9, 1915.

43. Burke, 58–59.

44. Marcosson and Frohman, 381.

45. Hughes, 239.

46. Marcosson and Frohman, 383.

47. *New York Herald,* May 10, 1915.

48. Marcosson and Frohman, 384–85.

49. Preston, 138.

50. Poirier and Kalafus, "The Jolivet Family," 169, 173–74.

51. Hoehling and Hoehling, 39; Marshall, 97; Poirier and Kalafus, "The Jolivet Family," 163.

52. Poirier and Kalafus, "The Jolivet Family," 164; Hoehling and Hoehling, 39.

53. *New York Times,* July 2, 1915; *Mixed Claims,* 259; Poirier and Kalafus, "The Jolivet Family," 168.
54. Dreiser, 9.

CHAPTER THREE

1. Hoehling and Hoehling, 61.
2. Ibid.; Hickey and Smith, 104; Protasio, 62.
3. Poirier, "Tragic Tale," 167.
4. *Lusitania Resource*; Hoglund; Mro, 76; *The Jeffery Automobile*; *The Motor World,* Volume 43, May 12, 1915, 37; *The Automobile,* Volume 32, May 13, 1915, 864.
5. Segger, 11, 16, 206–7, 216; Robinson, Hall, and Price, 3, 12, 35, 100.
6. Audain, 153–54.
7. Ibid., 154–57; Reksten, 232.
8. Audain, 154–57, 172; *Victoria Times Colonist,* March 2, 2008.
9. Audain, 154.
10. Boulton, CBC; Hickey and Smith, 103; Mosley, 1:332–33.
11. Boulton, CBC.
12. *The Times,* May 10, 1915; *New York Times,* May 11, 1915; Hickey and Smith, 201; Hoehling and Hoehling, 149.
13. *Townsville Daily Bulletin,* March 14, 1939.
14. *Lusitania Resource.*
15. Ibid.; Eddis.
16. *Lusitania Resource*; Molony, *Double Jeopardy.*
17. Ryerson, 184–86, 191.
18. Ibid., 192, 195–97.
19. Ibid., 204.
20. Irwin, 142.
21. Maurice, 19.
22. *New York Times,* May 26, 1915; Scannell, 1:228–29; Schapiro, 3–6.
23. *New York Times,* May 26, 1915; Scannell, 1:228–29; *New York Times,* October 30, 1956; Schapiro, 7–10.
24. Walker, 159.
25. Hoehling and Hoehling, 25; Walker, 159.
26. Reckitt, 19, 270.
27. *Lusitania Resource.*
28. *New York Times,* May 10, 1915.
29. Reckitt, 227–28.
30. Ibid., 19.
31. *New York Times,* May 10, 1915.
32. Ibid., May 11, 1915.
33. James Houghton, letter to Freeman family, from the collection of Chester Nimitz Lay and Richard Bailey, courtesy of Michael Poirier.

34. Hoehling and Hoehling, 28.
35. Loodts.
36. Hickey and Smith, 35.
37. *Philadelphia Inquirer,* May 12, 1915, courtesy of Michael Poirier.
38. Kellogg, 5–6.
39. Ibid., 6–7; Hoehling and Hoehling, 28.
40. Reckitt, 228.
41. Hoehling and Hoehling, 79.
42. Austin, 2.
43. Protasio, 60–61.
44. Davis, 368.
45. Warren, 15.
46. *New York Tribune,* June 19, 1913; Simpson, 26–32.
47. Bailey and Ryan, 10.
48. Ibid.
49. Michael Byrne, letter of June 8, 1915, in NARA: United States Department of State, 841.857 L97/72, courtesy of Michael Poirier.
50. Simpson, 31–32, 49; Bailey and Ryan, 6, 19–20; Ramsay, 34; O'Sullivan, 43–44; Sauder and Marschall, 69.
51. Bailey and Ryan, 56–58; Ramsay, 54.
52. *Washington Post,* April 23, 1915.
53. Decies, 211–14.
54. *New York Times,* May 8, 1915.
55. Lauriat, 6.
56. Pope, *And Then,* 99, in Hoehling and Hoehling Archive, MS Collection 45, Box 2, Folder 1.
57. *Liverpool Echo,* May 5, 1915, courtesy of Michael Poirier.

CHAPTER FOUR

1. Pope, *And Then,* 98, in Hoehling and Hoehling Archive, MS Collection 45, Box 2, Folder 1.
2. O'Gorman, 29, 31; Katz, 3–5, 27; Smith, *Theodate Pope Riddle.*
3. O'Gorman, 26, 29–31.
4. Ibid., 38; Wilson, 64; Smith, *Theodate Pope Riddle.*
5. O'Gorman, 38; Katz, 45.
6. Wilson, 68–70.
7. Hewitt, 157; O'Gorman, 40–45; Wilson, 73; Blackburn, 197–200; Smith, *Theodate Pope Riddle.*
8. James, 45–46.
9. O'Gorman, 80.
10. Gaddis, 178.
11. Katz, 87.
12. Ibid., 16–17, 24.

13. Ibid., 59.
14. Ibid., 32.
15. Ibid., 50.
16. Smith, *Theodate Pope Riddle.*
17. Allen, *William James,* 26–27.
18. Katz, 69.
19. Ibid., 90–91.
20. Ibid., 97.
21. Ibid., 102–3.
22. Pope, *And Then,* 98–99, in Hoehling and Hoehling Archive, MS Collection 45, Box 2, Folder 1.
23. Katz, 103–4, 110.
24. Hoehling and Hoehling, 69, 73; Katz, 105.
25. Pope, *And Then,* 98–99, in Hoehling and Hoehling Archive, MS Collection 45, Box 2, Folder 1; Smith, *Theodate Pope Riddle.*
26. Pope, *And Then,* 98–99, in Hoehling and Hoehling Archive, MS Collection 45, Box 2, Folder 1.
27. Kalafus and Poirier, *Lest We Forget, Part 2.*
28. Mayer Opinion, 4; Layton, 105–6; Preston, 132; Simpson, 27.
29. Michael Byrne, letter of June 8, 1915, in NARA: United States Department of State, 841.857 L97/72, courtesy of Michael Poirier; Bernard, *Cock Sparrow,* 149; *New York Sun,* May 11, 1915.
30. Mersey Report, 5–6; William Turner, testimony of June 15, 1915, Mersey Public Proceedings, 127, in Bailey and Ryan Archive, Box 2.
31. Michael Byrne, letter of June 8, 1915, in NARA: United States Department of State, 841.857 L97/72, courtesy of Michael Poirier.
32. Fletcher, 146.
33. *New York Times,* May 10, 1915; Hickey and Smith, 113.
34. *The Times,* September 15, 1920; Lehr, 28–29.
35. Bradshaw, 207–11.
36. Lehr, 54.
37. Ibid., 32, 65.
38. Ibid., 28–29.
39. Beebe, *Big Spenders,* 106.
40. *New York Times,* May 12, 1902; Edwards, 15; Guy, 33.
41. *The Call,* March 28, 1906; *New York Times,* December 24, 1997; *American Menu.*
42. *Springfield Daily Republican,* June 21, 1915, courtesy of Michael Poirier.
43. Hickey and Smith, 89.
44. *Springfield Daily Republican,* June 21, 1915, courtesy of Michael Poirier.
45. Wells, 90; Hickey and Smith 88–89; *Springfield Daily Republican,* June 21, 1915, courtesy of Michael Poirier; Taylor, 28; *American Menu.*
46. Wells, 90.

47 Hoehling and Hoehling, 36.

48. Bernard, *Cock Sparrow,* 149.

49. Ibid., 22, 26, 45, 50, 94–95; Bernard, *Getting Over It,* 9.

50. Bernard, *Cock Sparrow,* 92.

51. Ibid., 95, 97, 115.

52. Ibid., 129.

53. Bernard, *Cock Sparrow,* 137; Hickey and Smith, 32–33.

54. Bernard, *Cock Sparrow,* 142–43.

55. Ibid., 145.

56. Ibid., 145–48.

CHAPTER FIVE

1. Hoehling and Hoehling, 70–71.

2. Maxtone-Graham, 191–92.

3. Hopkins, 128.

4. Fletcher, 145.

5. Hopkins, 96.

6. Alec-Tweedie, 308–9.

7. Quoted in Taylor, 28.

8. Schaller, 32; Hopkins, 66; Brinnin, 440.

9. Fletcher, 97–100.

10. Ibid., 117.

11. Hopkins, 131–32.

12. Ellis, 241.

13. Fletcher, 148.

14. Bailey and Ryan, 138; Hickey and Smith, 118; Layton, 124–25; Hopkins, 114.

15. *Ocean Liners of the Past,* 138; Warren, 52; Hoehling and Hoehling, 71.

16. Warren, 3, 52; Sauder and Marschall, 49; Layton, 32; Ramsay, 26; O'Sullivan, 40.

17. Hopkins, 114.

18. Maxtone-Graham, 219.

19. Preston, 119.

20. Fletcher, 147, 150–51.

21. Dreiser, 15–16, 32–34.

22. Post, 600.

23. Angela Papadopoulos account, from the Baffa Trasci Amalfitani di Crucoli family, courtesy of Michael Poirier.

24. McQueen, 27.

25. Ibid., 15.

26. Ibid., 37.

27. Brinnin, 340.

28. Davis, 367.
29. Warren, 52; Ramsay, 26; *Ocean Liners of the Past,* 138; Sauder and Marschall, 39–40.
30. Layton, 44.
31. Information from Mary Carpenter to the authors; McGroarty, 2:104; *Notables of the West,* 2:194.
32. Information from Mary Carpenter to the authors.
33. Lubet, 3–4.
34. Ibid., 171.
35. Ibid., 4–6; Roberts, 190–203.
36. Information from Mary Carpenter to the authors; *Notables of the West,* 2:194–97.
37. McGroarty, 2:105; *Mixed Claims,* 263–65.
38. Condon, 12.
39. *Los Angeles Times,* June 16, 1915.
40. Bilicke, undated clipping, in Hoehling and Hoehling Archive, MS Collection 45, Box 1, Folder 61.
41. *Lusitania's Victims,* 13.
42. Duveen, *Secrets,* 260; Pearce; *Lusitania's Victims,* 13.
43. Duveen, *Secrets,* 216–63, 269; *New York Times,* May 7, 1915.
44. *New York Times,* May 7, 1915; *New York Times,* May 9, 1915; Seacrest, 160; Duveen, *Rise,* 247.
45. *The Times,* May 10, 1915; O'Byrne, 10–11, 26–27; Bodkin, 1–2; Gregory, 19–20; *New York Times,* May 15, 1915; *Lusitania's Victims,* 11–13.
46. Gregory, 239.
47. Ibid., 19–20; O'Byrne, 19–20.
48. Gregory, 60.
49. *Lusitania's Victims,* 11–13.
50. Gregory, 246.
51. Ibid., 184.
52. O'Byrne, ix, 150–51.
53. *Lusitania's Victims,* 11–13.
54. Chidsey, 13; see O'Byrne, 242–44, for a rebuttal of these tales.
55. Chidsey, 13.
56. Gregory, 244.

CHAPTER SIX

1. Lauriat, 68–69.
2. Frederick Orr-Lewis, undated letter, John Douglas Hazen Collection, University of New Brunswick, Fredericton, MG H13, Box 22, courtesy of Michael Poirier.
3. Hopkins, 101.

4. Maxtone-Graham, 187.
5. Hopkins, 101.
6. Post, 599.
7. Maxtone-Graham, 193–94; Hopkins, 115–16.
8. Robinson Pirie account, 1915, from the collection of Marika Pirie, courtesy of Michael Poirier.
9. Hopkins, 114–17; Maxtone-Graham, 197.
10. Layton, 32–34; Ramsay, 26; Sauder and Marschall, 52; Warren, 52.
11. Warren, 52.
12. Fletcher, 96; Hopkins, 110.
13. Michael Byrne, letter of June 8, 1915, in NARA: United States Department of State, 841.857 L97/72, courtesy of Michael Poirier.
14. Hopkins, 132.
15. Fletcher, 150.
16. Maxtone-Graham, 207.
17. Ibid., 205–6.
18. Fletcher, 148.
19. Hopkins, 115.
20. Maxtone-Graham, 206.
21. Ibid., 204; Fletcher, 169; Lauriat, 69; Hopkins, 116–17; Beebe, *Big Spenders*, 202.
22. Maxtone-Graham, 204–5; Fletcher, 169; Lauriat, 69; Hopkins, 116–17; Beebe, *Big Spenders*, 202.
23. Rhondda, *This Was*, 11.
24. Morgan, *Rhondda*, 10, 87, 114; Begbie, 126–27.
25. Rhondda, *D. A. Thomas*, 25.
26. Ibid., 34.
27. *Daily Express*, May 19, 1922.
28. Rhondda, *This Was*, 84.
29. Ibid., 108.
30. Ibid., 112.
31. Ibid., 120.
32. Ibid., 125–27.
33. Ibid., 145.
34. Ibid., 152.
35. Ibid., 153–59.
36. Cowles, 50.
37. Rhondda, *This Was*, 159–60; *The Times*, July 21, 1958.
38. Rhondda, *D. A. Thomas*, 195.
39. Ibid.
40. Ibid., 196.
41. Reckitt, 229.
42. *New York Times*, May 16, 1915.

43. Kalafus, *Henry Sonneborn.*
44. Ibid.
45. Ibid.

CHAPTER SEVEN

1. *Ocean Liners of the Past,* 131; Warren, 3, 52; Sauder and Marschall, 45; Layton, 33–34; O'Sullivan, 38; Ramsay, 26; Alec-Tweedie, 306.
2. Fletcher, 116, 262–63; Hopkins, 102.
3. Frothingham, 5.
4. MacKay, 157.
5. Rémillard, 20; MacKay, 7, 157; Westley, 80–81.
6. Ryerson, 144.
7. Leacock, 231.
8. Westley, 26–26; Collard, *Call Back,* x; Rémillard, 12, 20–21; MacKay, 157.
9. Smith, *George,* 165; Atherton, 3:561–62; *The Times,* November 21, 1921; Frederick Orr-Lewis, undated letter, John Douglas Hazen Collection, University of New Brunswick, Fredericton, MG H13, Box 22, courtesy of Michael Poirier.
10. Morgan, *Canadian Men,* 474; MacKay, 161, 190.
11. Westley, 182, 202.
12. MacKay, 146; Rémillard, 59.
13. MacKay, 36, 67, 78; Rémillard, 80; Borthwick, 165–67; Atherton, 2:205–6, 2:542, 3:635–37.
14. Collard, *Montreal Yesterdays,* 150.
15. MacKay, 146–47.
16. Rémillard, 27, 55–57, 79; MacKay, 71, 73, 81, 147; Bianchini, 5, 9, 13–14; Appleton, 10, 14; Gersovitz, 6, 8–9; Collard, *Montreal Yesterdays,* 150; Collard, *Montreal: The Days,* 264–65; Hinshelwood, 85.
17. Collard, *100 More Tales,* 146.
18. MacKay, 81.
19. Collard, *Montreal Yesterdays,* 150.
20. MacKay, 147, 151.
21. Grant, 274.
22. *The Times,* September 25, 1957.
23. MacKay, 175; Hoehling and Hoehling, 194.
24. Smith, *George,* 138–39.
25. Atherton, 2:501, 3:661.
26. Appleton, 173; Rémillard, 81; MacKay, 153; Atherton, 3:661–62; *Canadian History Makers,* 15.
27. Collard, *100 More Tales,* 146.
28. Casgrain, 19.
29. MacKay, 153.
30. Dufferin, 62; Collard, *Montreal: The Days,* 221–25; Collard, *Montreal Yesterdays,* 106.

NOTES

31. Appleton, 173; MacKay, 150–51; Wagg, 61–63; *Cacouna: Sir Hugh Montague Allen*; Rémillard, 83; Westley, 97; Atherton, 3:661.

32. Dubé, 69–75; Westley, 97; Jillson, 37; Wrong, iii.

33. Leacock, 235.

34. MacKay, 182.

35. Ibid., 151, 183.

36. Appleton, 182; Collard, *Montreal Yesterdays*, 92.

37. MacKay, 184.

38. Appleton, 182; MacKay, 147, 182, 184.

39. Smith, *George*, 142, 149.

40. Ibid., 151–52.

41. Ibid., 171.

42. Morton, 101–2. It has been suggested that Morton's identification of the two girls as Anna and Gwen Allan is wrong, and that he actually encountered the two Crompton daughters on deck—an alternative scenario impossible to confirm or refute.

43. Boulton, CBC.

44. *New York Times*, May 16, 1915.

CHAPTER EIGHT

1. *Ocean Liners of the Past*, 144, 162–63; Warren, 22, 25–26, 52; Sauder and Marschall, 42; Ramsay, 26; Layton, 102.

2. Warren, 52.

3. Layton, 44.

4. Sauder and Marschall, 43, 123; Bailey and Ryan, 92.

5. Ballard, 32.

6. Allen, *Vanderbilts*, 86.

7. Beebe, *Big Spenders*, 1.

8. Andrews, 288; Patterson, 134; Vanderbilt, *Queen*, 20; Allen, *Vanderbilts*, 25.

9. Auchincloss, 39; Patterson, 83; Churchill, *Splendor*, 72–73; Kathrens, 38–39; King, *Season*, 152–53; Craven, 133–45; King, *Homes*, 39; Allen, *Vanderbilt*, 30; Foreman and Stimson, 54–60; Andrews, 346; Vanderbilt, *Fortune's Children*, 183.

10. Andrews, 348; Smales, 12, 17–19, 25–26; Patterson, 137, 154–56; Foreman and Stimson, 252–53; Craven, 174–83; Benway, 51–54; Hoyt, 290.

11. Hoyt, 289.

12. Allen, *Vanderbilts*, 48; Vanderbilt, *Farewell*, 8–9.

13. Hoyt, 298.

14. Allen, *Vanderbilts*, 25; *New York Times*, September 13, 1899; Balsan, 3; Vanderbilt, *Queen*, 20.

15. Vanderbilt, *Queen*, 18; Vanderbilt, *Fortune's Children*, 185.

16. King, *Season*, 52.

17. Vanderbilt, *Queen,* 200.
18. Churchill, *Splendor,* 168; King, *Season,* 121; Wecter, 345.
19. Vanderbilt, *Queen,* 24, 43–44, 89–90; Friedman, 103; Patterson, 215; Hoyt, 299; information from the late Lady Sarah Spencer-Churchill to Greg King; Churchill, *Splendor,* 177.
20. *New York Times,* June 11, 1896.
21. Vanderbilt, *Queen,* 66; Hoyt, 306; Friedman, 141.
22. Allen, *Vanderbilts,* 52; Patterson, 217.
23. Patterson, 156; Foreman and Stimson, 253; Benway, 51–52; Smales, 19–21; Vanderbilt, *Fortune's Children,* 222.
24. Andrews, 354–55; Patterson, 218; Foreman and Stimson, 64.
25. Friedman, 166; *New York Times,* March 1, 1942; Vanderbilt, *Queen,* 132–33; Patterson, 221.
26. Beebe, *Mansions,* 10, 258–59; Andrews, 391; Kirschenbaum, 9, 13–18, 21–25; Bridger, 33, 46; King, *Homes,* 98, 140–43; Hoyt, 348; Hoehling and Hoehling, 30.
27. Garman, 68, 72–75; Beebe, *Big Spenders,* 218; Wecter, 440–41; King, *Homes,* 144–46; Andrews, 348; Foreman and Stimson, 245; Patterson, 245; Allen, *Vanderbilts,* 89; Chase and Mendillo, 26.
28. Decies, 228.
29. Lehr, 13–14; Wecter, 440–41.
30. Decies, 228.
31. Morris, 17; Lord, 106–7.
32. *New York Tribune,* October 27, 1901.
33. Beebe, *Big Spenders,* 122; Lord, 108.
34. Bridge, 12.
35. Garman, 79; Andrews, 393.
36. Gittelman and Gittelman, Chapter 12.
37. Vanderbilt, *Fortune's Children,* 456; *New York Times,* June 11, 1908, May 10, 1915; Hoyt, 358; Patterson, 244; Hickey and Smith, 27; Ramsay, 59; Hoehling and Hoehling, 29; *New York Herald,* April 2, 1908, April 4, 1908, August 26, 1908; Andrews, 394; Gittelman and Gittelman, Chapters 11 and 12.
38. Vanderbilt, *Fortune's Children,* 456; *New York Times,* May 10, 1915; Hoyt, 358; Patterson, 244; Hoehling and Hoehling, 29; *New York Herald,* April 2, 1908, April 4, 1908, August 26, 1908; Andrews, 394; Beebe, *Mansions,* 358–59.
39. *New York Times,* June 11, 1909, May 10, 1915; Hoyt, 358; Vanderbilt, *Fortune's Children,* 456; Beebe, *Mansions,* 359; Hoehling and Hoehling, 29.
40. Gittelman and Gittelman, Chapter 12; Hickey and Smith, 29.
41. Hickey and Smith, 28–29, 90; *New York Tribune,* May 9, 1915; *New York Times,* June 11, 1909, May 10, 1915; Gittelman and Gittelman, Chapter 12.
42. *New York Times,* May 10, 1915; Ramsay, 59.

43. Bridger, 18; *New York Times,* May 10, 1915.
44. Bridger, 18; Allen, *Vanderbilts,* 83; Patterson, 244; Hickey and Smith, 28; *New York Herald,* December 8, 1911; Andrews, 394.
45. *Vanderbilt Hotel,* 1–2; Patterson, 242; Andrews, 390.
46. Hoehling and Hoehling, 29.
47. William H. Vanderbilt, letter of June 17, 1955, in Hoehling and Hoehling Archive, MS Collection 45, Box 1, Folder 57.
48. Patterson, 245.
49. Hoehling and Hoehling, 29.
50. *New York Times,* May 10, 1915.
51. Geis, 78–80.
52. *Lusitania's Victims,* 14; Morris, 17–18; Lord, 106–7, 114; Amory, *Who Killed Society?,* 520; Beebe, *Big Spenders,* 124; King, *Season,* 406.
53. *Lusitania's Victims,* 14; *Mixed Claims,* 256–57.
54. Beebe, *Big Spenders,* 125–30; Logan.
55. Ouse, 4.
56. Ibid., 5; *Lusitania Resource.*
57. *New York Times,* May 16, 1915.
58. Maxtone-Graham, 210–11.
59. *Lusitania Resource.*
60. *New York Times,* May 16, 1915.

CHAPTER NINE

1. Hoehling and Hoehling, 79.
2. Hopkins, 102.
3. Sauder and Marschall, 55.
4. Hopkins, 111–12.
5. Dreiser, 16.
6. Post, 601.
7. Eddington, 12.
8. Warren, 26; *Ocean Liners of the Past,* 160–61.
9. Fletcher, 288.
10. Eddington, 91; Layton, 190.
11. Dreiser, 16.
12. Maxtone-Graham, 239.
13. *Ocean Liners of the Past,* 22; Warren, 3, 51–52; Sauder and Marschall, 47–48; Layton, 36.
14. Sauder and Marschall, 48.
15. Ibid., Color Illustration Insert No. 17.
16. Hickey and Smith, 98; O'Sullivan, 38.
17. Post, 601.
18. Maxtone-Graham, 188.
19. Hopkins, 100; Fletcher, 250.

20. Poirier and Kalafus, "The Jolivet Family," 169.
21. Bernard, *Cock Sparrow*, 148–49.
22. Post, 601–2.
23. Lauriat, 71; information from Michael Poirier to the authors.
24. James Houghton, letter to Freeman family, from the collection of Chester Mimitz Lay and Richard Bailey, courtesy of Michael Poirier.
25. Hickey and Smith, 98; Ballard, 48; O'Sullivan, 38–39; Eddington, 60; Layton, 226; Fletcher, 284.
26. Alec-Tweedie, 303.
27. *New York Times,* May 16, 1915.
28. Poirier and Kalafus, "The Jolivet Family," 164.
29. *New York Times,* May 16, 1915; Poirier and Kalafus, "The Jolivet Family," 164, 170.
30. James Houghton, letter to Freeman family, from the collection of Chester Nimitz Lay and Richard Bailey, courtesy of Michael Poirier.
31. Angela Papadopoulos account, from the collection of the Baffa Trasci Amalfitani di Crucoli family, courtesy of Michael Poirier.
32. Layton, 34, 123.
33. Fletcher, 169; Chidsey, 49; Preston, 138; Hoehling and Hoehling, 57, 61; Layton, 281.
34. Champney, 3–4.
35. Hamilton, 186.
36. Champney, 22.
37. Ibid., 43–44; Winter, 137.
38. Barter, 87.
39. Champney, 58, 92; Hoehling and Hoehling, 42, 58; Barter, 88.
40. Champney, 4; Hoehling and Hoehling, 42; Hickey and Smith, 24; Barter, 89.
41. Winter, 137.
42. Barter, 89.
43. *In Memoriam: Elbert and Alice Hubbard,* 20.
44. Champney, 4.
45. Hubbard, *Philosophy,* 7–8, 27, 32.
46. Champney, 37–38; Hoehling and Hoehling, 57–59; Preston, 144.
47. Champney, 76.
48. Ibid., 97–99.
49. Hamilton, 194.
50. Hoehling and Hoehling, 59.
51. Champney, 109; *In Memoriam: Elbert and Alice Hubbard,* 43–44.
52. *Mixed Claims,* 273.
53. Hubbard, *Hollyhocks,* 91–94.
54. Ellis, 107; *New York Times,* May 9, 1915; Hickey and Smith, 25; Hoehling and Hoehling, 58; Champney, 159–60, 195.
55. Champney, 193.

56. Ellis, 103–6; Champney, 194.
57. Lauriat, 8.
58. Hoehling and Hoehling, 41.
59. Ellis, 107–10.
60. Hoehling and Hoehling, 58, 61.
61. *New York Times,* May 7, 1916.
62. Warren, 52; Fletcher, 126, 149.

CHAPTER TEN

1. Hoehling and Hoehling, 71; Butler, *Cunard,* 169.
2. *Ocean Liners of the Past,* 145.
3. Hoehling and Hoehling, 72; Chidsey, 19.
4. Ballard, 31.
5. Warren, 53; Layton, 39; Sauder and Marschall, 58.
6. Warren, 3, 53; Layton, 39; Sauder and Marschall, 60.
7. Hoehling and Hoehling, 74.
8. Holbourn, *Foula,* 197.
9. Ibid., 201, 208.
10. Hoehling and Hoehling, 74; Hickey and Smith, 114.
11. Holbourn, *Foula,* 9, 193, 219.
12. *Worcester Daily Times,* May 15, 1915, in Hoehling and Hoehling Archive, MS Collection 45, Box 2, Folder 70.
13. Ballard, 35; Hoehling and Hoehling, 73; Holbourn, *Foula,* 227; Hickey and Smith, 36; *Worcester Daily Times,* May 15, 1915, in Hoehling and Hoehling Archive, MS Collection 45, Box 2, Folder 70.
14. Ballard, 35; Hoehling and Hoehling, 73; Holbourn, *Foula,* 227.
15. Preston, 129.
16. Avis Dolphin, letter to mother, May 1915, in Sauder and Marschall, 86.
17. Holbourn, *Child,* 2; Holbourn, *Foula,* 230; Hickey and Smith, 138.
18. *Worcester Daily Times,* May 15, 1915, in Hoehling and Hoehling Archive, MS Collection 45, Box 2, Folder 70.
19. *Lusitania Resource*; *Daily Telegraph,* April 21, 2008.
20. Poirier, *Remembering Barbara,* 221.
21. *Kansas City Star,* June 27, 1915, courtesy of Michael Poirier.
22. *Kansas City Times,* August 26, 1950; *Kansas City Star,* August 26, 1950.
23. *Kansas City Star,* June 27, 1915, courtesy of Michael Poirier; *Kansas City Star,* June 15, 1919, courtesy of Michael Poirier.
24. *Kansas City Star,* June 15, 1919, courtesy of Michael Poirier.
25. Ibid.
26. *Marshall News-Statesman,* August 16, 1915, courtesy of Michael Poirier.
27. Ellis, 240; Warren, 20; *Ocean Liners of the Past,* 151, 162; Sauder and Marschall, 61; Peeke, Walsh-Johnson, and Jones, 21.

28. Kalafus and Poirier, *William Meriheina*; *The Motor World*, Volume 43, May 12, 1915, 37; *The Automobile*, Volume 32, May 13, 1915, 864.
29. *The Motor World*, Volume 43, May 12, 1915, 37; *The Automobile*, Volume 32, May 13, 1915, 864; *Indianapolis News*, May 22, 1915.
30. Kalafus and Poirier, *William Meriheina*.
31. *New York Evening Post*, May 24, 1915; *New York Times*, May 25, 1915; Hickey and Smith, 185; *Chester Reporter*, February 28, 1924.
32. Amory, *Death*, 8.
33. *Alfred Howard Amory*.
34. *Toronto World*, August 17, 1915.
35. Amory, *Death*, 9.
36. Warren, 3, 20; Layton, 40.
37. Amory, *Death*, 14–15.
38. Layton, 208, 224–25, 227, 306; Ballard, 54.
39. Holbourn, *Foula*, 227; Hoehling and Hoehling, 74.

CHAPTER ELEVEN

1. Bailey and Ryan, 117–18.
2. Ibid., 116; Ramsay, 64; Preston, 150.
3. Bailey and Ryan, 162.
4. Thomas, 91.
5. Kortemeier, 319.
6. Thomas, 91.
7. Bailey and Ryan, 162.
8. Thomas, 83, 91.
9. Forstner, 7.
10. Thomas, 89.
11. Forstner, 33–34.
12. Thomas, 90–91.
13. Forstner, 6, 18.
14. Bailey and Ryan, 53–55.
15. Ibid., 115, 122.
16. Molony, *Lusitania*, 9.
17. Bailey and Ryan, 124.
18. Ibid., 125–26; Beesly, 103–4.
19. Bailey, 335; Bailey and Ryan, 164.
20. Bailey and Ryan, 127.
21. Beesly, 3–7, 97–99.
22. Pope, *And Then*, 4, in Hoehling and Hoehling Archive, MS Collection 45, Box 2, Folder 1.
23. Bailey and Ryan, 133; Hoehling and Hoehling, 82; Mayer Opinion, 9–10, 15; Lauriat, 137.

24. *New York Times,* May 11, 1915.
25. Wynne testimony, 95, in Mayer, in Bailey and Ryan Archive, Box 7.
26. Admiralty Instruction, January 13, 1915, Mersey, In Camera, June 15, 1915, 2, in Bailey and Ryan Archive, Box 2; *Papers Relating to the Foreign Relations,* 1915 Supplement, 653.
27. Mayer Opinion, 9–10, 16; Lauriat, 137.
28. *New York Times,* May 10, 1915.
29. Ibid.
30. Ibid., May 11, 1915.
31. Lauriat, 4–5.
32. *New York Times,* May 10, 1915.
33. Lott Gadd, letter of December 20, 1929, to Elbert Hubbard II, copy in Hoehling and Hoehling Archive, MS Collection 45, Box 1, Folder 18.
34. Angela Papadopoulos account, from the collection of the Baffa Trasci Amalfitani di Crucoli family, courtesy of Michael Poirier.
35. Hoehling and Hoehling, 85; Hickey and Smith, 152.
36. Avis Dolphin, letter to mother, May 1915, in Sauder and Marschall, 86.
37. Poirier and Kalafus, "The Jolivet Family," 165.
38. Boulton, CBC.
39. Fletcher, 176.
40. Hickey and Smith, 154; Ellis, 37.
41. Spedding, 16–17.
42. Bernard, *Cock Sparrow,* 151.
43. Frederick Orr-Lewis, undated letter, John Douglas Hazen Collection, University of New Brunswick, Fredericton, MG H13, Box 22, courtesy of Michael Poirier.
44. Poirier and Kalafus, "The Jolivet Family," 165.
45. Amory, *Death,* 15–16.
46. Bernard, *Cock Sparrow,* 135, 151, 155.
47. Angela Papadopoulos account, from the collection of the Baffa Trasci Amalfitani di Crucoli family, courtesy of Michael Poirier.
48. Kalafus and Poirier, *Albert Arthur Bestic.*
49. Michael Byrne, letter of June 8, 1915, in NARA: United States Department of State, 841.857 L97/72, courtesy of Michael Poirier.
50. Hickey and Smith, 155; *New York Tribune,* May 10, 1915; Report of Wesley Frost to Secretary of State, in NARA: United States Department of State, 341.111 L97/61.
51. *New York Times,* May 10, 1915.
52. Lauriat, 6.
53. *New York Times,* May 10, 1915.
54. Boulton, CBC.
55. Bernard, *Cock Sparrow,* 150–51.
56. Josephine Brandell deposition, 1915, courtesy of Michael Poirier.

57. *New York Sun,* May 12, 1915.

58. Hoehling and Hoehling, 57.

59. *New York Sun,* May 25, 1915; Ellis, 42.

60. Francis Jenkins, testimony of June 17, 1915, Mersey Public Proceedings, 1850–1864, in Bailey and Ryan Archive, Box 2.

61. Charles Jeffery deposition, 1915, for Mersey Inquiry, from the collection of Christine Anagnos, courtesy of Michael Poirier.

62. Michael Byrne, letter of June 8, 1915, in NARA: United States Department of State, 841.857 L97/72, courtesy of Michael Poirier.

63. *New York Times,* May 11, 1915.

64. Angela Papadopoulos account, from the collection of the Baffa Trasci Amalfitani di Crucoli family, courtesy of Michael Poirier.

65. *Pittsburgh Press,* August 11, 1935, courtesy of Michael Poirier.

66. Angela Papadopoulos account, from the collection of the Baffa Trasci Amalfitani di Crucoli family, courtesy of Michael Poirier.

67. Boulton, CBC.

68. Bailey and Ryan, 133; Lauriat, 5; Hoehling and Hoehling, 60.

CHAPTER TWELVE

1. Poirier and Kalafus, "The Jolivet Family," 167.

2. Bernard, *Cock Sparrow,* 150.

3. *Kansas City Star,* June 15, 1919, courtesy of Michael Poirier.

4. *Townsville Daily Bulletin,* March 14, 1939, courtesy of Michael Poirier.

5. Bailey and Ryan, 138; Layton, 295.

6. Boulton, CBC.

7. Ibid.

8. Frost, 192.

9. Michael Byrne, letter of June 8, 1915, in NARA: United States Department of State, 841.857 L97/72, courtesy of Michael Poirier.

10. *New York Evening Post,* May 24, 1915.

11. Lauriat, 5, 70.

12. *New York Times,* May 10, 1915, May 16, 1915.

13. Rhondda, *This Was,* 254.

14. Hoehling and Hoehling, 140; Hickey and Smith, 208.

15. *Pittsburgh Press,* August 11, 1935, courtesy of Michael Poirier.

16. *New York Times,* May 16, 1915.

17. Rhondda, *This Was,* 253.

18. Michael Byrne, letter of June 8, 1915, in NARA: United States Department of State, 841.857 L97/72, courtesy of Michael Poirier; James Brooks, undated letter, in Hoehling and Hoehling Archive, MS Collection 45, Box 1, Folder 10; Wesley Frost to State Department, May 14, 1915, in NARA: United States Department of State, 841.857 L97/29.

19. Bernard, *Cock Sparrow,* 151.

20. Hoehling and Hoehling, 101; Bernard, *Cock Sparrow,* 152.

21. Pope, *And Then,* 99, in Hoehling and Hoehling Archive, MS Collection 45, Box 2, Folder 1.

22. Howard Fisher, undated letter to son, courtesy of Michael Poirier.

23. Rhondda, *This Was,* 242.

24. *Kansas City Star,* June 15, 1919, courtesy of Michael Poirier.

25. Amory, *Death,* 17–18.

26. *New York Times,* May 8, 1915.

27. Ramsay, 245.

28. *New York Times,* May 11, 1915.

29. Bestic undated clipping, 1955, in Hoehling and Hoehling Archive, MS Collection 45, Box 1, Folder 60.

30. Bailey and Ryan, 41.

31. Simpson, 125–29; Bailey and Ryan, 144–45, 174; Beesly, 96, 110; Ramsay, 75, 200–201, 246; O'Sullivan, 70.

32. Bailey and Ryan, 133–35.

33. Bailey and Ryan, 136; *New York American,* May 8, 1915.

34. Bailey and Ryan, 140.

35. "Lusitania," *American Journal of International Law,* 865. Later allegations that the query about the Merchant Code was actually a secret instruction for Turner to divert *Lusitania* to Queenstown are easily refuted by Turner's own insistence that he received no such order. See Simpson, 150; Beesly, 105; Peeke, Walsh-Johnson, and Jones, 71–75; and, for refutation, Bailey and Ryan, 138–39, and the *New York Times,* May 11, 1915.

36. Beesly, 117; Bailey and Ryan, 209–12, 280.

37. Simpson, 177.

38. Bailey and Ryan, 142; Hoehling and Hoehling, 63; Bestic, undated clipping, 1955, in Hoehling and Hoehling Archive, MS Collection 45, Box 1, Folder 60; Ramsay, 142; Preston, 321; William Turner, testimony of June 15, 1915, In Camera, in Bailey and Ryan Archive, Box 2; Beesly, 97; Layton, 264; "Lusitania," *American Journal of International Law,* 881.

39. Bestic, undated clipping, 1955, in Hoehling and Hoehling Archive, MS Collection 45, Box 1, Folder 60.

40. Simpson, 176; Beesly, 97; Bailey and Ryan, 143.

41. William Turner, testimony of June 15, 1915, In Camera, in Bailey and Ryan Archive, Box 2; Beesly, 97; Layton, 264; Bailey and Ryan, 143; "Lusitania," *American Journal of International Law,* 881.

42. "Lusitania," *American Journal of International Law,* 869–70; Bailey and Ryan, 144; Ramsay, 79.

43. Hoehling and Hoehling, 95; Bailey and Ryan, 285.

44. Charles Jeffery, deposition for Mersey Inquiry, from the collection of Christine Anagnos, courtesy of Michael Poirier.

45. *New York Times,* May 25, 1915.

46. Beesly, 117; Bailey and Ryan, 209–12, 280.
47. "Lusitania," *American Journal of International Law,* 869–70; Bailey and Ryan, 209–12; Layton, 296.
48. Thomas, 96–97.
49. Walther Schwieger, War Diary for U-20, in Bailey, 335.
50. Ibid.
51. Bailey and Ryan, 11, 22, 152–55.
52. Thomas, 97.
53. Walther Schwieger, War Diary for U-20, in Bailey, 335.

CHAPTER THIRTEEN

1. Bernard, *Cock Sparrow,* 152–53.
2. Ibid., 154.
3. Ibid.; *New York Times,* May 10, 1915.
4. *Chicago Tribune,* May 10, 1915, courtesy of Michael Poirier.
5. Bernard, *Cock Sparrow,* 154–55; *New York Times,* May 10, 1915.
6. Brinnin, 345.
7. Warren, 3; Layton, 34; Maxtone-Graham, 33; Sauder and Marschall, 54.
8. *Townsville Daily Bulletin,* March 14, 1939, courtesy of Michael Poirier.
9. Angela Papadopoulos account, from the collection of the Baffa Tasci Amalfitani di Crucoli family, courtesy of Michael Poirier.
10. *New York Times,* June 2, 1915; Isaac Lehmann account, in NARA: United States Department of State, 841.857 L97/29; Isaac Lehmann, Mayer testimony, 262–72, 294–312, in Bailey and Ryan Archive, Box 6.
11. *New York Times,* June 2, 1915.
12. *Chicago Tribune,* May 10, 1915, courtesy of Michael Poirier.
13. Ryerson, 205; Ryerse, 8.
14. Frederick Orr-Lewis, undated letter, John Douglas Hazen Collection, University of New Brunswick, Fredericton, MG H13, Box 22, courtesy of Michael Poirier.
15. *Toronto Daily Star,* May 10, 1915, courtesy of Michael Poirier.
16. Robinson Pirie account, from the collection of Marika Pirie, courtesy of Michael Poirier.
17. Ogden Hammond, deposition of May 21, 1915, in NARA: United States Department of State, 841.857 L/97/48.
18. *New York Times,* May 10, 1915.
19. Ogden Hammond, deposition of May 21, 1915, in NARA: United States Department of State, 841.857 L97/48.
20. William Adams, April 15, 1918, examination, 5–6, in Mayer Opinion, 13.
21. Jessie Taft Smith account, May 9, 1915, courtesy of Michael Poirier.
22. *New York Times,* May 11, 1915.
23. Rhondda, *This Was,* 242.
24. Rhondda, *Recalling,* 635, in Hoehling and Hoehling Archive, MS Collection 45, Box 2, Folder 1.

25. Rhondda, *This Was*, 242–43.
26. Thomas Home, undated letter, courtesy of Michael Poirier.
27. Michael Byrne, letter of June 8, 1915, in NARA: United States Department of State, 841.857 L97/72, courtesy of Michael Poirier.
28. *New York Times*, May 10, 1915; James Brooks, letter of March 31, 1955, in Hoehling and Hoehling Archive, MS Collection 45, Box 1, Folder 10.
29. Undated clipping, 1955, in Hoehling and Hoehling Archive, MS Collection 45, Box 1, Folder 62.
30. Hoehling and Hoehling, 46.
31. Undated clipping, 1955, in Hoehling and Hoehling Archive, MS Collection 45, Box 1, Folder 62.
32. *New York Times*, May 10, 1915; Mayer Opinion, 14–15; James Brooks deposition, in NARA: United States Department of State, 841.857 L97/80; undated clipping, 1955, in Hoehling and Hoehling Archive, MS Collection 45, Box 1, Folder 62.
33. *New York Times*, May 11, 1915.
34. James Houghton, letter to Freeman family, from the collection of Chester Nimitz Lay and Richard Bailey, courtesy of Michael Poirier.
35. Ellis, 41.
36. *New York Times*, May 10, 1915, May 16, 1915.
37. Lauriat, 7.
38. Ibid., 7–8, 72–73.
39. Elbert Hubbard II, letter of May 4, 1955, in Hoehling and Hoehling Archive, MS Collection 45, Box 1, Folder 30.
40. Pope, *And Then*, 99–100, in Hoehling and Hoehling Archive, MS Collection 45, Box 2, Folder 1.
41. Bernard, *Cock Sparrow*, 172.
42. *Oldham Chronicle*, undated clipping, 1915, courtesy of Michael Poirier.
43. Thomas, 102.
44. Josephine Burnside, undated clipping, *Toronto Star*, courtesy of Michael Poirier.
45. Josephine Brandell deposition, courtesy of Michael Poirier.
46. *New York Times*, June 6, 1915.
47. *Pittsburgh Press*, August 11, 1935, courtesy of Michael Poirier.
48. Robert Timmis, testimony of June 17, 1915, Mersey Public Proceedings, 1967–68, in Bailey and Ryan Archive, Box 2.
49. Howard Fisher, undated letter to son, courtesy of Michael Poirier.
50. Rhondda, *This Was*, 242–43.
51. Amory, *Death*, 17–18.
52. Titanic International Society.
53. Kroeger; *Lusitania Resource*; *Daily Telegraph*, April 21, 2008.
54. *New York Times*, May 25, 1915.
55. *New York Evening Post*, May 24, 1915.

56. Kalafus and Poirier, *William Meriheina.*
57. Amory, *Death,* 18–19.
58. Avis Dolphin, letter to mother, May 1915, in Sauder and Marschall, 86; *Worcester Daily Times,* May 15, 1915, in Hoehling and Hoehling Archive, MS Collection 45, Box 2, Folder 70.
59. Hickey and Smith, 192.
60. Avis Dolphin, letter to mother, May 1915, in Sauder and Marschall, 86.
61. Avis Dolphin Foley, letter of August 25, 1955, in Hoehling and Hoehling Archive, MS Collection 45, Box 1, Folder 16.
62. *Marshall News-Statesman,* August 16, 1915, courtesy of Michael Poirier.
63. *Kansas City Star,* June 15, 1919, courtesy of Michael Poirier; *Marshall-News-Statesman,* August 16, 1915, courtesy of Michael Poirier.
64. Brown, *Imperial,* 103.
65. Alice Lines, testimony of June 17, 1915, Mersey Public Proceedings, 1778–82, in Bailey and Ryan Archive, Box 2.
66. Hickey and Smith, 200.
67. Brown, *Imperial,* 102–3.
68. *Auburn Citizen,* June 15, 1915, courtesy of Michael Poirier.
69. Poirier and Kalafus, "The Jolivet Family," 165.
70. Boulton, CBC.
71. Rita Jolivet, Mayer testimony, in Kalafus and Poirier, *Lest We Forget, Part 2.*
72. Marcosson and Frohman, 386.
73. Ellis, 37.
74. *Townsville Daily Bulletin,* March 14, 1939, courtesy of Michael Poirier.
75. Hoehling and Hoehling, 118.
76. Boulton, CBC.
77. Layton, 309.
78. Ibid., 103.
79. *Townsville Daily Bulletin,* March 14, 1939, courtesy of Michael Poirier; Boulton, CBC; Hoehling and Hoehling, 110; Preston, 210–11. There is some question about this most persistent of *Lusitania* stories, which seems to have cropped up only several years after the disaster; Boulton, however, was adamant that he witnessed the scene, and several other passengers also later confirmed the details.
80. Boulton, CBC.

CHAPTER FOURTEEN

1. Morton, 102–3.
2. Leslie Morton, testimony of June 16, 1915, Mersey Public Proceedings, 416, in Bailey and Ryan Archive, Box 2; Mayer Opinion, 15.
3. Leslie Morton, testimony of June 16, 1915, Mersey Public Proceedings, 426, 422, in Bailey and Ryan Archive, Box 2.
4. Morton, 103.

5. Thomas Quinn, testimony of June 16, 1915, Mersey Public Proceedings, 15, in Bailey and Ryan Archive, Box 2.

6. William Turner, testimony of June 15, 1915, Mersey Public Proceedings, 92, in Bailey and Ryan Archive, Box 2.

7. *New York Times,* May 11, 1915.

8. Walter Schwieger, War Diary for U-20, in Bailey, 335–36.

9. Layton, 302; Preston, 448; Ramsay, 208.

10. Ramsay, 208; Layton, 302; Preston, 448; Bailey and Ryan, 169.

11. Thomas, 97.

12. Walther Schwieger, War Diary for U-20, in Bailey, 336.

13. Preston, 448, 451–52; Bailey and Ryan, 167.

14. Preston, 201.

15. Hoehling and Hoehling, 124; *New York Times,* May 11, 1915.

16. Mayer Opinion, 28; Gentile, 2:297.

17. *New York Times,* May 10, 1915.

18. Bernard, *Cock Sparrow,* 155.

19. *New York Times,* May 10, 1915.

20. Ellis, 75.

21. Ibid., 69.

22. Michael Byrne, letter of June 8, 1915, in NARA: United States Department of State, 841.857, L97/72, courtesy of Michael Poirier.

23. *New York World,* May 10, 1915.

24. *New York Times,* May 10, 1915.

25. *Oldham Chronicle,* undated clipping, 1915, courtesy of Michael Poirier.

26. Bestic, undated clipping, 1915, in Hoehling and Hoehling Archive, MS Collection 45, Box 1, Folder 60.

27. Lauriat, 16.

28. Morton, 105.

29. Frederick Orr-Lewis, undated letter, John Douglas Hazen Collection, University of New Brunswick, Fredericton, MG H13, Box 22, courtesy of Michael Poirier.

30. Smith, *George,* 175–76.

31. *Toronto Daily Star,* May 10, 1915, courtesy of Michael Poirier.

32. Frederick Orr-Lewis, undated letter, John Douglas Hazen Collection, University of New Brunswick, Fredericton, MG H13, Box 22, courtesy of Michael Poirier.

33. Bernard, *Cock Sparrow,* 155–57.

34. *New York Evening Post,* May 24, 1915; *New York Times,* May 25, 1915.

35. *New York Times,* May 10, 1915; James Brooks deposition, in NARA: United States Department of State, 841.857 L97/80; Mayer Opinion, 64.

36. Ellis, 44.

37. Bernard, *Cock Sparrow,* 157.

38. Lauriat, 11.

39. *Pittsburgh Press,* August 11, 1935, courtesy of Michael Poirier.
40. Unidentified newspaper clipping, May 31, 1915, courtesy of Michael Poirier.
41. Lauriat, 13–14; *Philadelphia Inquirer,* May 12, 1915, courtesy of Michael Poirier.
42. Lauriat, 14–15.
43. Marshall, 44–45; Hoehling and Hoehling, 138, 171.
44. Lauriat, 76–77.
45. Ellis, 42–43.
46. William Turner, testimony of June 15, 1915, 106, Mersey Public Proceedings, in Bailey and Ryan Archive, Box 2.
47. Simpson, 159.
48. Preston, 218–19.
49. Hoehling and Hoehling, 117.
50. Simpson, 159; Preston, 132; Layton, 105–6.
51. Lauriat, 15, 74.
52. James Brooks, letter of July 13, 1955, in Hoehling and Hoehling Archive, MS Collection 45, Box 1, Folder 10; *Washington Post,* June 18, 1915; David Thomas, testimony of June 17, 1915, Mersey Public Proceedings, in Bailey and Ryan Archive, Box 2.
53. Michael Byrne, letter of June 8, 1915, in NARA: United States Department of State, 841.857 L97.72, courtesy of Michael Poirier.
54. Alice Lines, testimony of June 17, 1915, Mersey Public Proceedings, 1776–86, in Bailey and Ryan Archive, Box 2.
55. *New York Times,* May 11, 1915; *Lusitania Resource.*
56. *Daily Telegraph,* April 21, 2008.
57. Mayer Opinion, 51.
58. Charles Bowring testimony, Mayer Hearings, 477, in Bailey and Ryan Archive, Box 6; Mayer Opinion, 44.
59. Hoehling and Hoehling, 115.
60. *New York Sun,* May 11, 1915.
61. Droste and Tantum, 163.
62. Layton, 105–6; Preston, 132.
63. Droste and Tantum, 163.
64. Preston, 229–30; Ellis, 44.
65. Thomas Home, undated letter, courtesy of Michael Poirier.
66. William Adams, statement, in NARA: United States Department of State, 841.857 L97/4.
67. *New York Times,* June 2, 1915.
68. *Los Angeles Times,* June 4, 1915, courtesy of Michael Poirier.
69. Josephine Brandell deposition, courtesy of Michael Poirier.
70. Angela Papadopoulos account, from the collection of the Baffa Trasci Amalfitani di Crucoli family, courtesy of Michael Poirier.
71. Holbourn, *Foula,* 227–28.

72. Avis Dolphin, letter to mother, May 1915, in Sauder and Marschall, 86.

73. Angela Papadopoulos account, from the collection of the Baffa Trasci Amalfitani di Crucoli family, courtesy of Michael Poirier.

74. Holbourn, *Foula*, 227–28.

75. Howard Fisher, undated letter to son, courtesy of Michael Poirier.

76. Rhondda, *This Was*, 243–44.

77. Rhondda, *Recalling*, 636, in Hoehling and Hoehling Archive, MS Collection 45, Box 2, Folder 1.

78. Rhondda, *This Was*, 244.

79. Pope, *And Then*, 100–101, in Hoehling and Hoehling Archive, MS Collection 45, Box 2, Folder 1.

80. *New York Times*, May 25, 1915.

81. Ibid., June 2, 1915.

82. Thomas, 97.

83. Walther Schwieger, War Diary for U-20, in Bailey, 335–36.

84. Bailey and Ryan, 159.

85. Thomas, 97.

86. Walther Schwieger, War Diary for U-20, in Bailey, 336.

CHAPTER FIFTEEN

1. Mayer Opinion, 38–39.

2. *New York World*, May 10, 1915.

3. *Townsville Daily Bulletin*, March 14, 1939, courtesy of Michael Poirier.

4. Elisabeth Lassetter, testimony of June 17, 1945, Mersey Public Proceedings, in Bailey and Ryan Archive, Box 2.

5. Lauriat, 9–11.

6. Ellis, 42–43.

7. Ogden Hammond, deposition of May 21, 1915, in NARA: United States Department of State, 841.857 L/97/48.

8. Rhondda, *This Was*, 244.

9. *Kansas City Star*, June 15, 1919, courtesy of Michael Poirier.

10. Ellis, 42–43.

11. Bernard, *Cock Sparrow*, 156, 158.

12. *Chicago Tribune*, May 10, 1915, courtesy of Michael Poirier.

13. Amory, *Death*, 20–22.

14. Michael Byrne, letter of June 8, 1915, in NARA: United States Department of State, 841.857 L97/72, courtesy of Michael Poirier.

15. Rhondda, *This Was*, 244.

16. Ellis, 127.

17. Bestic, undated clipping, 1955, in Hoehling and Hoehling Archive, MS Collection 45, Box 1, Folder 60.

18. Morton, 106.

19. Ogden Hammond, deposition of May 21, 1915, in NARA: United States Department of State, 841.857 L/97/48.

20. *New York Times,* May 10, 1915.

21. Ibid., June 2, 1915.

22. Robinson Pirie account, 1915, from the collection of Marika Pirie, courtesy of Michael Poirier; *New York Times,* June 2, 1915; Mayer Opinion, 48.

23. Hoehling and Hoehling, 115; Marshall, 32.

24. Bernard, *Cock Sparrow,* 156.

25. *New York Tribune,* May 9, 1915.

26. *New York Times,* May 9, 1915.

27. *Amsterdam Evening Recorder,* May 17, 1915, courtesy of Michael Poirier.

28. Strange, 134–35.

29. Bernard, *Cock Sparrow,* 159–60.

30. Ellis, 41.

31. *New York Times,* May 11, 1915.

32. James Houghton, letter to Freeman family, 1915, from the collection of Chester Nimitz Lay and Richard Bailey, courtesy of Michael Poirier.

33. Pope, *And Then,* 100–101, in Hoehling and Hoehling Archive, MS Collection 45, Box 2, Folder 1.

34. Boulton, CBC.

35. Gregory, 216–17.

36. Frederick Orr-Lewis, undated letter, John Douglas Hazen Collection, University of New Brunswick, Fredericton, MG H13, Box 22, courtesy of Michael Poirier.

37. *Toronto Daily Star,* May 10, 1915, courtesy of Michael Poirier.

38. Unidentified newspaper clipping, May 31, 1915, courtesy of Michael Poirier.

39. *New York Times,* May 25, 1915.

40. *Kansas City Star,* undated May 1915 clipping, courtesy of Michael Poirier; *Toronto Daily Star,* undated 1980 clipping, courtesy of Michael Poirier.

41. *Auburn Citizen,* June 15, 1915, courtesy of Michael Poirier.

42. Lott Gadd, letter of February 2, 1930, to Elbert Hubbard II, copy in Hoehling and Hoehling Archive, MS Collection 45, Box 1, Folder 18.

43. *Auburn Citizen,* June 15, 1915, courtesy of Michael Poirier.

44. Ryerson, 205.

45. Bestic, undated clipping, 1955, in Hoehling and Hoehling Archive, MS Collection 45, Box 1, Folder 60.

46. Morton, 107.

47. Hoehling and Hoehling, 158.

48. Leslie Morton, letter of August 29, 1955, in Hoehling and Hoehling Archive, MS Collection 45, Box 1, Folder 43.

49. Hoehling and Hoehling, 133; James Brooks, letter of July 13, 1955, in Hoehling and Hoehling Archive, MS Collection 45, Box 1, Folder 10.

50. James Brooks, undated 1955 article, in Hoehling and Hoehling Archive, MS Collection 45, Box 1, Folder 62; *New York Times,* May 10, 1915; James Brooks statement, undated, in NARA: United States Department of State, 841.857 L97/80.

51. Howard Fisher, letter to son, courtesy of Michael Poirier.

52. Rhondda, *Recalling,* 636, in Hoehling and Hoehling Archive, MS Collection 45, Box 2, Folder 1.

53. Reckitt, 229.

54. Rhondda, *This Was,* 244.

55. Ibid., 245; Rhondda, *Recalling,* 637, in Hoehling and Hoehling Archive, MS Collection 45, Box 2, Folder 1.

56. *Pittsburgh Press,* August 11, 1935, courtesy of Michael Poirier.

57. Robert Timmis, testimony of June 17, 1915, Mersey Public Proceedings, 1967–68, in Bailey and Ryan Archive, Box 2.

58. *Pittsburgh Press,* August 11, 1935, courtesy of Michael Poirier.

59. *New York Times,* May 26, 1915.

60. *New York Sun,* May 25, 1915.

61. *Marshall News-Statesman,* August 16, 1915, courtesy of Michael Poirier.

62. *Kansas City Star,* June 15, 1919, courtesy of Michael Poirier.

63. Marshall, 25.

64. Frohman, 250.

65. *New York Times,* May 11, 1915; Hickey and Smith, 222.

66. *New York Times,* May 11, 1915; Hoehling and Hoehling, 157.

67. Kalafus and Poirier, *Lest We Forget, Part 2.*

68. *New York Times,* May 10, May 11, 1915.

69. *Retford, Gainsborough, and Worksop Times,* June 11, 1915, courtesy of Michael Poirier.

70. *New York Times,* May 11, 1915.

71. Warren Pearl statement, May 21, 1915, in NARA: United States Department of State, 842.857 L98/31.

72. *New York Times,* May 11, 1915; Hoehling and Hoehling, 149.

73. Bates, 126–28.

74. *New York Times,* May 11, 1915; *New York Herald,* May 10, 1915.

75. William Adams, undated statement, in NARA: United States Department of State, 841.857 L97/4.

76. Lauriat, 16–18, 84; Mayer Opinion, 53.

77. Bernard, *Cock Sparrow,* 161.

78. David Thomas, testimony of June 17, 1915, Mersey Public Proceedings, 1984–87, in Bailey and Ryan Archive, Box 2.

79. Bernard, *Cock Sparrow,* 161–62.

80. *Chicago Tribune,* May 10, 1915, courtesy of Michael Poirier.

81. *New York Times,* May 25, 1915.

82. Kalafus and Poirier, *William Meriheina*; information from Michael Poirier to the authors.

83. Lauriat, 84.

84. *New York Times,* May 10, 1915.

85. *Oldham Chronicle,* undated clipping, 1915, courtesy of Michael Poirier.

86. Lauriat, 18–19, 86.

87. Kalafus and Poirier, *William Meriheina.*

88. Lauriat, 18–19.

89. Brown, *Imperial,* 103.

90. James Brooks, undated clipping, 1955, in Hoehling and Hoehling Archive, MS Collection 45, Box 1, Folder 62.

91. *New York Times,* May 10, 1915.

92. *Toronto Daily Star,* May 10, 1915, courtesy of Michael Poirier.

93. Lauriat, 21.

94. *New York Evening Post,* May 24, 1915.

95. Bernard, *Cock Sparrow,* 174.

96. *New York Times,* May 10, 1915.

CHAPTER SIXTEEN

1. Lauriat, 20.

2. *New York Times,* May 10, 1915.

3. Lauriat, 86.

4. Bestic clipping, undated, 1955, in Hoehling and Hoehling Archive, MS Collection 45, Box 1, Folder 60.

5. *New York Times,* May 11, 1915.

6. Boulton, CBC.

7. *New York Times,* May 25, 1915.

8. Frost, 204.

9. *New York Times,* May 11, 1915.

10. Josephine Brandell deposition, undated, courtesy of Michael Poirier.

11. Bernard, *Cock Sparrow,* 162.

12. *New York Times,* May 10, 1915.

13. Hoehling and Hoehling, 159.

14. *New York Times,* June 6, 1915.

15. *Auburn Citizen,* June 15, 1915, courtesy of Michael Poirier.

16. Ryerson, 205.

17. James Houghton, undated letter to Freeman family, 1915, from the collection of Chester Nimitz Lay and Richard Bailey, courtesy of Michael Poirier.

18. *New York Times,* May 11, 1915; *Washington Post,* May 10, 1915.

19. *New York Times,* May 11, 1915; *Saratogian,* May 11, 1915, courtesy of Michael Poirier.

20. *Kansas City Star,* undated clipping, May 1915, courtesy of Michael Poirier.

21. *New York Times,* June 2, 1915.
22. Ibid., May 25, 1915.
23. Robinson Pirie account, 1915, from the collection of Marika Pirie, courtesy of Michael Poirier.
24. *Toronto Daily Star,* May 10, 1915, courtesy of Michael Poirier.
25. Frederick Orr-Lewis, undated letter, John Douglas Hazen Collection, University of New Brunswick, Fredericton, MG H13, Box 22, courtesy of Michael Poirier.
26. *Toronto Daily Star,* May 10, 1915, courtesy of Michael Poirier.
27. Reckitt, 19; *New York Times,* May 10, 1915.
28. Boulton, CBC.
29. *Retford, Gainsborough and Worksop Times,* June 11, 1915, courtesy of Michael Poirier.
30. *Townsville Daily Bulletin,* March 14, 1939, courtesy of Michael Poirier.
31. Boulton, CBC.
32. *Townsville Daily Bulletin,* March 14, 1939, courtesy of Michael Poirier.
33. Frederic Lassetter, testimony of June 17, 1915, Mersey Public Proceedings, 1964, in Bailey and Ryan Archive, Box 2; *New York Times,* May 11, 1915.
34. *Townsville Daily Bulletin,* March 14, 1939, courtesy of Michael Poirier.
35. *Pittsburgh Press,* August 11, 1935, courtesy of Michael Poirier.
36. Michael Byrne, letter of June 8, 1915, in NARA: United States Department of State, 841.857 L97/72, courtesy of Michael Poirier.
37. *New York Times,* May 26, 1915.
38. Amory, *Death,* 24–25.
39. *Los Angeles Times,* June 4, 1915, courtesy of Michael Poirier; Bilicke clipping, undated, in Hoehling and Hoehling Archive, MS Collection 45, Box 1, Folder 61.
40. Angela Papadopoulos account, from the collection of the Baffa Tasci Amalfitani di Crucoli family, courtesy of Michael Poirier.
41. *New York Times,* May 10, 1915; Ogden Hammond statement, May 21, 1915, in NARA: United States Department of State, 841.857 L/97/48.
42. *New York Sun,* May 11, 1915.
43. Warren Pearl statement, May 21, 1915, in NARA: United States Department of State, 842.857 L98/31; *New York Times,* May 11, 1915.
44. *Kansas City Star,* June 15, 1919, courtesy of Michael Poirier.
45. *Marshall News-Statesman,* August 16, 1915, courtesy of Michael Poirier.
46. *Kansas City Star,* June 15, 1919, courtesy of Michael Poirier.
47. Poirier and Kalafus, "The Jolivet Family," 166.
48. Boulton, CBC.
49. Kalafus and Poirier, *Lest We Forget, Part 2;* Poirier and Kalafus, "The Jolivet Family," 169.
50. Ellis, 43.

51. *Worcester Daily Times,* May 15 1915, in Hoehling and Hoehling Archive, MS Collection 45, Box 2, Folder 70.

52. Holbourn, *Foula,* 228–29; Hoehling and Hoehling, 166–69.

53. Avis Dolphin, letter to mother, May 1915, in Sauder and Marschall, 86.

54. *Gaelic American,* May 22, 1915, in Droste and Tantum, 163.

55. James Brooks, undated statement, in NARA: United States Department of State, 841.857 L97/80; Lauriat, 22–26.

56. Lauriat, 88.

57. *New York Times,* May 10, May 11, June 2, 1915; Ellis, 77; Hoehling and Hoehling, 209; *Chicago Tribune,* May 10, 1915, courtesy of Michael Poirier.

58. *Chicago Daily News,* undated, from the collection of Paul Latimer, courtesy of Michael Poirier; *Chicago Tribune,* May 10, 1915, courtesy of Michael Poirier.

59. Unidentified newspaper clipping, May 31, 1915, courtesy of Michael Poirier.

60. *New York Evening Post,* May 24, 1915.

61. *New York Times,* May 25, 1915.

62. *New York Evening Post,* May 24, 1915.

63. Pope, *And Then,* 101–2, in Hoehling and Hoehling Archive, MS Collection 45, Box 2, Folder 1.

64. Hoehling and Hoehling, 157, 177.

65. Howard Fisher, undated letter to son, courtesy of Michael Poirier.

66. Kalafus and Poirier, *William Meriheina.*

67. Rhondda, *Recalling,* 638–39, in Hoehling and Hoehling Archive, MS Collection 45, Box 2, Folder 1; Rhondda, *This Was,* 245–47.

68. Norman Turner, letter of July 9, 1955, in Hoehling and Hoehling Archive, MS Collection 45, Box 1, Folder 55.

69. Maude Thompson, statement, July 8, 1915, courtesy of Michael Poirier.

70. Hoehling and Hoehling, 180.

71. Ramsay, 86.

72. *New York Times,* May 10, 1915.

73. Preston, 254.

74. McQueen, 37.

75. Lott Gadd, letter of February 2, 1930, to Elbert Hubbard II, copy in Hoehling and Hoehling Archive, MS Collection 45, Box 1, Folder 18; Marshall, 32; Morton, 108–9.

76. Frost, 205.

77. Lauriat, 26–31, 88.

78. Simpson, 176; Bailey, 175.

79. Bernard, *Cock Sparrow,* 162.

80. Amory, *Death,* 27–28.

81. *Toronto Daily Star,* May 10, 1915, courtesy of Michael Poirier.

82. *New York Times,* May 10, 1915; Morton, 109; Ellis, 43–44.

83. *Kansas City Star,* June 15, 1919, courtesy of Michael Poirier.
84. *New York Times,* June 2, 1915.
85. Ibid., May 26, 1915.
86. Ibid., May 10, 1915.
87. Angela Papadopoulos account, from the collection of the Baffa Trasci Amalfitani di Crucoli family, courtesy of Michael Poirier.
88. *Worcester Daily Times,* May 15, 1915, in Hoehling and Hoehling Archive, MS Collection 45, Box 2, Folder 70.
89. Frost, 211–12.
90. Pope, *And Then,* 102, in Hoehling and Hoehling Archive, MS Collection 45, Box 2, Folder 1.
91. *New York Times,* May 10, 1915.
92. Preston, 265–66.
93. *New York Times,* May 10, 1915; Molony, *Lusitania,* 90.
94. Ogden Hammond statement, May 21, 1915, in NARA: United States Department of State, 841.857 L/97/48; Lauriat, 36.
95. Lauriat, 34–39.
96. Bernard, *Cock Sparrow,* 164.
97. Lauriat, 39.
98. Rhondda, *D. A. Thomas,* 198–99.
99. Thomas, 104.
100. Rhondda, *Recalling,* 638–40, in Hoehling and Hoehling Archive, MS Collection 45, Box 2, Folder 1; Rhondda, *This Was,* 248–50.
101. *The Times,* May 10, 1915.
102. Rhondda, *Recalling,* 638–40, in Hoehling and Hoehling Archive, MS Collection 45, Box 2, Folder 1; Rhondda, *This Was,* 248–50.
103. *New York Times,* May 16, 1915.
104. Rhondda, *Recalling,* 638–40, in Hoehling and Hoehling Archive, MS Collection 45, Box 2, Folder 1; Rhondda, *This Was,* 248–51.

CHAPTER SEVENTEEN

1. Frost, 4.
2. Unidentified, undated newspaper clipping, 1955, in Hoehling and Hoehling Archive, MS Collection 45, Box 1, Folder 62.
3. Thomas, 102.
4. Boulton, CBC.
5. Hoehling and Hoehling, 215; Preston, 286.
6. Rhondda, *This Was,* 251; Rhondda, *D. A. Thomas,* 200.
7. Hoehling and Hoehling, 215–16.
8. Rhondda, *D. A. Thomas,* 199.
9. *Kansas City Star,* June 15, 1919, courtesy of Michael Poirier.
10. *New York Times,* May 25, 1915.

11. *Pittsburgh Press*, August 11, 1935, courtesy of Michael Poirier.

12. Robinson Pirie account, 1915, from the collection of Marika Pirie, courtesy of Michael Poirier.

13. *New York Times*, June 2, 1915.

14. Reckitt, 229; *New York Times*, May 10, 1915; Rhondda, *D. A. Thomas*, 199.

15. UPI Report, May 8, 1915.

16. *Pittsburgh Press*, August 11, 1935, courtesy of Michael Poirier.

17. *Philadelphia Inquirer*, May 12, 1915, courtesy of Michael Poirier.

18. *New York Times*, May 9, 1915.

19. *Chicago Tribune*, May 10, 1915, courtesy of Michael Poirier.

20. Lauriat, 45.

21. Molony, *Lusitania*, 154.

22. Lauriat, 43–48.

23. Ambassador Walter Page to Secretary of State William Jennings Bryan, May 18, 1915, in NARA: United States Department of State, 841.857.L97/2.

24. Wesley Frost to Secretary of State William Jennings Bryan, May 11, 1915, in NARA: United States Department of State, 841.857 L97/27; Frost, 216–17.

25. *New York Times*, June 2, 1915.

26. Frost, 220; Preston, 282; Schapiro, 23.

27. *New York Sun*, May 11, 1915.

28. *Kansas City Star*, undated newspaper clipping, May 1915, courtesy of Michael Poirier.

29. Avis Dolphin, letter to mother, May 1915, in Sauder and Marschall, 87.

30. Pope, *And Then*, 102, in Hoehling and Hoehling Archive, MS Collection 45, Box 2, Folder 1; Hoehling and Hoehling, 14.

31. Rhondda, *This Was*, 254, 257.

32. *New York Times*, May 9, 1915.

33. Frost, 208.

34. Ibid., 226.

35. *New York Times*, May 9, 1915.

36. Robinson Pirie account, 1915, from the collection of Marika Pirie, courtesy of Michael Poirier.

37. Bernard, *Cock Sparrow*, 165–66.

38. *Chicago Tribune*, May 10, 1915, courtesy of Michael Poirier.

39. *New York Times*, May 11, 1915.

40. *Marshall News-Statesman*, August 16, 1915, courtesy of Michael Poirier.

41. Leslie Morton, letter of July 25, 1955, in Hoehling and Hoehling Archive, MS Collection 45, Box 1, Folder 43.

42. Appleton, 10.

43. Ibid., 183.

44. Smith, *George*, 186.

45. *New York Times,* May 10, 1915.

46. Ibid., May 12, 1915.

47. Frost, 224–25; Wesley Frost to Secretary of State William Jennings Bryan, May 11, 1915, in NARA: United States Department of State, 841.857 L97/27.

48. Hoehling and Hoehling, 224–25; Molony, *Lusitania,* 122–25; *New York Times,* May 11, 1915; Ellis, 79–83.

49. Preston, 278–79.

50. Wesley Frost to Secretary of State William Jennings Bryan, May 11, 1915, in NARA: United States Department of State, 841.857 L97/27.

51. Michael Byrne, letter of June 8, 1915, in NARA: United States Department of State, 841.857, L97/72, courtesy of Michael Poirier.

52. Molony, *Lusitania,* 154.

53. *New York Times,* May 9, 1915.

54. Horgan, 274; *New York Times,* May 11, 1915.

55. Hoehling and Hoehling, 219.

56. *New York Tribune,* May 10, 1915.

57. Bernard, *Cock Sparrow,* 163.

58. Rhondda, *D. A. Thomas,* 200.

59. Wesley Frost to Secretary of State William Jennings Bryan, May 11, 1915, in NARA: United States Department of State, 841.857 L97/27.

60. *New York Times,* May 10, 1915.

61. Ibid., May 25, 1915.

62. *Chicago Tribune,* May 10, 1915, courtesy of Michael Poirier.

63. *New York Times,* May 11, 1915.

64. Ibid., May 10, 1915.

65. *New York Times,* May 25, 1915; Michael Byrne, letter of June 8, 1915, in NARA: United States Department of State, 841.857 L97/72, courtesy of Michael Poirier.

66. *New York World,* May 10, 1915.

67. *New York Sun,* May 25, 1915.

68. *Richmond Times Dispatch,* June 4, 1915, in Droste and Tantum, 174–75.

69. Bernard, *Cock Sparrow,* 151, 167, 171.

70. *New York Times,* May 10, 1915.

71. Ibid., May 11, 1915.

72. Gregory, 216.

73. Hoehling and Hoehling, 219; Frost, 230.

74. *New York Times,* May 12, 1915.

75. Kalafus and Poirier, *Lest We Forget,* Part 2.

76. *New York Times,* May 11, 1915.

77. Unidentified, undated newspaper clipping, in Hoehling and Hoehling Archive, MS Collection 45, Box 1, Folder 61.

78. Wesley Frost, telegram to Secretary of State William Jennings Bryan, May 11, 1915, in NARA: United States Department of State, 841.857 L97/22.

79. Frost, 234–35.
80. Bailey and Ryan, 193; Layton, 424; Preston, 303; Ramsay, 296.

CHAPTER EIGHTEEN

1. *Daily Mirror,* May 8, 1915; Preston, 308.
2. *The Times,* May 10, 1915.
3. Ibid., May 8, 1915.
4. Snyder, 52.
5. Preston, 3, 309.
6. *New York Tribune,* May 8, 1915.
7. *New York Herald,* May 8, 1915.
8. *New York World,* May 8, 1915.
9. *New York Times,* May 10, 1915.
10. Hurd, 15.
11. Bailey and Ryan, 229.
12. Gerard, *Four Years,* 179, 181.
13. Gerard, *Face to Face,* 42–43, 48.
14. Tirpitz, 2:155.
15. *New York Times,* May 10, 1915.
16. Bernstorff, 138–40.
17. *New York Times,* May 11, 1915.
18. *Papers Relating to the Foreign Relations,* 1915 Supplement, 385–86.
19. *Atlanta Constitution,* May 8, 1915, courtesy of Michael Poirier.
20. *New York Times,* May 11, 1915.
21. *Papers Relating to the Foreign Relations,* 1915 Supplement, 393–96.
22. Ramsay, 174.
23. Bailey and Ryan, 84–85.
24. Ramsay, 196; Preston, 362; Simpson, 16.
25. Horgan, 273–74; *New York Times,* May 11, 1915.
26. *New York Times,* May 11, 1915.
27. Horgan, 275.
28. Preston, 324.
29. Bailey and Ryan, 201.
30. Mersey Report, 8, in Bailey and Ryan Archive, Box 2.
31. Preston, 308.
32. Ibid., 363.
33. *New York Times,* May 11, 1915.
34. Webb Memorandum, May 12, 1915, in Bailey and Ryan, 179; Preston, 317.
35. Bailey and Ryan, 179–80.
36. William Turner, testimony of June 15, 1915, Mersey In Camera, in Bailey and Ryan Archive, Box 2.
37. Bailey and Ryan, 202.
38. Ibid., 206–7.

39. Mersey Report, 5–6, in Bailey and Ryan Archive, Box 2.

40. Ibid., 5–7.

41. Ibid., 6.

42. Ibid., 9.

43. Simpson, 232.

44. Lauriat, 155–58.

45. Bailey and Ryan, 272.

46. Ibid., 273–85.

47. Simpson, 34.

48. Winston Churchill to Walter Runciman, letter of February 12, 1915, in Gilbert, 3:501.

49. Bailey and Ryan, 191.

50. Beesly, 114, 122; Preston, 348.

51. Simpson, 194–96.

52. Beesly, 122.

53. *New York Post,* May 8, 1915.

54. Simpson, 106; Ramsay, 56.

55. *The Times,* July 20, 2008; *Daily Mail,* December 20, 2008.

56. Ballard, 148, 152; Gentile, 1:62–63; Snyder, 71; Preston, 373; Bailey and Ryan, 323; Ramsay, 189; Simpson, 9–10.

57. MacLeish, 37–45.

58. Ballard, 194–95; Gentile, 1:25.

59. Ballard, 194–95.

60. O'Sullivan, 101–5.

61. Ballard, 194–95; Gentile, 1:25; *Daily Telegraph,* July 1, 2012.

62. Bailey and Ryan, 166–67; Preston, 451–53.

63. See William Adams, Mayer testimony, 5–6, 21, 24, in Bailey and Ryan Archive, Box 7; Isaac Lehmann, Mayer testimony, 272, 294, in Bailey and Ryan Archive, Box 6; *Retford, Gainsborough and Worksop Times,* June 11, 1915, courtesy of Michael Poirier.

64. Charles Bowring, Mayer testimony, 472, 494, in Bailey and Ryan Archive, Box 6.

65. Bailey and Ryan, 158–59; Preston, 313–14, 417; Bailey and Ryan, 358, note 15, reports that these handwritten logs were usually destroyed after being handed over to an official for transcription.

66. Bailey and Ryan, 151; Preston, 418.

67. Walther Schwieger, War Diary for U-20, in Bailey, 335–36.

68. Bailey and Ryan, 151; Preston, 418.

69. Walther Schwieger, War Diary for U-20, in Bailey, 336.

70. Bailey and Ryan, 152.

71. Preston, 417, 419; Bailey and Ryan, 158–59.

72. Bailey and Ryan, 152; Preston, 417.

73. Bailey and Ryan, 83.

74. Ibid., 164.
75. Ibid., 122.
76. Gentile, 1:25–26.
77. Layton, 93; Preston, 445, 448; *Daily Telegraph,* July 1, 2012.
78. Thomas, 97–99.
79. Bailey and Ryan, 157; Tirpitz, 2:168.
80. Preston, 433.
81. Molony, *Double Jeopardy.*
82. Thomas, 107; Sauder and Marschall, 78; Gray, 261; Preston, 434.
83. Bailey and Ryan, 162; Gray, 268.
84. Bailey and Ryan, 162; Preston, 378–79.
85. Preston, 420.
86. Bailey and Ryan, 154–55.
87. Ibid., 340.
88. *News of the World,* London, June 6, 1937.

EPILOGUE

1. *New York Times,* May 10, 1915.
2. Lauriat, 50–51.
3. Ibid., 53–54, 67.
4. Ryerse, 16–17.
5. Poirier, *Tragic Tale,* 167.
6. Reksten, 235.
7. Walker, 160.
8. *Auburn Citizen,* June 15, 1915, courtesy of Michael Poirier.
9. *Loney Family; Lusitania Resource.*
10. Marion Holbourn, letter of June 21 1955, in Hoehling and Hoehling Archive, MS Collection 45, Box 1, Folder 27.
11. Ibid.
12. *Worcester Daily Times,* May 15, 1915, in Hoehling and Hoehling Archive, MS Collection 45, Box 2, Folder 70.
13. Marion Holbourn, letter of June 21, 1955, in Hoehling and Hoehling Archive, MS Collection 45, Box 1, Folder 27.
14. Holbourn, *Moat,* 2.
15. Avis Dolphin Foley, letter of August 25, 1955, in Hoehling and Hoehling Archive, MS Collection 45, Box 1, Folder 16.
16. *Lexington Herald,* May 16, 1915, courtesy of Michael Poirier.
17. James Houghton, letter to Freeman family, 1915, from the collection of Chester Nimitz Lay and Richard Bailey, courtesy of Michael Poirier.
18. *Lusitania Resource.*
19. *Chester Reporter,* February 28, 1924.
20. *Lusitania Resource*; Kroeger; Titanic International Society; *Daily Telegraph,* April 21, 2008.

21. *Lusitania Resource.*
22. Amory, *Death*, 25.
23. Information from Michael Poirier to the authors.
24. Mosley, 1:333.
25. *Townsville Daily Bulletin*, March 14, 1939, courtesy of Michael Poirier.
26. Appleton, 183.
27. Ibid., 184.
28. Ibid., 174, 184.
29. *Los Angeles Times*, June 16, 1915, courtesy of Michael Poirier.
30. Mixed Claims, Docket No. 266, *United States of America, on Behalf of Gladys Bilicke, Claimant, v. Germany*, courtesy of Michael Poirier.
31. *Berkeley Square.*
32. Gentile, Book 1:48; Ramsay, 167; Bailey and Ryan, 321–22.
33. Mixed Claims, Docket No. 266, *United States of America, on Behalf of Gladys Bilicke, Claimant, v. Germany*, courtesy of Michael Poirier.
34. *The Times*, September 15, 1920; *Lusitania Resource*; *American Menu.*
35. Angela Papadopoulos account, 1915, from the collection of the Baffa Trasci Amalfitani di Crucoli family, courtesy of Michael Poirier.
36. *New York Times*, May 9, 1915.
37. Ibid., May 10, 1915.
38. *New York Herald*, May 10, 1915.
39. *Philadelphia Inquirer*, May 12, 1915, courtesy of Michael Poirier.
40. *New York Times*, May 22, 1915.
41. Ibid., May 28, 1915.
42. Molony, *Lusitania*, 20.
43. Bernard, *Getting Over It*, 39.
44. *Pittsburgh Press*, August 11, 1935, courtesy of Michael Poirier; *Gainesville Evening Sun*, August 9, 1939.
45. *Lusitania Resource.*
46. Kalafus and Poirier, *William Meriheina.*
47. Information from Michael Poirier to the authors.
48. Poirier and Kalafus, "The Jolivet Family," 169–70, 172, 174.
49. Hoehling and Hoehling, 232.
50. Boulton, BBC.
51. *The Times*, January 31, 1916.
52. Poirier and Kalafus, "The Jolivet Family," 170, 172.
53. Kalafus and Poirier, *Lest We Forget, Part 2.*
54. Ibid.
55. *Lusitania Resource.*
56. *New York Times*, May 9, 1915.
57. Ibid., May 26, 1915.
58. Ibid., May 9, 1915.
59. Hoehling and Hoehling, 191.

60. *New York Times,* May 24, 1915.

61. Champney, 196.

62. Rhondda, *Recalling,* 639, in Hoehling and Hoehling Archive, MS Collection 45, Box 2, Folder 1.

63. Rhondda, *This Was,* 259.

64. Rhondda, *D. A. Thomas,* 214–15.

65. *The Times,* December 22, 1922.

66. Hoffert, 186–90.

67. *The Times,* July 21, 1958.

68. Katz, 121.

69. Pope, *And Then,* 99, in Hoehling and Hoehling Archive, MS Collection 45, Box 2, Folder 1.

70. *Kansas City Star,* June 27, 1915, courtesy of Michael Poirier.

71. Ibid., June 15, 1919, courtesy of Michael Poirier.

72. Katz, 248.

73. *Kansas City Times,* August 26, 1950.

74. James Brooks, letter of June 13, 1955, in Hoehling and Hoehling Archive, MS Collection 45, Box 1, Folder 10.

75. James Brooks, letter of August 5, 1955, in Hoehling and Hoehling Archive, MS Collection 45, Box 1, Folder 10.

76. Sauder and Marschall, 6.

77. Audrey Lawson-Johnston.

78. *Independent,* February 14, 2011.

79. BBC report, January 11, 2011.

80. Norman Turner, letter of September 18, 1955, in Hoehling and Hoehling Archive, MS Collection 45, Box 1, Folder 55.

81. Bailey and Ryan, 224; *New York Times,* June 24, 1933.

82. Norman Turner, letter of July 9, 1955, in Hoehling and Hoehling Archive, MS Collection 45, Box 1, Folder 55.

83. *New York Times,* May 7, 1932.

84. Molony, *Lusitania,* 76.

85. Lott Gadd, letter of February 2, 1930, to Elbert Hubbard II, copy in Hoehling and Hoehling Archive, MS Collection 45, Box 1, Folder 18; information from Michael Poirier to the authors.

86. Morton, 124; *The Times,* August 7, 1915.

87. Leslie Morton, letter of July 25, 1955, in Hoehling and Hoehling Archive, MS Collection 45, Box 1, Folder 43.

88. Leslie Morton, letter of June 20, 1955, in Hoehling and Hoehling Archive, MS Collection 45, Box 1, Folder 43.

89. Leslie Morton, letter of July 25, 1955, in Hoehling and Hoehling Archive, MS Collection 45, Box 1, Folder 43.

90. Leslie Morton, letter of August 29, 1955, in Hoehling and Hoehling Archive, MS Collection 45, Box 1, Folder 43.

91. Bailey and Ryan, 3.
92. Avis Dolphin, letter to mother, May 1915, in Sauder and Marschall, 87.
93. Gentile, 1:63; Gentile, 2:217–19; Snyder, 71; Ballard, 144–48, 152; Preston, 374–76; *The Times,* July 20, 2008; *Daily Mail,* December 20, 2008.
94. Gentile, 2:278.

BIBLIOGRAPHY

Abbreviations and archival references used within the Notes:

Bailey and Ryan Archive: The Thomas A. Bailey and Paul B. Ryan Archive, at the Hoover Institution on War, Revolution and Peace, Stanford University, Stanford, California. Includes transcripts of Mayer interrogatories, oral arguments, testimony, trial, and opinion; Mersey testimony, in camera testimony, and opinion; and documents from the Public Records Office.

Boulton, CBC: Interview with Harold Boulton, 1965, CBC Radio Archives, Toronto, Ontario.

Hoehling and Hoehling Archive: A. A. and Mary Hoehling Archive, *Lusitania* Collection, MS 45, at the Library, Mariners' Museum, Newport News, Virginia. Includes correspondence with survivors, newspaper clippings and accounts, and other data collected for their book *The Last Voyage of the Lusitania*.

Mayer: Interrogatories, Oral Arguments, Testimony, Trial, and Opinion of the Honorable Justice Julius M. Mayer in the Matter of the Petition of the Cunard Steamship Company, Owners of Steamship *Lusitania,* for Limitation of Liability, United States District Court, Southern District of New York. Copies are in the Bailey and Ryan Archive.

Mersey: Loss of the Steamship *Lusitania,* Shipping Casualties, British Wreck Commissioner's Inquiry, Wreck Commissioners' Court, Central Hall, Westminster, Proceedings on a Formal Investigation Ordered by the Board of Trade, before the Right Honorable Lord Mersey, Wreck Commissioner of the United Kingdom, et al., Public Proceedings, In Camera Hearings, and Report. Copies are in the Bailey and Ryan Archive.

NARA: National Archives and Records Administration of the United States, Maryland: Includes archives of the Department of State, dispatches from American

Queenstown consul Wesley Frost; telegrams from survivors; queries from relatives of those aboard *Lusitania;* and passenger accounts of the sinking. Most *Lusitania* files are in 341.111 and 841.857, grouped under 197 and 198 *Lusitania.*

Michael Poirier: Private collection, provided by *Lusitania* historian Michael Poirier to the authors. Includes unpublished accounts and letters by survivors, official documents, statements, and newspaper clippings.

BOOKS

Alec-Tweedie, Ethel. *My Table Cloths: A Few Reminiscences.* New York: George H. Doran, 1916.

Allen, Armin Brand. *The Cornelius Vanderbilts of the Breakers: A Family Retrospective.* Newport, RI: Preservation Society of Newport County, 1995.

Allen, Gay Wilson. *William James.* Minneapolis: University of Minnesota Press, 1970.

Amory, Cleveland. *Who Killed Society?* New York: Harper & Brothers, 1960.

Amory, Phoebe. *The Death of the Lusitania.* Toronto: William Briggs, 1917.

Andrews, Wayne. *The Vanderbilt Legend: The Story of the Vanderbilt Family, 1794–1940.* New York: Harcourt, Brace and Co. 1941.

Appleton, Thomas. *Ravenscrag: The Allan Royal Mail Line.* Toronto: McClelland & Stewart, 1974.

Atherton, William Henry. *Montreal: From 1535 to 1914.* 3 Volumes. Montreal: Clarke, 1914.

Auchincloss, Louis. *The Vanderbilt Era.* New York: Charles Scribner's Sons, 1989.

Audain, James. *From Coalmine to Castle: The Story of the Dunsmuirs of Vancouver Island.* New York: Pageant, 1955.

Austin, Walter. *A War Zone Gadabout: Being the Authentic Account of Four Trips to the Fighting Nations.* Boston: R. H. Hinkley, 1917.

Bailey, Thomas A., and Paul B. Ryan. *The Lusitania Disaster: An Episode in Modern Warfare and Diplomacy.* New York: Free Press, 1975.

Ballard, Robert D., with Spencer Dunmore. *Exploring the Lusitania: Probing the Mysteries of the Sinking That Changed History.* New York: Warner, 1995.

Balsan, Consuelo Vanderbilt. *The Glitter and the Gold.* New York: Harper, 1952.

Barrymore, Ethel. *Memoirs: An Autobiography.* New York: Harper & Brothers, 1955.

Barter, Judith A., ed. *Apostles of Beauty: Arts and Crafts from Britain to Chicago*. New Haven: Yale University Press, 2009.

Bates, Lindon, Jr. *The Path of the Conquistadors*. Boston: Houghton Mifflin, 1912.

Beebe, Lucius. *The Big Spenders*. New York: Doubleday, 1966.

———. *Mansions on Rails: The Folklore of the Private Railway Car*. Berkeley: Howell-North, 1959.

Beesly, Patrick. *Room 40: British Naval Intelligence, 1914–18*. New York: Harcourt Brace Jovanovich, 1982.

Begbie, Harold. *The Mirrors of Downing Street: Some Political Reflections by a Gentleman with a Duster*. New York: G. P. Putnam's Sons, 1921.

Benway, Ann. *A Guide to Newport Mansions*. Newport, RI: Preservation Society of Newport County, 1984.

Berhman, S. N. *Duveen*. New York: Harmony, 1951.

Bernard, Oliver P. *Cock Sparrow*. London: Jonathan Cape, 1936.

Bernard, Oliver P., Jr. *Getting Over It: An Autobiography*. London: Peter Owen, 1992.

Bernstorff, Count Johann von. *My Three Years in America*. New York: Charles Scribner's Sons, 1920.

Bestic, Albert. *Kicking Canvas*. London: Evans Brothers, 1957.

Bethmann-Hollweg, T. von. *Reflections on the World War*. London: Thornton Butterworth, 1920.

Bianchini, Robert. *Ravenscrag*. Montreal: McGill University School of Architecture, 1985.

Bisset, Sir James. *Tramps and Ladies*. New York: Criterion, 1959.

Bisset, Sir James, and P. R. Stephenson. *Commodore: War, Peace, and the Big Ships*. London: Angus & Robertson, 1961.

Blackburn, Roderic H. *Great Houses of New England*. New York: Rizzoli, 2008.

Bodkin, Thomas. *Hugh Lane and His Pictures*. Dublin: Browne & Nolan, 1934.

Borthwick, J. Daniel. *History and Biographical Gazetteer of Montreal to the Year 1893*. Montreal: John Lovell, 1892.

Braynard, Frank O., and William H. Miller. *Fifty Famous Liners*. Volume I. New York: W. W. Norton, 1982.

Bridger, Beverly. *Great Camp Sagamore: The Vanderbilts' Adirondack Retreat*. Charleston, SC: History Press, 2012.

Brinnin, John Malcolm. *The Sway of the Grand Salon.* London: Arlington, 1986.

Brown, Henry Collins. *Fifth Avenue, Old and New.* New York: Fifth Avenue Association, 1924.

Brown, Malcolm. *The Imperial War Museum Book of the First World War.* London: Pan Macmillan, 2002.

Browne, Walter, and E. De Roy Koch, eds. *Who's Who on the Stage, 1908: The Dramatic Reference Book and Biographical Dictionary of the Theatre, Containing Careers of Actors, Actresses, Managers and Playwrights of the American Stage.* New York: B. W. Dodge, 1908.

Burke, Billie. *With a Feather on My Nose.* New York: Appleton-Century-Crofts, 1949.

Butler, Daniel. *The Age of Cunard: A Transatlantic History, 1839–2003.* Annapolis: ProStar, 2003.

———. *Lusitania: The Life, Loss and Legacy of an Ocean Legend.* Mechanicsburg, PA: Stackpole, 2000.

Canadian History Makers: A Volume Containing Accurate and Concise Sketches of Men Who Have Done Things in the Dominion of Canada Past and Present, Together with Photogravures Made from Their Latest Photographs. Montreal: Canadian Publication Society, 1913.

Casgrain, Thérèse. *A Woman in a Man's World.* Toronto: McClelland & Stewart, 1972.

Champney, Freeman. *Art and Glory: The Story of Elbert Hubbard.* Kent, OH: Kent State University Press, 1983.

Chase, David, and Bernard Mendillo, eds. *Historical and Architectural Resources of Portsmouth, Rhode Island: A Preliminary Report.* Providence, RI: Rhode Island Historical Preservation Commission, 1979,

Chatterton, E. Keble. *Steamships and Their Story.* London: Cassell, 1910.

Chidsey, Donald. *The Day They Sank the Lusitania.* New York: Award, 1967.

Churchill, Allan. *The Splendor Seekers.* New York: Grosset & Dunlap, 1974.

Churchill, Winston S. *The World Crisis, 1911–1918.* New York: Charles Scribner's Sons, 1931.

Clews, Henry. *Fifty Years in Wall Street.* New York: Irving, 1908.

Collard, Edgar Andrew. *Call Back Yesterdays.* Toronto: Longmans Canada, 1965.

———. *The Days That Are No More.* Toronto: Doubleday, 1976.

————. *Montreal Yesterdays: More Stories from All Our Yesterdays.* Montreal: Montreal Gazette, 1989.

————. *100 More Tales from All Our Yesterdays.* Montreal: *Montreal Gazette,* 1990.

Condon, James Edward. *Southern California Blue Book of Money: Taxpayers Assessed on $5,000 and Upwards.* Los Angeles: James Edward Condon, 1913.

Cowles, Virginia. *1913: The Defiant Swan Song.* London: Weidenfeld & Nicolson, 1967.

Davis, Richard Harding. *Adventures and Letters of Richard Harding Davis.* New York: Charles Scribner's Sons, 1918.

Dawson, Philip, and Bruce Peter. *Ship Style: Modernism and Modernity at Sea in the 20th Century.* London: Conway, 2010.

Decies, Elizabeth, Lady. *Turn of the World.* Philadelphia: Lippincott, 1937.

Dreiser, Theodore. *A Traveler at Forty.* New York: Century, 1913.

Dressler, Marie. *My Own Story.* Boston: Little, Brown and Co., 1934.

Droste, C. L., and William Tantum. *The Lusitania Case.* Riverside, CT: 7 C's Press, 1972.

Dubé, Philippe. *Charlevoix: Two Centuries at Murray Bay.* Montreal: McGill-Queen's University Press, 1990.

Dufferin, Marchioness of and Ava. *My Canadian Journal, 1872–78: Extracts from My Letters Home Written While Lord Dufferin was Governor-General.* New York: Appleton, 1891.

Dulles, Foster Rhea. *America Learns to Play: A History of Popular Recreation, 1607–1940.* New York: Appleton-Century, 1940.

Duveen, James Henry. *The Rise of the House of Duveen.* London: Longmans, Green, 1957.

————. *Secrets of an Art Dealer.* New York: E. P. Dutton, 1937.

Eaton, Walter Prichard. *At the New Theatre and Others: The American Stage, Its Problems and Performances, 1908–1910.* Boston: Small, Maynard and Co., 1910.

Edington, Sarah. *The Captain's Table: Life and Dining on the Great Ocean Liners.* London: National Maritime Museum, 2005.

Edwards, Michael. *The Finest Wines of Champagne: A Guide to the Best Cuvées, Houses, and Growers.* Berkeley: University of California Press, 2009.

Ellis, Frederick D. *The Tragedy of the Lusitania.* New York: George Bertron, 1915.

Fisher, Admiral of the Fleet Lord John. *Memories*. London: Hodder & Stoughton, 1919.

Fletcher, R. A. *Traveling Palaces: Luxury in Passenger Steamships*. London: Sir Isaac Pitman & Sons, 1913.

Foreman, John, and Robbe Pierce Stimson. *The Vanderbilts and the Gilded Age: Architectural Aspirations, 1879–1901*. New York: St. Martin's Press, 1991.

Forstner, Georg Guenther von. *The Journal of Submarine Commander von Forstner*. Boston: Houghton Mifflin, 1917.

Friedman, B. H. *Gertrude Vanderbilt Whitney*. Garden City, NY: Doubleday, 1981.

Frohman, Daniel. *Daniel Frohman Presents: An Autobiography*. New York: Claude Kendall & Willoughby Sharp, 1935.

Frost, Wesley. *German Submarine Warfare*. New York: Appleton, 1918.

Frothingham, Helen Losanitch. *Mission for Serbia: Letters from America and Canada, 1915–1920*. New York: Walker, 1970.

Gaddis, Eugene R. *Magician of the Modern: Chick Austin and the Transformation of the Arts in America*. New York: Alfred A. Knopf, 2000.

Garman, James E. *A History of the Gentlemen's Farms of Portsmouth, Rhode Island*. Portsmouth: Hamilton Printing, 2003.

Geis, M. Christina. *Georgian Court: An Estate of the Gilded Age*. Philadelphia: Art Alliance Press, 1982.

Gentile, Gary. *The Lusitania Controversies, Book One: Atrocity of War and a Wreck-Diving History*. Philadelphia: Gary Gentile Productions, 1998.

———. *The Lusitania Controversies, Book Two: Dangerous Descents into Shipwrecks and Law*. Philadelphia: Gary Gentile Productions, 1999.

Gerard, James W. *Face to Face with Kaiserism*. New York: George H. Doran, 1918.

———. *My Four Years in Germany*. New York: Grosset & Dunlap, 1927.

Gersovitz, Julia. *Ravenscrag*. Montreal: McGill University School of Architecture, 1975.

Gilbert, Martin. *Winston S. Churchill, 1914–1916*. Companion Volume 3. London: Heinemann, 1973.

Gittelman, Steven H., and Emily Gittelman. *Alfred Gwynne Vanderbilt: The Unlikely Hero of the Lusitania*. New York: Hamilton, 2013.

Grant, Hamil. *Two Sides of the Atlantic*. London: Grant Richards, 1917.

Gray, Edwyn. *The Killing Time: The German U-Boats, 1914–1918*. London: Seeley Service, 1972.

Gregory, Lady Augusta. *Hugh Lane's Life and Achievement*. London: John Murray, 1921.

Guy, Kolleen M. *When Champagne Became French: Wine and the Making of a National Identity*. Baltimore: Johns Hopkins University Press, 2003.

Hamilton, Charles Franklin. *As Bees in Honey Drown: Elbert Hubbard and the Roycrofters*. New York: A. S. Barnes, 1973.

Hewitt, Mark Alan. *The Architect and the American Country House*. New Haven: Yale University Press, 1990.

Hickey, Des, and Gus Smith. *Seven Days to Disaster: The Sinking of the Lusitania*. New York: G. P. Putnam's Sons, 1981.

Hinshelwood, N. M. *Montreal and Vicinity*. Montreal: Desbarats, 1903.

Hoehling, A. A., and Mary Hoehling. *The Last Voyage of the Lusitania*. New York: Madison, 1956.

Hoffert, Sylvia. *Alva Vanderbilt Belmont*. Bloomington: Indiana University Press, 2012.

Holbourn, Ian B. Stoughton. *The Child of the Moat: A Book for Girls*. London: Arnold Shaw, 1916.

———. *The Isle of Foula*. Lerwick, Scotland: Johnson & Grieg, 1938.

Hopkins, Albert A. *The Scientific American Handbook of Travel, with Hints for the Ocean Voyage, for European Tours and a Practical Guide to London and Paris*. New York: Munn, 1910.

Horgan, J. J. *Parnell to Pearce: Some Reflections*. Dublin: Browne & Nolan, 1948.

Hoyt, Edwin. *The Vanderbilts and Their Fortune*. Garden City, NY: Doubleday, 1962.

Hubbard, Elbert. *Hollyhocks and Goldenglow*. East Aurora, NY: Roycrofters, 1913.

———. *The Philosophy of Elbert Hubbard*. East Aurora, NY: Roycrofters, 1916.

Hughes, Glenn. *A History of the American Theatre, 1700–1950*. New York: Samuel French, 1951.

Huldermann, Bernhard. *Albert Ballin*. London: Cassell, 1922.

Hurd, Archibald. *Murder at Sea*. London: Fischer Unwin, 1915.

In Memoriam: Elbert and Alice Hubbard. East Aurora, NY: Roycrofters, 1915.

Irwin, Will. *Herbert Hoover: A Reminiscent Biography*. New York: Century, 1928.

James, Henry. *The American Scene*. London: Chapman & Hall, 1907.

Jillson, Herbert. *Northward-ho! Covering Maine's Inland Resorts, Moosehead Lake, the Rangeleys, Belgrade Lakes and Poland Spring*. Bangor, ME: Herbert Jillson, 1909.

Jones, John Price. *The German Spy in America: The Secret Plotting of German Spies in the United States and the Inside Story of the Sinking of the Lusitania*. London: Hutchinson, 1917.

Kathrens, Michael. *Great Houses of New York, 1880–1930*. New York: Acanthus, 2005.

Katz, Sandra L. *Dearest of Geniuses: A Life of Theodate Pope Riddle*. Windsor, CT: Tide-Mark, 2003.

Kellogg, Charlotte. *Women of Belgium: Turning Tragedy into Triumph*. New York: Funk & Wagnalls, 1917.

King, Greg. *A Season of Splendor: The Court of Mrs. Astor in Gilded Age New York*. Hoboken, NJ: John Wiley & Sons, 2009.

King, Moses. *King's Handbook of New York City*. New York: Moses King, 1892.

King, Robert B. *The Vanderbilt Homes*. New York: Rizzoli, 1989.

Kirschenbaum, Howard. *The Story of Sagamore*. Raquette Lake, NY: Sagamore Institute, 1990.

Kludas, Arnold. *Great Passenger Ships of the World, Volume I: 1858–1912*. London: Patrick Stephens, 1972.

Kortemeir, Siegfried. *U-Boote am Feind: Umschlag und Einband*. Berlin: Bertelsmann, 1937.

Lauriat, Charles. *The Lusitania's Last Voyage*. Boston: Houghton Mifflin, 1915.

Layton, J. Kent. *Lusitania: An Illustrated Biography*. London: Amberley, 2010.

Leacock, Stephen. *Montreal: Seaport and City*. Toronto: McClelland & Stewart, 1941.

Lehr, Elizabeth Drexel. *King Lehr and the Gilded Age*. London: Constable, 1935.

Logan, Andy. *The Man Who Robbed the Robber Barons*. New York: W. W. Norton, 1965.

Lord, Walter. *The Good Years*. New York: Harper & Row, 1960.

Los Angeles, the Old and the New. Los Angeles: Los Angeles Chamber of Commerce, 1911.

Lubet, Steven. *Murder in Tombstone: The Forgotten Trial of Wyatt Earp*. New Haven: Yale University Press, 2004.

MacKay, Donald. *The Square Mile: Merchant Princes of Montreal*. Vancouver: Douglas & McIntyre, 1987.

Marcosson, Isaac, and Daniel Frohman. *Charles Frohman, Man and Manager*. New York: Harper & Brothers, 1916.

Marks, Paula Mitchell. *And Die in the West: The Story of the O.K. Corral Gunfight*. New York: William Morrow, 1998.

Marshall, Logan. *Horrors and Atrocities of the Great War*. New York: L. T. Myers, 1915.

Martin, Frederick Townsend. *The Passing of the Idle Rich*. Garden City, NY: Doubleday, Page and Co., 1911.

Maurice, Arthur Bartlett. *Fifth Avenue*. New York: Dodd, Mead and Co., 1918.

Maxtone-Graham, John. *The Only Way to Cross*. New York: Macmillan, 1972.

McGroarty, John Steven. *Los Angeles, from the Mountains to the Sea: With Selected Biography of Actors*. New York: American Historical Society, 1921.

McQueen, Rod. *The Eatons: The Rise and Fall of Canada's Royal Family*. Toronto: Stoddart, 1998.

Miller, William H. *The First Great Ocean Liners in Photographs*. New York: Dover, 1984.

Mixed Claims Commission, Report: United States and Germany, Administrative Decisions and Opinions of a General Nature and Opinions on Individual Lusitania Claims and Other Cases to June 30, 1925. New York: United Nations, 1956.

Molony, Senan. *Lusitania: An Irish Tragedy*. Douglas Village, Cork, Ireland: Mercier, 2004.

Morgan, Henry James. *The Canadian Men and Women of the Time*. Toronto: William Briggs, 1898.

Morgan, J. Vyrnwy. *Life of Viscount Rhondda*. London: H. R. Allenson, 1919.

Morris, Lloyd. *Postscript to Yesterday*. New York: Random House, 1947.

Morton, Leslie. *The Long Wake*. London: Routledge and Kegan Paul, 1968.

Mosely, Charles, ed. *Burke's Peerage and Baronetage*. 106th Edition, 2 Volumes. Crans, Switzerland: Burke's Peerage, 1999.

Mro, Albert. *American Military Vehicles of World War I*. Jefferson, NC: McFarland, 2009.

Notables of the West: Being the Portraits and Biographies of Progressive Men of the West Who Have Helped in the Development and History Making of This Wonderful Country. 2 volumes. San Francisco: Press Reference Library/International News Service, 1915.

O'Byrne, Robert. *Hugh Lane*. Dublin: Lilliput, 2000.

Ocean Liners of the Past: The Cunard Express Liners Lusitania and Mauretania. Reprinted from *The Shipbuilder*. London: Patrick Stephens, 1970.

O'Gorman, James F., ed. *Hill-Stead: The Country Place of Theodate Pope Riddle*. New York: Princeton Architectural Press, 2010.

O'Sullivan, Patrick. *Lusitania: Unraveling the Mysteries*. Staplehurst, Kent, UK: Spellmount, 2000.

Ouse, David. *Forgotten Duluthians*. Duluth, MN: X-presso Books, 2010.

Papers Relating to the Foreign Relations of the United States. 1915 Supplement. Washington, D.C.: United States Government Printing Office, 1915.

Papers Relating to the Foreign Relations of the United States. 1916 Supplement. Washington, D.C.: United States Government Printing Office, 1916.

Patterson, Jerry E. *The Vanderbilts*. New York: Harry N. Abrams, 1989.

Peeke, Mitch, Kevin Walsh-Johnson, and Steven Jones. *The Lusitania Story*. Annapolis: Naval Institute Press, 2002.

Post, Emily. *Etiquette*. New York: Funk & Wagnalls, 1922.

Preston, Diana. *Lusitania: An Epic Tragedy*. New York: Walker, 2002.

Protasio, John. *The Day the World Was Shocked: The Lusitania Disaster and Its Influence on the Course of World War I*. Philadelphia: Casemate, 2011.

Ramsay, David. *Lusitania: Saga and Myth*. New York: W. W. Norton, 2001.

Read, James M. *Atrocity Propaganda, 1914–1919*. New Haven: Yale University Press, 1941.

Reckitt, Harold J. *V.R. 76: A French Military Hospital*. London: William Heinemann, 1921.

Reksten, Terry. *The Dunsmuir Saga*. Vancouver: Douglas & McIntyre, 1991.

Rémillard, François. *Mansions of the Golden Square Mile, 1850–1930*. Montreal: Meridian, 1987.

Rhondda, 2nd Viscountess of (Margaret Haig Thomas, Lady Mackworth). *D. A. Thomas, Viscount Rhondda*. London: Longmans, Green, 1921.

———. "Recalling a Tragedy." Published in *The Spectator,* London; copy in Hoehling and Hoehling Archive.

———. *This Was My World.* London: Macmillan, 1933.

Roberts, Gary L. *Doc Holliday.* Hoboken, NJ: John Wiley & Sons, 2006.

Robinson, Maurice, Beverly Hall, and Paul Price. *Royal Roads: A Celebration.* Victoria, BC: Natural Light Productions, 1995.

Ryerse, Phyllis. *Ryersons on the Lusitania.* Electronic Book: Amazon Digital Services, 2012.

Ryerson, George Sterling. *Looking Backward.* Toronto: Ryerson, 1924.

Saelcett, William, ed. *Scannell's New Jersey's First Citizens: Biographies and Portraits of the Notable Living Men and Women of New Jersey.* Paterson, NJ: J. J. Scannell, 1917.

Sauder, Eric, and Ken Marschall. *RMS Lusitania: The Ship and Her Record.* London: History Press, 2009.

Schaller, Mary W. *Deliver Us from Evil: A Southern Belle in Europe at the Outbreak of World War I.* Columbia: University of South Carolina Press, 2011.

Schapiro, Amy. *Millicent Fenwick: Her Way.* New Brunswick, NJ: Rutgers University Press, 2003.

Secrest, Meryle. *Duveen: A Life in Art.* New York: Alfred A. Knopf, 2004.

Segger, Martin. *The Buildings of Samuel Maclure: In Search of Appropriate Form.* Victoria, BC: Sono Nis Press, 1986.

Simpson, Colin. *The Lusitania.* Boston: Little, Brown and Co., 1972.

Skinner, Otis. *Footlights and Spotlights.* New York: Blue Ribbon Books, 1924.

Sloane, Florence Adele. *Maverick in Mauve.* Garden City, NY: Doubleday, 1983.

Smales, Herbert T. *The Breakers.* Newport, RI: Preservation Society of Newport County, 1979.

Smith, Nina Slingsby. *George: Memoirs of a Gentleman's Gentleman.* London: Century, 1986.

Snyder, Louis A. *The Military History of the Lusitania.* New York: Franklin Watts, 1965.

Spedding, Charles. *Reminiscences of Transatlantic Travelers.* London: T. Fisher Unwin, 1926.

Strange, Michael (Blanche Oelrichs). *Who Tells Me True*. New York: Charles Scribner's Sons, 1940.

Taylor, Edmond. *The Fall of the Dynasties and the Collapse of the Old Order, 1905–1922*. Garden City, NY: Doubleday, 1963.

Thomas, Lowell. *Raiders of the Deep*. Garden City, NY: Garden City Publishing, 1928.

Tirpitz, Grand Admiral Alfred von. *My Memoirs*. New York: Dodd, Mead and Co., 1919.

Turner, Alford E. *The O.K. Corral Inquest*. College Station, TX: Creative Publishing, 1981.

Vanderbilt, Arthur. *Fortune's Children: The Fall of the House of Vanderbilt*. New York: William Morrow, 1992.

Vanderbilt, Cornelius, Jr. *Farewell to Fifth Avenue*. New York: Simon & Schuster, 1935.

———. *Queen of the Golden Age: The Fabulous Story of Grace Wilson Vanderbilt*. New York: McGraw-Hill, 1956.

Vanderbilt Hotel: Two Weeks' Vacation in New York; The Nation's Best Summer Resort. New York: Kalkhoff, 1918.

Viereck, George. *Spreading Germs of Hate*. London: Duckworth, 1931.

Wagg, Susan. *Architecture of Andrew Thomas Taylor: Montreal's Square Mile and Beyond*. Montreal: McGill-Queen's University Press, 2013.

Walker, Pierre A., ed. *Henry James on Culture: Collected Essays on Politics and the American Social Scene*. Omaha: University of Nebraska Press, 1999.

Warren, Mark D. *The Cunard Turbine-Driven Quadruple-Screw Atlantic Liner Lusitania*. Reprinted from *Engineering*, 1907. Wellingborough, Northamptonshire, UK: Patrick Stephens, 1986.

Wecton, Dixon. *The Saga of American Society: A Record of Social Aspiration, 1607–1937*. New York: Charles Scribner's Sons, 1937.

Wells, H. G. *The Future in America: A Search After Realities*. New York: Harper & Brothers, 1906.

Westley, Margaret W. *Remembrance of Grandeur: The Anglo-Protestant Elite of Montreal, 1900–1950*. Montreal: Libre Expression, 1990.

Wilcox, Herbert. *Twenty-Five Thousand Sunsets*. London: Bodley Head, 1967.

Williamson, Ellen. *When We Went First Class: A Recollection of Good Times.* Ames: Iowa State University Press, 1977.

Wilson, Richard Guy. *The Colonial Revival House.* New York: Harry N. Abrams, 2004.

Winter, Robert. *Craftsman Style.* New York: Harry N. Abrams, 2004.

Wrong, George M. *A Canadian Manor and Its Seigneurs: The Story of a Hundred Years, 1761–1861.* Toronto: Bryant, 1908.

JOURNALS AND MAGAZINES

The Automobile, Volume 32, May 13, 1915.

Bailey, Thomas A. "German Documents Relating to the Lusitania." In *The Journal of Modern History,* Volume 8, No. 3, September 1936, 320–37.

Bradshaw, William R. "Mr. George A. Kessler's Bachelor Apartments." In *The Decorator and Furnisher,* Volume 25, No. 6, March 1895, 207–11.

Chamberlain, Eugene Tyler. "The New Cunard Steamship Contract." In *The North American Review,* Volume 177, 1904, 533–43.

Doubleday, F. N. "A Trip on the Two Largest Ships." In *The World's Work: A History of Our Time,* Volume 15, No. 3, January 1908, 9803–10.

"Leadership in Ocean Service." In *The World's Work: A History of Our Time,* Volume 15, No. 1, November 1907, 9503–4.

"Lusitania." In *The American Journal of International Law,* Volume 12, October 1, 1918, 862–88.

"Lusitania's Victims." In *American Art News,* Volume 13, May 15, 1915.

MacLeish, Kenneth. "Was There a Gun?" In *Sports Illustrated,* Volume 17, No. 73, December 24, 1962, 37–43.

The Motor World, Volume 43, May 12, 1915.

Poirier, Michael. "Remembering Barbara: A Life Well-Lived." In *Voyage Magazine,* Titanic International Society, No. 64, 2008, 221–24.

———. "Tragic Tale of Jessie Taft Smith." In *Voyage Magazine,* Titanic International Society, Issue 44, 2003, 163–72.

Poirier, Michael, and Jim Kalafus. "The Jolivet Family and the Lusitania." In *Voyage Magazine,* Titanic International Society, Issue No. 48, 2004, 163–74.

NEWSPAPERS

Individual newspapers are referenced by date in the citations.

BIBLIOGRAPHY

Australia

Townsville Daily Bulletin

Canada

Toronto Daily Star
Toronto Star
Toronto World
Victoria Times Colonist, Victoria, British Columbia

United Kingdom

Daily Express, London
Daily Mail, London
Daily Mirror, London
Daily Sketch, London
Daily Telegraph, London
The Independent, London
Liverpool Echo
News of the World, London
The Observer, London
Oldham Chronicle
Retford, Gainsborough and Worksop Times, Nottingham
Sunday Express, London
The Times, London

United States

Amsterdam Evening Recorder, New York
Atlanta Constitution
Auburn Citizen, New York
The Call, San Francisco
Chester Reporter, Hill County, Montana
Chicago Daily News
Chicago Tribune
Evening Sun, Gainesville, Texas
Indianapolis News
Kansas City Star, Kansas
Kansas City Times, Missouri
Lexington Herald, Kentucky
Los Angeles Herald
Los Angeles Times
Marshall News-Statesman, Michigan
New York American

BIBLIOGRAPHY

New York Evening Post
New York Herald
New York Morning Post
New York Nation
New York Post
New York Sun
New York Times
New York Tribune
New York World
Philadelphia Inquirer
Pittsburgh Press
Plain Dealer, Cleveland
Saratogian, Saratoga Springs, New York
Springfield Daily Republican, Massachusetts
The Sun, Baltimore
Washington Post

WEB SITES

"Alfred Howard Amory," *Canadian Great War Project,* at http://canadiangreat
warproject.com/searches/soldierDetail.asp?ID=98685.

The American Menu: Compliments of George Kessler, at http://www.theameri
canmenu.com/2012/04/compliments-of-george-kessler.html.

Audrey Lawson-Johnston, at http://mmmatmelchbourne.yolasite.com/audrey
-lawson-johnston.php.

Berkeley Square: Historic Los Angeles, at http://www.berkeleysquarelosangeles
.com/2011/05/7-llewellyn-milner-house.html.

Cacouna, Sir Hugh Montague Allan, at http://cacouna.net/montaguAllen_e.htm.

Eddis, Charles. *The Story of a Sacred Place,* at http://www.canadianuuhistorical
society.ca/Charles%20Eddis%20Story%20of%20a%20Sacred%20Space%20
ver2.pdf.

Hoglund, Laura. *Charles Jeffery: Wisconsin's Lusitania Connection,* at http://
www.examiner.com/article/charles-jeffery-wisconsin-s-lusitania-connection.

The Jeffery Automobile and the Thomas B. Jeffery Company, at http://www.
american-automobiles.com/Jeffery.html.

Kalafus, Jim. *Lest We Forget: Henry Sonneborn,* 2006, at http://www.encyclopedia
-titanica.org/lest-we-forget-henry-sonneborn.html.

Kalafus, Jim, and Michael Poirier. *Lest We Forget, Part 2: As the Lusitania Went
Down,* 2005, at http://www.encyclopedia-titanica.org/lusitania-lest-we-forget-2.html.

————. *Lest We Forget: Albert Arthur Bestic,* 2010, at http://www.encyclopedia -titanica.org/lusitania-bestic.html)http://www.encyclopedia-titanica.org/lusitania -bestic.html.

————. *William Meriheina: An Inventive Survivor,* 2014, at http://www.encyclo pedia-titanica.org/william-meriheina-an-inventive-survivor.html.

Kroeger, Judy. *Bullskin Man Recalls Mother's Survival After Sinking of Lusitania,* 2009, at http://www.pittsburghlive.com/x/dailycourier/news/s_617382. html#ixzz1KvHYrF71.

Last Known Lusitania Survivors Dies, BBC News, January 11, 2011, at http:// www.bbc.co.uk/news/uk-england-beds-bucks-herts-12161194.

The Loney Family, at http://kihm3.wordpress.com/2008/03/27/the-loney-family/.

Loodts, Patrick. *The Extraordinary Destiny of Dr. Depage, Related to Three White Angels of Exceptional Character,* at http://www.1914-1918.be/docteur _depage_ocean.php?PHPSESSID=4b3dfa57057a2e63500351015b1548b5.

Lusitania Resource, at www.rmslusitania.info.

Molony, Senan. *Double Jeopardy: Lusitania's Unique Victim,* 2007, at http:// www.encyclopedia-titanica.org/double-jeopardy-lusitania-double-victim.html.

Pearce, Nick. *Gorer v. Lever: Edgar Gorer and William Hesketh Lever,* at http:// www.liverpoolmuseums.org.uk/ladylever/collections/chinese/goreressay/index.aspx.

Sauder, Eric. *The Lusitania Disguised? Unraveling the Mystery,* 1995–2002, at http://marconigraph.com/lusitania/mfa_camo.html.

————. *Probing the Mysteries of the Lusitania: A Journal of the 1993 Expedi- tion,* at http://www.northatlanticrun.com/367%201993%20expedition/ 367exp1993Intro.html.

Smith, Sharon Dunlap. *Theodate Pope Riddle: Her Life and Architecture,* 2002, at http://www.valinet.com/~smithash/theodate/.

Titanic International Society Mourns the Loss of Lusitania Survivor, April 13, 2008, at http://titanicinternational.wordpress.com/2008/04/13/tis-mourns-the -loss-of-lusitania-survivor.

INDEX

INDEX

INDEX